Dialogues in Urban and Regional Planning 1

Dialogues in Urban and Regional Planning offers a selection of the best urban planning scholarship from each of the world's planning school associations. The award-winning papers presented illustrate the concerns and the discourse of planning scholarship communities and provide a glimpse into planning theory and practice by planning academics around the world. All those with an interest in urban and regional planning will find this collection valuable in opening new avenues for research and debate.

Set in context by the editors' introductory chapter, these essays draw on local concerns but also reflect three international issues: The first, the relationship between planning and economy, is raised in situations ranging from mixed urban land-use in Canada via Olympic stadiums in Sydney to the effect of market forces on urban space in Buenos Aires. Concerns over the environment and conservation, the second issue, are raised in papers on biodiversity in Britain; the difficulties of balancing conservation and regeneration in Shanghai; and the effects of ecological–economic zoning in the Brazilian Amazon. The third issue: the nature of the planning process and decision-making, is raised through participation and communication in Belfast, Jerusalem, Johannesburg and Canada; the application of normative planning theory to Africa; and in the use of storytelling as a way of gaining mutual understanding. The final chapter questions the ability of Critical Planning Theory to acknowledge the presence of power in the planning process.

This book is published in association with the Global Planning Education Association Network (GPEAN), and the nine planning school associations it represents, who have selected these papers based on regional competitions.

Editors: **Bruce Stiftel** is professor of urban and regional planning at Florida State University, USA. **Vanessa Watson** is professor in the City and Regional Planning programme and deputy director of the School of Architecture, Planning and Geomatics at the University of Cape Town, South Africa.

Contributors: **Henri Acselrad, Scott A. Bollens, Dick Cobb, Paul M. Dolman, Leonardo Fernández, Jill Grant, Thomas L. Harper, Tazim B. Jamal, Juan D. Lombardo, Andrew Lovett, Raine Mäntysalo, Tim O'Riordan, Leonie Sandercock, Glen Searle, Stanley M. Stein, Bruce Stiftel, Karen Umemoto, Mercedes DiVirgilio, Vanessa Watson** and **Jiantao Zhang**.

Dialogues in Urban and Regional Planning

Prize winning papers from the World's Planning School Associations

This biennial series is published in association with the Global Planning Education Association Network (GPEAN). The nine members of the GPEAN are:

the Association of African Planning Schools (AAPS)
the Association of Collegiate Schools of Planning (ACSP) in the USA
the Association of Canadian University Planning Programs (ACUPP)
the Association of European Schools of Planning (AESOP)
the Association of Latin American Schools of Urbananism and Planning (ALEUP)
the National Association of Urban and Regional Postgraduate and Research Programmes (ANPUR) in Brazil
the Australia and New Zealand Association of Planning Schools (ANZAPS)
the Association for the Development of Planning Education and Research (APERAU)
the Asian Planning Schools Association (APSA)

International editorial board

Dialogues in Urban and Regional Planning 1

Edited by
Bruce Stiftel and Vanessa Watson

Routledge
Taylor & Francis Group

LONDON AND NEW YORK

First published 2005
by Routledge
2 Park Square, Milton Park, Abingdon, Oxon OX14 4RN

Simultaneously published in the USA and Canada
by Routledge
270 Madison Ave, New York, NY 10016

Routledge is an imprint of the Taylor & Francis Group

© 2005 Taylor & Francis, selection and editorial; individual
chapters, the contributors

Typeset in Galliard by
HWA Text and Data Management, Tunbridge Wells
Printed and bound in Great Britain by
MPG Books Ltd, Bodmin

British Library Cataloguing in Publication Data
A catalogue record for this book is available from the British Library

Library of Congress Cataloging in Publication Data
A catalog record for this book has been requested

ISBN 0–415–34693–2

Contents

Contributors

Henri Acselrad is professor in the Institute for Urban and Regional Research at the Federal University of Rio de Janeiro (Brazil), and researcher at the Brazilian National Council for Scientific Development. He writes on environmental conflicts and planning. Editor of *Revista Brasileira de Estudos Urbanos e Regionais*, and former editor of *Cadernos*, his PhD was earned in economics at the University of Paris I (Panthéon-Sorbonne)(France).

Scott A. Bollens is professor of urban and regional planning in the Department of Planning, Policy and Design at the University of California, Irvine (USA). A PhD graduate of the University of North Carolina at Chapel Hill (USA), his research concerns ethnicity and public policy, regionalism and intergovernmental planning.

Dick Cobb is lecturer in environmental sciences and researcher in the Centre for Environmental Risk at University of East Anglia (UK). His research concerns agricultural and rural policy, and environmental legislation and accountability.

Mercedes DiVirgilio is a member of the faculty of the Institute of Urban Areas at General Sarmiento National University (Argentina). She holds a bachelor's degree in sociology and a master's degree in research in social sciences, both from the University of Buenos Aires (Argentina), and has been a visiting scholar at the University of Texas at Austin (USA).

Paul M. Dolman is lecturer in ecology at the University of East Anglia (UK). His primary interest has always been in biodiversity conservation and predicting the consequences of environmental and land-use change. Specialising in population analysis, spatial and landscape ecology he also works in interdisciplinary programmes such as the work presented in this volume

Leonardo Fernández is research assistant at the Urban Institute of the General Sarmiento National University (Argentina).

Jill Grant is professor and director of the School of Planning at Dalhousie University (Canada). Her research focuses on residential environments and the cultural context of community planning. She is editor of *Plan Canada*, the professional journal of the Canadian Institute of Planners (CIP), and serves on the editorial boards of the *Journal of the American Planning Association* and *Landscape and Urban Planning* journal. Her article on mixed use won a CIP Award for Impact on the Profession.

Thomas L. Harper is professor and director of the Planning Programme, Faculty of Environmental Design at the University of Calgary (Canada). His inter-disciplinary research, done collaboratively with Stanley Stein, focuses on normative planning theory. Professor Harper is past president of the Association of Canadian University Planning Programs, and is currently that association's representative to the Global Planning Education Association Network. He holds the professional designation 'Member of the Canadian Institute of Planners', and has worked with a variety of clients, community, educational and religious organizations.

Tazim B. Jamal is assistant professor in the Department of Recreation, Park and Tourism Sciences, at Texas A&M University (USA). A PhD graduate of the University of Calgary (Canada), her primary research areas are on community-based planning for sustainable tourism and heritage tourism development. Related to the planning process, she also conducts participatory research in projects involving multi-stakeholder processes for addressing tourism-related conflict and natural resource sustainability.

Juan D. Lombardo is associate professor and head of the research division the Department of Urbanism at General Sarmiento National University (Argentina), and Vice-President of the Association of Latin American Schools of Urbanism and Planning. Holder of a doctorate in urbanism from the University of Aachen (Germany), he has served on the faculties of the University of Aachen and the University of Rosario (Argentina), as well as consultant to UNESCO. His publications have appeared in Argentina and abroad.

Andrew Lovett is senior lecturer in environmental sciences at University of East Anglia (UK). A PhD graduate of University College Wales, Aberystwyth (UK), his research concerns geographic information systems, environmental epidemiology and hazardous waste disposal.

Raine Mäntysalo teaches strategic and participatory urban planning in the Department of Architecture, University of Oulu (Finland). Currently he manages multi-disciplinary research projects concerned with sustainability of growing and declining urban areas and participatory rural planning. His doctoral thesis 'Land-use Planning as Inter-organizational Learning' was completed in 2000 at the University of Oulu.

Tim O'Riordan is professor of environmental sciences at the University of East Anglia (UK). He has completed extensive research on landscapes and is currently working on governance for sustainable development. He is a member of the UK Sustainable Development Commission, a Deputy Lieutenant of the County of Norfolk, and a fellow of the British Academy, a society for advancement of the humanities and the social sciences.

Leonie Sandercock is professor in urban planning and social policy in the School of Community and Regional Planning at University of British Columbia (Canada), where she chairs the PhD programme. She writes on planning theory and history, multicultural planning, participatory planning, and the importance of stories and storytelling in planners' work. She is an editor of *Planning Theory & Practice*.

Glen Searle is senior lecturer in urban planning at the University of Technology, Sydney (Australia). He was previously deputy manager of policy in the New South Wales Department of Planning and senior research officer in the UK Department of the Environment. Articles editor of *Urban Policy and Research*, his research is primarily concerned with the political economy of Sydney's recent planning and secondarily with the urban functioning of advanced economy industry clusters.

Stanley M. Stein is senior instructor of philosophy in the Faculty of Environmental Design at the University of Calgary (Canada). He has published on the practical implications of philosophical and ethical aspects of planning theory, the ethical and economic justifications of government intervention, environmental ethics, social institutions, and theories of aesthetics and design. His recent work seeks to articulate a theoretical basis for a broadly communicative ('dialogical') approach for public planning.

Bruce Stiftel is professor of urban and regional planning at Florida State University (USA). He writes on collaborative processes in environmental decision-making, as well as the development of urban planning educational institutions. He was editor of the *Journal of Planning Education and Research*, and president of the Association of Collegiate Schools of Planning. A fellow of the American Institute of Certified Planners, currently, he serves as co-chair of the Global Planning Education Association Network.

Karen Umemoto is associate professor in the Department of Urban and Regional Planning at the University of Hawaii at Manoa (USA). Her academic focus is planning and governance in a multicultural society. Her research areas include community planning, race relations, community development and urban violence. She also works with various public and non-profit organizations in strategic planning and community development.

Vanessa Watson is professor in the City and Regional Planning Programme and deputy director of the School of Architecture, Planning and Geomatics at the University of Cape Town (South Africa). She writes on planning theory and researches in the area of planning practices in Africa. She is the winner of the 2003 South African Distinguished Women in Science Award, and represents the Association of African Planning Schools to the Global Planning Education Association Network.

Jiantao Zhang graduated from the University of Liverpool (UK) and currently a post-doctoral research assistant in the Urban Planning Department of Tongji University (China). His research converns urban morphology and urban design, urban policy analysis, urban conservation and regeneration. He is a member of International Seminar on Urban Form.

Preface

Dialogues in Urban and Regional Planning began as a conversation among leaders of ten planning school associations in Shanghai in 2001. The hope was to improve entry to 'foreign' scholarship for urban planners working in each of the world's nations and languages and, as a result, to promote better integration, cross-fertilization and criticism. Papers were nominated by each of the nine member associations of the Global Planning Education Association Network (GPEAN) and then chosen by an international editorial board. This is the inaugural English-language volume in what will be a biennial series available in print and electronic editions. Translations to additional languages will be made available as funding permits.

Urban planning scholarship has been constrained by limited communication across national and language boundaries. Legal, institutional and cultural consider-ations have often been assumed as givens in planning scholarship because the degree of variation among them may be quite limited within individual nations. Efforts to promote international exchange in planning scholarship, accelerated in the past decade, and highlighted by the first World Planning Schools Congress held in Shanghai in 2001, suggest that the potential value of comparative work is quite high. At the same time, language and library budgets limit access to planning scholarship worldwide. The *Dialogues* book series seeks to offer a sampling of the best urban planning scholarship from each of the world's planning scholarship communities to scholars in the other communities. While a small sample of papers can only do so much, we believe the current level of access is such that a book series featuring some of the best scholarship from each community will be powerful in suggesting models and in leading scholars to new resources.

Submissions were chosen by each planning school association through editorial committees. Specific methods of choice varied by association, with some selecting the best papers in certain journals, and others reviewing open suggestions from their member faculty. The International Editorial Board then reviewed all association-submitted papers and selected those to be included in this book. The objective was to select examples of the best urban and regional planning scholarship including work from each of the world's regions. You won't find national or regional consensus views of planning issues here. Rather, the papers presented illustrate the concerns and the discourse of planning scholarship communities around the world. They provide a peek into the theories and methods of use by planning academics around the world, and they are suggestive of sources that may lead to further useful exploration.

Each biennial volume will be published in English and marketed worldwide in print and electronic editions by Routledge. Then, with support of national and multi-lateral organizations, translations of the papers will be made available in other languages through GPEAN's web facility (www.gpean.org). The expectation is for broad coverage in university libraries worldwide, purchase by individual planning scholars, as well as use as a text in doctoral coursework.

The nine member associations of GPEAN are: the Association of African Planning Schools (AAPS), the Association of Collegiate Schools of Planning (ACSP) in USA, the Association of Canadian University Planning Programs (ACUPP), the Association of European Schools of Planning (AESOP), the Association of Latin-American Schools of Urbanism and Planning (ALEUP), the National Association of Urban and Regional Postgraduate and Research Programmes (ANPUR)in Brazil, the Australia and New Zealand Association of Planning Schools (ANZAPS), the Association for the Development of Planning Education and Research (APERAU), and the Asian Planning Schools Association (APSA).

We are indebted to our colleagues on the International Editorial Board: Sigmund Asmervik, Marco Gomes, Tom Harper, Alain Motte, Roberto Rodriguez, Angus Witherby and Anthony Yeh; and the members of the nine national and regional editorial committees: Tunde Agbola, Peter Bikam, David Brown, Fermin Carreño, Jeremy Dawkins, K.D. Fernando, Michael Ginder, Mike Gillen, Phillip Harrison, Michael Hibbard, Debra Howe, Irene Layrisse de Niculescu, Lik Meng Lee, Alberto Lovera, Frank Marcano, Barrie Melotte, A. Mosha, Yukio Nishimura, Ken Odero, Mark Oranje, Daniel Phiri, Rosa Maria Sanchez, Luis Jaime Sobrino, Andrejs Skaburskis, Ian Skelton, Alison Todes, and Zhiqiang Wu. These scholars laboured under the difficult task of choosing from among many high-quality submissions. Helen Ibbotson and her colleagues at Routledge went well beyond the usual support as this project evolved. We are grateful to the staffs of the various journals in which chapters in this book first appeared, who provided assistance in text, graphics and permissions, including: Huw Alexander, Robin Bloxsidge, Pilar Espíndola, Katie Halliday, Patsy Healey, Kim Henderson, Rene Kane, Sarah King, Allison LaBott, Peter Link, Peter Marino, David Shaw, John Shaw, Ginny Smith, and Ian Thompson; as well as to J.P. John Peter, Shawn Lewers and Deden Rukmana of Florida State University, who assisted with many of the challenges the project offered. Tina Behet, Ramiro Berardo, and Heather Portorreal performed able translations essential to the work. Many among the leaders of the planning school associations offered historical memory, including David Amborski, Jay Chatterjee, Andreas Faludi, David Forkenbrock, Klaus Kunzmann, Cristina Leme, Johanna Looye, Hans Mastop, and Martim Smolka. The project was advanced, in part, with funds granted to ACSP and ANPUR by the Fannie Mae Foundation and the Lincoln Institute of Land Policy. The errors, of course, are our own.

Bruce Stiftel
Tallahassee, USA

Vanessa Watson
Cape Town, South Africa

Chapter 1
Introduction
Building global integration in planning scholarship

Bruce Stiftel and Vanessa Watson

In the fall of 1985, Patsy Healey of the University of Newcastle and Klaus Kunzmann of the University of Dortmund sat in a restaurant in Atlanta, USA, discussing the potential for a new pan-European affiliation of urban planning schools. Unbeknownst to them, similar conversations about the value of learned societies for planning were taking place that fall in Brazil; others had recently concluded in France. These conversations were to lead to a quantum leap in communication among urban planning educators worldwide. Today, the Planning Schools Movement has the potential to facilitate growth and maturation of scholarship in urban planning in ways that could not have been imagined 20 years ago. This volume is a significant step in that movement.

Healey and Kunzmann were in the United States for the 27th annual meeting of the Association of Collegiate Schools of Planning (ACSP). This was only the sixth such meeting that featured presentation of scholarly papers, as opposed to discussions of institutional issues facing university programmes. ACSP had begun in 1959 as a vehicle for department chairs and deans to share tactics and develop common projects that might advance the interests of planning education within universities, as had the Association of Canadian University Planning Programs (ACUPP), begun in neighbouring Canada in 1977. Then, in the late 1970s, the ACSP leadership debated stepping beyond those boundaries and working directly to improve the quality of scholarship in the field. ACSP president Ed McClure, vice-president Jay Chatterjee and others, had to push hard to convince the elected leadership that an independent scholarly conference and a journal devoted to planning education would be feasible. Both these projects began in 1980. By the mid-1980s, ACSP had 86 full-member schools and its own journal with over 800 subscribers, and was a partner with the national professional institute in the accreditation of planning schools. (Chatterjee 1986)

So, when Healey and Kunzmann sat down over steak dinner in 1985, they had observed several days in which 348 urban planning researchers (ACSP 2000a: 5–3) presented, contrasted and questioned their research. The impact was obvious. A venue that permitted serious discussion of research and pedagogy in planning, absence of the incessant calls for immediate policy relevance that characterize most professional conferences in a practice-based field like urban planning, was leading to meaningful improvements in research design and the quality of theory. It seemed that it might be possible to build a *discipline* of urban and regional planning that could sustain a rigorous level of growth in ideas, that could hold its own in university assessments of performance, and that could foster innovation in professional practice based on realistic, empirically-grounded but theoretically informed scholarship. Could this happen in Europe? Healey and Kunzmann thought it must.

Fifteen months later, 12 European planning academics met at Castle Cappenberg in Germany's Ruhr valley to found the Association of European Schools of Planning (AESOP). Dieter Bökermann from the Technical University in Vienna, Andreas Faludi of the University of Amsterdam, Dieter Frick of the Technical University in Berlin, Jean-Claude Hauvuy of the University of Paris VIII, Luigi Mazza of the Polytechnic in Milan, Giorgio Piccinato of the University Institute of Architecture in Venice, Willy Schmid of the Swiss Federal Institute of Technology, René Perrin of the University of Tours, and Gerd Hennings and Michael Wegener from the University of Dortmund, joined Healey and Kunzmann at Cappenberg. Kwasi Ardakwa from Ghana also participated in the discussions. The group imagined that a pan-European learned society of planners could foster an increased appreciation for the value of planning as a discipline, and could enable national communities of planners to learn from each other across the continent. Programmes for exchange of scholars could be arranged; a journal could be developed. Officers were selected, and in the next months, incorporation papers prepared, so that when formal membership was opened in October 1987,

1.1 AESOP's founders

67 schools of planning from 21 countries became original members. That November, over 100 scholars met in AESOP's first congress in Amsterdam, chaired by Andreas Faludi. It had taken just two years for a pan-European association of planning academics to move from notion to reality. (Kunzmann 1998)

Meanwhile in Brazil, 1985 was a time of social pressure for re-democratization. In the aftermath of over 20 years of military control of government, Brazil's planning schools found themselves between pressures for technocratic control of urbanization and critical interpretation of the social realities of urban life. The national Council of Urban Development was pushing for a clear national agenda for cities and wanted the five urban planning schools to play significant ancillary roles. Not everyone in the schools was comfortable with the implied directions. When the Council proposed to assess the state of the art in technology, planning and the built environment, the schools knew they needed to respond.

Lucio Grinover at the University in São Paulo took the initiative to bring representatives of the five Brazilian postgraduate planning programmes together. The meeting in São Paulo included Martim Smolka of the Federal University in Rio de Janeiro, Ricardo Fariet of the University of Brasília, Warama Parizza of the Federal University of Rio Grande do Sul in Porto Alegre and Guillerme Varella of the Federal University of Pernambuco in Recife. They recognized that, if the schools were to be effective as independent voices, they would have to band together. In São Paulo, they named themselves as the provisional board of a new association of urban planning programmes, and committed to preparing by-laws.

In 1986, Smolka hosted an open meeting of planning academics in Rio de Janeiro, for what became the formal creation of ANPUR, the National Association of Urban and Regional Postgraduate and Research Programmes. With about 40 persons in attendance, the group hammered out by-laws in a meeting that lasted until three in the morning. The underlying sentiment was that school curricula should be determined in the schools and that planning needed to have an identity that could not be manipulated by the authorities. As a result, in 1988, when ANPUR held its first official national meeting in Terasópolis, it was prepared to have a voice responding to a government programme for rating all postgraduate schools that would determine future funding levels. (Smolka 2004)

French planning schools were no strangers to stress in the mid-1980s. As early as 1982, national institutional reforms had led to challenges in the authority of urban planners, retrenchment from many of the social aspects of public policies championed by planners, and re-definition in universities that tied planning to secondary status. Seven French planning programs responded to these challenges by creating an association in May 1984. APERAU, the Association for the Development of Planning Education and Research, was founded by the planning institutes at the universities of Aix-Marseille III, Grenoble II, Lyon II, Paris

VIII, Paris XII, and Tours, and the Paris Institute of Political Study, to promote the discipline, reflect the interests of the schools, and facilitate cooperation with professional bodies. (Motte 1991)

The 1980s forces prompting creation of AESOP, ANPUR and APERAU, and stimulating ACSP to branch beyond its early charter, are consistent, if regionally distinct. As the ideas of the Reagan–Thatcher revolution developed, supplanting Keynesianism, urban planning came under considerable pressure in many nations. Schools connected to the profession experienced lowered student demand, and reductions in opportunity for funded work. At the same time, universities were increasingly attentive to unit productivity and many planning schools found themselves under criticism, if not outright threat. The twin incentives of organization to combat national challenges to the planning profession, and integration to promote better scholarship that might lead to stronger positions within universities, led planning schools on three continents to independently create or strengthen school associations. By the end of the 1980s, the Planning Schools Movement was an idea whose time had come.

Since 1990, the number of associations linking urban planning schools has continued to increase. The Asian Planning Schools Association (APSA) was formed in 1993, following a successful pan-Asian conference in Tokyo convened by Sadao Watanabe of the University of Tokyo in 1991, and a similar event in Hong Kong convened by Anthony Yeh of the Unversity of Hong Kong in 1993. APSA's original membership included 19 schools in 15 countries (Asian Planning Schools Association 2004).

The Australia and New Zealand Association of Planning Schools (ANZAPS) began with a resolution taken on 7 July 1995 at a national meeting of Australian planning schools hosted by Jeremy Dawkins at the University of Technology, Sydney. This momentum for the association was built at two workshops in 1994 hosted by Martin Payne and Greg Mills at the University of Sydney and by C. Tong Wu at the Queensland University of Technology. The several dozen participants in these meetings believed that the small size of Australian planning schools necessitated better communication among the nation's planning faculty. They also wanted to find a way to provide input into a review of education policy underway by the Royal Australian Planning Institute. ANZAPS chose less formal organization than the other planning schools associations existing at the time: it has no constitution, no elected officers, nor formal membership criteria, but rather prides itself on its status as a peer-to-peer network. (Witherby 2004)

The Association of Latin-American Schools of Urbanism and Planning (ALEUP) began in 1999 with five member schools in Argentina, Mexico and Venezuela. Roberto Rodriguez of Simon Bolivar University, hosted a meeting in Caracas in September, called for the purpose of founding the association, which had been under informal discussion since 1995. Antonio Ruiz Tenorio of the

Benemerita Autonomous University in Puebla, Lucia Andrade of the Autonomous University of Aguacalientes, Alberto Villar of the Autonomous University of the State of Mexico, Juan Lombardo of the General Sarmiento National University, and Rodriguez sought a mechanism to address the void in communication across national boundaries among planning academics in Central and South America. (Rodriguez 2004)

Just two years ago, a new association was created linking planning schools in sub-Saharan Africa. This association followed from discussions beginning in 1999 in Dar-es-Salaam during a PhD workshop funded, in part, by the Danish Danida Foundation. Staff from the planning school at the University of Dar-es-Salaam, including Tumsifu Nnkya, were joined by Kofi Diaw from Komasi University in Ghana and Vanessa Watson from the University of Cape Town. They discussed the often inappropriateness of African planning school curricula for the African context, and sought to use Danida funding to support efforts to address such issues through a network of planning academics. Danida funding did not materialize, but through contacts with other planning school associations, the idea of the ANZAPS model of peer-to-peer networking emerged, and in 2002, 16 schools in 10 countries agreed to become founding members of the Association of African Planning Schools (AAPS).

Nineteen years after Healey and Kunzmann dined in Atlanta, AESOP has 141 full and associate member schools in 29 countries, draws as many as 400 scholars to its annual congress, sponsors *European Planning Studies*, and has served as the conduit for European Union student and scholar exchange and curricular development. Its PhD student summer workshops, begun in 1991, are thought to have led to great strides in bridging the academic cultures of the various European nations and language groups.

ANPUR has grown to 32 institutional members. Its most recent biennial conference in May 2003 drew 550 persons to Belo Horizonte. The association publishes *Revista Brasileira de Estudos Urbanos e Regionais*, has fostered a national identity among urban planning students, has opened up international linkages for Brazilian planning scholars, and has influenced government actions on a national planning school entrance exam, and national response to habitat.

APERAU has 28 members in eight French-speaking countries (APERAU 2004). It hosts an annual conference, conducts research, and represents the French planning schools to university and government authorities involved with accreditation, school organization and European integration.

ACSP has 99 full and affiliate member schools in the US, publishes the *Journal of Planning Education and Research*, draws as many as 900 persons to its annual conference, conducts a biennial administrators conference and an annual workshop for doctoral students, is a partner in school accreditation, and has committees active in a variety of curricular, institutional and faculty interest areas.

APSA has 19 members schools in 13 countries, conducts a biennial congress, most recently drawing 199 presenters to Hanoi. ANZAPS has active faculty in 17 universities in Australia and New Zealand and is actively considering expansion to Papua New Guinea and other island Pacific nations. Its annual conference draws about 50. ALEUP has ten member schools and sponsors two conferences each year. Leaders of ACUPP's 16 member schools meet annually in conjunction with the conference of the Canadian Institute of Planners. AAPS has 16 member schools.

Also in these past 19 years, the world's planning school associations have begun to do things together. In 1991, AESOP and ACSP held a joint congress in England. In 1997, ANPUR sent a delegation of 27 scholars to the ACSP conference in Florida. Most notably, in 2001, four planning school associations joined together to hold the first World Planning Schools Congress (WPSC) in China. This successful congress, organized by Tongji University in Shanghai, drew 650 planning scholars from over 250 planning schools in 60 countries.

In Shanghai, leaders of ten planning school associations met to exchange information about their organizations and to discuss the potential for further cooperation. They shared information, discussed common objectives and possible future actions. The discussions were diplomatic, with a spirit of good will and a sense of historic purpose. They reflected considerable differences among the associations: national and multi-national; formal and informal; old and new; well-

1.2 World Planning Schools Congress 2001 opening assembly

financed and poorly financed. They considered the potential for future world congresses, mechanisms for internet linkages and other electronic communication, publication of joint scholarship, communications among persons with similar functions in the various regions, advocacy of the visibility of planning, and student exchanges. At the conclusions of the meetings, they unanimously agreed to what has become known as the Shanghai Statement, signed by representatives of all ten associations at the closing ceremony of the Shanghai Congress. This statement reads:

> Representatives of national and international planning education associations gathered at Tongji University in Shanghai and agreed on the goal of increasing mutual communication in order to improve the quality and visibility of planning and planning education. To achieve this, it was agreed to establish a global planning education association network and committees to plan holding the second World Planning Schools Congress and to develop an inclusive communication network.

The Shanghai Statement was subsequently formally endorsed by nine of the associations, each of which sent representatives to a first meeting of the Global Planning Association Network (GPEAN) in conjunction with the AESOP Congress in Volos, Greece in July 2002. In Greece, the GPEAN delegates crafted an action program and agreed to principles for operation of the network; officers were selected. Ten months later in Belo Horizonte, Brazil, in conjunction with an ANPUR Congress, a charter was developed, which has since been ratified by all nine founding member associations. The GPEAN charter sets up two standing committees: a coordinating committee, now chaired by Angus Witherby of ANZAPS, and a World Congress Steering Committee, co-chaired by Louis Albrechts of AESOP, Johanna Looye of ACSP, and Zhiqiang Wu of APSA. All together, the associations linked in GPEAN represent over 350 planning schools on all six continents.

This volume, the first in a series of books presenting selections of quality urban planning scholarship from each of the world's regions, originated with discussions in Shanghai. The discourse among scholars from the various countries represented at the first world congress demonstrated that much of the work planning scholars do is not known outside their home countries. The benefits of expanding our scholarly discourse to the global scale were seen as potentially very powerful. Face-to-face conferences were an important step, but other methods would be equally valued. They left Shanghai hoping to find ways to expand the sharing of published scholarship. In Volos the idea was honed, and in Belo Horizonte, Routledge was chosen as publisher and an international editorial board was named.

Each association formed its own editorial committee and made submissions in its own fashion. Most associations solicited open nominations and a jury chose the selections to put forward. In some associations, this meant putting forward the winner of a standing competition, such as AESOP's Prize Paper award and ACSP's Chester Rapkin and *JAPA* Best Paper awards. APSA selected its submissions from among the papers presented at its 2003 congress in Hanoi. APERAU chose not to submit for this first volume, but is committed to making submissions for the second volume to be published in 2006. In the final round, papers to be published were chosen by the international editorial board from among the submissions from the eight associations.

Looking back on the history of the various associations, the first World Planning Schools Congress, and the birth of GPEAN, it is clear that the Planning Schools Movement serves important scholarly and institutional purposes. Planning scholarship and planning education have been weaker because of the relative isolation of the various schools and the various national corps of planning educators. Cooperation, first nationally and regionally, and now globally, has made us stronger and has the potential to make us much stronger still.

As a relatively small profession, it has been difficult for us to have rich debates about our scholarship – debates informed by a variety of perspectives and many active research projects. In the USA, for instance, there are about 800 full-time planning faculty and ACSP's Guide lists 36 distinct areas of study (ACSP 2000b). That works out to 22 full-time faculties per area of study nationwide. This is often too few for effective discourse. In other countries, of course, the numbers are smaller still. Communication across borders is increasing the size of the groups of investigators who are aware of each other's work, resulting in more robust debates.

As a profession with widely disparate traditions and broad interdisciplinary connections, we have significant differences across national boundaries. International comparisons force us to re-evaluate our national decisions about the structure and nature of our discipline and to understand better why we choose to do what we do, and the way we do it.

As a profession entangled with national legal and institutional structures, our scholarship has often lacked variation in key variables. Communication across national boundaries has the potential to increase variation in our scholarship and to therefore reduce the level of assumption which we must use in our work.

Finally, given the extent of difficulty planning schools often have explaining their purposes and justifying their cost structures within universities, the growth of international cooperation allows us to gain new ideas about how to effectively represent our accomplishments and our purposes to our own institutional leaders.

International cooperation brings difficulties, of course. The various corps of planning scholars are as different in outlook and resources as the cultures they represent. Centuries of colonial history leave no shortage of concerns about exportation of hegemonic views. But, the early experience of GPEAN cooperation suggests that these fears need not dominate our interactions. The spirit of GPEAN's development has been one of cooperation and sensitivity. We have moved slowly in recognition of the need to respect different views, different decision cultures and different resources of the various associations. We have undertaken only that which is in harmony with the needs of *all* the associations. We have consciously adopted principles of exchange. These first steps position us as colleagues joined together to explore a common future.

So many times in Oxford, Toronto, Shanghai and Leuven, sites of the various multi-association congresses, we heard scholars exclaim surprise at alternative approaches used to study the very issues they study, by people they previously did not know existed. So often we have heard complaints that whole journals exist in one country, that students and teachers in other countries do not know about. So often we hear frustrations about the limitations in international exchange posed by language differences and differences in educational systems. The *Dialogues* project is a small but significant step toward remediation of global isolation in planning scholarship.

Global themes

The chapters in this volume indicate some key themes in current international planning scholarship. Significantly, while these contributions come from very different parts of the world, and while some authors stress the particularity of their context, it appears that certain planning issues and concerns are common across a wide range of countries. The emerging commonalities, we would suggest, make the task of bringing together these regional contributions both an interesting and a necessary one.

Three central themes are identified here. A first theme has to do with the relationship between planning and economy. *Grant's* article (Chapter 2) focuses on a common and contemporary planning strategy: the promotion of mixed urban land use in order to achieve more accessible, efficient and sustainable cities. Using empirical material from Canadian cities, she finds that while the policy and legal environment has been changed to facilitate mix, important cultural and economic barriers continue to promote the separation of land uses and social groupings. *Searle* (Chapter 3) also explores an attempt by planning to intervene in an urban economy. He analyzes the impact of the construction of two large stadiums for the Olympic Games in Sydney, Australia. Both were developed in partnership with government on the grounds that they would generate wider economic benefits for the city. In commenting on the lack of financial viability of the stadiums and the questionable economic impacts of the investments, Searle points to planning's increasing subordination to market forces in a context of economic uncertainty, and hence planning processes that are more reactive, short-term and unpredictable in their consequences.

The article by *Lombardo, Di Virgilio and Fernández* (Chapter 4), which analyzes the shaping of urban land use by forces of capital in Buenos Aires, echoes the conclusions of the other two articles in this group. Space is being shaped by market forces, causing a fragmentation of the city and isolation of lower-income people. Upper-income residential forms increasingly occur in gated villages and country clubs, while the excluded or devalued zones of the city are left to the public sector and the poor. Private capital, and not government or planning, has become the main organizer of the city.

The second theme evident in these articles is that of environment and conservation. The *Dolman, Lovett, O'Riordan and Cobb* article (Chapter 5) describes a 'whole-landscape' approach to rural management in Britain that ensures conservation and the enhancement of biodiversity in farmed landscapes. Drawing on the emerging discipline of landscape ecology, they consider how the structure and juxtaposition of landscape elements affects their function in terms of ecosystem processes, resilience to change, the regulation of environmental quality and the dynamics of species assemblages and individual populations. *Zhang's* article (Chapter 6), concerned with the rapidly changing urban setting of Shanghai, looks at the common problem of balancing needs for conservation with the management of urban regeneration. Drawing on case study material, Zhang shows how China's incomplete urban conservation policy framework, and the lack of a theoretical foundation to conservation efforts, results in insufficiently effective planning tools, difficulties in countering pressure from both the market and other local government departments, and variable interpretations by different agents of how landscapes should change.

The article by *Acselrad* (Chapter 7) takes as its subject the process of ecological-economic zoning in the Brazilian Amazon region, but he uses this to explore the theoretical issue of the use of planning as a means of surveillance and control of people and territory. Drawing on the theoretical resources of Foucault and de Certeau he highlights the gap between the conception of space informing the planning process and the lived reality within that space. Planning in this case forms a mechanism through which power can be exercised, and its effectiveness in protecting environment and livelihoods has been minimal.

The third theme of the collection gathers together those articles primarily concerned with the nature of planning processes and decision-making. An important issue in all of these contributions is that of how to manage, or how to understand, consensus-seeking decision-making processes in contexts characterized by multiple stakeholders and interest groups, and increasingly, by cultural diversity as well.

Umemoto (Chapter 8) and *Bollens* (Chapter 9) both begin their pieces with a common concern: the problem of participation in situations of cultural diversity, and communication across culture-based epistemologies. Both address the US planning profession, yet both are drawing on empirical material on cross-cultural planning efforts from very different parts of the world: Umemoto from Hawai'i and Bollens from three 'polarized' cities – Belfast, Jerusalem and Johannesburg. Both authors draw attention to the need for planning to accommodate difference, and to develop methods and epistemologies that can bridge the gap between different worldviews. *Jamal, Stein and Harper* (Chapter 10) offer planning practitioners and theorists a way around multi-stakeholder and multicultural dilemmas. They consider how a neopragmatic approach to collaborative planning, in a situation involving nature-based tourism in a remote region of Canada, could have avoided conflict between stakeholders. Neopragmatism suggests an inter-active, learning-based approach to planning under conflict, where term definitions and categories are not imposed on participants but are left to evolve over time through debate. *Watson* (Chapter 11) tackles this issue from a different perspective, and asks how appropriate are current normative theories of planning which deal with communication and multiculturalism, and with equitable city form, in the very different context of Africa. She concludes that while these theories have value, they are all based on assumptions about culture, economy and place that do not hold in this very different context.

Two further articles make important theoretical contributions to the planning themes of difference, communication and consensus. *Sandercock* (Chapter 12) advocates the use of stories in planning: as a way of gaining mutual understanding (particularly between people with different worldviews); as a way of communicating and debating; as a form of persuasion and policy shaping; and as a way of teaching. Stories, she suggests, can form the basis of both an epistemology and a methodology that is particularly appropriate to planning in the contemporary world. *Mantysalo*'s (Chapter 13) article is aimed at criticizing the currently hegemonic position in planning theory: critical planning theory, which draws on Habermas for its theoretical base and which has informed communicative and collaborative planning action. He asks if critical planning theory can really be considered a new paradigm in planning and concludes that it should be seen as no more than a partial theory of legitimacy in participatory planning. It fails to acknowledge the presence of power in all planning actions and fails to inform the organizing, problem-shaping and problem-solving aspects that are central to any planning process.

This collection of articles, which has emerged from selection processes at both regional and global level, creates the opportunity to consider what the planning community currently regards as 'good scholarship'. The *Dialogues* International Editorial Board did not set standard criteria for selection by the associations, but it became clear as the articles were assembled that there are commonalities in terms of what is regarded as a good article.

In the first instance they are all contemporary and speak to current and pressing regional concerns in planning. Thus it is not surprising that many of the contributions from the United States, Canada and Europe show a concern with decision-making processes in planning in the context of increasing multiculturalism and multi-stakeholder societies, as it is these parts of the world which represent the destinations for the largest global migration flows. Similarly, it is not surprising that in those parts of the world that have been experiencing rapid urban growth and change, there are concerns about the ability of planning to protect local heritage and environmental resources, to create more accessible and sustainable cities, and to accommodate the poor in the face of strong and often global market forces.

A second characteristic is the ability to ground an argument in an analysis of concrete practice, and to link this analysis to a broader theoretical debate. Such practice can be illustrative of a more general argument that is being made, or can itself generate new theoretical propositions. Many of the articles use this methodology to produce new understanding, and the Sandercock article fits well with these in suggesting the use of stories as a way of gaining and presenting situated knowledge.

Following from the above, a third characteristic of the good scholarship represented here is a familiarity with broader theoretical debates in the field of concern. The articles here all indicate a good knowledge of relevant literature and an understanding of the need to be able to frame current debates and then to take them forward. For some of the authors, assembling such debates has meant crossing language and geographical divides, but the rewards for testing ideas outside of their original context are certainly high.

A final issue to be explored here is the extent to which thinking about planning in various parts of the world is cross-connected and integrated. We argue here that such integration in scholarship is something to be fostered as it exposes all of us to the widest possible range of ideas and debates, and allows us to better understand the complexity and diversity of situations in which planners find themselves. One rather simple way of gauging the extent of cross-connection is to examine the literature sources cited by various authors, and the degree to which these sources are geographically local or more widespread. A quick scan of the literature sources used by the authors in this volume suggests that while there may be common themes and issues that connect them, the integration of intellectual traditions and ideas is partial.

The chapters in this volume indicate a tendency for authors to draw primarily on local sources. This is particularly true of authors in regions with good publishing outlets for planning scholars, efficient marketing and distribution networks for planning literature, and larger concentrations of planning academics. North America and Europe fit these criteria, as does South America (where planning is part of a broader urbanism field). Authors from regions less well equipped in these terms may have little option but to look elsewhere both for intellectual input and publishing opportunities. Africa, for example, does not have a single supra-national, dedicated, planning journal, and Australia and New Zealand are only a little better off. This gives rise to a degree of (uni-directional) integration, but there may be little incentive for authors from literature-rich regions to reciprocate, unless they are drawing on case material from these other parts of the world. Both the Bollens and Umemoto chapters fall into this category.

Authors also draw on local sources when language barriers prevent them from accessing literatures more widely. The Zhang chapter, originally produced in Mandarin, is a good example of a breach of this barrier, allowing the author to draw on the extensive British literature on heritage management. But there is little evidence of English-speaking authors drawing on literature sources produced by other language groups, and little evidence of authors crossing barriers between languages other than English.

It is in relation to the overcoming of such barriers that the GPEAN publishing project is intended to play an important role. The aim is to make available best scholarship from whatever source languages, to English-speaking readers, and to use both websites and publishers to make the contents of the book available in languages other than English. The promotion and distribution of this material through the organizational structures of the nine planning school associations which make up GPEAN will help to make this wide-ranging material available in parts of the world where it would not normally be accessible, and will, it is hoped, help to make intellectual connections which will integrate and enrich the body of planning scholarship.

The growth of the Planning Schools Movement onto a global stage offers potential to reduce the problems of scholarly isolation in urban planning, and to build a stronger, more rigorous, richer profession of urban planning. This volume is a significant step in the very young global history of planning schools coopera-tion. We hope that you will find these papers stimulating and that they will suggest new directions, bibliographically, methodologically, theoretically or substantively, that will lead directly or indirectly, to improvements in your own work, changes in your schools and improvements in the practice of urban planning in your communities.

References

ACSP (Association of Collegiate Schools of Planning) (2000a) *Executive Committee Background Notebook*. Tallahassee: ACSP.

—— (2000b) *Guide to Undergraduate and Graduate Education in Urban and Regional Planning*. Tucson, AZ: ACSP.

APERAU (2004) Association pour la Promotion de l'Enseignement et de la Recherche en Aménagement et Urbanisme. Available online http://www.aperau.org/organismes.htm/ (accessed 13 July).

Asian Planning Schools Association (2004) Asian planning schools association. Available online http://www.apsaweb.org/ (accessed 14 January).

Chatterjee, J. (1986) 'Presidential address', *Journal of Planning Education and Research*, 6(1): 3–8.

Kunzmann, K.R. (1998) *AESOP: Raumplanung in Europa vernetzt*, working paper. Reprint 33. Dortmund: Universität Dortmund, Facultät Raumplanung.

Motte, A. (1991) 'Education in town and regional planning in France', paper presented at the Joint Congress of the Association of European Schools of Planning and the Association of Collegiate Schools of Planning, Oxford, England, July.

Rodriguez, R. (2004) E-mail correspondence, 10 January.

Smolka, M. (2004) Telephone interview, 23 January.

Witherby, A. (2004) E-mail correspondence, 11 March.

Chapter 2
Mixed use in theory and practice
Canadian experience with implementing a planning principle

Jill Grant

This article explores the theory and practice of mixed use, from its origins in the critiques of Jane Jacobs to the recent prescriptions of New Urbanism. Drawing on experiences in Canada, where mixed use has become firmly established as a key planning principle, we identify some of the problems and barriers encountered in seeking mix in several cities. We find that mixed use promises economic vitality, social equity, and environmental quality, but it cannot readily deliver such benefits in a context where cultural and economic forces promote separation of land uses.

As the twentieth century opened, North American cities began segregating land uses, regulating noxious industries and creating single-purpose districts. Early city planning sought to enhance safety and efficiency by putting distance and buffers between activities deemed incompatible. By the close of the century, however, the philosophy of separation had turned full circle, with planners advocating mixing land uses for vibrancy and sustainability. "Mixed use" has become a mantra in contemporary planning, its benefits taken for granted. Few question its premises or endeavor to clarify its meaning. Mixed use forms an integral premise of the popular paradigms of New Urbanism and sustainable development (Bernick and Cervero, 1997; Berridge Lewinberg Greenberg Ltd., 1991; Calthorpe, 1993). In theoretical discussions, proponents promise social and economic gains from mixing uses; in design exercises, various approaches promote mix; in planning practice, an increasing number of jurisdictions implement mixed-use zones.

This article examines mixed use in theory and in practice in nine cities across Canada, shown in Figure 2.1. I begin by exploring the premises of mixed use. The proponents of mixed use see modern town planning's effort to separate uses in the twentieth century as unnatural. New planning approaches treat mixing as necessary and desirable, yet often provide insufficient clarity about intended

Article submitted by the Association of Canadian University Planning Programs.

2.1 Locations of Canadian cities cited in this article

objectives or appropriate strategies. I analyze the meanings of mixed use to introduce greater clarity into the discussions and suggest that various levels of mixed use imply different objectives and divergent strategies.

Canadian planners rallied early and strongly to the call for mixed use. I review Canadian experiences in promoting mixed use through redeveloping the inner city and in greenfield projects.[1] The New Urbanists suggest that Canadian planning is far ahead of that in America (Wight, 1995), but has mixed use succeeded in Canadian cities? This article examines some of the problems and barriers encountered in Canada and tries to explain why some planners and many developers remain skeptical of the idea of mixed use. While mixed-use strategies have revived many declining inner-city districts and may add new dimensions to large greenfield projects, not all urban residents nor all uses benefit from such changes.

Premises: mixed-use theory

Congestion, pollution, and generally poor urban conditions led to modern town planning in the early twentieth century. By the 1920s, zoning became firmly entrenched as a strategy for separating uses seen as incompatible in proximity. For much of the century, planners played an important role in keeping land uses in their places in the urban environment.

By mid-century, however, changing transportation and economic patterns had transformed North American cities. Inner-city districts suffered decline as suburban areas grew. Postwar governments responded with urban renewal schemes designed to restore vitality to moribund downtown areas. Within a decade of the initiation of renewal projects, skeptics began challenging dominant modern planning premises.

Jane Jacobs, an influential early critic, released her powerful book, *The Death and Life of Great American Cities*, in 1961. She argued that fine-grain mixing of diverse uses creates vibrant and successful neighborhoods. As urban renewal continued, its impacts grew more evident, and Jacobs' comments seemed increasingly cogent. By the late 1960s, community activists and progressive planners saw neighborhood planning and mixed use for the urban core as desirable strategies.

By the 1980s, support for mixing uses had become increasingly common in the literature (see, e.g. Van der Ryn and Calthorpe, 1986) and a popular topic of discussion at professional conferences. Mixed use regained favor with its promise of restoring vitality, environmental quality, equity, and efficiency to the post-industrial city. Its proponents suggested many benefits.

- Mix creates an urban environment active at all hours, making optimum use of infrastructure.
- Smaller, post-baby-boom households can have a greater range of options (rather than just detached homes).
- Mixing housing types could increase affordability and equity by reducing the premium that exclusive, segregated areas enjoy.
- By providing housing near commercial and civic activities, planners could reduce the dependence of the elderly and children on cars.
- Enabling people to live near places where they can shop, work, or play could reduce car ownership and vehicle trips, increase pedestrian and transit use, and thus alleviate the environmental consequences associated with automobile use.

Mixing uses thus forms part of a strategy for sustainable development as well as a theory of good urban form, with the objectives of economic vitality, social equity, and environmental quality.

Mixing land uses seems like a relatively straightforward concept. However, as we examine the objectives and strategies used by those advocating mix, we find at least three conceptual levels. At the first level, proponents suggest increasing the intensity of land uses. Within a given category of land use, usually residential, planners may enhance the range of choices available. Instead of differentiating zones by density or type of housing, we could encourage a mix of forms and tenures. This would have the effect of increasing overall density. Moreover, if we believe that households choose housing type based on life-cycle stage or income level, then we could argue that mixing types of housing brings different households together (Vischer, 1984). This is the aim of social mix, a popular concept in the 1970s.

Another level of mixing involves increasing the diversity of uses within the urban fabric by encouraging compatible mix. Compatible uses do not create conflict and may generate synergies. For instance, adding high-density residential uses to commercial and office districts may prove compatible because residents who live near businesses may patronize or work in those businesses. Their presence could enliven the area after work hours, creating new business opportunities. Flexibility to allow such mixing, say its advocates, will enable markets to restore conditions common in the preregulated city.

The third level of mixing involves integrating segregated uses. Bringing categories of use together in proximity may require overcoming regulatory barriers. For instance, jurisdictions often require spacing or buffers between heavy industry and other urban uses. Such separations reflect concerns about environmental impacts, noise, or traffic. In larger cities, economic patterns (more than government regulation) also contribute to the development of special areas (e.g. a "garment district"). While integrating some segregated uses may prove desirable and possible, the term compatible recognizes that not all uses mix well.

What have planners generally meant by "mixed use"? Although the term appears frequently in the planning literature, it is rarely defined (Molinaro, 1993). In its text on the subject, the Urban Land Institute (1987) suggests that a mixed-use project develops according to a coherent plan with three or more functionally and physically integrated revenue-producing uses. Large-scale urban redevelopment projects dominated urban renewal in the 1960s to 1980s; for instance, Marina City in Chicago, The Watergate in Washington, and Scotia Square in Halifax featured a mix of office, retail, hotel, leisure, and residential uses in a pedestrian-oriented environment (Collier, 1974; Urban Land Institute, 1987). These mega-projects, which typically displaced earlier mixed-use districts rendered obsolete or deemed unattractive by the ravages of time, shared the philosophy of increasing diversity while also increasing density and intensity.

Attempts to mix uses reveal significant fears about mixing. People do not want certain land uses near them. Adopting mixed-use zoning and providing for urban intensification in the 1980s generated a public response. Agencies that needed to find sites for group homes, day care centers, waste management facilities, high-density housing, halfway houses, or prisons typically encountered resistance from residents. Even parks and playgrounds sometimes met opposition. NIMBYism, the "Not-In-My-Back-Yard" phenomenon, grew along with pressures for mixing (Dear, 1992; Hornblower, 1988; Rural and Small Town Research and Studies Programme, 1992). Experience shows that the residents of established communities may resent mixing, especially those uses seen as most "incompatible" or likely to increase urban densities (Clark-Madison, 1999; McMahon, 1999; Pendall, 1999).

New Urbanism is probably the most important movement for entrenching mixed use within North American planning in recent years. With roots in the neotraditional town planning of Andres Duany and Elizabeth Plater-Zyberk (1992, 1996; Katz, 1994; Krieger, 1991) and influenced by the transit-oriented development concepts of Peter Calthorpe (1993), New Urbanism became veritable gospel in the 1990s. Its advocates traveled the conference and talk-show circuit, describing their vision (Hume, 1991; McInnes, 1992), while the print media disseminated the word (e.g. Adler, 1994; Anderson, 1991; *Newsweek*, 1995). Extensively promoted by professional organizations in journals, workshops, and conferences, New Urbanism came to dominate late twentieth-century planning principles. Many communities revised their policies, plans, and regulations to incorporate the concepts.

The two streams within New Urbanism have different visions of mixed use. Duany and Plater-Zyberk's traditional neighborhood design (TND) involves intensification and mixing compatible uses at a fine grain (Bressi, 1994; Duany and Plater-Zyberk, 1994). TND promotes apartments over garages to intensify uses, residential units over stores in a diverse but low-rise town center, and zoning codes to allow people to work from home. Duany and Plater-Zyberk (1994) say that special districts accommodate industrial and other uses that cannot integrate into neighborhoods.

Transit-oriented development (TOD) concentrates development in nodes associated with transit stations (Bernick and Cervero, 1997; Berridge Lewinberg Greenberg Ltd, 1991; Calthorpe, 1993; Kelbaugh, 1989, 1997; Nelessen, 1993). Commercial, office, entertainment, and high-density residential uses colocate near the station. Low-density residential development disperses toward the edges of the node within a five-minute walk. Thus TOD creates an urban region structure with clusters of uses aligned in a density gradient from transit stations. This concept has proven popular as a rationale for redevelopment in cities with good or improving transit systems. It has relatively little to say, however, about options for integrating industrial uses.

These two models of New Urbanism thus expound different strategies for mixed use (Katz, 1994). The TOD approach supports urban infill and redevelopment approaches. The TND model works best with greenfield development on new suburban sites. Those committed to urban sustainability (with efficient use of infrastructure and reduced environmental impacts) prefer TOD. Others argue that the TND approach seems more practical, given that most growth occurs at the urban edge.

When contemporary planners and designers speak of mixed use, they do not advocate a jumble of uses. The proponents of contemporary mixed use promote either the planned community, with its clusters of compatible uses oriented to encourage walking and transit use (Bernick and Cervero, 1997; Calthorpe, 1993; Nelessen, 1993), or they suggest what the Urban Land Institute (1987) calls "multiuse projects" (several uses within one or more buildings) in inner core areas. Mixed uses are part of the "Smart Growth" agenda promoted by organizations such as the Urban Land Institute (O'Neill, 2000; Urban Land Institute, 1998), the American Planning Association (APA, 2001), and the Congress for the New Urbanism (CNU, 2001). APA's guide on best development practices suggests mixing at the finest grain the market will bear (Ewing, 1996), while acknowledging that the market may not tolerate a great deal of mixing.

Commercial, office, retail, institutional, and residential uses feature prominently in discussions about mixed use. Industrial activities are less commonly included, although some planners promise a place for them. As Berridge Lewinberg Greenberg Ltd (1991: 22) write:

> While some uses are not compatible with some others, particularly heavy industry, noxious, or noisy uses, many new industries are small in scale and clean. Industries which meet "good neighbour" environmental criteria regarding noise or emissions should be permitted to be part of the local urban fabric.

Nonetheless, few New Urbanist-inspired suburbs or villages provide an industrial component. Ewing (1996) suggests relegating industry to "harmless" locations, reflecting the difficulty of mixing. Planners see industrial uses as less desirable and perhaps incompatible with other uses in the postindustrial city.

Encouraged by theories such as sustainable development and New Urbanism, today professional discourse (e.g., in journals, books, and conferences) treats mixed-use zoning as an established "planning principle," especially for downtown areas and "town centers." As Berridge Lewinberg Greenberg Ltd. (1991: 22–3) assert, "Mixing land uses is a necessary but not sufficient condition for a better city and environment. ... Promoting mixed use development is the most fundamental land use principle." Many cities amended zoning bylaws in the 1980s and 1990s to provide districts to permit, encourage, and intensify mixed uses – usually combinations of residential, commercial, open space, and institutional (Tomalty, 1997). While single-use zones have not disappeared, they appear increasingly as anachronisms. The next section considers how mixed use became gospel in Canada and the impact it has had on planning practice.

Promises: the Canadian experience

Mixed use downtown

Jane Jacobs (1961) had a great influence on planning in Canada. Although she wrote about American cities, Jacobs struck a chord with Canadian activists. Her book, taught in most planning schools, remained on the "must read" list of planners for decades (Martin et al.,1988). Jacobs had moved to Toronto by the

1970s and joined the Canadian debate full force. The timing proved auspicious, as a reform slate of councillors and mayor took control of Toronto city government in 1972 (Gordon and Fong, 1989; Sewell, 1993). Council set about changing planning in the city, with Jacobs' admonitions in mind.

Infill projects in Toronto reveal Jacobs' influence. In 1974, the St Lawrence neighborhood, an industrial site needing redevelopment, provided an opportunity to test Jacobs' ideas of fine-grain mixed use (Gordon and Fong, 1989). With government financing, the project aimed for a mix of market-rate and affordable housing and commercial and institutional uses. Although the consultant originally recommended light industry near Parliament Street, industrial uses were omitted in the end because City staff feared destabilizing the industrial district at King and Parliament. As the project took shape, it received praise and abundant publicity.

During the 1970s and 1980s, older Toronto neighborhoods became trendy (Caulfield, 1994). Gentrification changed their character, improving the tax base, but driving out working-class residents. Districts such as Cabbagetown and the waterfront experienced rejuvenation and intensification of uses through to the 1990s (Berridge Lewinberg Greenberg Ltd, 1991). City planners, supported by local government, sought to accommodate growth without letting it spill into the suburbs. Land use planning for mixed use along transit lines and in the urban core formed part of the strategy of intensification and reurbanization (Municipality of Metropolitan Toronto 1987, 1991, 1992).

Toronto's experience influenced other cities. Vancouver, BC, followed suit with mixed use projects along its waterfront. Through conferences and professional journals, interest in mixed use and social mix grew. In the 1980s, an increasingly conservative political environment supported deregulating markets. By the mid-1980s, many Canadian communities had added "mixed use" zones to their land use bylaws and applied them to the urban core. Mixed use became a planning principle.

Other Canadian municipalities hoped to follow Toronto and Vancouver's lead by redeveloping declining inner cities. They rezoned central business districts to allow mixed use. While Toronto and Vancouver experienced rapid change as residential and commercial uses displaced aging industrial districts, many smaller cities saw little return from efforts to revitalize their downtowns. Some communities, such as Halifax and Vancouver, can point to waterfronts or former industrial sites transformed into entertainment or residential districts through federal and provincial initiatives. For most cities, however, growth continued to funnel into suburban areas as city cores slid into potential irrelevance. Government initiatives could not change urban development patterns (Tomalty, 1997).

The late 1980s and early 1990s brought widespread interest in environmental issues. Maurice Strong, a prominent Canadian diplomat, participated in the World Commission on Environment and Development (1987), playing a major role in promoting "sustainable development." The federal government's Green Plan (Government of Canada, 1990) presented an agenda of environmental responsibility, while a Royal Commission (1992) replanned the Toronto water-front. Agencies such as Health Canada, Environment Canada, and Canada Mortgage and Housing Corporation initiated programs to encourage sustainability in Canadian communities. Planners began to consider how to adjust their practice to accommodate sustainability concerns (Grant, 1997; Grant *et al.*, 1994; Paehlke, 1991; Pomeroy, 1999).

As Canadian planners worried about reducing the environmental impacts of urban development, interest in applying the ideas of New Urbanism grew (City of Calgary, 1998; Isin and Tomalty, 1993; Tomalty, 1997). New Urbanism offered a theory of urban form to fit the predispositions of influential groups in Canadian planning practice, especially in the largest centers. During the 1990s, cities such as Calgary, Vancouver, Ottawa, Toronto, Waterloo, Winnipeg, and Edmonton revised their plans to incorporate constructs from New Urbanism and sustainable development. The Ontario provincial government prepared reports describing New Urbanism and sponsoring design contests to illustrate its potential (Government of Ontario, 1995, 1997; Warson, 1994). Organizations such as the Federation of Canadian Municipalities, the Canadian Institute of Planners, the Canadian Institute of Transportation Engineers, the Canadian Urban Transit Association, and the National Roundtable on Environment and Economy advocated transit-oriented urban development with mixed-use nodes (Berridge *et al.*, 1996; National Roundtable, 1997; Transportation Association of Canada, 1998). The Canadian planning profession's journal, *Plan Canada*, had articles promoting New Urbanism and sustainable development in half its issues in 1992 and 1993 and in every issue from 1994 through 1996. Feature editors of *Plan Canada* referred to traditional suburbs in negative terms (e.g. Wight, 1995, 1996). For several years, Canadian Institute of Planners conferences featured sessions and keynote speakers on New Urbanism. Thus, in the 1990s, Canadian planners practiced in a context where New Urbanism dominated discourse and became infused with overtones of environmental responsibility.

With the professional bodies clearly behind New Urbanism, planners across Canada adjusted plans and regulations accordingly (Pomeroy, 1999). Larger cities hired consultants to work with staff to examine plans and regulations to reorient their policies with the new ideas (e.g. Bogdan, 1992; Greenberg and Gabor, 1992; Lewinberg, 1993). New Urbanism (with its rhetoric of sustainable develop-ment) provided a reinvigorated rationale for planning practice.[2]

Cities across Canada promote mixed use today, arguing for its benefits on social, economic, and environmental grounds. Mixed use remains most common in inner-city districts, especially as a strategy to revitalize derelict properties. Thus, for instance, Toronto plans to turn abandoned industrial districts, known as "The

Kings,"[3] into "reinvestment areas" (City of Toronto, 1998; Porte, 1998). They will renovate old brick buildings largely for residential use. In Ville Saint-Laurent in Montreal, a former air strip has become the site of a "new town," Bois Franc (Hutchinson, 1998; Sauer, 1998). The project seeks to reproduce attributes of older Montreal neighborhoods; however, proposals to allow convenience stores in Bois Franc faced resident opposition. Efforts to develop comprehensive urban plans promoting intensification and mixed use can meet resistance.

While infilling core areas with new mixed uses has benefits, it also carries costs. Some uses are pushed out. For example, in Halifax, two bars had to close even though zoning policies allowed them as part of the mix. In one case, in the 1990s, residents of a new apartment building in the core successfully fought the renewal of a bar's liquor license, claiming that the establishment (which predated their tenure in the neighborhood) ruined their quiet enjoyment. In another instance, the landlord of a multiuse building refused to renew a nightclub's lease after a new tenant complained about noise. Those who resist mixed use have other mechanisms to employ if zoning facilitates "incompatible" mix.

In Toronto and Vancouver, deindustrialization has opened land in the inner city for redevelopment. Manufacturing jobs are leaving the city, taking the working class with them. Some cities are becoming gentrified, with older neighborhoods changing from industrial to upscale residential use.[4] At the same time, housing costs escalate, vacancy rates decrease, and homelessness becomes a significant concern. Revitalization solves the problems of some declining neighborhoods, but not without generating other dilemmas.

Mixing land uses in the inner city has become part of a strategy for replacing disappearing industrial uses. Although many sources suggest that industry is changing to become clean and quiet and thus no longer needs be segregated, in most cases industry remains unwanted. Relegated to the periphery, industrial areas still provide significant employment opportunities. Their isolation and distance from transit routes may force workers to drive to get to them. Could a strategy of increasing mixed use in industrial parks prove viable?

We explored this question with a case study of Burnside Industrial Park in the Halifax region of Nova Scotia (Grant *et al.*, 1994). This industrial park, a clean and relatively quiet site with a spectacular view of Bedford Basin, hosts 1,200 businesses. Our analysis demonstrated ample opportunities for residential infill. However, interviews with business owners, park managers, local councillors, and planners revealed considerable reluctance to alter the mix of uses. Respondents worried that residents would destabilize the business environment by complaining about noise, traffic, and risk. Businesses felt more confident about their investments knowing that zoning constrained the mix of uses and limited uncertainty about the future. We found the prospects for mixing residential with industrial uses no more favorable in the industrial park than in the urban core.

In sum, then, infill development and intensification are popular with Canadian planners; TOD-style New Urbanism affects development in major cities such as Toronto, Vancouver, and Calgary. However, it has not become the dominant form of growth, and industrial uses do not form part of the mix. Greenfield sites remain cheap, especially in slowly growing regions. Powerful interests promote suburban development. Moreover, Canadians often fear high density or affordable housing and remain attached to their cars. They resist intensification (Tomalty, 1997). In the next section, I briefly review the planning of new greenfield sites in Canada to consider whether planners are implementing mixed use there.

Mixed use in the suburbs

In 1997 the Congress for the New Urbanism held its well-publicized conference in Toronto. New Urbanists raved about the city, its neighborhoods, and projects proposed or underway in Canada (Everett-Green, 1997). By 2000, some 30 suburban communities showed the influence of New Urbanism. The first of these communities to break ground, McKenzie Towne in Calgary, projected developing some 2,400 acres. By mid-2000, the developers, Carma, had constructed two neighborhoods (or "villages") and a "town center." Designed in consultation with Andres Duany and described as a mixed-use community, McKenzie Towne has a range of housing types, from apartments to single detached units. It features neighborhood commercial property on the village square. Consistent with Calgary's plans (City of Calgary, 1995a, 1995b), McKenzie Towne plans a light rail transit stop at the town center. Through the 1990s, McKenzie Towne enjoyed positive press and a high profile in planning discussions (Chidley, 1997; Hygeia, 1995; MacDonald and Clark, 1995).

The research revealed several difficulties in making this mixed-use plan work, at least in the early years of development. Carma has invested millions of dollars in commercial structures that it cannot sell; instead, it leases the properties but faces high vacancy rates. The neighborhood commercial property on the square is largely empty. A private school proposed to move into the building but faced resident opposition and backed out. The developer cancelled plans for apartments above stores in the town center because market rents would not cover building costs; apartments over garages on the alleys suffered the same fate. The light rail station is years away, and residents express concern about the length of the bus trip into the city.

Carma representatives found that builders had trouble selling high-end homes where mixing of housing types was greatest. For that reason, the developers reduced mixing in the second village. Based on the experience in Calgary, where growth is strong and the housing market very tight, Carma says New Urbanism appeals to a small market segment. Residents like the architectural details and public spaces, but buyers prefer homogeneous neighborhoods with single-family detached homes.

TND forms cost more to build and service than conventional development but do not create a premium value for sales. McKenzie Towne is becoming a "starter" housing area because the "move-up" market seeks a more conventional built form and mix. Thus the suburb will offer affordable housing,[5] but the upper end of the mix originally envisioned will not materialize. In subsequent phases of the project, Carma has decided it will abandon the TND concept in favor of conventional development. The developer discovered that mix can be dangerous to the corporate bottom line even in a high-growth area.

In the Toronto suburbs, New Urbanism is proliferating. Following amalgamation of the city with its suburbs in the late 1990s, the focus of development may be shifting from the inner city. In wealthy Markham, northeast of the city, local officials seem committed to changing regulations to promote New Urbanism (Hutchinson, 1998). Buildings in these upscale suburbs often replicate features of early-twentieth-century neighborhoods but include a mix of housing types (see Figure 2.2). By the summer of 2000, several Toronto suburbs featured "heritage-inspired" communities with back lanes and a mix of housing types. By and large, however, these high-priced suburbs do not include commercial uses.

The largest New Urbanist community in Markham is Cornell, commissioned by the Province of Ontario in the mid-1990s but later sold to private interests.

2.2 Suburban mix in Markham, ON. Service bollards in the grass strip along the street disrupt the "old town" image

The design shows the influence of Duany and Plater-Zyberk (*Financial Post*, 1996; *Toronto Life*, 1996). With 11 neighborhoods, Cornell draws on the Toronto vernacular; Duany said it will resemble treasured Cabbagetown if the code remains simple (Bentley Mays, 1997). Although rapid transit does not reach Cornell, bus links are available.

New Urbanist communities in Ontario struggle to attract commercial tenants (*Toronto Life*, 1996) and appeal only to a small segment of the market. As a New Urban form, they present a risk to investors. The early experience of some builders may scare other developers away, because mixed use and back lanes are not proving popular with purchasers.

"In the ultimate New Urbanist scenario, home owners live next to renters. Merchants live above their own shops" (Hutchinson, 1998: 120). This situation does not apply in Canadian projects. If we find both apartments and houses, most are occupied by owners; few are rented. Stores, with false stories above, are leased to franchisees. These new "towns" are in danger of becoming caricatures of a real community: a theme park "olde" town (Saunders, 1997). In some suburbs, New Urbanism means little more than gingerbread trim and front porches. Stripped to a few essentials, the concept is a marketing ploy for placing narrow houses on small lots.

Judging from interviews with planners and from statements in Canadian plans, the planners of growing suburban municipalities seem positive about New Urbanism and its precepts (see also Pomeroy, 1999). They actively encourage developers to try elements of New Urbanism. They are adjusting planning and zoning rules to promote flexibility and are trying to convince engineers and others in local government to cooperate. Why? New Urbanism seems progressive. It responds to the market by allowing developers to maximize yield. It draws on powerful values in planning, such as efficiency, equity (affordability), amenity, and environment – even if it cannot fully deliver. In the face of continuing sprawl, planners see few alternatives to promoting New Urbanism. If mixed use promises vitality, efficiency, and equity, how could planners oppose it?

Our interviews revealed, however, that planners in slow-growing communities remain skeptical of the potential benefits of New Urbanism in suburban development (even though they reflect its premises in documents). They focus on trying to prevent further deterioration of the inner city while managing growth on the fringe. They see the "old urbanism" (i.e. existing neighborhoods) as needing support. They believe that people make conscious choices in buying homes: suburbanites want space, a rural feel, and separation from other uses. In this scenario, mixed uses are best placed in the urban core. Planners who hold such views are cautious in expressing them because they face the disdain of the proponents of New Urbanism. For instance, the editor of a *Plan Canada* issue called the skeptics of New Urbanism "effectively anti-urban and favouring a lower, sub-form of truly urban life" (Wight, 1995: 20).[6] If the weight of the profession advocates a particular paradigm, those who dispute it may feel marginalized.

Prospects: targets and barriers

Surveys conducted by planners in the City of Waterloo (1998) and the City of Calgary (1998) indicate that most suburban areas accommodate limited mixed use. For instance, many allow day nurseries, libraries, worship, personal services, repair shops, restaurants, retail shops, and medical clinics, but do not permit group homes, lodging houses, row housing, hospitals, industry, or supermarkets. Some communities, however, are removing permitted uses from their lists: For instance, in Montreal, Council may change residential zones to control places of worship (Fischler, 2000).[7]

What is appropriate mix? Will we know it when we achieve it? In the early 1990s, Toronto set a target of one job for every 1.5 residents (Municipality of Metropolitan Toronto, 1991), but does that give sufficient direction to know what kind of mix to generate or what uses to permit? Is the number of grocery stores in a neighborhood a reasonable indicator of commercial and residential mix (IBI Group, 2000)? If not, what would be? Given the lack of specificity in our prescriptions about mixed use, how can we set targets that will allow us to know when we have succeeded in meeting our goals?

What level of mixing are we seeing in Canadian communities? We do find evidence of potential for greater intensity, but largely due to smaller lot sizes rather than to mixing. Figure 2.3, for example, shows a mix of housing types and sizes on narrow lots, even though single detached units remain the norm. In

2.3 Skinny mix in a suburban neighborhood of Calgary, AB

part, cost drives this process (especially in fast-growing communities), as do greater returns to development interests. However, the desire of planners to achieve efficiency and sustainability clearly enhances the trend. We should note, however, that most new housing in Canada remains clustered by type and tenure within suburban and urban projects. Mixing is the exception, not the rule.

Some inner-city areas show more residential units as part of the mix than they did a decade ago. Does this reflect increasing diversity of use? The mix has certainly changed, but residential and entertainment uses have largely replaced industrial uses. We find a different mix. Land uses such as prisons and heavy industry show little sign of being integrated into the urban fabric. Regulatory barriers may be coming down, but the market prefers a degree of land use segregation.

Infill development and mixed use have proven popular in Toronto and Vancouver, where heavy immigration led to high growth and diverse populations. For example, in central Toronto a mix of residential, office, entertainment, and retail uses are reanimating former industrial neighborhoods (see Figure 2.4). Mixed use helps to increase housing stock, facilitate transit use, and reduce cost in a tight housing market. More people in those cities may seek urban lifestyles, and good transit systems are already in place to facilitate life without cars. Ken Greenberg has called Toronto a model of New Urbanism, suggesting that Canadian tax policies have not encouraged people to abandon the city, as happened in the US. (*Financial Post*, 1997). Mixing does, however, affect the inner city in both positive and negative ways. Gentrification contributes to new forms of class-based spatial segregation. By filling in the crevices left as industry abandons its northern base, mixing eases the transformation to a postindustrial city. Faced with the choice of empty lots or acres of parking in formerly productive districts, municipal officials welcome new office, residential, or entertainment-based projects (Schmandt, 1999). Inner-city districts become leisure and commercial theme parks heavily marketed to attract tourists and accommodate the wealthy (Gottdiener, 1997; Ward, 1998).

With its promise of character and sustainability, New Urbanism provides the theory to justify mixed use in Canada today. The concept of TOD appears widely in the plans of larger cities, but has been slower to affect practice. Even Toronto's plan to intensify around the subway system has met local resistance. In most communities, mixed-use nodes, with commercial, office, and multifamily housing, typically develop in suburban locations at highway interchanges: the "edge city" phenomenon Garreau (1991) describes. The streetcar suburbs of the early twentieth century provide the model of TOD many planners hope to see, but the realities of land ownership patterns, consumer preferences, and rates of urban growth make it difficult to implement today.

2.4 Mixed use in a former industrial neighborhood in Toronto, ON

With the development of designer suburbs in affluent cities, Leung (1995) suggests the result of New Urbanism may simply be more picturesque sprawl; he notes that mix forms part of the package of the self-contained, privileged enclave. We find few good-sized examples of "new towns" with the range of mix promoted by the TND style of New Urbanism. Given the limited market for mix at high density, these projects can succeed only in areas of high growth and high cost. For much of Canada those conditions do not hold. In less affluent areas, builders adorn starter "skinny" houses with New Urbanist architectural touches. "High Street" shops in new suburbs like McKenzie Towne (Calgary) give the illusion of mixed use, but false windows front the second stories (see Figure 2.5). The developer

2.5 False fronts on shops in McKenzie Towne, a suburb of Calgary, AB

omitted apartments and offices over the retail space because the economics of mixed use proved unviable for the suburban new town. The concept of mixed use appears in local plans but does not influence practice in an unreceptive market.

Thus while many engineering and planning barriers to mix have fallen in recent years, and planners and local economic development authorities welcome mix, hesitation derives from cultural barriers that planners cannot easily overcome. People want security, predictability, and tranquillity in their environments. They fear mix. The success of zoning in the twentieth century reflects that reality (Foglesong, 1986; Moore, 1979). Only a small segment of the population accepts the risks of investing in mixed-use projects. Where costs are modest, mixed-use projects have trouble taking off. As long as experience shows that mixing uses slows market absorption, builders and developers will avoid it. While cultural barriers remain, the resulting economic barriers will limit experimentation with mixed use to a few markets where it has a chance of succeeding.

Is mixed use a means or an end? Its proponents cite it as a means to social integration, economic strength, and environmental improvement. Canadian experience with mixed use is discouraging. Mixed use districts are becoming more segregated by class, and affordability has not improved. Efforts to mix uses have not staunched the loss of economic vitality for most Canadian cities. Land is consumed at a rapid rate, vehicle miles traveled are increasing, and we see no end to consumption. In sum, we are making slim progress on the proposed ends of mixed use. Yet planners continue to advocate it. Perhaps they see mixed use as good in and of itself, regardless of its consequences.

Cities are dynamic artifacts, shaped by human intervention. As our cultural values and social behaviors change, we alter the cities we inhabit. The mix of uses reflects many factors such as cultural beliefs, means of production, transportation technology, shelter technology, and level of affluence. The post-industrial city will differ in mix from the industrial city, just as the industrial contrasted with the medieval. As planners, we evaluate current practice against community goals and adjust policies and regulations to help residents achieve their objectives. The Canadian experience with implementing mixed use serves as important feedback in that process.

Acknowledgements

I would like to acknowledge the help of two research assistants who facilitated this work. Jaime Orser worked for the past two years on the study of Canadian cities and prepared the map. Darrell Joudrey participated in the research on industrial park planning. I owe them a great debt. Thanks also to colleagues who read earlier versions of this paper and to the anonymous referees who forced me to elaborate and clarify my arguments.

Notes

1 The Social Sciences and Humanities Research Council of Canada provided funding for recent research on the impact of New Urbanism on Canadian planning practice (1999–2001). This project involves extensive review of planning documents, field visits to suburban developments, and interviews with planners, developers, and realtors in a sample of Canadian cities. Research for the Halifax industrial park case study was supported by Canada Mortgage and Housing Corporation under the terms of the External Research Program. The views expressed are those of the author and do not represent the official view of the funding agencies.

2 In the US and Australia a similar process was occurring. For instance, the American Planning Association began promoting "smart growth," which features mixed use. The American approach, however, pays less attention to environmental issues.

3 When the St Lawrence Project began in 1974, planners worried about the long-term viability of the industrial area at King and Parliament. Within a decade, this area also succumbed to deindustrialization.
4 Zukin (1989) documents the same process in New York.
5 In Calgary, homes under $150,000 are considered "affordable," although a majority of households may not be able to purchase a house in that range.
6 The gurus of the movement, such as Andres Duany and James Kunstler, are even less tolerant, as discussion on the Pro-Urb e-mail list quickly demonstrates.
7 Ethnic diversity brings a proliferation of small religious congregations. Residents who find a house of worship opening on their quiet street may take exception to the noise and extra traffic generated.

References

Adler, J. (1994) 'The new burb is a village', *Newsweek*, December 26: 109.
American Planning Association (2001) 'Senate committee may consider community character act'. Available online: http://cw2k.capweb.net/planning/.
Anderson, K. (1991) 'Oldfangled new towns', *Time*, May 20: 52–5.
Bentley Mays, J. (1997) 'The high priest of New Urbanism', *The Globe and Mail*, March 8: C17.
Bernick, M. and Cervero, R. (1997) *Transit Villages in the 21st Century*, New York: McGraw-Hill.
Berridge Lewinberg Greenberg Ltd (1991) *Guidelines for the Reurbanisation of Metropolitan Toronto*, Toronto: Municipality of Metropolitan Toronto.
Berridge Lewinberg Greenberg Dark Gabor, Cosburn Patterson Wardman, and Glatting Jackson Kercher Anglin Lopez Rinehart (1996) *The Integrated Community: A Study of Alternative Land Development Standards*, Ottawa: Canada Mortgage and Housing Corporation.
Bogdan, J. (1992) 'The design of Queensville new town', *Plan Canada*, 32(3): 14–15.
Bressi, T. (1994) 'Planning the American dream', In P. Katz (ed.) *The New Urbanism*, New York: McGraw-Hill.
Calthorpe, P. (1993) *The Next American Metropolis*, New York: Princeton Architectural Press.
Caulfield, J. (1994) *City Form and Everyday Life: Toronto's Gentrification and Critical Social Practice*, Toronto: University of Toronto Press.
Chidley, J. (1997) 'The new burbs', Maclean's, July 21: 16–21.
City of Calgary (1995a) *Calgary Transportation Plan*, Calgary: Author.
City of Calgary (1995b) *Sustainable Suburbs Study: Creating More Fiscally, Socially and Environmentally Sustainable Communities*, Calgary: Planning and Building Department.

City of Calgary (1998) *Summary Report: Transit-oriented Suburban Community Design. A Survey of Municipalities in Canada and the USA*, Calgary: Planning and Building Department, New Communities Planning.

City of Toronto (1998) *Tracking the Kings: A Monitor Statement on the King–Parliament and King–Spadina Reinvestment Initiative*, Toronto: City of Toronto Urban Development Services.

City of Waterloo (1998) 'West side nodes zoning study discussion paper', Waterloo, ON: City of Waterloo Development Services.

Clark-Madison, M. (1999) 'Urban on the rocks: neighborhood juries still out on smart growth', *The Austin Chronicle*, 18(35). Available online: http://www.auschron.com/issues/_vol18/issue35/pols.htm.

Collier, R. (1974) *Contemporary Cathedrals*, Montreal: Harvest House.

Congress for the New Urbanism (2001) *Smartening up Growing Smart*. Available online: http://www.cnu.org/cnu_updates/Smartening-notes-wkshops.pdf.

Dear, M. (1992) 'Understanding and overcoming the NIMBY syndrome', *Journal of the American Planning Association*, 58(3): 288–300.

Duany, A. and Plater-Zyberk, E. (1992) 'The second coming of the American small town', *Plan Canada*, 32(3): 6–13.

Duany, A. and Plater-Zyberk, E. (1994) 'The neighborhood, the district and the corridor', in P. Katz (ed.) *The New Urbanism*, New York: McGraw-Hill.

Duany, A. and Plater-Zyberk, E. (1996) 'Neighborhoods and suburbs', *Design Quarterly*, 164: 10–23.

Everett-Green, R. (1997) 'Model cities for the next millennium', *The Globe and Mail*, May 31: C21.

Ewing, R. (1996) *Best Development Practices: Doing the Right Thing and Making Money at the Same Time*, Chicago: APA Planners Press.

Financial Post (1997) 'Homescaping: there's a revolution occurring in town planning and it's led by rebels who call themselves the New Urbanists', *Financial Post*, 10(25): 24–6

Financial Post Daily (1996) '1,500-acre housing project set for Toronto area' (Cornell), October 11: 5.

Fischler, R. (2000) *More on Storefront Churches*. Available by e-mail: planet@listserv.acsu.buffalo.edu.

Foglesong, R. (1986) *Planning the Capitalist City: The Colonial Era to the 1920s*, Princeton, NJ: Princeton University Press.

Garreau, J. (1991) *Edge City: Life on the New Frontier*, New York: Anchor Books.

Gordon, D. and Fong, S. (1989) 'Designing St Lawrence', in D. Gordon (ed.) *Directions for new Neighbourhoods: Learning from St Lawrence*, Conference proceedings (unpaginated) Toronto: Ryerson Polytechnic Institute, School of Urban and Regional Planning.

Gottdiener, M. (1997) *The Theming of America: Dreams, Visions, and Commercial Spaces*, Boulder, CO: Westview Press.

Government of Canada (1990) Canada's Green Plan. Ottawa: Environment Canada.

Government of Ontario (1995) *Making Choices: Alternative Development Standards. Guideline, Planning Reform in Ontario*, Toronto: Queen's Printer for Ontario.

Government of Ontario (1997) *Breaking Ground: An Illustration of Alternative Development Standards in Ontario's New Communities*, Toronto: Queen's Printer for Ontario.

Grant, J. (1997) 'Next generation neighbourhoods: finding a focus for planning residential environments', *Canadian Journal of Urban Research*, 6(2): 111–34.

Grant, J., Joudrey, D. and Klynstra, P. (1994) *Next Door to the Factory: Housing People in Modern Industrial Parks* (Report), Ottawa: Canada Mortgage and Housing Corporation, External Research Program.

Greenberg, K. and Gabor, A. (1992) 'The integration of urban design and planning', *Plan Canada*, 32(3): 26–8.

Hornblower, M. (1988) 'Not in my backyard you don't. Too often, that's the answer to a community in need', *Time*, June 27: 58–9.

Hume, C. (1991) 'They dare to critique our cities: designer wants suburbs that work', *Toronto Star*, August 31: K10.

Hutchinson, B. (1998) 'Good porches make good neighbors' (a back-to-basics movement called New Urbanism is threatening the suburban model), *Canadian Business*, June 26: 120–3.

Hygeia Consulting Services and REIC Ltd (1995) *Changing Values, Changing Communities: A Guide to the Development of Healthy, Sustainable Communities*, Ottawa: Canada Mortgage and Housing Corporation.

IBI Group (2000) *Greenhouse Gas Emissions from Urban Travel: Tool for Evaluating Neighbourhood Sustainability*, Ottawa: Canada Mortgage and Housing Corporation and Natural Resources Canada.

Isin, E. and Tomalty, R. (1993) *Resettling Cities: Canadian Residential Intensification Initiatives*, Ottawa: Canada Mortgage and Housing Corporation.

Jacobs, J. (1961) *The Death and Life of Great American Cities* New York: Vintage Books.

Katz, P. (1994) 'Preface', in P. Katz (ed.) *The New Urbanism*, New York: McGraw-Hill.

Kelbaugh, D. (1989) *The Pedestrian Pocket Book: A New Suburban Design Strategy*, New York: Princeton Architectural Press.

Kelbaugh, D. (1997) *Common Place: Toward Neighborhood and Regional Design*, Seattle: University of Washington Press.

Krieger, A. (1991) *Andres Duany and Elizabeth Plater-Zyberk: Towns and Town Making Principles*, New York: Harvard Graduate School of Design.

Leung, H.L. (1995) 'A new kind of sprawl', *Plan Canada*, 35(5): 4–5.

Lewinberg, F. (1993) 'Reurbanization: the context for planning growth', *Plan Canada*, 33(2): 10–14.

MacDonald, D. and Clark, B. (1995) 'New Urbanism in Calgary: McKenzie Towne', *Plan Canada*, 35(1): 20–2.

Martin, L., Filion, P. and Higgs, E.S. (1988) A survey of the preferred literature of Canadian planners', *Plan Canada*, 28(1): 6–11.

McInnes, C. (1992) 'Drawing happiness into the blueprints', *The Globe and Mail*, April 27: A17.

McMahon, E. (1999) 'Cooperation instead of confrontation' (from *Planning Commissioners Journal*, 33). Available online: http://www.plannersweb.com/trends/_1coop._html.

Molinaro, J. (1993) 'Agree on how to disagree or how to have useful discussions' (from *Planning Commissioners Journal*, 12). Available online: http://www.plannersweb.com/_trends/__1coop.html.

Moore, P. (1979) 'Zoning and planning: the Toronto experience, 1904–1970', in A. Artibise and G. Stelter (eds) *The Usable Urban Past*, Toronto: Macmillan.

Municipality of Metropolitan Toronto (1987) *Housing Intensification* (Metropolitan Plan Review Report No. 4), Toronto: Author.

Municipality of Metropolitan Toronto (1991) *Guidelines for the Reurbanization of Metropolitan Toronto*, Toronto: Author.

Municipality of Metropolitan Toronto (1992) *The Liveable Metropolis* (Municipality of Metropolitan Toronto, Draft Plan), Toronto: Author.

National Roundtable on the Environment and the Economy (1997) *The Road to Sustainable Transportation in Canada*, Ottawa: Author.

Nelessen, A.C. (1993) *Visions for a New American Dream: Process, Principles, and an Ordinance to Plan and Design Small Communities*, Chicago: APA Planners Press.

Newsweek, 'Paved paradise. Fifteen ways to fix the suburbs', May 15: 40–53.

O'Neill, D.J. (2000) *The Smart Growth Tool Kit*, Washington, DC: Urban Land Institute.

Paehlke, R.C. (1991) *The Environmental Effects of Urban Intensification*, Toronto: Ontario Ministry of Municipal Affairs.

Pendall, R. (1999) 'Opposition to housing NIMBY and beyond', *Urban Affairs Review*, 35(1): 112–36.

Pomeroy, S. (1999) *Professional Attitudes Towards Alternative Development Standards*, Toronto: ICURR Publications.

Porte, D. (1998) 'Toronto – an urban design approach' (from *Urban Design Quarterly*, 66). Available online: http://_ww2.rudi.net/ej/udq/66/internat_1.htm.

Royal Commission on the Future of the Toronto Waterfront (1992) *Regeneration: Toronto's Waterfront and Sustainable City*, Toronto: Ministry of Supply and Services Canada.

Rural and Small Town Research and Studies Programme (1992) *Guidelines for action: Understanding Housing-related NIMBY*, Sackville, NB: Mount Allison University.

Sauer, L. (1998) 'Creating a "signature" town: the urban design of Bois Franc', *Plan Canada*, 34(9): 22–7.

Saunders, D. (1997) 'Ye new Olde town', *The Globe and Mail*, March 8: C17.

Schmandt, M. (1999) 'The importance of history and content in the postmodern urban landscape', *Landscape Journal*, 18(2): 152–65.

Sewell, J. (1993) *The Shape of the City: Toronto Struggles with Modern Planning*. Toronto: University of Toronto Press.

Tomalty, R. (1997) *The Compact Metropolis: Growth Management and Intensification in Vancouver, Toronto, and Montreal*, Toronto: ICURR Publications.

Toronto Life (1996) 'Introducing the invisible garage: the New Urbanists are mounting a savage attack on subdivisions', *Toronto Life*, October: 77–80.

Transportation Association of Canada (1998, November) 'Achieving livable cities' (Briefing), Ottawa: Author.

Urban Land Institute (1987) *Mixed-use Development Handbook*, Washington, DC: Author.

Urban Land Institute (1998) *Smart Growth: Economy, Community, Environment*, Washington, DC: Author.

Van der Ryn, S. and Calthorpe, P. (1986) *Sustainable Communities: A New Design Synthesis for Cities, Suburbs and Towns*, San Francisco: Sierra Club.

Vischer, J. (1984) 'Community and privacy: planners' intentions and residents' reactions', *Plan Canada*, 23(4): 112–21.

Ward, S.V. (1998) *Selling Places: The Marketing and Promotion of Towns and Cities, 1850–2000*, London: E&FN Spon.

Warson, A. (1994) 'Born-again urbanism in Canada', *Progressive Architecture* (P/A), November: 51–2.

Wight, I. (1995) 'New Urbanism vs. conventional suburbanism', *Plan Canada*, 35(5): 20–2.

Wight, I. (1996) 'In search of grander humane visions', *Plan Canada*, 36(4): 3–4.

World Commission on Environment and Development [Brundtland Commission] (1987) *Our Common Future* (Report), New York: Oxford University Press.

Zukin, S. (1989) *Loft Living: Culture and Capital in Urban Change*, Rutgers, NJ: Rutgers University Press.

Chapter 3
Uncertain legacy
Sydney's Olympic stadiums

Glen Searle

The two main stadiums for the Sydney Olympic Games were developed by the private sector with state assistance to reduce government costs and risks. In the post-Olympic period, both stadiums have experienced major revenue shortfalls which threaten their viability. This has been caused by competition from pre-existing, though smaller, state-owned stadiums and lack of potential major sporting and other events. In part to help the Olympic stadiums, the government has produced a master plan for a major urban development at the Olympic Park. The article illustrates the risks of partnership development of specialized infrastructure, and the way in which special events can lead urban development.

Hosting the 2000 Olympic Games has given Sydney a legacy of large, state-of-the-art, sporting stadiums sufficient to meet a range of post-Olympic sporting needs for decades to come. This legacy was always secondary to the primary objective of providing facilities to successfully handle the Games themselves. But the New South Wales government, the provider of Olympic venues and facilities, cited it as a major benefit to the people of the state to increase popular support. The post-Olympic situation has assumed particular importance because the two major new Olympic stadiums involved significant private sector funding which depended on substantial spectator numbers after the Olympics.

The local context has threatened the viability of Olympic stadiums in two main ways. The stadiums are in competition with pre-existing state government stadiums, all newly built or extensively redeveloped in the previous decade and a half. They also face the reality of national sporting leagues which generate relatively small attendances at games in Sydney for reasons of local history and culture. There are very few other major stadium events which are feasible in Sydney's market to make up the shortfall. This situation has been influential in causing the state government to seek proposals for major urban development around the

Article submitted by the Australia and New Zealand Association of Planning Schools.

two Olympic stadiums. A draft master plan for Olympic Park has been prepared, and development proposals sought.

This article analyses the process of developing the Sydney Olympic stadiums, and their post-Olympic aftermath. In doing so, the paper illustrates several new planning concerns, including the potential risks of public–private partnerships to develop specialized urban infrastructure, the problems of such partnerships in situations where there is competition from existing state infrastructure, and the way in which major urban development can be led by belated attempts to offset the costs of specialized infrastructure.

Cities and stadium development

Nearly all academic analysis of cities and stadium development has been of United States cases. The US context involving national sporting leagues with big crowds at each game, and team franchises which are mobile between cities, is distinctive. Nevertheless, the US experience has general lessons for the analysis of cities and stadiums in Europe and other developed regions.

A principal issue involves the extent to which stadium development generates economic development. This is usually the main reason put forward to justify the large taxpayer subsidies which are used to build major stadiums in US cities in order to keep or attract mobile team franchises in baseball, gridiron and basketball (Rich 2000a). However, the academic literature has consistently failed to identify positive economic development impacts from US stadium development commensurate with the subsidies given by cities for new stadiums (Baade 1996; Rich 2000a). The primary beneficiaries of subsidies are team owners and players (Baade 1996; O'Kaer 1974). Nevertheless, the building of stadiums with city subsidies has become more important as the emphasis in local political agendas has shifted from redistribution to economic development since the 1970s (Euchner 1993). A wider development logic has emerged in this period. While the economic development benefits from having a team may be unquantifiable, 'cities that have teams and lose them are likely to encounter an image problem' (Zimbalist 1992).

More generally, cities have increasingly incorporated stadium development as a central component in wider local economic and urban development strategies. For example, Indianapolis made a downtown economic development strategy emphasizing sports venues, although it did not produce significant shifts in actual economic development (Rosentraub et al. 1994). In Cleveland, a new stadium complex came to be seen as part of the strategy for major redevelopment of the downtown (Sidlow and Henschen 2000). The Detroit Renaissance civic group saw a new stadium as integral to rebuilding the city (Sidlow and Henschen 2000). Conversely, stadium subsidies may have negative impacts on urban development by diverting taxes which would otherwise have been spent on social infrastructure and services. In Cleveland, the gateway Sports Complex was relieved of taxes which would otherwise have gone to schools and local government (Bartimole 1994). City funding of Birmingham's (UK) National Indoor Arena had similar effects (Beazley *et al.* 1997).

As this would suggest, the provision of subsidies for stadium development in US cities has been a contested process. In this, relationships between different interest groups, politicians and owners are critical (Rich 2000a). As Sidlow and Henschen put it, the decision to build a stadium with public funds is

> often the culmination of years of demands by a variety of interested parties, numerous proposals floating in the policy primeval soup, politicians worried about their political reputations and legacies, and events that create an opportunity for an idea to become a done deal.
>
> (Sidlow and Henschen 2000: 168)

The role of city elites can be critical in this. Rich (2000b) suggests that stadium development is attractive to politicians because securing a sports franchise is one of the few things the economic elite desire; they often show less enthusiasm about solving other needs of the city. Co-opting of the media can also be crucial in securing stadium development (Rich 2000b).

In considering the relevance of US experience for stadium development in Sydney and elsewhere, the particular context of US inter-city stadium competition needs to be borne in mind. In particular, US sporting leagues are monopolies in which the supply of teams is less than the demand for them by cities (Zimbalist 2000: 57). In addition, team franchises are saleable and therefore potentially mobile between cities. These factors create the conditions for inter-city bidding for franchises via new stadium subsidies. Other factors in US stadium competition are more universal. For example, new technology has allowed simple stadium constructions which maximize opportunities for revenue generation from luxury suites, club boxes, concessions, catering, signage, parking, advertising and theme activities. New stadiums can incorporate these features and thus have an immediate advantage over older facilities (Zimbalist 2000: 57). The potential for rapid obsolescence from changes in viewing fashion is also significant. Domed stadiums and artificial turf are now less preferred than traditional open-air stadiums (Rich 2000b: 224).

In Australia, the themes of public subsidies, inter-stadium competition and urban development have been prominent in recent stadium projects, as the Sydney case studies in this chapter will show. The political limits to public subsidies have also been starkly shown. The largest Australian stadium built in recent years, other than Sydney's main Olympic stadium, is Colonial Stadium in Melbourne, with

52,000 seats. It was originally conceived as a state-funded soccer and rugby stadium (Maiden 2001) as the first project in the Victorian government's Docklands redevelopment scheme covering 220 hectares. The government claimed that integrated redevelopment of the area around the stadium would be a first for Australia (Office of Major Projects 1997). An alternative stadium scheme was then developed in which a guarantee of 30 Australian Football League (AFL) matches each year allowed the project to be privately financed (Chandler 1999). The stadium consortium of private investors, which included News Corp and the national Seven TV network which held AFL telecasting rights, won the right to build the stadium and redevelop an adjacent area, principally for a television studio. The $A150 million in equity was supplemented by $A100 million from Seven for 25-year rights to ticketing, premium seating, naming rights and signs (Maiden 2001). The Stadium opened in 2000. But the failure to secure off-season activity and lower than expected attendances meant that revenue was well below expectations. Its first full financial year generated revenue of $A22.5 million instead of the $A55 million that had been forecast (Maiden 2001). There was a pre-tax loss of $A41.2 million, and the value of the stadium was written down by $A156 million to $A200 million (Maiden and Milovanovic 2001). To avoid liquidation, Seven paid $A75 million plus a future annual fee to the owners to lease and manage the stadium for 23 years (*Sydney Morning Herald* 26 October 2001). By contrast, Melbourne's main stadium, the Melbourne Cricket Ground, is being redeveloped by the Victorian government at a cost of $A400 million for the 2006 Commonwealth Games, which will increase its capacity from 96,000 to just over 100,000 spectators (*Australian Financial Review* 15 August 2001). This situation of private sector losses in the face of state-funded redevelopment of competing stadiums parallels the story of Sydney's Olympic stadiums described below.

In Colonial Stadium's case, the private sector has had to bear the costs. On the other hand, two Olympics-related stadium developments in Adelaide and Canberra involved government subsidies and generated their own political costs. The developments both involved cost overruns of stadium upgrades for rounds of the year 2000 Olympic soccer competition. In Adelaide, the cost of upgrading the Hindmarsh Soccer Stadium went from an original estimated cost of $A8.5 million to an eventual cost of $A30 million, borne by the state government (*Weekend Australian* 22–23 April 2000). This caused the resignation of the state tourism minister and the cabinet secretary (*Australian Financial Review* 19 October 2001). In Canberra, the cost of upgrading Bruce Stadium went from an initial estimate of $A27.3 million, with a national territory contribution of $A12.3 million, to a final cost of $A60 million, with territory taxpayer liabilities eventually totalling $A64 million (Harris 2001). The expectations of at least 6,000 extra covered seats were misplaced, with only 1,600 eventually being built. The Bruce Stadium debacle was a major factor in the resignation of the national territory chief minister just after the Olympic Games (*Sydney Morning Herald* 18 October 2000). Such political repercussions were avoided in the development of Sydney's Olympic facilities, though these were not without their own problems as we shall now see.

Development of Homebush Bay and the Olympic stadiums

In 1993 Sydney won the right to host the year 2000 Olympic Games. The bid for the Olympic Games had proposed mostly new stadiums and other venue facilities. The main venues were to be constructed on a redundant state abattoir site of 760 hectares at Homebush Bay close to the Parramatta River arm of

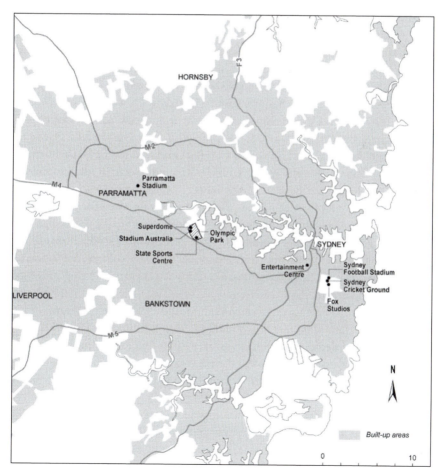

3.1 Sydney stadiums and sporting venues mentioned in text

Sydney Harbour, 14 km from the city centre (Figure 3.1). The site had become available with the election of a neo-liberal (Liberal-National) state government in 1988. The new government, taking its cue from the UK (Thatcher) and US (Reagan) governments, closed several state businesses, including the abattoirs and brickworks at Homebush Bay, as part of a 'small government' philosophy.

The Homebush Bay site, which also contained a large old federal armaments depot, had been proposed for redevelopment in various government plans from the early 1970s (Homebush Bay Corporation and Property Services Group 1994). In 1973, the state government investigated possible sites in Sydney for international sporting facilities, then limited to the aging Sydney Cricket Ground. Homebush Bay was selected for several reasons, including its size and central metropolitan location, predominant public ownership, and relative lack of development. The scheme produced for the government proposed international sporting uses in two locations on the site. In 1982, government studies produced land-use options for the site, based on whether or not the abattoirs closed and Silverwater prison (next to the armaments depot) shifted. A sport and exhibition area, industry use and parkland were included in both options. A consultant report in 1983 recommended Homebush Bay as the site of Sydney's first technology industry and prestige business park. This led to the government developing surplus abattoirs land for the Australia Centre technology park under private sector management.

A draft Regional Environmental Plan was produced by the Department of Planning in 1986 (Homebush Bay Corporation and Property Services Group 1994). This designated parkland over almost half the site, incorporating the regional Bicentennial Park which was then being developed by the government on residual state land east of the abattoirs. A sports centre zone was designated at what would be the southern end of Olympic Park, where a State Sports Centre had recently been built. A sports village area was shown in two alternative locations nearby. Industrial uses (including Australia Centre) were placed at the site's core and along the western shore of Homebush Bay. Two years later, in 1988, the state prepared a plan for its unsuccessful bid for the 1996 Olympic Games. This reduced the amount of industrial and parkland areas contained in the 1986 plan, significantly extended the sporting areas (now sport and exhibition zones), and included a large housing area next to the main sporting zone. This reflected the bid's focus on Homebush Bay as the principal site for sporting facilities and accommodation.

The government then proceeded to start planning to win the year 2000 Games. A new development strategy was prepared in 1989 for the Homebush Bay precinct and surrounding sites (Homebush Bay Corporation and Property Services Group, 1994). The strategy included establishment of a central sports complex including a stadium, athletics centre and aquatic centre capable of hosting major international sporting events, and additional recreational facilities. Royal Agricultural Society Showground facilities would be relocated next to the sports complex from the inner city as part of an overall sport and exhibition core zone. Housing development was proposed for the armaments site and along the western bay shore. The amount of industrial land included was significantly greater than in the 1988 plan. This, together with two designated commercial and retail areas adjacent to the sport zone, was intended to generate development yielding financial returns to the government from its land, in line with the strong asset realisation philosophy of the state's neo-liberal government. A master plan was completed in 1990 incorporating key elements of the 1989 strategy, including major international sporting venues, new Royal Agricultural Society facilities, and a retail/commercial centre.

To assist in winning the year 2000 Games, the state government then commenced building the international aquatic centre for swimming and diving events as well as the athletics stadium (useable as an Olympics warm-up track) on the abattoir site in time for the bid. The existing State Sports Centre contained a hockey stadium and basketball and other indoor sporting venues which were also incorporated into the Olympic bid. The master plan was revised in 1992 principally to incorporate the requirements of Sydney's bid for the year 2000 Olympics as an option for development. This was the culmination of a decade of regeneration plans for Sydney's largest brownfield site, all of which (excepting the 1983 scheme) contained precincts for major sporting facilities as a central element in combination with varying mixes of industry, parklands and housing.

In the event, Sydney's bid won the Games and the master plan provided the starting point for Olympic development at Homebush Bay. The win had significant implications for the regeneration of Homebush Bay. It brought the regeneration forward and at a scale probably not otherwise possible. Without the Olympics it is highly doubtful, for example, whether a new rail line to Homebush Bay would have been built. The win skewed the regeneration toward construction of Olympic venues, a large housing area and a regional park which helped Sydney's claim of a 'green games'. The industrial areas in former plans disappeared. Planning since the Games, discussed later, has further skewed the nature of the area's regeneration toward major commercial and retail development.

The new facilities to be built there for the Games were the main Olympic stadium, a coliseum (which would be replanned as the SuperDome, for major indoor events), a small outdoor playing field and indoor venues which would eventually house Sydney's annual Royal Agricultural Show, a tennis complex, and an archery field. The bid also included a velodrome at Homebush Bay which was eventually built in Bankstown to the south west. It proposed to use the existing Exhibition Centre and Entertainment Centre at Darling Harbour for various indoor events. New facilities for rowing, equestrian events, beach volleyball, shooting and mountain biking were to be built in other parts of Sydney. The re-establishment of Royal Agricultural Society facilities at Homebush Bay freed up the Society's old state site in the inner city. Later in the decade that site would be successfully offered, along with significant government subsidies, to Fox Studios to establish its first production studio outside the US (Searle and Cardew 2000). Proposed redevelopment of the inner east White City tennis court complex for housing, following Tennis New South Wales' shift to the new complex at Olympic Park, has been thwarted by strong local resident opposition.

The Fox studio and associated theme park, and retail and entertainment facilities were a significant, if unforeseen, urban development consequence of Sydney's successful bid for the Olympic Games. The bid itself incorporated three major urban development initiatives at Homebush Bay. The first was the construction of the Athletes Village on an 84-hectare surplus defence site just to the north of Olympic Park, as the Homebush Bay venue complex would become known. The village was to be built on strong ESD (ecologically sustainable development) principles, notably the incorporation of solar energy using photovoltaic roof panels on all residences and recycled grey water and storm water runoff. After the Games, the village would be the core of the new suburb of Newington, housing 5,000 people at a medium density, which would alleviate Sydney's urban sprawl.

The second significant urban development initiative in the bid was the creation of Sydney's largest urban park, Millennium Parklands, on 450 hectares of remaining abattoir and defence land between Olympic Park and Parramatta River. The park would contain wetlands and grassland habitats regenerated from degraded industrial land, a remnant of threatened native woodland, and cycle routes and footpaths. The third initiative was the construction of a rail line to Olympic Park so that the use of public transport by spectators was maximised. All of these developments supported the bid's selling of Sydney 2000 as the 'green games', fully committed to ecologically sustainable development. This was to be a crucial factor in winning the Games (Olympic Coordination Authority 1996: 14). Since the Games, the state government has produced a master plan for major mixed use development at Olympic Park. This is discussed later in the paper.

The state government ensured mechanisms were in place to achieve construction and operation of Olympic venues from the start. A state Homebush Bay Development Corporation was set up in 1992, in the final stages of the bid, as coordinator of land use planning and site development of Homebush Bay, and the corporation assumed ownership of state land in the Olympic Park area. A draft state planning instrument, Sydney Regional Environmental Plan No. 24 – Homebush Bay (SREP 24) was made to enable the Development Corporation to prepare and adopt guidelines for development and conservation of land in the area consistent with the master plan.

Following the winning of the bid in 1993, the Development Corporation was reconstituted as the Olympic Co-ordination Authority (OCA) in 1995 to deliver sporting facilities and venues for use during the 2000 Olympic and Paralympic Games and to manage development of Homebush Bay. SREP 24 was signed into law. State Environmental Planning Policy No. 38 – Olympic Games (SEPP 38) was introduced to facilitate the development of all Olympic facilities. SEPP 38 set out site development guidelines, including the requirement that all development be ecologically sustainable. It also exempted major Olympic projects from the requirement to prepare environmental impact statements. It made the Minister for Urban Affairs and Planning the consent authority for development of Olympic facilities. The NSW government did not intend that the local council, which would otherwise have been the consent authority, would be able to hold up development of the Olympic venues with their non-negotiable deadline. Indeed, local government was excluded from significant Olympics planning stages, and even from much detailed development information (Dunn and McGuirk 1999: 29). In 1995 a new master plan was published. The plan, and supporting documents on environment, transport and landscape strategies, provided transport and infrastructure frameworks and urban design, accessibility, environmental and other guidelines under SREP 24 for the development of facilities at Olympic Park for the 2000 Games. SREP 24 was amended in 1998 to address planning for the post-Olympic period, allowing the minister to approve new master plans (Olympic Co-ordination Authority 2001a).

From the start, the NSW state government budgeted for a small profit from the Games as a demonstration of its good management. The state's Olympic bid estimated the gross costs of staging the Olympics would be $A1.7 billion., underwritten by the government. A profit of $A15 million, later revised down to $A6 million, was forecast. By 1996 the estimated final capital costs of the Olympics had increased by $A375 million over the 1992 bid budget, but it was still claimed that this represented 'value for money for the taxpayer' given the legacy the games would leave to NSW (Olympic Coordination Authority 1996: 43). The escalation in costs was ultimately balanced by revenue increases, particularly by higher ticket prices, the sale of US television rights above the forecast level, and a higher than expected contribution from the private sector to main stadium costs. In order to keep state costs down, the two major new venues – the main stadium and the SuperDome – used significant private sector funding. This strategy was not without risks to private investors and, ultimately, the state's existing stadiums, as the article now analyses.

Stadium Australia

Sydney's lack of a major stadium holding more than 45,000 spectators was expected to make the main stadium a viable proposition after the Games, although concern was expressed from the start that the stadium would make the existing state-controlled Sydney Football Stadium a 'white elephant' (MacDonald 1992; Byrne 1995). The Olympic bid estimated the 80,000 seat stadium's cost to be $A307 million, including $A15 million of private sector funding. By 1995 the government envisaged that around half the cost could be raised from the private sector, allocating $A185 for the stadium in the 1995–6 state budget (*Australian Financial Review* 24 January 1996). To achieve this and minimize costs and risks to the state, the government invited private sector bids to design, build, operate and maintain the Stadium until 2031 under a lease from OCA.

The winning bid from the Stadium Australia consortium exceeded the government's hopes. It offered to build the stadium for a state government contribution of only $A135 million. Nearly all of the rest of the total cost of $A463 million would be raised by an innovative public float of $A300 million. The float would issue 30,000 units in a trust (later increased to 34,400 to raise $A344 million), which entitled holders to buy tickets to Olympic events in the stadium and to seats at other stadium sporting events until 2031 (*Weekend Australian* 27–28 January 1996). To accommodate unit holders, the capacity of the stadium would be increased to 110,000 for the Olympics, reverting to 80,000 afterwards. The consortium's proposal offered little risk to the government, as the float would be fully underwritten by five financial companies (*Australian Financial Review* 24 January 1996).

The float failed, however, mainly because no contracts for major rugby league, rugby union and soccer matches after the Olympics at the Stadium had been signed (Moore 1998). Only $A108 million was raised, leaving a shortfall of $A236 million (*Sydney Morning Herald* 10 April 1997). Concern about the possibility of tens of thousands of empty seats at major Olympic events in the stadium prompted the Sydney Organising Committee for the Olympic Games (SOCOG) to act after a year of rescue talks. It agreed to allow Stadium Australia underwriters to sell their remaining Olympic seats, and SOCOG itself would then sell any seats still unsold (*Australian Financial Review* and *Sydney Morning Herald* 19 December 1997).

This measure still left the problem of empty underwriters' seats after the Games, threatening the financial viability of Stadium Australia. A financial restructuring plan approved by unit holders in 1998 was a first step to address the problem. This involved 17,200 of the 22,950 unsold Stadium memberships being bought by Stadium Australia from underwriters for $A20.6 million using funds lent by the underwriters (Carr 1998). These would then be sold on to the major football codes – rugby union, rugby league and Australian Rules – for sale by them as code memberships entitling holders to buy tickets to the code's games at the stadium.

After the opening of Stadium Australia in 1999, some major international, interstate and club finals matches in rugby league, rugby union and soccer were played at the stadium. But in most months the stadium remained empty. There were not enough major football matches or rock concerts in Sydney each year. Stadium Australia operated at a loss of $A24 million in its first year, 1998–9, $A11 million in 1999–2000, and nearly as much in the next year (*Australian Financial Review* 7 September 2001). The state government rejected requests for financial assistance (*Sydney Morning Herald* 16 March 2001) in line with its philosophy that the state's strong internationalized economy did not warrant such measures (McGregor 1999). However the government did contribute $A8 million toward the $A68 million cost of reconfiguring the stadium for use by the Australian Football League (Australian Rules) (*Sydney Morning Herald* 16 March 2001). Stadium Australia's major creditor then agreed to extend its $A125 million loan to avoid liquidation when the Sydney's AFL team agreed to play their three best games at the stadium over the next seven years, plus pre-season and home finals matches (*Australian Financial Review* 7 September 2001).

Stadium Australia's problems have resulted not only from the paucity of major events in Sydney suitable for an 80,000-seat arena, but also from competition for those events. This competition has come from existing new or redeveloped state-controlled stadiums. The main competition was from the Sydney Cricket and Sports Ground Trust (SCSGT), a government agency directed by the Minister for Sport and Recreation. It controlled the Sydney Cricket Ground and the adjacent Sydney Football Stadium located two kilometres east of the city centre. Each venue accommodated around 40,000 spectators.

In the 1980s the SCSGT, under the chairmanship of politically well-connected ex-state Labor minister and ex-Lord Mayor Pat Hills, commenced redevelopment and expansion of its old cricket ground and sports ground complex using its own funds and government grants and loans. The Sydney Cricket Ground (SCG) was the city's chief venue for major rugby union, rugby league and cricket matches. From 1980, private boxes were put in and general seating capacity slowly expanded, reaching 42,000 by 2000 (Auditor-General 1981; Auditor-General 1985; Audit Office of NSW 2001), increasing spectator comfort by replacing standing areas so as to compete with other venues and with increasing television coverage.

But the main competition for Stadium Australia has come from the Sydney Football Stadium (SFS), opened by the SCSGT on the old Sports Ground site in 1987. The SFS was constructed with an all-seated capacity of 42,000. To finance the $A58 million cost, the Trust used a technique subsequently adopted with modifications by Stadium Australia. Gold and corporate memberships of the SCG-SFS complex were sold, entitling holders to lifetime access to all events there. The proceeds of the memberships were used to fund construction (Auditor-General 1986). In an ominous preview of Stadium Australia's financial problems, however, the new memberships did not sell at the required rate. The Trust had had to borrow from the state Treasury (Auditor-General 1987, 1988; Byrne 1995), and construction of the SFS eventually cost state taxpayers more than $A80 million (Byrne 1995).

When the Olympic stadium decision was announced, the Trust set about securing what major matches it could for the SFS and SCG. In 1997 it signed the NSW Rugby Union, with its popular international Super 12 matches, for nine years to the SFS. International soccer matches had already been contracted to the SFS until 2009. In 1999, the Trust re-signed the Sydney AFL team, committing it to seven games a year for ten years at the SCG (Carr 1999). More generally, the attractiveness of the SCG and SFS for spectators has been increased in the last few years with much improved car access following the opening of the Eastern Distributor city–airport motorway ahead of the Olympic Games, and development of the Fox Studios entertainment complex adjacent to the SCG and SFS (Kennedy 2001).

Further competition for Stadium Australia has come from another modern state-run venue, Parramatta Stadium, to the west of Homebush Bay. The stadium was opened in 1986 at a cost of $A15 million, funded jointly by the NSW and Federal governments (Auditor-General 1986). The stadium was developed with an all-seated capacity of 30,000. The stadium's gestation had been a highly contested process, requiring a special act of parliament to overcome a successful legal challenge by the Friends of Parramatta Park community group (Fitzallen *et al.* 1982). Although Parramatta has the smallest capacity of the competing stadiums, it is reckoned to be perhaps the most successful. Its size and seating layout, generating strong crowd atmosphere with attendances of 10–15,000, has made it attractive to national league clubs in soccer and rugby (Cowley 1997). It has also provided a suitable venue for one-off events such as international boxing title fights and international rock concerts (such as one featuring Paul McCartney).

This experience reflects two factors undermining the long-term viability of Stadium Australia. The first is the relatively modest attendance at nearly all football matches and other events suitable for stadiums in Sydney. The number of events in Sydney which are too big for the SFS or SCG are few, certainly less than one per month.

There are sporadic opportunities for Stadium Australia to attract events to Sydney which would previously have by-passed the city because it had no stadium to accommodate the minimum viable crowd size, such as the Three Tenors and the Bee Gees concerts (Dennis 1999a, 1999c). This capacity has also allowed Sydney to be the front runner to host the major matches in the 2003 Rugby Union World Cup. Yet such events are very infrequent. On the other hand, the post-Olympic Stadium Australia capacity of 80,000 may indeed be too small for the very largest events. The annual Australia–New Zealand rugby union test twice drew 107,000 or more spectators to the Stadium before the Olympic Games. With the capacity now scaled back to 80,000 the ARU may consider holding the test at the larger MCG (Dennis 2000).

The second factor undermining Stadium Australia's viability, and which helps explain Sydney's paucity of regular large sporting crowds, is the nature of Australia's national sporting leagues and Sydney's place in them. In North America, the market is big enough to make viable the provision of large stadiums (very often with significant help from local taxpayers) for teams in single US or US–Canadian leagues in football, baseball, basketball and ice hockey. In Europe, soccer so dominates the sporting scene that every decent-sized urban area can draw good crowds to large stadiums built for national league soccer teams.

In Australia, the main spectator attendances for outdoor stadium sports in a nation of 19 million are split between Australian football, rugby league, soccer, rugby union, and cricket. For the latter two, large crowds are confined to international matches, with few of them played in Sydney each year. Australian football is dominant outside New South Wales and Queensland. Its popularity in Melbourne allows the MCG to regularly take in crowds over 50,000 to national league matches. In Sydney the main national league sport is rugby league, but its spectator support is much weaker than that of AFL in Melbourne. Attendances at NRL matches in Sydney are relatively modest, and crowds of more than 20,000 are rare. Average attendances at the Sydney AFL team's matches are larger, but within the capacity of the SCG for most matches. Soccer is a secondary football code in Australia, and its national league matches in Sydney invariably draw crowds of less than 10,000. The upshot is that the only non-finals national league matches requiring Stadium Australia's capacity are the few AFL matches sold out at the SCG. Thus Stadium Australia cannot rely on regular national league matches to sustain it unlike, for example, the main stadium for the Atlanta Olympic Games which was converted to a national baseball league stadium.

The SuperDome

The problems of Stadium Australia, and their genesis, are largely mirrored in the story of the SuperDome. This was built to accommodate Olympic Games basketball and gymnastics. Its 21,000 seat capacity makes it the largest indoor stadium in Australia. The development was a 'build own operate transfer' scheme, like Stadium Australia, with the SuperDome being built and operated by the

Abigroup development company for a concession period of 30 years. The state government contributed $A142 million of the total cost of $A197 million, and Abigroup contributed the rest (Olympic Co-ordination Authority 1999). As with the main stadium, the government was anxious to attract private sector funding for the project to reduce the state's Olympic costs and risks. To help the SuperDome's prospects after the Games, the government built an adjoining car park with 3,400 spaces at a cost of $A63 million, contrary to the ESD objective for Olympic developments.

Like Stadium Australia, the long term viability of the SuperDome depends on its ability to compete with a smaller state facility, in this case the Sydney Entertainment Centre. The latter has a capacity of 10,000 seats, and is located near Darling Harbour in Sydney's southern central business district (CBD). The Centre was opened in 1983, at a total development cost to the state of $A49.5 million (Auditor-General 1983). It marked the first state investment for redevelopment of the Darling Harbour area, which had been proposed for several years and which was given full effect with the setting up of the Darling Harbour Authority the following year.

The SuperDome failed to attract audiences from the Entertainment Centre right from the SuperDome's opening in 1999. Almost no indoor events in Sydney required a capacity of more than 10,000 seats. Promoters preferred to put on their shows in the Entertainment Centre rather than in a half-empty SuperDome (*Sydney Morning Herald* 23 August 2000). Audiences preferred the Entertainment Centre's central location and the after-show dining, drinking and nightlife opportunities nearby in Chinatown and the CBD (Moore 1999). The revenue potential from national league basketball and ice hockey which sustained arenas in the US like the SuperDome was absent in Sydney. There was no ice hockey, and although the Sydney Kings national basketball team relocated from the Entertainment Centre to the SuperDome, their crowds averaged only 4,000 or 5,000 with only a dozen or so home matches per season. Moreover, another state-funded arena, the State Sports Centre on the other side of Olympic Park, was now also in competition with the SuperDome because it was the home to Sydney's new second national basketball team. By the middle of 2000, the Entertainment Centre was winning virtually all the big indoor events coming to Sydney (*Sydney Morning Herald* 30 May 2000). Within nine months of opening, SuperDome's operating losses were estimated to be running at $A5 million per year (Moore 2000b).

The situation concerned the government, with its substantial investment of taxpayers' money in the SuperDome. It commissioned a review to investigate whether live shows at the Entertainment Centre should be banned in favour of conventions and the like, in order to divert business to the SuperDome (*Sydney Morning Herald* 6 June 2000). Under the contract between the government and Abigroup, the government would receive $A7 million from Abigroup if it banned live acts at the Entertainment Centre after the Centre's original operating lease expired in 2003 (*Australian Financial Review* 6 June 2000). The review came down in favour of the Centre, however (*Sydney Morning Herald* 1 November 2000).

At the same time Sydney's third biggest indoor venue, the Hordern Pavilion, was being refurbished at a cost of $A27 million (Dennis 1999b). This was part of the former Royal Agricultural Society's inner city complex, and thus had the advantage of being adjacent to the Fox Studios entertainment complex, like the SCG and SFS. The refurbished pavilion would be 'sold as an alternative to the Entertainment Centre and SuperDome, as well as other smaller venues' (Dennis 1999b).

A better future for the SuperDome seemed to lie, in part, in creating a vibrant urban neighbourhood at Olympic Park to match those of its competitors. New plans for Olympic Park, discussed in the next section, now offer the potential to achieve this.

Olympic Park post-Olympic master plan

Ensuring that Olympic sporting facilities would be properly used after the Games was one of the Olympic Co-ordination Authority's (OCA's) principal functions. Even before the Games had been held, it seemed that this issue could be addressed in concert with another principal OCA function, ensuring the orderly economic development of the Homebush Bay area. The 1998 metropolitan strategy (Department of Urban Affairs and Planning 1998) started by showing Olympic Park as a focus of major economic development for the first time. As a first step toward this, the OCA circulated a development options paper for Homebush Bay to operators of venues there in May 2000. The paper included proposals to make Homebush Bay a centre of excellence for sports, with a sports university and sports medicine centre. It also proposed extending the area's role as a leisure and cultural centre, with a cinema complex, an Aboriginal centre, an arm of the Australian (NSW) Museum, and a tertiary education centre (Moore 2000b).

The venue operators apparently felt the proposals were insufficient, and formed a lobby group, the Sydney Olympic Park Business Association, to press their arguments. The Association wanted the OCA to recommend several things in the Homebush Bay development review paper to be submitted to state cabinet. These included government capital grants for more car parks close to venues, development of another hotel, clubs, cinemas and shops, and ongoing subsidies, especially for cross-Sydney bus routes to major Olympic Park events (Moore 2000a, 2000c). Soon after the Games, the state premier said the government would respond to the problems of Olympic Park venues by 'pack[ing] in activity' around Homebush Bay, drawing a parallel with the Darling Harbour redevelopment scheme of the 1980s (Lawson 2000).

A parallel factor was the leasehold revenue the government stood to gain from intensified activity at Olympic Park, which would offset the ongoing costs of maintaining and operating the Park and its public sporting venues. The 'realizing [of] development potential of the Homebush Bay site' to offset long-term maintenance costs had already been mooted by the OCA in 1999, in response to the auditor-general's estimate that the management and upkeep of Olympic park would cost $A5 million per annum (Audit Office of NSW 1999). The 2001 state budget allocated $A50 million to the new Sydney Olympic Authority (which has replaced the OCA) for post-Olympic expenses at the Park and former Olympic venues (Moore 2001).

The options paper submitted to Cabinet generated a decisive response. Early in 2001, the OCA commissioned four architectural and urban design practices to develop alternative design scenarios or visions for Olympic Park. After considering these, the OCA then prepared a draft post-Olympic master plan for Olympic Park, which was published in June 2001 (Olympic Co-ordination Authority 2001a).

The draft master plan envisaged future development being guided by a precinct structure. The precincts comprised a 'vibrant' Town Centre around the railway station, a Major Events precinct (Stadium Australia and the SuperDome), the Showgrounds precinct, Australia Centre (part of the old abattoir site zoned as a business park), the Brickpit Edge, the Participation Precinct (including the State Sports Centre, International Tennis Centre, Hockey Centre, Aquatic Centre and Athletics Centre), and Parklands. The plan aimed to increase employment to at least 10,000 jobs, focused on the Town Centre. Residential development would also be facilitated with a target urban core population of 3,000 to contribute to the critical mass needed for town centre retail activities. High-rise development of up to 30 storeys would be permitted in the Centre. The plan envisaged a nucleus of retail uses within the Town Centre providing restaurants, food outlets, cafés and convenience retailing for visitors, workers and residents. It saw potential for a major cultural institution on the southern rim of the Brickpit. A previously proposed rapid-transit way from the area to Parramatta regional centre was incorporated in the plan. Overall, the draft plan envisaged that existing under-used or vacant land at Olympic Park, such as open-air car parks, would provide opportunities for significant further development.

It could be argued that the plan failed to draw on imaginative elements contained in the four commissioned proposals. It was essentially a developers' *tabula rasa*, containing little more than simple land-use and density controls. Even these would not be binding: the plan was released as a draft so that developer proposals would not be rejected on the ground that they did not comply with a final master plan (Moore 2001). The Royal Australian Institute of Architects criticized the plan for ignoring a number of design principles that were in the four commissioned scenarios. These included links to the surrounding areas, reducing the huge scale of the site by introducing a grid of streets, and planning the precinct and surroundings together. It also criticized the draft master plan's emphasis on the current commercial potential of the site at the expense of its long-term potential as a new sustainable community (Royal Australian Institute of Architects 2001). Nevertheless the revised draft master plan (Government Architect's Design Directorate and Urban Design Group 2002) kept the general structure of the initial draft. It increased the emphasis on uses associated with sport and entertainment in the centre of the main stadium zone and shifted the focus of the high-rise residential uses from the rail station to the adjacent main entry boulevard, to form a prominent edge and to reduce potential noise and other conflicts with main venue activities.

Along with publication of the initial draft master plan, the OCA requested proposals for commercial development at Olympic Park based on the draft. Assessment of proposals would be based on conformity with the draft master plan (though it seemed this would be generously interpreted – see Moore 2001), financial return to the OCA, capacity to deliver the project, risks to the OCA, and the approach to ecologically sustainable development (including impact on public transport) (Olympic Co-ordination Authority 2001b).

Thus the stadiums and other venues built for the Olympic Games at Homebush Bay seem likely to generate a significant metropolitan centre not envisaged at the time of Sydney's Olympic bid (although general retail and commercial development had been proposed in the 1990 Master plan). This will have a positive impact on the fortunes of Stadium Australia and the SuperDome. But the parameters of the draft 2001 Master plan do not give confidence that they will generate a vibrant, fine-grained neighbourhood of the kind that attracts patrons to rival venues.

In strategic planning terms, a major commercial centre at Homebush Bay could reduce the expansion potential of nearby Parramatta (Figure 3.1), the government's long-designated regional centre for western Sydney. Parramatta has not grown as fast as previously planned, and the current government target requires a doubling of existing employment to 80,000 (Department of Urban Affairs and Planning 1998). Commercial jobs at Homebush Bay are likely to be heavily car-based as the rail service is infrequent outside major event occasions, although there is obviously potential for a better service if commercial development becomes significant. The proposed higher density residential development has strategic planning pluses, by assisting the government's urban consolidation policy and taking advantage of excellent recreation possibilities, water views and rail access. It can also be argued that the latest master plan suitably recognizes the synergistic potential of the Olympic venues to generate entertainment and sports-related activity, although planning to realize the area's unique tourist potential as the site of the year 2000 Olympic Games is still virtually absent.

Other metropolitan redevelopment consequences of the Olympic Games are significant, although they vary in their degree of longer-term strategic intention. The Fox Studios redevelopment of the vacant old showgrounds site was the result of an opportunistic bid for the studios by the state government. Proposed redevelopment of the former Tennis NSW complex for housing is being strongly fought and the outcome is uncertain. On the other hand, new hotel construction was promised in the Games bid and was encouraged in the CBD by city council planning bonuses. Construction of the CBD–airport rail line and motorway was hastened by the winning of the Games, but was in accordance with strategic planning objectives. The same was true of the development of Millennium Park. The Olympic Village itself is a centrepiece of the government's urban consolidation strategy (Department of Planning 1995).

Conclusion

The development of large new stadiums was an integral element of Sydney's bid for, and successful running of, the year 2000 Olympic Games. But their lack of pre- and post-Games events reflects the risks for cities building specialized infrastructure for sporadic or once-only special events. The main issue in Sydney has been the very large size of the stadiums which were necessary for Olympic Games crowds. Similar crowds for other events in Sydney are very uncommon. Other modern stadiums operating before the Games can handle all but a few of the sports matches and concerts which are viable in Sydney's market. In this, the size and structure of national sports leagues has been critical, with very few regular season national league matches able to generate crowds beyond the capacity of pre-Olympic stadiums.

Sydney's experience also shows that partnerships between the state and the private sector do not necessarily eliminate such risks. Private investor decisions do not guarantee profits. In the case of the Olympic stadiums, private investor expectations have been very wide of reality. The Stadium Australia prospectus predicted that by 2002 there would be 41 football games at the stadium with an average attendance of 40,000 (Moore 1998), a far cry from the seven or eight games likely to be played there in 2002. For the investors, redressing this misjudgement has been made more difficult by the state equity in competing venues. This has made the state government reluctant to grant concessions in favour of the Olympic Park stadiums.

The case of Sydney's Olympic stadiums thus raises the general issue of whether public–private projects are justified in relation to potential risks to government. The main advantages to government lie in public expenditure savings in a contemporary context of fiscal restraint and debt reduction (Quiggin 1997; Searle 1999). It is also argued that infrastructure and services are likely to be provided with greater innovation and efficiency (Hunt 1994). The experience of public–private motorways in Sydney suggests that a major issue is the tendency of governments to allow the profits of infrastructure provision to be privatised, while socializing the attendant risks (Quiggin 1997). Pressures by Sydney Olympic stadium operators to restrict state competition (in the case of the SuperDome) and use the state to produce a more attractive precinct environment are essentially post-construction attempts to socialize some of the emergent risks. The overall outcomes of public–private infrastructure projects in Sydney range from those which are very profitable (the motorways) to those which have made large losses (the airport rail line and the Olympic stadiums). One possible conclusion is that infrastructure which has a steady stream of revenue under monopolistic conditions, such as urban motorways, is a surer bet than infrastructure operating under oligo-polistic conditions, especially where revenue is very lumpy.

The development and operation of Stadium Australia and the SuperDome also illustrate the nature and problems of planning in a postmodern era. Their development was a response to a passing opportunity to attract a major global special event to Sydney, kindled by the opportunity for the Olympic Games to generate economic development and a global profile for further investment. Planning considerations about whether Sydney's long-term recreational and entertainment needs required them were absent. Moreover, the construction of stadiums and other venues at Olympic Park has set significant urban development in train nearby, much of it largely unforeseen at the time of the bid for the Games. Planning's increasing subordination to economic development, the need for partnerships with the private sector to achieve outcomes, and the uncertain competitive environment all this entails means a planning process that is more reactive, more short term and more unpredictable in its consequences. This becomes part of the price of participating in the city competition game.

References

Audit Office of NSW (1999) 'The Sydney 2000 Olympic and Paralympic Games – review of estimates', Sydney: Audit Office of NSW.

Audit Office of NSW (2001) 'New South Wales Auditor-General's Report for 2001', Sydney: Audit Office of NSW.

Auditor-General (1981) 'Report of the Auditor-General … for the period ended 30th June 1981', Sydney: NSW Government Printer.

Auditor-General (1983) 'Report of the Auditor-General … for the period ended 30th June 1983', Sydney: NSW Government Printer.

Auditor-General (1985) 'Report of the Auditor-General under the Public Finance and Audit Act 1983, 1984–85', Sydney: NSW Government Printer.

Auditor-General (1986) 'Report of the Auditor-General under the Public Finance and Audit Act 1983, 1985–86', Sydney: NSW Government Printer.

Auditor-General (1987) 'Report of the Auditor-General under the Public Finance and Audit Act 1983, 1986–87', Sydney: NSW Government Printer.

Auditor-General (1988) 'Report of the Auditor-General under the Public Finance and Audit Act 1983, 1987–88', Sydney: NSW Government Printer.

Baade, R.A. (1996) 'Professional sports as catalysts for metropolitan economic development', *Journal of Urban Affairs*, 18: 1–17.

Bartimole, R. (1994) 'If you build it, we will stay', *The Progressive*, June, 28–31.

Beazley, M., Loftman, P. and Nevin, B. (1997) 'Downtown redevelopment and community resistance: an international perspective', in N. Jewson. and S. MacGregor (eds) *Transforming Cities: Contested Governance and New Spatial Divisions*, London: Routledge.

Byrne, A. (1995) 'Power games: fair play fears in the battle to build Sydney's Olympic stadium', *Sydney Morning Herald*, 25 March.

Carr, M. (1998) 'Investors attack stadium board', *Australian Financial Review*, 10 September.

Carr, M. (1999) 'Sports wars to find winning turf', *Australian Financial Review*, 29 October.

Chandler, M. (1999) '"Hello, darling and here's your megaplex"', *Australian Financial Review*, 10 November.

Cowley, M. (1997) 'Sydney's sporting heart', *Sydney Morning Herald*, 3 April.

Dennis, A. (1999a) 'New arena for inter-city rivalry', *Sydney Morning Herald*, 13 March.

Dennis, A. (1999b) 'Barns battle in $250m. fight for concert cash', *Sydney Morning Herald*, 22 May.

Dennis, A. (1999c) 'A capital event', *Sydney Morning Herald*, 9 June.

Dennis, A. (2000) 'Rugby plea: don't shrink the stadium', *Sydney Morning Herald*, 23 August.

Department of Planning (1995) *Cities for the 21st Century*, Sydney: Department of Planning.

Department of Urban Affairs and Planning (1998) *Shaping Our Cities*, Sydney: DUAP.

Dunn, K.M. and McGuirk, P.M. (1999) 'Hallmark events', in R. Cashman. and A. Hughes (eds) *Staging the Olympics: The Event and its Impact*, Sydney: University of New South Wales Press.

Euchner, C.C. (1993) *Playing the Field: Why Sports Teams Move and Cities Fight to Keep Them*, Baltimore: Johns Hopkins University Press.

Fitzallen, L., Goldfinch, P., Routh, N. and Gregory, J. (1982) *Parramatta Stadium and the Law*, Sydney: Law School, Macquarie University.

Government Architect's Design Directorate and Urban Design Group (2002) 'Draft Sydney Olympic Park Post Olympic Master Plan', Sydney: Department of Public Works and Services.

Harris, T. (2001) 'ACT stadium shocker', *Australian Financial Review*, 3 October.

Homebush Bay Corporation and Property Services Group (1994) 'Urban design studio brief: the future redevelopment of Homebush Bay and the XXVII Olympiad 2000 AD Sydney, Australia', Sydney: Property Services Group.

Hunt, A. (1994) 'Providing and financing urban infrastructure', *Urban Policy and Research*, 12: 118–23.

Kennedy, A. (2001) 'Homebush Bay looking isolated as Sydney turns back to Moore Park roots', *Sydney Morning Herald*, 14 April.

Lawson, M. (2000) 'Homebush works on post-games agenda', *Australian Financial Review*, 25 October.

MacDonald, J. (1992) 'Off the beat', *Sydney Morning Herald*, 4 November.

Maiden, M. (2001) 'Stokes carries the Colonial team', *Sydney Morning Herald*, 26 November.

Maiden, M. and Milovanovic, S. (2001) 'Colonial Stadium facing collapse', *Sydney Morning Herald*, 23 November.

McGregor, C. (1999) 'Making history', *Sydney Morning Herald*, 30 January.

Moore, M. (1998) 'Stadium is still looking for someone to pay for it', *Sydney Morning Herald*, 30 July.

Moore, M. (1999) 'Domebush home to future fun', *Sydney Morning Herald*, 16 July.

Moore, M. (2000a) 'Millions sought to "save" Games site', *Sydney Morning Herald*, 30 May.

Moore, M. (2000b) 'Superdoom', *Sydney Morning Herald*, 10 June.

Moore, M. (2000c) 'What do we do with Olympic Park?', *Sydney Morning Herald*, 26 October.

Moore, M. (2001) 'Call for new dreams to revive Olympic site', *Sydney Morning Herald*, 19 June.

Office of Major Projects (1997) *Agenda 21 Quarterly*, Melbourne: Office of Major Projects, Department of Infrastructure, 13: 7.

O'Kaer, B.A. (1974) 'Subsidies of stadiums and arenas', in R.G. Noll (ed.) *Government and the Sports Business*, Washington, DC: Brookings Institute.

Olympic Co-ordination Authority (1996) 'State of play – a report on Sydney 2000 Olympics planning and construction', Sydney: OCA.

Olympic Co-ordination Authority (1999) 'Development fact sheet: Sydney SuperDome', Sydney: OCA.

Olympic Co-ordination Authority (2001a) 'Sydney Olympic Park draft post Olympic Masterplan', Sydney: OCA.

Olympic Co-ordination Authority (2001b) 'Sydney Olympic Park: request for proposals for commercial development', Sydney: OCA.

Quiggin, J. (1997) 'Private and public ownership and urban transport', *Urban Policy and Research*, 15: 56–8.

Rich, W.R. (ed.) (2000a) *The Economics and Politics of Sports Facilities*, Westport: Quorum.

Rich, W.R. (2000b) 'Conclusion', in W.R. Rich (ed.) *The Economics and Politics of Sports Facilities*, Westport: Quorum.

Rosentraub, M.S., Swindell, D., Przybylski, M. and Mullins, D.R. (1994) 'Sport and downtown development strategy: if you build it, will jobs come?', *Journal of Urban Affairs*, 16: 221–39.

Royal Australian Institute of Architects (2001) 'Draft post Olympic Masterplan', *Architecture Bulletin*, October/November: 5–6.

Searle, G. (1999) 'New roads, new rail lines, new profits: privatisation and Sydney's recent transport development', *Urban Policy and Research*, 17: 111–21.

Searle, G. and Cardew, R. (2000) 'Planning, economic development and the spatial outcomes of market liberalisation', *Urban Policy and Research*, 18: 355–76.

Sidlow, E.L. and Henschen, B.M. (2000) 'Building ballparks: the public-policy dimensions of keeping the game in town', in W.R. Rich (ed.) *The Economics and Politics of Sports Facilities*, Westport: Quorum.

Zimbalist, A. (1992) *Baseball and Billions: A Probing Look Inside the Big Business of Our National Pastime*, New York: Basic Books.

Zimbalist, A. (2000) 'The economics of stadiums, teams, and cities', in W.R. Rich (ed.) *The Economics and Politics of Sports Facilities*, Westport: Quorum.

Chapter 4

Land markets, social reproduction and configuration of urban space

A case study of five municipalities in the Buenos Aires Metropolitan Area

Juan D. Lombardo, Mercedes DiVirgilio, and Leonardo Fernández
with assistance from Natalia DaRepresentaçao and Victoria Bruschi

This study examines the concrete practice of the shaping of urban space. It explores the convergence of transformations initiated by worldwide neoliberal processes, which are producing the "megacity," and the urban landscape, imagined by some authors as being superimposed on the global, informational or postmodern city. The subject of this study is the Buenos Aires Metropolitan Area, particularly five of its municipalities. Our scope is limited to the period from 1991 to 2001. In order to explain this structuring of urban space, the study is organized around the following questions: How is the articulation between society and space produced? What logic lies behind it? What are the predominant social relations that currently support the structuring of urban space? Regarding the market that drives the structuring of urban space, how is it organized, and who are its primary agents? Finally, what are the contours of the resulting urban space?

The 1990s brought to the Buenos Aires Metropolitan Area (BAMA) a wide variety of important socioeconomic changes, many of which pertained to the realm of urban space, consisting of both territory and constructed space. The transformations that have been made and that are still being made in the city[1] are not isolated cases, especially when seen in relation to those changes that began to emerge in Argentinean society early in 1976, that have been even more pronounced since 1991,[2] and that have "naturally" coincided with the neoliberal socioeconomic and technological trends that are developing worldwide (Lombardo 2000a).[3]

Translated from Spanish by Heather Portorreal. Chosen as the best paper in *Quivera* Journal, volume 4, and submitted by the Association of Latin-American Schools of Urbanism and Planning. © Faculty of Urban and Regional Planning of the Autonomous University of the State of Mexico. Originally published in Spanish as 'Mercado del suelo: reproducción del espacio urbano. El caso de cinco municipios en la region metropolitana de Buenos Aires', in *Quivera: Revista de Estudios Territoriales*, 4(7) (2002): 49–72. By kind permission of the Autonomous University of the State of Mexico. © Juan D. Lombardo, Mercedes DiVirgilio and Leonardo Fernández. www.plazayvaldes.com.

The recent spatial transformations to which we refer to in this study are reshaping the territory in profound ways: in the distribution and organization of the functions and resources in certain spaces, in the select outfitting of urban areas, in the prioritization of places, in the assignment of prices to both land and urban spaces, in the way in which agglomeration comes about, in the distribution of that space among the local people, and in the pronunciation of spatial segregation, reaching a magnitude of unheard-of proportions. In short, there have been changes in the configuration of this urban space, of urban dimensions, that now rather than being defined by the reproduction of life, is defined by the capitalist logic of accumulating (reproducing) capital. This urban space does not come about "naturally" and sporadically, but rather through the actions of social agents, of specific social relations, and of investments.

From the variety of complex questions that may emerge from these affirmations, we will concentrate here on just two of them:

- What are the social relations and the main social agents that presently support the shaping of urban space?
- What are the characteristics of the urban space that is being shaped?

We are going to observe this in the BAMA, focusing particularly on the organization and the articulation of land markets in this area and on the effect they've had in the municipalities of San Miguel, Malvinas Argentinas, José C. Paz, Hurlingham, and Tigre (see Map 4.1). The answers to these questions point to the historic specificity of the relationship between space and society.

The shaping of urban space

To understand how diverse determinants link socioeconomic processes with spatial organization, we must first understand the legal relationships established among socioeconomic processes, social relations, and spatial forms. These relationships are complex in nature (Coraggio 1989). The shape of the urban space as it is functionally divided, outfitted, defined, and organized is a product of the social relations established in a given society. This shape is supported by a multitude of environmental, socioeconomic, political, cultural, and spatial trends and processes, which are dialectally defined as part of a system generated primarily for social reproduction. This system constructs a framework within which individual, family and institutional agents from distinct socioeconomic levels carry out their practices – their actions – reproducing themselves according to the set of options presented to them by the framework. This set of options encompasses not only housing, but also capital, institutions, etc. – all of those agents that comprise the system of social reproduction. This implies the reproduction of the distinct social sectors,

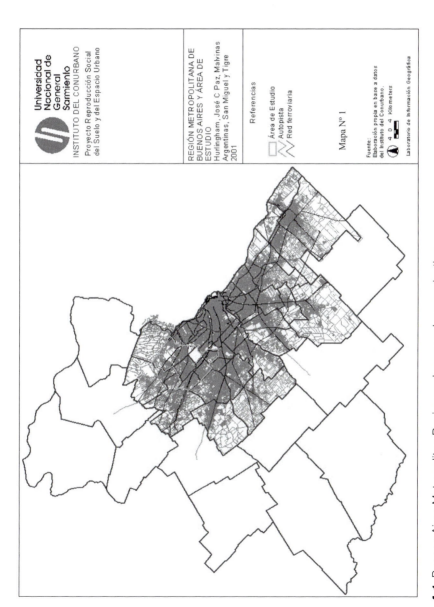

4.1 Buenos Aires Metropolitan Region and area under examination

Universidad
Nacional de
General
Sarmiento

INSTITUTO DEL CONURBANO

Proyecto Reproducción Social
del Suelo y del Espacio Urbano

REGIÓN METROPOLITANA DE
BUENOS AIRES Y ÁREA DE
ESTUDIO
Hurlingham, José C Paz, Malvinas
Argentinas, San Miguel y Tigre
2001

Referencias

Área de Estudio
Autopista
Red ferroviaria

Mapa Nº 1

Fuente:
Elaboración propia en base a datos
del Instituto del Conurbano.
4 0 4 Kilometers

Laboratorio de Información Geográfica

of distinct elements of capital, and of social structure itself. As such, reproduction strategies are shaped by each of the social agents who carries out and drives these processes. These strategies define and contextualize the social practices that the agents carry out in the process of their own reproduction.

The type of development adopted by a society conditions these strategies in that it determines the characteristics of the job market, of consumer spending, of government spending, of people's living conditions, of political process and practice, an operational framework for market growth, etc. This system relies on a number of closely-related dimensions – social, economic, cultural, spatial, etc. The practices of social reproduction operatively relate and concatenate these distinct dimensions. That is to say that they go on to produce an infinite number of combinations that operate upon the territory, giving concrete form to a system that reproduces relationships (social, economic, cultural, environmental, spatial, etc.). Within this system of social relations, these practices, contextualized within a system of reproduction, are articulated and interwoven. In this process, they generate a pragmatic support system for the territory. In other words, they generate their own social space so that they can actively develop.[4]

In turn, urban space (buildings, streets, zoned and organized space), in simultaneously being spatial support (Coraggio 1989) and also the site of the carrying out of social reproduction, becomes, consequently, the synthesis of a broad set of decisions, such as in politics, social programs and projects, legislation, regulations, and codes. These decisions or determinants are generated in the dimensions mentioned above, regulating the articulation among society, space, and territory. In this articulation, the laws of society govern over the laws of nature. This system gives shape, not mechanically, but rather contradictorily, to the city in the given territory.

The logic of capital gains (accumulation and capitalization of wealth), which reinforces in the territory an important apparatus sustained today by free market ideas (neoliberal engineering) and capital finance, holds hegemony over the process of social reproduction and the subsequent shaping of the city. Our own background analyses reveal important inequalities within the system of reproduction, using variables such as income, employment, unemployment and capital gains.

As an example of this shaping of urban space, we can look to the BAMA, where the new economic dynamic emergent from trends of liberalization and deregulation set the scene for a deployment of financial investments. This situation generated social and economic trends as well as spatial reorganization, all of which imply the recomposition and relocalization of secondary and tertiary urban activities, the creation of new ones, and the subsequent distribution of buildings, infrastructure, outfitting, sources of employment, the relocation of people, etc. This spatial organization traces out pragmatic circuits that allow for profit gain and the subsequent socio-spatial segregation in the region. These changes in land organization and development in the region appear to correlate with the inequalities present in the systems of social reproduction and of capital gain (Catenazzi *et al.* 2001).

Now then, when these processes of reorganization are realized in the region, we see a functionally divided space, a distribution of land uses, of productive activities, as well as a social and technical division of labor, as evidenced in infrastructure, service networks, schools, hospitals, housing, banks, public buildings, etc. We also see a cooperation – a spatial articulation, in other words – of these components. In this sense, the city operates as the operational foundation of the reproduction of a system whose main goal is the reproduction of capital. It plays a pivotal and complex role in the process of social reproduction (Topalov 1979).

Hence, the city weaves together all those elements necessary for urban life, elements such as the general conditions for reproduction, the population itself, financial and productive capital, space divided among diverse social sectors, distribution of merchandise, centers of financial capital, etc. Within urban space, these elements work in relation to one another, interwoven in such a way that they become functional components of the dominant system of reproduction, in which the ruling logic is that of capital gains. The spatial dimension is therefore pivotal to the process of social reproduction for the simple reason that it is the site where such reproduction is concretely realized; without its existence or systematization, social reproduction would not be insured in any of its dimensions. For this reason, the analysis of this space provides an ideal vantage point for observing the articulation between space and society. At the same time, spatial analysis, contextualized in the processes of social reproduction, presents a theoretical framework for understanding how a society expands, organizes itself and creates order within its territory.

The process of capital reproduction actually consists of a multitude of reproductive processes, of varied causes, which encompass the different social sectors and the distinct sources of private capital that compete in the city's economy. In this sense, the resulting layout of capital and economic value in the city is functional, contradictory and unequally distributed among the population.

Within this context, the state, in our case Argentina, acts mainly upon two important points related to the issues mentioned above: the implementation of social policies whose objectives are containing unemployment and supporting and encouraging the investment of private capital (for the most part financial capital as well as that coming from public service companies) in the region.

Within this integrated system, urban space and its organization become concrete; they become a commodity that needs to be produced, circulated, consumed and distributed.

Urban space, systems of reproduction, land markets, and land

Distribution

This established, how can we understand the spatial transformations taking place in the BAMA within the framework of what we have just outlined? While on a day-to-day basis we observe only some of these transformations, there is a city that is taking shape as a whole. What are its contours? What city is it becoming? And what social relationships are supporting these transformations of urban space in the BAMA?

The urban morphology to which we are referring is sustained by a system of social relations that has also given form to a market and a method of distributing land among the inhabitants of the region. The market to which we are referring is that of land, urban land, and urban space.[5] We see how in the development of this market a number of factors came together in relation to one another, factors such as some of the transformations we have, in general terms, mentioned here; the social practices of individuals with vested interests in this process; the individuals themselves (as social agents); a set of investments; norms; etc.

As part of the deregulation and decentralization of the national road system initiated in 1989 by the Argentinean government, the maintenance and operation of some 10,000 km of national highways and access routes to distinct cities was privatized. Included in this were the roads into, out of, and through the BAMA. This meant major investment in the improvement and maintenance of the highways servicing the BAMA. Between 1990 and 1998, one of the sectors receiving considerable investment was the infrastructure for commercial transport and local transit, an area which has received approximately $2 billion (Ciccolella 1999).

At the same time, there has been a considerable increase in the number of automobiles and in travel in private vehicles. Private automobile travel increased some 58 percent between 1970 and 1992 (Gutiérrez 1999). Meanwhile, vehicle registrations in the Buenos Aires Metropolitan Area went from 1,121,879 units in 1990 to 2,283,744 in 1998. In the municipalities of interest to this study – San Miguel, Malvinas Argentinas, J.C.Paz (municipalities that formed part of the former Partido de General Sarmiento), Hurlingam (of which Morón was a part until 1996), and Tigre – there were 192,768 registered vehicles in 1990, increasing to 425,745 in 1998 (Dirección Provincial de Estadística 1990–1998). Add to the number of automobiles a considerable increase in the number of gasoline stations in the BAMA, which rose to 5,000 within this period (Sabaté 1999).

On a similar note, we can examine the simultaneous increase in cellular telephone usage in the BAMA between 1990 and 1998, a fact that is complementary to the statistics given for automobile usage. This information becomes even more relevant when seen in light of the recent quantitative increase in the number of private, gated communities and neighborhoods, as well as country club style subdivisions located in the outskirts of the BAMA and serving as sites of permanent residence. This gains further relevance when we consider the social status of those inhabiting these developments between 1991 and 2001. Add to this the state of permanent "online" communication enjoyed by the inhabitants of these outlying neighborhoods, as well as the rapid migration facilitated by the highways connecting these neighborhoods to the urban center (the center of economic and political power) (De Mattos 1996).

The highways of the BAMA have become the new axes of urban expansion, along which the new developments and tertiary outfittings have been constructed. Some of the major highways in question are those of the northern and western corridors of the BAMA, along which the majority of these new subdivisions are concentrated. Between private, gated communities, and country club style subdivisions, there are some 356 such developments (*Diario Clarín* 2001). These highways create a rapid and direct connection between the economic and political centers located in Buenos Aires proper with the new subdivisions, now the permanent residence of the upper class, neighborhoods located in the primary, secondary and tertiary outlying regions of the BAMA (San Isidro, San Fernando, San Miguel, Malvinas Argentinas, Tigre, Pilar, Escobar, etc.).

This area of highways occupies space along the railroad lines and crosses areas of land that were not subdivided during previous periods of urban expansion (see Map 4.1). This has led to increased land value and investment in areas not previously subdivided, areas that can now be purchased in large plots at a low cost but that now call for investment in infrastructure and services. This brings with it, however, the possibility of generous economic returns.[6]

The territory of the BAMA has promoted investment in infrastructure in what are known as "areas of opportunity." Such areas have been brought into the economy through investments and have played a key role in the development of other private ventures. This development has been spurred by the changes occurring within the framework of the current processes of privatization and changes in regulations pertaining to public property.

Now then, how is capital organized in this region? And how does capital, in turn, organize the area?

Within the context of the situation faced by Argentina by the opening up of the domestic market to foreign capital, accentuated principally since the 1991 sanctions that offered an operational framework of inclusion and security for foreign investors, national business leaders wanting to carry out real estate ventures in the BAMA have been able to access significant amounts of money to finance their projects. This has meant high rates of return on their investments. In the words of one Argentinean developer, new sources of financing are now available in the market: pension funds, insurance companies, etc. Financing is carried out through the financial market, through titles, shares, the banks' own investment funds ...

(Patto 1998)

To summarize, since the late 1970s and especially since 1991, there have been changes in the following areas:

- the amounts of financing available to developers and general contractors[7] for the financing of their projects
- the types of financing available and
- the repayment period on the financing.[8]

Besides these development opportunities, we need to consider all of the other direct investments in developing the area along the new highways. Some of these projects (primarily shopping centers, supermarkets and hotels) have been carried out with private capital while domestic capital has been used for tertiary outfittings. The total of all these investments rose between 1990 and 1998 to some $4.65 billion (Ciccolella 1999). If the returns on these initial investments were tremendous, so were the business opportunities created by these projects. In addition to the returns gained from the investment in land, as explained above, we must add the secondary profits (Jaramillo 1989) resulting from the development of that land (now urbanized and zoned). Currently, it costs a developer approximately $450/m² to build a midsize house. Compare that with the market sale price of a midsize home located in the northern corridor (municipality of Pilar del Este): up to $984/m² (*Diario La Nación* 2001). As such, the developer's investment sees a gross return of 218 percent.

In addition to these changes (normative, financial, employment, etc.) that took place in the BAMA, we need must consider those changes related to the organization of real estate agencies, financial institutions, and other companies associated with the land market as other key agents in the reproduction of the land market in this region. This implies not only organizational changes in the management and organization of businesses, but also changes in technological equipment, time, rate of development work, and employment in the area.[9] These changes directly affect the construction companies, who are key players in this market and who are the ones determining the methods used in the actual construction, the technological equipment employed in the work, and the quantity and quality of the workers employed on the project.[10] "The companies that currently coordinate many of these development projects are financial institutions who are professionals working in the area of urban development" (IRSA 1998).

In this context, a new and important social agent emerges: the developer.

This agent is a key player in this new phase mentioned above and is the one coordinating, organizing and bringing together the various components and participants in this integrated system set to complete a project in a short period of time and to make the anticipated profit (IRSA 1998).

Normative concerns play a pivotal role in the reproduction of the market in question. In this respect, Aspizu's (2000) comments on privatization in Argentina adds to our understanding of this market:

> public policy creates mechanisms for transferring resources, for protection, for the consolidation of benefiting areas with extraordinary profits or privilege ... From there, we should understand this as the creation of a new market for the private groups, privileged with respect to the other areas of the economy.

One of the principal measures taken to regulate the use of urban land is Law 8912/77. This law governs the division and organization of land in the Province of Buenos Aires and regulates the use, occupation, subdivision and outfitting of this land.

Recent changes in legislation have been induced by pressure generated over land administration in light of several factors, two of which are 1) a lack of resources in the municipalities and 2) the intensity of competition, which has increased as a result of new conditions and changes implemented in the country, drawing private capital toward investments in the municipality. The pressure also comes from the investors themselves, pressure not only affecting the negotiations between the municipality and holders of private capital, but also producing changes in legislation. In this way:

1   The tension created between the advocates of development projects and the municipality, over the construction of these new projects, has brought about modifications in Law 8912. Accordingly, in 1998 the Province of Buenos Aires sanctioned Decree 27/98, which regulates the private, gated communities within its jurisdiction. Since then, the establishment of gated communities has been governed by national Law 13.512, without disregarding the stipulations contained in article 52 of Law 8912/77 or opting for what is pertinent according to the legal regimen established by Decree 9404/80. With the sanctioning of this land-regulating law (Law 8912/77) came the end to what were known as "popular lots," (lots created within the BAMA without infrastructure, services or equipment). These had become a mechanism by means of which the BAMA had extended outward along the railroad lines, mainly since the time of import substitution. These lots were accompanied by a very accessible system of financing

for the working class and the poor. Based on this system, the self-constructed city was created (Garay 1996). This regulation failed to produce the desired control over the land markets.[11]

2   In terms of taxation and in spite of local financial deficits, the framework established for negotiating land development has allowed the municipalities to develop the land, increase their tax base, privately resolve matters related to urban infrastructure (water, gas, sewer, paving, etc.) and attract services and outfittings (supermarkets and supermarket chains, private schools, etc.). However, it also means that certain areas, precisely those hosting such services and outfittings, have been inaccessible to certain sectors of the population. This way of developing the city – which did end up with new construction in the above-mentioned provinces – signified on a practical level more votes for those in office since, after all, there was certain development in the city as a whole. This development brought, for example, new facilities, new roads to the subdivisions (which were also used by non-residents) an extension of public transportation lines, improvements to shopping areas in the city due to the increased affluence of the population, and new sources of employment (in housekeeping, for example), etc.

This implies, furthermore, that those who invest in these private development projects, directed solely at affluent sectors of the population, will enjoy significant economic gains. Since such investments are made on land acquired at a low price, which is then outfitted with infrastructure, that land can be (and is) intentionally organized in such a way that the distribution of land parcels and the spatial outline of the territory are directly correlated to the sale price demanded by the developer. This is part of a very precise and scheduled plan.

In the case at hand, it is important to mention that in the five municipalities in question, between 1986 and 2000 the municipality approved 41 modifications to the division of land, modifications, including zoning changes as well as alterations to regulatory codes. These areas were for the most part designated for use by private subdivisions, high-rise apartment buildings, and commercial zones (Lombardo 2000). As such, the government has taken on a new role in this process of urban morphology. In the 1990s the government lessened its active role as planner and developer in the region and instead focused on promoting private investment in such endeavors. This was made possible by institutional and regulatory changes.

At the same time, as regulations give the municipalities in its jurisdiction the responsibility for the division of lands, it is the municipalities who, in light of their debts and limited budgets, are responsible for attracting the investment of private capital as one way of encouraging development in their territories. This process is facilitated by changes stemming from regulations (for instance, in Decree

27/98 as well as in the modifications in land use that the municipalities made to the division of land in order to optimize the investment of private capital). The introduction of this capital means the restructuring of certain sectors of the municipality (which will now have access to infrastructure, outfittings, and services) and the generation of a new tax base. But it also means that there will be certain "closed" sectors participating only sporadically in the greater community and that propose, in their private communities, a different type of socialization, one that is distinct from that of the other local residents and that stands in contrast to the social system prevalent in the area up to that point. "Neoliberalism incites each municipality to compete for global capital because with such investments comes modernization, development, tax revenues, etc." (Seminario, La Universidad como agente del desarrollo local 2001). In turn, the government supports the generation of capital and the growth of the land market. In light of widespread unemployment, it creates and enforces policies providing for compensatory social assistance in an effort to contain the spreading inequality produced by the free market.

Now then, what does the demand in this market look like? In order to have access to the land market (including the purchase of urban space), one must obtain financing. In this respect there are two major factors to consider: 1) offers for public and private financing and 2) the ability of the consumer to meet the conditions of these offers. In terms of public financing, this suggests a widespread offer primarily geared toward the construction of housing (delivery of a finished product), neighborhood improvement (providing infrastructure) and ownership regulation. The target sector for this type of offer is generally the lower class, whose basic needs are not being met and whose monthly income is at or below $450. But with the exception of the lending programs offered through the Blanco Hypothecation National (National Mortgage Bank), the loans offered as part of these programs are insufficient for the purchase of land valuing $200/m^2 or of a house in the range of $900/m^2, which is the going rate in the market we are considering. More than anything, this group of programs works collectively to contain the growing mass unemployment and to reinforce the government's efforts to support and promote the investment of private capital.

The offer of private mortgage financing, provided by international banks (Rio, City, Galicia, etc.), is made to salaried and self-employed individuals who finance 75 to 100 percent of their purchase. The terms of the mortgages range from 10 to 20 years, with an annual interest rate between 11 and 13 percent. The minimum monthly income required for these loans is somewhere between $1,000 and $1,800, with the mortgage payment lying between 35 to 40 percent of that monthly income. One also has to prove job security, and self-employed individuals must provide proof of income and payment of taxes in order to secure the loan. That said, is the population in a position to access this type of financing?

As shown in Table 4.1, in May of 2001 the total rate of unemployment in the BAMA was extremely high at 18.7 percent. In the Greater Buenos Aires Zone 4 (GBA4), however, 22.9 percent of the population was unemployed.

And, as shown in Table 4.2, the average income of those who were employed varied from $479/month in the most depressed – yet most densely populated – part of the region to as much as $1,008/month in GBA1.

The gap that exists between supply and demand appears to be great, especially in those sectors where the need is greatest and where the loan programs are focused. Containing these needs is a job that financial and real estate capital leaves in the hands of the government.

Table 4.1 Economically active population in Greater Buenos Aires (GBA), 2001* (in percentages)

	May 2001				
	GBA1	GBA2	GBA3	GBA4	Total
Active workers 14 and older	59.4	58.4	55.9	60.2	58.4
Employment rate	50.1	48.5	47.2	47.7	47.9
Unemployment rate	15.7	17	15.6	20.7	17.9
Occupational category					
Salaried workers	69.7	71.9	74.2	75.7	73.8
Workers without salary	30.3	28.1	25.8	24.3	26.2
Salaried workers without retirement	31.2	37.9	41.5	43.7	40.6

Source: EPH-INDEC.

Note

* Data from the Permanent Home Survey of the National Institute of Statistics and Census; added to the Buenos Aires Metropolitan Area are four homogeneous zones: GBA 1, 2, 3 and 4 that are made up of various municipalities whose people share similar socioeconomic characteristics.

Table 4.2 Average income of workers in various zones of Greater Buenos Aires (GBA), 2000

GBA and its areas	May 2000	May 2000 % of occupied homes in each GBA
GBA1	1,008	7.9
GBA2	617	27.8
GBA3	531	28.7
GBA4	479	35.6
Total	571	100

What results, then, is a financing offer directed toward a very concentrated demand, limited to private communities, country club style subdivisions, country clubs, old-fashioned style towns, etc., in other words, new developments. This fact is confirmed by the following statement made by a loan consultant: "60 percent of financed mortgages are located in areas where the average monthly income is between $1,500 and $1,200 to $1,000. To those earning monthly salaries of $1,000 to $900 and less, banks do not offer financing and builders have difficulty doing so" (Patto 1998).

In the context of a free market economy, sanctioned and supported by regulations in our country, the investments and actions of social agents have brought about the changes we have described and continue to shape the spatial-temporal systems in which we move daily. These transformations, taking place on various levels, and in diverse dimensions, and manifested in myriad ways, have also been instrumental in the reorganization and reestablishment of these social agents in the process of social reproduction, which takes place in accord with the predominant capitalist logic of making a profit. Practically speaking, this means that each participant – albeit individual or group – in this system occupies a designated space in accord with their participation in the established system. At the same time, this also means the reestablishment, the reorganization, and the redistribution of space among the distinct social sectors.

The logic governing this system is that which is established in today's society by the investment of private capital for the purpose of generating wealth. This is particularly the case with financial and real estate capital. It is no coincidence that the situation in the real estate market has unevenly distributed urban space among the different social sectors and has created among the different zones a heterogeneity and inequality in the standards of living. These changes, along with the practices and ventures of the distinct social agents and the investments coming from distinct sectors and branches of the financial market (funds made available for land development, investments made by the venture capitalists themselves, investments from domestic savings accounts, investments prompted by actions taken by the Argentinean government, etc.), have created a market founded upon the practices of its participants, whose investments in land, in accord with the new type of urban development that has resulted, have reproduced a space that is organized around the generation of profits. The distribution of investments over the land in question has redefined this land. It has also redefined the urban areas and activities affected by such investments.

Slowly, therefore, private capital has become the principle organizer – the directing agent – in the process of social reproduction and in the distribution of space. In this scenario, the state functions as facilitator and promoter of this process.

In order to give the approximate magnitude of the market that we are analyzing and that is perpetuating itself in the BAMA, we calculated the average capital gains earned from investment in urban land. We limited the calculations to what are referred to as "closed neighborhoods" (country club style subdivisions; private, gated communities; country clubs; and large subdivisions) located within 29 different municipalities of the BAMA. Over a span of approximately 19,000 hectares or 190,000,000 m² of urban space (A y DET 2001), (*Diario La Nación* 2001), taking into consideration a wholesale cost of $25/m² and an average sale price of $116/m² (*Diario La Nación* 2001) for the various areas of the BAMA, we arrive at an average capital gain of $91/m² and an average gross income of $17.3 billion for the BAMA. From these figures, of course, we must subtract the interest paid to finance these investments.

Figure 4.2 presents our model of the dynamics structuring space, as reproduced by the actions of social agents themselves.

So then, what are the characteristics of the urban space shaped by the market in this region?

The context generated by the changes that have been occurring on different levels in the BAMA, has reproduced a multi-dimensional operative framework for the earning of capital gains from private investment in land and urban space lying along the axes of expansion constituted by the new highways. This form of private venture is not new to the region, but rather is a pronunciation of the method used in real estate venture during a prior period of expansion in the region (the period of Substitution of Imports) (Lombardo 1999). The difference lies in that the interests of those holding the capital impose direction and predominance upon the process of accumulating wealth during the period in question. This process constitutes the reproduction of society. In this sense, the dynamics in this area, and the footprint left on the territory, are distinct from those emerging in previous decades.

The logic used by the private sector to organize and shape the region is the capitalist logic of profit gain, seen in action here in the case of land markets. This logic governs the real estate concerns in the distinct zones and areas of the different municipalities of the BAMA. It decides which areas are to be included or excluded and what set of expectations are held for each area. In deeming them not "financially viable" or "lucrative," private capital excludes certain devalued zones, leaving them in the hands of the government.

The main point in relation to land and urban space may be examined using Figures 4.3 and 4.4. The appreciation or depreciation of, or the profitability expectations for different urban zones varies by market value. A key factor in this situation is the functional division of space, which maps out specific places and in so doing determines the land market. This indicator reflects the desired distribution (municipal zoning) as compared to real distribution (existing zoning of the territory) of profits made off of urban space. This establishes the relationship between individuals, capital, and the state, a relationship mediated by the market

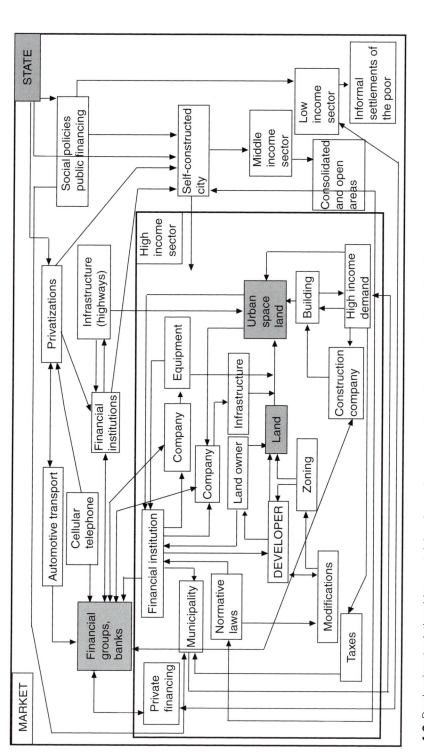

4.2 Predominant relationships sustaining the real estate market in five municipalities of the Buenos Aires Metropolitan Area

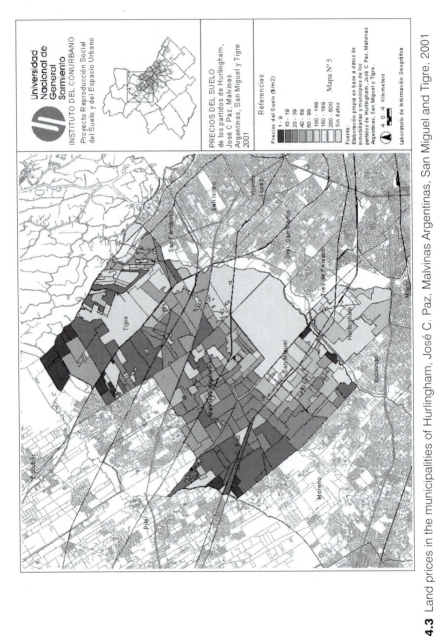

4.3 Land prices in the municipalities of Hurlingham, José C. Paz, Malvinas Argentinas, San Miguel and Tigre, 2001

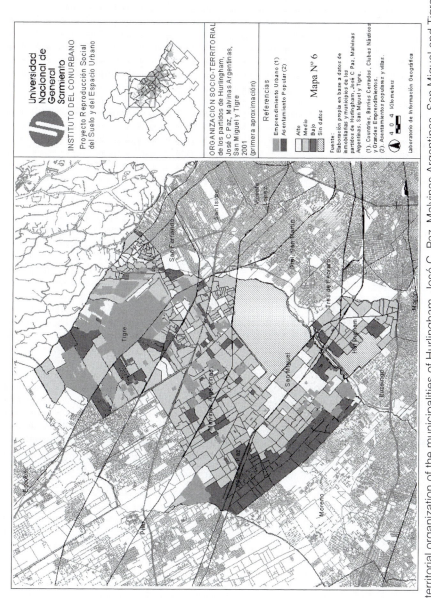

4.4 Socio-territorial organization of the municipalities of Hurlingham, José C. Paz, Malvinas Argentinas, San Miguel and Tigre, 2001

and its regulations. This phenomenon attempts to organize the territory by drawing an urban map based upon variables such as the prices of land, urban plots, and urban space. In this scenario, the highly valued areas are distributed among the high-income sector, who can afford the high prices of urban space. Middle-income zones, for the most part, are presented as having undetermined price expectations. And the lower-income areas, which are not attracting investment, are depreciating more and more. Nevertheless, within these latter areas there do appear some pockets of price expectations (mainly because the low price of land allows developers to buy low and sell high).

At the same time, the quality of infrastructure and outfittings is determined according to the price range of each distinct zone. The privatization of utilities (water, sewer, electricity, gas, etc.) that has taken place in the BAMA accentuates this process, giving private capital even more control over the shaping of urban space. The subdivision of these areas by private capital effectively facilitates social reproduction. A consequence of this is the increasingly marked socio-spatial segregation in the city, a divisive process that works differently in each social sector: isolating the lower class, marking the middle class with expectations for advancement, and promoting elitism among the upper class (Catenazzi *et al.* 2001). In other words, private capital, functioning through the practices and ventures of social agents, has become the principal organizer of the processes of social reproduction and of the distribution of urban space. The market is the mechanism integrating the process of social reproduction with the distribution of space. Again, in this scenario the government serves to facilitate and promote this process. This phenomenon is exemplified by five municipalities included in this study, as seen in Figures 4.3–4.7.

As a starting point, in Figure 4.5, we can see the distribution of distinct socioeconomic levels in the area under study in 1991. Figures 4.6 and 4.7 are provided to give a graphic impression of the magnitude of this urban morphology. They show vacant urban spaces (spaces not occupied for specific uses, for example INTA, Campo de Mayo, etc.) located within the territory in 1992 and then in 2001. The space occupied during this time period increased by 5,690 hectares. Figures 4.3 and 4.4 show the new spatial mapping of the area as a result of the land market described above. The latter of these two maps is intended to clearly represent the situation we are describing by showing both the new developments and the towns and neighborhoods populated by the lower class.

These maps represent a region being transformed. Social organization is characterized by a consolidated nucleus in the middle of two extremes, where the upper class and the lower class are distinctly concentrated each in their own space. In both the nucleus and along the boundaries of this space, there are areas of undetermined economic potential. The most consolidated areas are located in San Miguel and Hurlingham, nuclei of highly priced real estate. The middle class

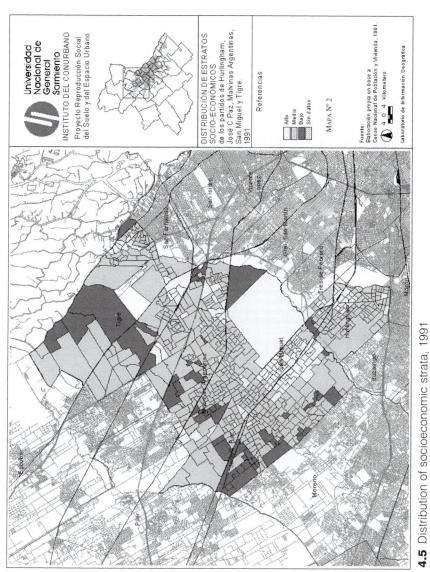

4.5 Distribution of socioeconomic strata, 1991

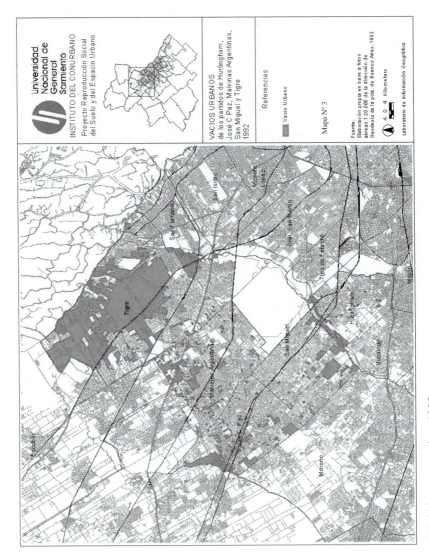

Universidad Nacional de General Sarmiento

INSTITUTO DEL CONURBANO

Proyecto Reproducción Social del Suelo y del Espacio Urbano

VACIOS URBANOS
de los partidos de Hurlingham,
José C Paz, Malvinas Argentinas,
San Miguel y Tigre
1992

Referencias

Vacío Urbano

Mapa N° 3

Fuente:
Elaboración propia en base a fotos
aéreas 1:20 000 de la dirección de
Geodesia de la pcia. de Buenos Aires, 1992

4 0 4 Kilometers

Laboratorio de Información Geográfica

4.6 Urban vacancies, 1992

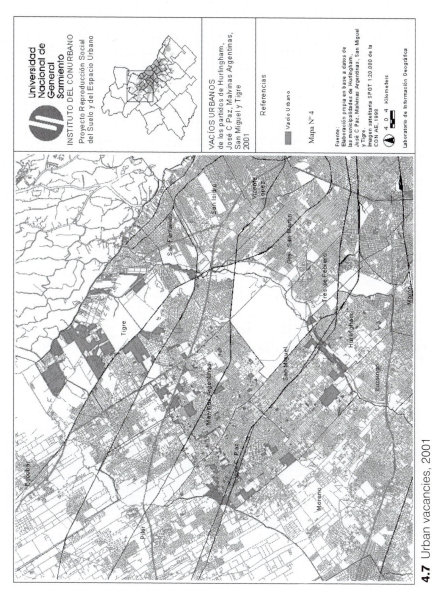

4.7 Urban vacancies, 2001

occupies the center of the area under study. Both the new developments and the lower-class neighborhoods are found dispersed throughout the territory, in many cases appearing adjacent to one another. In Partido del Tigre the new developments do not appear as isolated areas, but rather as a more consolidated agglomeration, primarily because of the relationship established in that area between capital and the municipal government, a relationship that has served to give shape to the city. Land prices, therefore, are the foundation for socio-territorial organization.

Finally, we can point out that, with respect to the shaping of urban space, the central contradiction presented by the system of social reproduction outlined here is one in which the logic, power and incentive for the reproduction of financial and real estate capital governs the organization, definition, and distribution of the space that should give priority to developing fair and egalitarian living conditions.

Conclusion

The present analysis of the shaping of urban space in the BAMA is situated within a conceptual framework based on the idea that space is one site of social reproduction and that the organization and mapping out of this space correlates with the organization of social relationships in this system. This perspective makes it possible to observe the effect of the free market economy, not in some remote, unspecified society in some other corner of the world, but rather in a historically-specific system of socioeconomic reproduction, where the abstract theories of the market are made concretely manifest by the strategies acted out by real social agents and by the footprint that their reproductive processes leave on the space they inhabit.

In other words, what happens when these financial, commercial, political, and economic networks – all international in nature – begin to operate directly upon the historically specific system of social reproduction that has already developed in a given city? It is in this unique, historically-specific context that urban morphology takes place, and it is in this context that we have tried to explain the dynamics of the market, the effect of capital investment, the importance of the various factors at work in the city, etc. In other words, these processes have left a footprint upon a specific and real society.

From this perspective, we can draw the following conclusions: the principal mechanism for shaping urban space (the shifting property values in a region and the profits earned from investing private capital in real estate) becomes more profound when inserted in another context, where it takes on another dimension. At the same time, in this new context and as part of this mechanism, two related phenomena gain importance: 1) the qualification of urban space, currently effected by private interests; and 2) the spatial segregation that has reached new levels and extremes. In other words, the effect that the general socioeconomic processes have had on society has altered the variables that mediate and regulate the articulation between space and society (regulations, the practices of social agents, etc.). It has also altered the social relationships formed by individuals as part of the process of social reproduction, relationships that support and sustain the articulation of society and space. In this context, the mechanism (for shaping social space) studied here repositions and perpetuates itself, reaching new dimensions.

The indicated variations in land value have to do primarily with the appraisal of a commodity (urban space), with the territory (providing infrastructure, out-fittings and services), with the maintenance of the existing urban space, and with the urban morphology prompting changes in these attributes. The mechanisms currently employed to meet these ends differ from those used up until the 1980s in the BAMA. During that period, urban expansion passed through three main phases: expansion, consolidation, and densification. This resulted in what is referred to as the "self-constructed city" (Garay 1995). Expansion took place primarily in the areas populated by the lower class, situated along the principle axes of that stage of urban sprawl: the railroad lines. These lots represented the subdivision of lands in the outskirts, which were made accessible through long-term loans to the lower class by the landowners and important real estate companies. This subdivided land generally lacked infrastructure and basic outfittings and was not regulated nor clearly zoned; thus, the location of these subdivisions was in accord with the demands of the market.

As time passed, pressure coming from the residents as well as government actions (paving of streets, extension of highways and public transit systems, construction of schools, etc.) meant the creation of infrastructure and outfittings in the area. This phase is known as "urban consolidation." Along with this new infrastructure (though incomplete in some municipalities, many of which lacked proper sewage systems) and with improved transportation, the population of the area slowly began to densify.

The system of land appraisal was based primarily on the availability of infra-structure and outfittings on every level (from national highways to neighborhood streets, for example), all of which remained the responsibility of the state. The appreciation of a tract of land was directly related to its present (or future) proximity to the infrastructure that the state alone was in charge of constructing.

Now, as part of the neoliberal socioeconomic processes (of the free market economy), these mechanisms have been reorganized primarily through the following means:

- the sanctioning of Law 8912/77, which regulates land arrangement in the Province of Buenos Aires and which prohibits the division of land into lots for sale in the absence of infrastructure
- the decision to privatize the operation and maintenance of infrastructure and the distribution of related services. In other words, the qualification of land was privatized so that the market played a key role in the decision to develop or not certain areas of the city. These decisions, which were previously in the hands of the state, are now made by individuals who, working through established contracts of privatization, hold considerable power over decisions related to the creation of these services. These individuals are motivated by the possibility of making a profit. This is happening in spite of the fact that it is the state who should be regulating and controlling these services.
- the new relationship established between the municipalities and private investors in order to bring about these development projects (subdivisions, new infrastructure, etc.), which implies that real estate projects will be limited to geographical areas favorable for capital investment, and which also means modifications to Law 8912/77 (mentioned above). This is to say that the municipal government delegates the ordering and arranging of land to private capital, which operates according to the whims of the market. These developments are carried out in self-contained zones, controlled by private capital, where the functional division of space imposed upon the land is directed by the desire to make the largest profit possible, and where the landowners and investors do not wait for the future expansion of infrastructure to increase property values.
- the government's decision to create an operational framework for the market and for the investment of private capital in the region, which implies the creation of "areas of opportunity" in which to do business, areas in which the government has made major investments (in important infrastructure) toward raising property values in the territory.
- the presence of considerable, previously unavailable funds now made available in the capitalist market by the opening up of the economy. These funds can be used to finance real estate investment projects.
- the reorganization of real estate and development companies, now looking to maximize the returns on their investments.

This process of land appraisal, rather than acting homogeneously in the territory, creates a heterogeneous space of distinct zones in which the different land prices reflect the arbitrary qualification (value) of that land. The location of these distinct zones depends primarily on the actions of capital within the market and also on the relationship between that capital and the municipal government.

The relatively poorer zones, inhabited by lower income sector, remain the government's responsibility.

This coincides with the socioeconomic restructuring of society, a process in which society is reproduced in accord with its participation in the system, as explained above. The simultaneous occurrence of these two phenomena results in the redistribution of land among distinct social sectors. The real estate industry is established and formalized as part of the market and, in accord with the logic of greatest capital gains, as part of the socioeconomic framework imposed by neoliberal socioeconomic processes. The urban space that emerges in this way is based on a different logic than was the case in previous eras.

Notes

1 For more information see Lombardo 2000b.
2 Among other important measures are the following: the law of state reform; the privatization of a large number of public businesses; the law of convertibility; the opening up of the domestic market to foreign capital; the effect of foreign investments; the reform and deregulation of the labor market; the changing role of the state with respect to economic controls; etc. For more on this topic, see Sabaté 2001.
3 The principal characteristics of these processes are: the deregulation of both international and domestic financial institutions; the predominance of financial capital with respect to other forms of capital investment; the revolution of information and communication systems; the displacement of employment as the central category around which class and identity were structured; the predominance of the market as the central institution in society; the reorganization of the relationship between capital and work; the technological revolution; economic, political and social restructuring within the countries as key factors in adapting to the conditions of the new international economy (De Mattos 1996; Harvey 1997; Borja and Castells 1997; Coraggio 1997).
4 For a thorough exploration of this theme, see Bordieu and Passeron 1995; Coraggio 1999; García Canclini 1990, 1995; Hintze 1989; Margulis 1986; Marx 1994; De Oliveira and Sales 1986; Lombardo 2000a.
5 Here, "land" is understood as that portion of territory subdivided into lots and located within the city limits. By "urban land," we mean urban lots, dedicated to infrastructure (water, drainage, electricity, light, gas, telephone, etc.) and mapped within a functional division of land (zoning). And the term "urban space" refers to zoned urban land containing buildings.
6 For example, there have been considerable financial returns on investments in the northern tract of urban expansion. The average price of land for an investor, with the costs of development and subdivision included, varied between $20/m²

and $25/m². The sale price, on the other hand, varied between $40/m² and $200/m² (*Diario La Nación* 2001). This reveals dramatic returns ranging from 100 percent to 900 percent on real estate investments when based on an initial investment of $20/m², over the cost of the invested capital, subtracting the interest on the money lent to the investor from the financial institution in order to carry out the project. This clearly is of considerable importance.

7   Financial capital acts principally and differently upon the different social agents participating in the construction of the city: the construction industry (production of cement, steel, construction materials, etc.); the construction company (of buildings or infrastructure); private providers of public services; the developer (businesses, consultants, arquitects, etc.); the landowner; real estate agents; and the consumer (of land or of a home).

8   Since the transformation, the country has been revalued in terms of the real estate market. Before this, short term ventures were more prevalent. The goal was to see how quickly the fixed assets (house, building) could pass from the hands of the developer to the consumer and the developer, in turn, could collect the return on his investment. Now there is more planning involved. There is stability. Investments are planned out for 10, 15 to 20 years. In the new scheme of things, banks play a new role than they did 50 years ago. Real estate agencies have to make business plans when before their only task was to bring together buyer with seller. The same is happenning with construction companies, who now have to plan construction developments carefully due to the strictly limited time allowed for each investment project. Now construction is carried out not with private capital but rather with money lent from third parties, through the use of stocks and securities.

(Patto 1998)

On the other hand, since the 1980s there has been greater variation in the amount of money invested in the real estate projects carried out. In 1989, during a slump in the construction industry, the cost of one m² of construction varied between $800 and $1,000. The primary building type constructed in the capital during that time were highrises built on horizontal tracts of land. As such, a building constructed on a 30m × 50m plot of land, with a square footage of 100m² per story, and consisting of 10 stories (which was most common at the time), was worth approximately $1,000,000. These highrises could reach a value of up to $3,000,000 (Garay 1998).

The amounts invested in more recent development projects has varied considerably from these figures. In "Marinas Golf" (Partido de Tigre) approximately $200,000,000 was invested. In "Nordelta" (Partido de Tigre), total investment was $250,000,000, while in "Pilar del Este" it reached $450,000,000 (*Diario Clarín* 2000).

9   A complex set of factors such as the type of financing, its total amount, and the period and conditions of the loan granted for the project all produced changes, not only in the organization of the businesses carrying out these projects since the 1980s, but also in the way in which they operated in order to meet the established deadlines for the various phases of each project. As a result it became necessary to create and adhere to a strict plan for the projects, for their financing and investments, for the period of execution, for commercial and real estate plans, for the period needed to pay back loans, etc. This organization and planning affects all players in and stages of the development projects: financial institutions, real estate agents, construction companies, etc. (Patto 1998).

10   They use industrial construction methods and heavy equipment (cranes, PLUMAS, hoists MONTACARGA, lifts, and workers) that allow them to complete the work more quickly with fewer man-hours of labor.

11   "The Province of Buenos Aires, in a broad sense, lacks clear public policy concerning land organization, planning and development, leaving these regulations as empty formalities, incapable of shaping the city as is truly desired." (Colegio de Arquitectos de la Provincia de Buenos Aires 2001).

References

Aspaizu, D. (2000) "Las privatizaciones en Argentina y la concentración del poder económico." Conference presented at Seminario Internacional. Las Grandes Regiones Metropolitantas del Mercosur y México entre la competitividad y la complementariedad. Mimeo. Buenos Aires: ICO, INGS.

A y DET (2001) "Localización y características de la residencia del alto y medio standard en diez ciudades argentinas." Mimeo. Buenos Aires.

Borja, J. and Castells, M. (1997) *Local y global. La gestión de las ciudades en la era de la información*, Madrid: Santillana, Taurus.

Bordieu, P. and Passeron, J.C. (1995) *La reproducción. Elementos para una teoría del sistema de enseñanza*. Mexico: Laia.

Catenazzi, A., Lombardo, J. and Wagner, R. (2001) "Notas sobre la nueva cuestión urbana." Taken from Seminario Megaciudades. Mimeo. Buenos Aires: Instituto del Conurbano, UNGS.

Ciccolella, P. (1999) "Globalización y dualización en la RMBA. Grandes inversiones y reestructuración socio territorial en los años noventa," *Eure*, 25(76): 5–27.

Colegio de Arquitectos de la Provincia de Buenos Aires (2001) *Decreto Ley 8912/77*, Mimeo. La Plata.

Coraggio, J.L. (1989) "Sobre la espacialidad social y el concepto de región," in J.L. Coraggio, F.A. Sabaté and O. Colman (eds) *La cuestión regional en América Latina*, Quito: CIUDAD.

Coraggio, J.L. (1999) *Política social y economía del trabajo*, Buenos Aires: UNGS and Miño & Dávila.

Coraggio, J.L. (2001) "Conferencia," presented at el Seminario: La Universidad como agente del desarrollo local. Mimeo. Buenos Aires.

De Mattos, C. (1996a) "Reestructuración, globalización, nuevo poder económico y territorio en Chile en los '90," in C. De Mattos, D. Hiernaux and D.R. Botero (eds) *Globalización y territorio*, Mexico: FCE.

De Mattos, C. (1996b) "Avances de la globalización y nueva dinámica metropolitana," *Eure*, 65.

De Oliveira, O. and Sales, V. (1986) "Reproducción social, población y fuerza de trabajo," taken from III Reunión nacional sobre investigación demográfica. Mimeo. México.

Diario Clarín (2000) "Countries." October

Diario Clarín (2001) "Countries," November.

Diario La Nación (2001) "Countries," March.

Dirección Provincial de Estadística (1990–8) *Estadísticas Bonaerenses*, La Plata: Dirección Provincial de Estadística.

Garay, A. (coordinador) *et al.* (1995) *El Conurbano Bonaerense*, Buenos Aires: Consejo Federal de Inversiones.

Garay, A. (1998) *'Conferencia,'* presented at *Seminario: Desarrollo urbano y mercado inmobiliario*, UNGS, Buenos Aires.

García Canclini, N. (1990) *Culturas híbridas*, Buenos Aires: Grijalbo.

García Canclini, N. (1995) "La sociologa de la cultura de Pierre Bourdieu," in P. Bourdieu (ed.) *Sociologa y cultura*, Mjico: Grijalbo.

Gutiérrez, A. (1999) "Transporte público y producción del espacio urbano: El caso de la RMBA," in Seminario el Milenio y lo urbano, Buenos Aires: CEUR, ICO, Instituto Gino Germani.

Harvey, D. (1997) "Globalización y urbanización," *Graphikos*, 8: 13–20.

Hintze, S. (1989) *Estrategias alimentarias de sobrevivencia*, Buenos Aires: Centro Editor de América Latina.

IRSA (1998) "Conferencia," presented at: Seminario: Desarrollo urbano y mercado inmobiliario, Buenos Aires: UNGS.

Jaramillo, S. (1989) *El precio del suelo y la naturaleza de sus componentes*, Mexico: Sociedad Interamericana de Planificación.

Lombardo, J.D. (1999) *Pensamiento urbanístico y desarrollo urbano en la RMBA*, Buenos Aires: UNGS.

Lombardo, J.D. (2000a) *La cuestión urbana en los '90*, Buenos Aires: Universidad Nacional General Sarmiento.

Lombardo, J.D. (2000b) "Transformaciones socio económicas, procesos de globalización, ciudad y procesos de reproducción social en la Región Metropolitana de Buenos Aires," Mimeo. Buenos Aires: UNGS.

Margulis, M. (1986) *Cultura y reproducción social en México*, Mexico: El Colegio de México.

Marx, K. (1994) *El capital*. Vol. I, Book I: 476–99; Vol. II, Book II: 27–77, México: Fondo de Cultura Económica.

Patto, M. (1998) "Conferencia" presented at Seminario: Desarrollo urbano y mercado inmobiliario, Buenos Aires: UNGS.

Sabaté, F.A. (1999) "Los ejes centrales de las áreas temáticas para abordar la cuestión urbana en la RMBA. resumiendo transformaciones desde la economía y algunas consecuencias ya conocidas." Mimeo. Buenos Aires: UNGS.

Sabaté, F.A. (2001) "Economía y sociedad de la RMBA en el contexto de la reestructuración de los '90." Mimeo. Buenos Aires: INGS.

Topalov, C. (1979) *La urbanización capitalista*, Mexico: Edicol.

Chapter 5
Designing whole landscapes

Paul M. Dolman, Andrew Lovett, Tim O'Riordan and Dick Cobb

A whole landscape approach is critical to ensuring conservation and enhancement of biodiversity in farmed landscapes. Although existing agri-environmental schemes are constrained by property boundaries and voluntary take up, the potential for adopting a whole landscape approach to planned countryside management is currently favoured by a number of factors. These include economic uncertainty in some agricultural sectors; the introduction of a reformulated rural development policy; increased understanding of relationships between biodiversity and management; and the introduction of geographical information systems technology that allows future landscapes to be visualised to stakeholders. We report on ecological and socio-economic aspects of whole landscape planning in a study covering 31 neighbouring farms in west Oxfordshire. A baseline was first compiled that included information on property boundaries; land cover; relationships between hedge and field margin management and key taxa; and farmer socio-economics and attitudes towards agri-environmental measures, conservation and sustainable agriculture. We then developed future scenarios of integrated whole landscapes management, designed to deliver amenity, environmental and biodiversity benefits. These scenarios were presented and interpreted to farmers, conservation and amenity stakeholders with the aid of GIS-based maps and three-dimensional virtual reality visualisations. We report farmers responses and discuss the potential for implementing whole landscape planning.

This paper considers the potential for implementing a whole landscape approach to rural management for amenity, biodiversity conservation and other environmental benefits. We describe novel methodological developments that incorporate geographical information systems software and visualisation techniques into the

Selected as 2002 AESOP Prize Paper and submitted by the Association of European Schools of Planning process of developing and representing scenarios of desired future landscape states to farmers and stakeholders. We illustrate this by a case study in Oxfordshire that assessed socio-economic constraints and opportunities for biodiversity and landscape enhancement.

The concept of landscape itself has diverse origins. Meinig (1979), Cosgrove (1984) and Matlass (1997) all seek to show how landscape images are constructed out of social history and morality, personal preferences and ideals, and the imprimatur of agricultural, forestry and conservation policy. Culture and biota intertwine through individual land management, social interpretation and associated policy drivers. The result is an amalgam of influences resulting in a composition of features that may be loved or loathed. What is not the case at present is the conscious and premeditated design of whole landscapes that cross many farm boundaries, yet link culture and ecology in creative and purposeful ways in order to deliver specific benefits. Matlass (1997) quotes John Dower (1944: 95–6) the architect of national parks in England and Wales. Dower looked for a 'team of experienced landscape lovers' to determine the characteristics and typology of beauty and cultural association in protected landscapes. Dower believed that self-claimed groups of landscape champions would assume a leadership for whole landscape design that the next generation would be eager to endorse. Matlass (1997) suggests that hidden in this call is a preference for order and control over landscape ecology and aesthetics that generate pre-determined outcomes.

Despite the adoption of apparently objective techniques such as Landscape Character Analysis (CC, 1987, 1996), aesthetic landscape appreciation and design remain value laden and subjective. Furthermore, they are predisposed to the reactive preservation of relatively recent cultural landscapes, rather than enhancement through visionary change. In contrast, the emerging quantitative discipline of landscape ecology considers how the structure and juxtaposition of landscape elements affects their function; in terms of ecosystem processes, resilience to change, regulation of environmental quality and the dynamics of species assemblages and individual populations (Dunning *et al.*, 1992; Forman, 1995; Fry and Sarlov-Herlin, 1995). It provides a predictive basis for designing 'whole landscapes'.

A 'whole landscape' approach may be defined as a process of integrated planning across property boundaries, that optimises the amount, location, configuration and management of habitats and other landscape elements, to deliver explicit environmental, amenity and biodiversity benefits (Cobb *et al.*, 1999). There is increasing recognition of the importance of such an approach in attaining biodiversity conservation. On the one hand, where individuals of a species range widely throughout the landscape then management to achieve a viable regional population requires more than a site-based approach. More generally, a combination of small size, edge effects and a lack of appropriate patch disturbance dynamics are gradually eroding the biodiversity value of many key designated sites, leading to an emphasis on the restoration and creation of extensive blocks and networks of habitat (e.g. Kirby, 1995; CNP, 1997; Dolman and Fuller, 2003). This emphasis is complemented by the statutory designation of contiguous landscapes as Special Protection Areas and Special Areas of Conservation under the EC Birds Directive and the Habitat and Species Directive (CEC, 1979 and 1992 respectively). In addition, the latter directive explicitly emphasises wider countryside measures and extensive habitat restoration, as means to restore favourable conservation status (Andrews, 1994). An emphasis on wider-scale restoration measures also arises from the Biodiversity Action Plans (DOE, 1994, 1995), and the development of Natural Area Profiles by English Nature.

However, various constraints currently impede the realisation and implementation of a whole-landscape approach. One is the reluctance of policy and statute makers to challenge individual property rights. Consequently, planning tools and agri-environmental schemes are inadequate to ensure cross-boundary co-operation of neighbouring farmers except on a voluntaristic basis (Cobb *et al.*, 1999; MacFarlane, 2000b). This is a serious shortcoming, as reliance on voluntary take-up of agri-environmental prescriptions in an uncoordinated and ad-hoc manner, does not guarantee conservation of either biodiversity or landscape, let alone its restoration or enhancement. This is illustrated by substantial erosion of aesthetic amenity and biodiversity within farmed landscapes, that in cases continues despite Environmental Sensitive Area and/or National Park designation (e.g. Buckingham *et al.*, 1999; RSPB, 2001). Related to this is the more general shortcoming of property rights law; under British common law there is no responsibility beyond ownership, while the collectivity of the landscape has no formal legal status (O'Riordan and Sayer, 1999).

Another impediment has been the lack, until recently, of a mechanism for visualising how a future integrated landscape might look 'across the horizon'. The advent of sophisticated GIS technology, has been recognised as a powerful tool in designing landscape scale futures (e.g. Harms, 1995; Swetnam *et al.*, 1998; MacFarlane, 2000a). As we demonstrate below, by linking GIS data to visualisation software it is now possible to both shape and present a multi-farm future in such a way as to be meaningful for owners and managers on a field-by-field basis.

Other opportunities have also arisen to greatly enhance the prospects for whole landscape design. The introduction of the Rural Development Regulation (RDR) (CEC, 1997) represents a further and important shift of EC policy; away from the Common Agricultural Policy support for intensive agricultural output that has substantially reduced the species and habitat diversity contained within farmed landscapes (e.g. Kleijn and Verbeek, 2000; Siriwardena *et al.*, 2001).

This potentially radical development opens up substantial opportunity for planned landscape restoration.

The RDR combines nine existing rural measures aimed at switching the basis for support towards sustainable rural development. The policy of integrating environmental measures into sustainability is enshrined in the EU Treaty of Amsterdam. Since the passage of that treaty in 1997, the European Commission has steadily turned its attention to bringing these two fundamental objectives into line with agricultural policy. All member states must widen the basis of agri-environment measures for the RDR to be accepted as regional rural development programmes. In addition, through 'modulation' member states may now redirect up to 20 per cent of existing production subsidy payments into 'accompanying measures' such as wider agri-environment programmes, afforestation, and early retirement schemes. Each of these measures attracts grant of up to 50 per cent from the Commission, with the member state providing the other half. Initial estimates for the RDR budget for England are given in Box 5.1.

More recently, the UK Government has created a new Department for Environment, Food and Rural Affairs (DEFRA) that has taken over the responsibilities of the former MAFF. This represents a concomitant shift of emphasis towards a rural policy that delivers wider benefits. At the same time as falling output prices across the British agricultural industry, the livestock sector particularly is in a state of upheaval, following both BSE and foot and mouth. This has led to renewed calls for a fundamental reappraisal of the structure and practice, and also the purpose, of the agricultural food chain sectors (e.g. ENDS, 2001: 33; Everett, 2001).

It is now possible to link GIS and visualisation tools to integrated scenarios for ecological and scenic whole landscapes. Farmers can now visualise how a

---

Box 5.1 Preliminary estimate of RDR budget for England

In England, over the seven-year period 2000–6 as much as £1.6 billion may be pumped into RDR schemes through the financing of the England Rural Development Plan (MAFF, 2000). In the 2000/3 UK Comprehensive Spending Review some £1 billion of new money was allocated to RDR measures, primarily targeted in the England Rural White Paper. Agri-environmental expenditures absorb about 75 per cent of the total England Rural Development Plan, rising from £90 million in 2000 to £150 million in 2006/7. Modulation is expected to yield £50 million in shifted income by the same time, with similar funding from the Treasury. For a further analysis, see Rutherford and Hart (2000).

dramatically different landscape might look, and also seek the funds to work collectively to create it. What follows is a first attempt to show how such an opportunity may be grasped.

The west Oxfordshire study

To investigate the scope for achieving a contiguous agricultural landscape it was necessary to find a block of land capable of being managed as a whole. The National Trust suggested their Buscot and Coleshill estate as a suitable location. This estate is situated on the boundary between Oxfordshire, Gloucestershire and Wiltshire (see Figure 5.1), encompassing land on the floodplain of the upper River Thames and part of the Midvale Ridge and includes 11 farms, totalling 3,000 hectares. These farms are tenanted and have a large degree of freedom over their individual management. Nevertheless, when negotiating and renewing farm rental agreements, the National Trust may offer incentives and guidelines for on-farm environmental management. The opportunity that this offers for integrating farm management across farm boundaries is unusual. Consequently, we extended the study area to include an additional 23 independent farms, contiguous with the National Trust estate, giving a total study area of some 110 km².

Our research objectives may be summarised as follows:

- obtain participation of farmers in the study and identify their current management practices, plans for the future and attitudes to participating in agri-environmental grant schemes
- develop and implement a methodology for baseline ecological appraisal of a contiguous piece of countryside
- incorporate information from this appraisal, along with other physical data, within a GIS database
- develop four plausible scenarios for future landscapes in the study area, in co-operation with a group of knowledgeable land management agencies covering wildlife conservation, amenity, planning, forestry and land management generally
- produce large format (A0) maps and computer-generated 3D visualisations of the current landscape and of the scenarios, to provide complementary views of the potential landscape changes, and allow the different visualisation methods to be compared
- interpret and visually summarise ecological and environmental benefits of implementing the various scenario prescriptions at a landscape scale
- assess the responses of land owners and managers in the area to the alternative scenarios, and identify the potential implications for their future management and farm economies should each scenario be pursued.

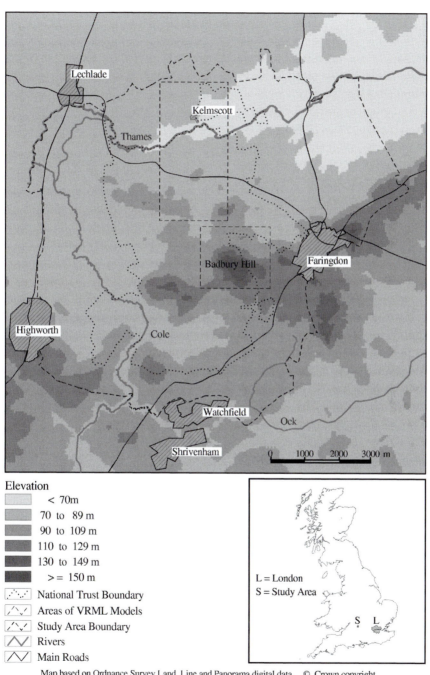

Elevation

      < 70m
      70 to 89 m
      90 to 109 m
      110 to 129 m
      130 to 149 m
      >= 150 m
      National Trust Boundary
      Areas of VRML Models
      Study Area Boundary
      Rivers
      Main Roads

L = London
S = Study Area

Map based on Ordnance Survey Land Line and Panorama digital data. © Crown copyright.

5.1 Map showing location of study area

Methodology: farmer surveys, landscape attributes and wildlife habitat

The study area consists of 34 farms. There were only three refusals amongst these farmers when asked to take part in the study and none of these cases represented significant amounts of land in the study area. We conducted three sets of interviews with the farmers. After making initial contact we first visited the 31 farms participating in the study to explain the purpose and methodology of the project, and at the same time determined which land they managed and the nature of their farm operations. In a second set of visits in April and May 1998, again to all 31 farms, we collected detailed socio-economic data and then focused on their responses to agri-environmental initiatives and feelings about future landscape options and the potential for collaborating across property boundaries. A final visit was made to a sub-set of farmers at the conclusion of the study, in order to assess their response to the visualised landscape scenarios.

Key landscape attributes in the 110 km² study area were identified and surveyed for incorporation into the GIS database. Woods were noted and characterised. Sites of nature conservation importance (SSSIs and County Wildlife Sites) were identified from county registers. Much of the survey concentrated on characterising and mapping hedgerows and fields within the farmed landscape. Field boundaries were identified from 1:25,000 scale OS maps; all boundaries were visited and categorised by type (ploughed out/crop change/field bank/fence/hedge). For each of the 745 field boundaries that supported a hedgerow, species composition of shrubs and standards were recorded using the DAFOR scale, and the physical structure of the hedge was also recorded (height and width in metres, gappiness on an ordinal scale from 0, hedge entire, to 5, gaps dominant). Adjoining crop species and margin vegetation types were also recorded.

Additional detailed ecological surveys focused on selected indicator groups; flowering plants, birds and butterflies. The abundance and species composition of hedgerow birds and butterflies was recorded from a sub-set of 98 independent 50 metre sections of hedgerow, stratifying for structure, adjacent crop type and farm type (recognising five categories on the basis of farm management and levels of biocide application: organic, converting or transition, conventional arable, conventional mixed stock and arable, conventional diary). Species were recorded adopting the methodology of Green *et al.* (1994) for hedgerow birds and standard techniques for butterfly transect monitoring (Pollard, 1977). Each hedge section was visited twice for the avian survey (May and June) while three visits were made to record butterflies (June, July and August); records for each section were combined across visits. Species composition was then related to hedgerow charac-teristics including structure and management, shrub composition and the composition of hedge margin vegetation. The plant species composition of arable headlands was surveyed in replicate headlands from organic and conventional fields (both sympathetically and intensively managed). Results of these surveys characterised the wildlife resource of the existing agricultural landscape and their analysis showed effects of differing farm management on species composition and abundance.

Structure of farms within the study area

Overall, the 31 farms studied included a range of owner-occupied and tenanted farms, of varying size and a balance of farming operations. Of the 11 National Trust farms, all apart from one have other land off the estate that they manage. One farmer owns a substantial hectarage south of the estate, five others have additional rented and owned land, and the remaining four rent other farms and fields. The first programme of interviews generated the data in Table 5.1.

This structure has been changing over the last five years. Both the farms of 700+ hectares have increased in size; six farms in the 300–700 ha band and five in the 100–300 ha group have also expanded. In the latter group, four out of the five bought more land compared with two in the 300–700 ha band. Three other farms in the 300–700 ha group have also used the contract farming route to increase their activities. Of the two largest operations, one has a policy of rapid expansion by purchasing any land in the region (over 1,000 hectares were acquired during 1993–8), while the other is expanding via contract farming. The smallest farms have not increased in size. Individual management circumstances are clearly influencing structural change.

In terms of the classification of the farms for the whole study area, ten are mainly arable, five mainly dairy, 12 mixed with arable, dairy and beef, one concentrates on arable and pigs (adding value by feeding much of the arable produce to the livestock), one operates some arable but mainly dairy and beef, and two farms have a high proportion of long term set-aside (one of which has additional grass supporting a flock of sheep).

Turning to the economics of the farms, 14 of the farms derive all their household income from the farm or related activities (diversification on the farm),

Table 5.1 Profile of the 31 farms

Size (ha)	Number of farms
50–100	3
100–300	13
300–700	13
700+	2

another 14 receive over 50 per cent, with another farm relying on the farmed land for only 25 per cent. In terms of profitability, when surveyed in 1998, 26 of the farms had made profits in each of the previous five years, three made losses in the last year, and two had more mixed results.

Response of farmers to environmental measures

During the second set of interviews, farmers were asked to respond to a series of statements on farming, conservation, landscape, property rights and rural economy issues, ranking these on a 'strongly agree' to 'strongly disagree' scale. Table 5.2 summarises their responses. Of the 31 respondents, 20 agreed that private land should be managed in the interest of the countryside and landscape (with only seven disagreeing). The suggestion that investing in conservation was a waste of time and effort, unless it made a profit, was rejected by 18 respondents, with only nine agreeing. The stronger statement that a land users only concern is profitability was also opposed by most. This indicates that a majority of the farmers felt some sense of stewardship or concern for conservation and landscape beyond the immediate demands of their business. Despite this most retained a pragmatic attitude to public subsidy for environmental and conservation measures – although eight believed conservation could still be achieved in the absence of public support, the overwhelming majority (22 of 31) thought such public subsidy was necessary. However a forceful minority remain, who rejected landscape and biodiversity concerns or any moral obligation to protect societies wider needs. In many instances it is these farmers who control the largest areas of land and who are most ruthlessly pursuing a policy of expansion. In addition, a substantial proportion of the farmers felt that environmental measures, conservation and sustainable agriculture infringed their property rights and freedom to manage 'their' land as they chose.

Specific questions on wider take up of agri-environment measures gave the following responses. Sixteen farmers said they would consider the option. Of these, six were already in the Countryside Stewardship Scheme (CS) and three were members of the Environmentally Sensitive Area Scheme (ESA). Ten farmers said they would not participate in further agri-environment measures, though one of these was in the CS, and three in the ESA.

Fifteen farmers said they would consider participating in wider landscape management policies, five of whom were in CS and four in the ESA. Seven farmers were not inclined to be involved in the wider landscape option, one of these was in CS, and three in the ESA. One of the factors that could be affecting this response is the landlord–tenant relationship. On the NT farms four farmers have some land in CS and two eligible farmers have entered the ESA. Four have not applied to CS, and one farmer has not entered the ESA scheme. Outside the

Table 5.2 Responses to management and property rights statements. The number of farmers giving each response is shown (total number of respondents = 31)

Statements offered for consideration	Strongly disagree	Disagree	Indifferent	Agree	Strongly agree
Modernisation of land management has improved the amenity and quality of the countryside	1	7	10	13	0
Disappearance of natural features like hedgerows reduces the number of wildlife species and the amenity of the countryside	0	0	1	16	14
Adapting business management to changing demands on the countryside could help to maintain and revive rural communities	1	7	8	14	1
The countryside would benefit from the abolition of the subsidy system	6	15	6	4	0
Private land should be managed in the general interest of countryside and landscape	2	5	4	18	2
Unless it can make money, investing in conservation is a waste of time and effort	4	14	4	7	2
A land user's only concern is the impact of management decisions on the profitability of the business	9	12	2	8	0
All nature conservation activities should be financially rewarded by subsidies	1	18	0	10	2
Conservation in the countryside can only be achieved with the help and support of public money	2	6	1	19	3
Dependence on public subsidy means that environmental conservation infringes private property rights	0	7	8	15	1
Sustainable agriculture is a means of telling farmers what to do with their land, and reducing the freedom of choice to make a decent living	6	20	1	4	1

estate, only two farms joined CS, and six the ESA. Eighteen have taken none of the CS options, and three of those eligible have not entered the ESA. Pressures from the landlord, together with lower rents, may have had an influence.

Farmers future management intentions

All the farmers interviewed were uncertain about what they might do over the coming decade. This was partly due to the deteriorating economic circumstances, but is also a function of ownership, opportunity, investment fund availability, and changing patterns of food markets. We found that two livestock farmers had begun the road to organic production in the belief that the organic milk premium would enable them to offset falling milk prices. One was seriously considering total conversion to organic, though the lack of guarantees in the organic transitional aid scheme was causing him to delay.

In general, the interviewees did not plan to do much that was different over the coming decade. They would seek to be more efficient, they would intensify where possible, they would contract out their labour and machinery where practical, they might reduce their labour force, and they would seek to maintain the wildlife and amenity value of their property wherever feasible. The conclusions from this element of the study were:

- no farmer planned to go out of business
- the labour force would probably decline by 10 per cent
- a small amount of wildlife loss was envisaged due to changes in field management, but this would be modest
- the overall landscape would probably not look much different.

Ecological condition of the landscape

Overall, the study area contained some rich and varied wildlife habitats, however these were invariably non-agricultural features, such as ancient woodlands or rivers protected by statutory or county-level designation. In contrast, the farmland itself was biologically and ecologically impoverished, despite the superficial retention of some aesthetically pleasing 'landscape furniture'.

The study area contained 42 km² of arable fields; most of which is intensively managed to the field boundaries, with virtually no wildlife habitat. Headlands of conventionally managed arable fields had very low species richness of flowering plants, however those of organic and converting fields supported significantly more plant species (see Table 5.3).

Although 422 km of hedgerows were identified from the study area, a further 138 km of field boundaries lacked a hedgerow, being marked by a grass

Table 5.3 Species richness of arable headland vascular plants in fields of five farms with differing management

Organic	Converting	Conventional/ sympathetic (farm 1)	Conventional/ intensive (farm 2)	Conventional/ intensive	Anova
6.8[a] 0.3	6.1[a] 0.3	4.2[b] 0.2	3.8[b] 0.3	2.4[c] 0.2	$F = 50.17$,
(40)	(48)	(48)	(36)	(48)	$p < 0.001$

Note
For each farm/management category, the mean and standard error of plant species richness per m^2 are given. Data were collected in a nested sampling structure; with 5–7 replicate headlands from each farm and a mean of seven quadrats per headland. Sample sizes in parentheses are the number of quadrats. Results of analysis of variance (incorporating headland as a nested factor within farm category) and subsequent multiple comparison test are shown; category means that share a common superscript do not differ significantly (Tukey test, $p > 0.05$). a, b and c indicate homogenous sub-sets identified by the Tukey multiple comparison test in Table 5.3.

strip, fenceline or change in crop. Many hedges in the study area were in poor physical condition, due to being cut too closely and too frequently; of 745 hedgerows surveyed, 44 per cent are cut every year, 38 per cent were less than 2m high and 12 per cent had gaps 'abundant' or 'dominant'. This greatly reduces their ecological interest and value as wildlife habitat.

Although there was a moderate diversity of trees and shrubs species within the hedgerows themselves (mean of 5.0 shrub species per 50m, s.d. = 2.2, $n = 97$), the species richness of associated taxa was generally low, with an average of 9.2 vascular plant species in the margins (s.d. = 5.1, $n = 97$), only 2.5 bird species (s.d. = 2.0, $n = 93$) and just 2.0 butterfly species (s.d. = 1.5, $n = 97$) per 50m section. Hedge margins of organic arable fields in the study area supported significantly more plant species than margins adjacent to conventionally managed arable fields (see Table 5.4). Table 5.5 shows the frequency of occurrence of the 14 butterfly species recorded during the survey. The most abundant species tended to be those predominantly associated with agriculture (e.g. *Pieridae*). Even species considered to be ubiquitous nationally, such as peacock, gatekeeper and meadow brown, were uncommon in the farmed landscape, while more specialist species like common blue and small copper were represented by only a handful of records. This emphasises the ecologically degraded nature of the current agricultural landscape.

GIS database construction and visualisation

A digital map database was created for the study area using the Arc/Info GIS (ESRI, 1997). Two main sources were used, 1:2500 scale digital vector maps (Land-Line®) and Land-Form Panorama® elevation data, both provided by the

Table 5.4 Species richness of hedge-margin vascular plants in relation to management of adjacent fields

Organic	Converting	Conventional arable	Conventional mixed	Conventional dairy	Anova
12.9[a] 3.8	8.5[a,b] 5.4	6.1[b] 2.9	8.3[a,b] 5.6	8.5[a,b] 5.7	$F = 3.06$,
(15)	(13)	(8)	(28)	(14)	$p = 0.0217$

Note
For each management category, the mean and standard error of margin plant species richness per 50 metre section are given; sample sizes in parentheses are the number of replicate sections. Results of an analysis of variance and subsequent multiple comparison test are shown; means that share a common superscript do not differ significantly (Tukey test, $p > 0.05$). a and b indicate homogenous sub-sets identified by the Tukey multiple comparison test in Table 5.4.

Table 5.5 Rank abundance of butterfly species recorded from hedgerow sections during survey work. Each hedgerow section received three visits using standardised methodology.

Species		Number of hedgerow sections from which species was recorded (total = 98 sections)
Small tortoiseshell	Aglais urticae	53
Small white	Pieris rapae	38
Green-veined white	Pieris napi	28
Speckled wood	Pararge aegeria	15
Gatekeeper	Pyronia ithonius	12
Ringlet	Aphantotpus hyperantus	10
Meadow brown	Maniola jurtina	8
Peacock	Inachis io	8
Large white	Pieris brassicae	7
Large skipper	Ochlodes venatus	5
Comma	Polygonia c-album	2
Common blue	Polyommatus icanus	2
Small copper	Lycaena phlaes	1
Red admiral	Vanessa atlanta	1

Ordnance Survey (OS). Considerable editing of the Land-Line data was required within the GIS, both to create closed polygons to define each field by combining various line details within the Land-Line data (Ordance Survey, 1997) and also to attach attributes from the ecological survey and farmer questionnaire. Vector coverages were created that included details of land cover, types of field boundaries and hedges, farm limits, and floodplain zones. This information on the current situation was subsequently modified to create equivalent map layers for the different scenarios. In some instances changes were so minor that it was straightforward to copy existing files and make the necessary alterations through manual editing and recoding. In more complex cases, GIS macros (i.e. sequences of commands) were written to implement sets of operations (e.g. to generate different sized buffer strips or to select field boundaries for hedge planting or restoration).

Visualisation methods

Two approaches were used to display current and potential future landscape characteristics. The first involved a series of large colour maps (A0 size). Figure 5.2 presents an excerpt from the map of current land cover for an area around the village of Kelmscott and the River Thames. This map has been designed specifically for purposes of greyscale display, and so the shadings and categories are different from the larger colour version, but it does illustrate the degree of geographical detail included in the database.

To complement the maps, 3D visualisations were created for key regions within the study area. These visualisations were thought necessary because it is difficult to get a sense of views across a landscape from a 2D map. This is primarily due to topographic influences, but also because of screening and texture effects from features such as buildings, trees and hedges. Several 3D modelling methods were investigated, but ultimately an approach based on virtual reality modelling language (VRML) was selected on grounds of cost, ease of generation from within a GIS, and flexibility of viewing using a freely available plug-in (e.g. Cosmo Player) for a standard web browser such as Internet Explorer or Netscape.

VRML is an open standard for 3D virtual environments on the Internet. A VRML 'world' consists of a series of files that together describe the geometry and attributes of objects in a 3D scene (Hartman and Wernecke, 1996; Doyle *et al.*, 1998). Several GIS programs now have the capability to generate VRML from map databases and in our study we used the Pavan authoring tools that operate with the MapInfo software (Smith, 1997). For details of VRML model construction see Lovett *et al.* (2002). Once the VRML files had been produced they were completely independent of the GIS software and could be viewed with a suitably enabled web browser. Figure 5.3 shows the appearance of a model for the Kelmscott area using Cosmo Player and Netscape. The controls towards the bottom of the browser window can be used to move around the landscape and it is also possible to link a series of viewpoints to create an animated tour. This latter feature proved very useful for demonstration purposes during our research.

Achieving a reasonable speed of response to the controls when viewing the VRML landscapes on a laptop computer required compromises in other respects.

Deciduous Woodland   Buildings

Coniferous Woodland   Roads and Tracks

Arable Fields   Other

Improved Grassland

Water Features

0   100   200   300   400   500   m

Map based on Ordnance Survey Land Line and Panorama digital data.   © Crown copyright.

5.2 Part of one of the A0 size maps of current landcover, reshaded for greyscale display

As is apparent in the foreground of Figure 5.4, several landscape components (e.g. field boundaries, trees and buildings) were depicted in a rather simplified and symbolic manner. It was also decided to give some narrow or small features (such as field margins and buffer zones) less realistic, but bright, colours so that they would be clearly visible. This was important for emphasising potential changes to the landscapes and allowed elements of the VRML models (where there was no legend) to be readily related to the colour maps.

5.3 View of a VRML model for the Kelmscott area, visualised using Cosmo Player and Netscape

5.4 A fixed viewpoint within a simplified VRML model, suitable for visualisation on a laptop computer

Four scenarios of future landscapes

Four scenarios for the future landscape of the study area were devised. One, named the 'Landscape Character' scenario, considered measures to enhance the visual and amenity value of the landscape. An alternative scenario was focused on conserving, and to some extent restoring, biodiversity within the landscape. This 'Biodiversity Conservation' scenario was divided into two variants. The basic scenario relied on generalised prescriptions that could potentially be delivered by cross-compliance. A second version incorporated further farm-specific and location-specific prescriptions that would require individual negotiation of management agreements for their implementation. In order to compare and evaluate these three prospective scenarios of desired future landscapes, we also investigated the likely changes that would take place in the absence of whole-landscape co-ordination. This scenario was termed the 'Business As Usual' landscape.

The three pro-active scenarios were primarily developed through detailed discussions with a range of stakeholder organisations, with further prescriptions incorporated from location-specific recommendations within published documents and planning guidance. These scenarios, still in text form and not yet visualised using GIS, were then validated by representative groups involved in their original formulation. Derivations of the detailed prescriptions for the Landscape Character and Biodiversity Conservation scenarios are given in Boxes 5.2 and 5.3 respectively. The main management prescriptions and landscape changes associated with each scenario are summarised below.

Scenario 1 (Business as usual) was based on each farmer's plans for future land management. The main sources of information were the baseline ecological survey and the questionnaire of farmers, as part of which each farmer was asked about current and past farming strategies and reactions to the proposals included in Agenda 2000 (CEC, 1997). In their responses, few farmers indicated that they were planning major changes to arable operations; none intended to cease dairying, and only five stated that they would abandon beef production (more as a result of difficulties arising from the BSE crisis than general changes in agricultural policy). As a consequence, the landscape changes in this scenario were relatively muted.

Main landscape changes:

- Limited conversion of arable to grassland on several farms.
- Creation of buffer strips and enhanced field margins on one farm.

Scenario 2 (Landscape character) focused on maximising visible amenity. The scenario was compiled based on discussions with stakeholder organisations and information in a variety of documents including local authority plans, Countryside Commission landscape character assessments, NT landscape plans, and ESA provisions. As biodiversity provides important amenity value, the proposals included some conservation management, but with a focus on superficial appearance rather than on ecologically effective prescriptions.

Main landscape changes:

• Conversion of selected riverside fields to improved grassland.
• New deciduous woodlands to screen urban areas.
• Planting of trees as linear features alongside roads, rivers and streams.
• Hedgerow restoration and replacement of some existing fences by hedges.
• Creation of an area of open space around the top of Badbury Hill, an archaeological site and viewpoint.

Box 5.2 Sources for prescriptions of scenario 2 – character landscape

Feature	Prescription
Thames Valley and floodplain (north of Thames, and south to rising ground)	
Grassland	Increase area of meadows and permanent pasture near river(3); increase area of extensively managed permanent grassland to strengthen landscape character (2).
Thames open views	Retain from river and towpath; do not obscure views from the river (3); river corridors an important source of open space (4); the Thames has a distinctive quality of peace and tranquillity as it meanders between remote meadows (5).
Willows	Retain and manage pollards, and create new pollarded trees along river bank and ditches to enhance landscape quality (1, 2, 3, 5).
River bank	Define river bank with more trees or changes in vegetation (3); manage the neglected small woods and copses (5).
Lombardy poplars	Regimented tree line along the flood bank to be broken, and remaining trees to be incorporated into new woodland (3).
Hedges	Improve the landscape quality by restoration of hedgerows (1, 2).

River Cole Valley (meanders north through the study area, joining the Thames west of Lechlade)

Grassland	More water meadows to be developed along the flood plain of the river (2, 6).
River valley	Delineate course of the river with more willows, trees and other riparian vegetation (3, 7).
Woodland	Any new woodland areas created not to close off the gap of the Cole Valley (7);
	river corridors make a significant contribution to the character of the landscape, also forming 'green chains' between areas of open space (4).

Oxford Clay Vale (between floodplain and Midvale Ridge)

Undulating, rolling farmland	Maintain and enhance landscape quality through restoration of hedges (1, 2, 3, 6);
	key hedges managed to become more substantial, plus more hedgerow trees (3);
Valleys and ridges	Define streams in valleys with trees to form a more distinct landscape (3).
Hilly areas, mainly wooded	Concentrate more on broad-leaved woodland with more variety; eliminate some of the coniferous forestry; more tree planting on the higher slopes (3).
Woodland	More areas of woodland to enhance the landscape and screen modern buildings (3);

Midvale Ridge (Corallian limestone band from Faringdon to Highworth; scarp to north, overlooking the Thames valley and Oxford clay vale; southern gentler slope across Lowland Vale to Downs)

Woodland	Badbury Hill coniferous forestry to be cleared around hillfort, and created as grassland (3);
	landscape has a moderately wooded character, and good woodland management will enhance this feature (3, 5);
	encourage planting of new woodland to enhance the landscape (3, 5, 7);
	more woodland cover around Faringdon to soften urban edge (2, 6).
Hedges	Whole farm hedgerow restoration (1, 3, 5, 6).

Lowland Vale (mainly Kimmeridge and Gault Clays, south of the Ridge)

Hedges
Replanting of hedges and tree planting within hedgerows to restore landscape (1, 3, 5);
recreate post enclosure landscape of hedgerows and hedgerow trees promoting good hedgerow management practices (clipped hedges with hedgerow trees) (5, 7).

Woods
Increase woodland around Watchfield and Shrivenham (7);
encourage planting of new woodland areas (in part to offset the loss of many elm trees) (5, 7).

A420 corridor
Screen and enhance with more substantial hedges and trees (3, 7).

References
1 Countryside Stewardship in Oxfordshire; supplement to The Countryside Stewardship Scheme, 1998, Ministry of Agriculture, Fisheries and Food.
2 Proposals for the future of the Upper Thames Tributaries Environmentally Sensitive Area 1999–2004: a consultation document, 1998, Ministry of Agriculture, Fisheries and Food.
3 Landscape Plan for Buscot and Coleshill Estate – report for the National Trust, Thames and Chiltern Region, 1996, Bronwen Thomas.
4 Swindon Borough Local Plan – Deposit Draft 1994; List of Proposed Modifications, 1998, Swindon Borough Council.
5 Vale of White Horse Local Plan – Deposit Draft 1995, Vale of White Horse District Council.
6 Whole Farm Plan, Stones Farm, Sherborne Estate, 1996, National Trust Estates Department, Cirencester.
7 Forest Implementation Plan – Faringdon-Shrivenham Framework Plan, 1996, Great Western Community Forest/Vale of White Horse District Council.

Scenario 3a (*Biodiversity conservation*) was designed to deliver substantial nature conservation and biodiversity benefits. It was based on detailed discussions with statutory and non-statutory organisations, including English Nature, local county wildlife trusts, and the RSPB, supplemented by the scientific literature and expertise of the research team. The proposals also reflected provisions in the Midvale Ridge, and Thames and Avon Vales Natural Area Profiles that applied to the study area as a whole, relevant prescriptions in the Countryside Stewardship scheme, and updated recommendations for the Upper Thames ESA. Blanket compliance was assumed across all habitats.

Main landscape changes:

*   Floodplain reversion along main rivers creating extensively grazed wet grasslands, wetlands and unmanaged areas.

- Creation of riparian woodlands (EC Habitats and Species Directive priority).
- Hedgerow restoration; in-fill planting of degraded hedges and re-planting hedges along all field boundaries that currently lack a hedgerow.
- Buffer strips around all streams and ditches, of unimproved grassland or unmanaged marsh/scrub habitat; width 10 m on arable land, 5 m on improved grassland.
- Uncropped margins around all remaining arable fields.

Scenario 3b (Supplemented biodiversity conservation) incorporated all the components of Scenario 3a, together with a number of measures for specific locations in the study area. The landscape implications of this option were therefore the most substantial of the four scenarios.

Main landscape changes:

- All elements of the basic Biodiversity Conservation Scenario, plus:
- Creation of 50 m buffer zones around designated wildlife sites,
- Conversion of fields around springs on Midvale Ridge to rough grassland.

Box 5.3 Sources for prescriptions of Scenario 3a – biodiversity conservation

Feature   Prescription
Applicable throughout

Arable fields   Uncultivated strips around fields, plus conservation headlands to link and buffer existing wildlife habitats (major priority for BBONT, primary objective for EN, and Priority for RSPB) (1, 2, 3, 4, 5, 6);
3m grassland strip along hedges: cut annually; low input (conservation headland) for 6m strip of crop (major priority for BBONT – detailed prescription agreed with by EN) (4, 6).

Hedges   Whole farm restoration (1);
restore hedge network: replant lost hedges and fill in discontinuous hedges (major priority for BBONT, primary objective for EN) (4, 6);
minimum 2m high × 2m wide thick bulky hedges preferred, cut in rotation (major priority for BBONT, primary objective for EN) (4, 6);
use native species for gaps and new hedges (priority for RSPB) (3, 5);

	increased numbers of hedgerow trees (especially oak, ash and willow, where appropriate) (primary objective for EN) (4).
Buffer strips along all water courses	Non-productive buffer strip at least 5m (10 m for arable land) from the ditches and streams for wildlife habitat (first priority for BBONT, major priority for EN, and priority for RSPB) (4, 5, 6, 7).
Within buffer	Encourage habitat variety: tall grass, scrub, reedbeds, some cut grass (in July); fencing may be appropriate but not required for arable; on grazed land retain some gaps for animal access (first priority for BBONT, major priority for EN) (4, 6).

Thames Valley and floodplain

Floodplain farmland	Reversion of arable and intensive floodplain grassland to extensive pasture (hay and grazing in summer – extensive flooding in winter); (priority for BBONT, major priority for EN, and priority for RSPB) (1, 4, 5, 6, 7);
	enhancement and protection of wet grassland (maintaining or raising water levels where possible) (1, 3, 6, 7).
Floodplain woodland	New riverside floodplain woodland (dominated by willows, alder and ash); (first priority for BBONT) (3, 6).

River Cole Valley

| Grassland | More extensive grassland in flood plain (priority for BBONT, major priority for EN) (4, 6). |
| Woodland | New riverside floodplain woodland (dominated by willows, alder and ash) to be created to increase habitat diversity (first priority for BBONT) (3, 4, 6). |

Midvale Ridge

| Arable fields | Encourage more spring sown crops to increase habitats for birds and spring flowers (esp. arable weeds) (primary objective for EN, primary priority for RSPB) (1, 3, 4); |
| | farm less intensively (reduce herbicide usage) (2, 4). |

Vale of the White Horse

Grassland	Restore extensive grassland to the low lying areas, where greatest ecological benefits accrue (high priority for EN) (4).

References
1 Countryside Stewardship in Oxfordshire; supplement to The Countryside Stewardship Scheme, 1998, Ministry of Agriculture, Fisheries and Food.
2 Midvale Ridge Natural Area Profile, 1997, English Nature.
3 Thames and Avon Vales Natural Area Profile, 1997, English Nature.
4 English Nature 1997: interview with Keith Payne, conducted by Paul Dolman, 7 October 1997.
5 RSPB 1997: interview with Frank Fuller and David Gibbons, conducted by Paul Dolman, 7 October 1997.
6 BBONT 1997: interview with Iain Corbyn, conducted by Paul Dolman, 23 July 1997.
7 Proposals for the future of the Upper Thames Environmentally Sensitive Area 1999 – 2004: a consultation document, 1998, Ministry of Agriculture, Fisheries and Food.

Scenario 3b – biodiversity conservation – supplemented

Feature	Prescription
Applicable throughout	
Farmland	More organic farming across the whole study area (lower priority for BBONT).
Woodland	Further woodland planting would add to wildlife habitat (lower priority for BBONT, low priority for EN).
Parkland trees	More parkland trees planted in pasture (lower priority for BBONT).
Wildlife sites	All designated wildlife sites to have a buffer zone restored around them, especially adjacent to existing wetlands; obligatory buffer zone up to 50m (major priority for BBONT); permanent grass and scrub margin created around designated semi-natural woodland sites (priority for EN).
Midvale Ridge	
Spring flushes	Fields with flushes should be managed extensively, allowing enhancement of quality and diversity of flush fauna and flora (need to be in grazing not arable (high priority for EN).

Grassland	Restoring semi-natural permanent grassland, although there is little conservation interest left in the grassland in the study area (low priority for EN); recreation of some acid grassland from arable, although (objective for CS).
Woodland	Promote woodland management that will restore a more natural character, especially on the drier soils: less conifers, more oak and birch (especially within existing semi-natural ('ancient') woodland); (priority objective for MVR, low priority for EN).

References
BBONT: interview with Iain Corbyn, conducted by Paul Dolman, 23 July 1997.
EN: interview with Keith Payne, conducted by Paul Dolman, 7 October 1997.
CS: Countryside Stewardship in Oxfordshire: supplement to The Countryside Stewardship Scheme, 1998, Ministry of Agriculture, Fisheries and Food.
MVR: Midvale Ridge Natural Area Profile, 1997, English Nature.

Implications of scenarios for land-cover and farm management

The future landscape composition that would result from implementing each of the scenarios is summarised in Table 5.6. This gives the aggregate area of different land cover categories, as well as the net change compared to the current situation. For each farm in each scenario, the GIS database was used to calculate the amount of arable and improved grassland that is either removed from production, or placed in extensively grazed grassland. Table 5.6 summarises these results, to show the number of farms affected by differing magnitudes of conversion of their productive land to non-agricultural or unproductive uses. This emphasises the highly asymmetric consequences to individual farmers, even of applying a simple blanket prescription throughout the landscape. For example, five properties would have over 60 per cent of their productive land altered by the biodiversity scenarios, while one property on the Thames flood plain would 'lose' almost all land to wet meadow. In the final farm survey, each farmer was shown the precise changes for their property, as illustrated for Farm 162 in Table 5.8.

Validating the scenarios

Before presenting the scenarios to the farmers, a final element of stakeholder validation was held at the ESRC offices in Swindon. This took the form of a day-long workshop, attended by 11 individuals who represented the following

Table 5.6 Extent of different landcover types in each scenario. The land area occupied by each landcover type is shown in hectares, with net changes from the current area shown in parentheses.

	Current use	Business as usual	Landscape character	Biodiversity conservation	Biodiversity conservation supplemented
Arable field	4,147	3,955 (−192)	3,844 (−303)	3,092 (−1,055)	3,031 (−1,116)
Improved grassland	2,803	2,964 (+161)	2,976 (+173)	1,952 (−851)	1,902 (−901)
Rough/ unimproved grassland	124	142 (+18)	124	95 (−29)	149 (+25)
Parkland	169	169	169	169	169
All woodland	474	474	609 (+135)	528 (+54)	528 (+54)
Riparian woodland only	–	–	–	(+54)	(+54)
Buffer strip	0	5 (+5)	0	146 (+146)	143 (+143)
Field margin	0	9 (+9)	0	420 (+420)	403 (+403)
Marshland and floodplain reversion	5	5	5	1,330 (+1,325)	1,330 (+1,325)
Scrub	27	26	27	26	103(+76)
Water or riverbank	113	113	113	112	112
Road, track or verge	157	157	157	157	157
Building	27	27	27	27	27
Other	178	178	173	170	170
Total	8,224	8,224	8,224	8,224	8,224

organisations, National Trust; Northmoor Trust; English Nature; Countryside Agency; National Farmers' Union; Farm and Conservation Agency; three local district councils; Oxfordshire County Council; the Wiltshire Wildlife Trust; and the Royal Society for the Protection of Birds. Participants heard of the basis of the research, examined interpretative material summarising ecological implications of each scenario, saw the VRML models projected from a laptop, reviewed the

Table 5.7 Farm-by-farm impacts of scenarios on the productive area, showing the number of farms that would experience differing percentage loss of productive land (defined as arable or improved grassland).

	0%	1–20%	21–40%	41–60%	61–80%	81–100%
Business as usual	25	6	0	0	0	0
Landscape character	14	17	0	0	0	0
Biodiversity conservation	0	16	8	2	4	1
Biodiversity – supplemented	0	16	8	2	4	1

Table 5.8 Proposed land-use changes for Farm 162. Note that areas are shown in acres, not hectares, and distances are shown in yards. Data were converted to imperial units as these are still the most familiar measure for practising farmers.

	Landscape character		Biodiversity conservation		Biodiversity conservation – supplemented	
	Acres	%	Acres	%	Acres	%
Arable	−11	1.0	−86	8	−101	9
Improved grassland	−5	0.4	−181	15	−215	18
Rough/unimproved grassland			−21	2	+25	2
Field margins			+47	4	+43	3
Woodland	+16	1.0				
Buffer strips to watercourses			+23	2	+22	2
Scrub buffer around designated sites					+8	1
Floodplain restoration			+218	19	+218	19
Hedgerow restoration			7,000 yds		7,000 yds	

large format maps and discussed their reactions. In relation to the overall approach of the study, and the techniques used, reactions were as follows:

- all participants were enthusiastic about the quality of the maps, the clarity of the scenarios, and the potential of the whole landscape approach,
- there was broad agreement that the 2D maps were accurate and particularly effective in portraying the shift from the present to the future; however to

improve interpretability, topography should be included and designated sites and planning guidelines highlighted

• the potential of the 3D virtual reality visualisation of future landscape scenarios was appreciated; however it was felt that VRML models needed additional detail and realism for specific locations to be immediately recognisable to local residents.

Responses of farmers to scenarios

A final set of visits to the farmers were conducted in June 1999, eighteen months after the initial questionnaire surveys. Due to limited research time and difficulties in arranging visits during the harvest period, not all farmers were interviewed in this phase of the project. Instead we explored the reactions of 17 of the 31, taking care to include all farms that would be substantially affected by the proposed floodplain reversion and all farmers who initially had been most hostile to participating in whole landscape management. At the beginning of each interview, we referred to their previous responses to see if their financial situation or management plans had changed. We then presented the scenarios of future landscapes in the form of the GIS generated maps, supported by visual and text material that interpreted and summarised key ecological benefits of the prescriptions. Each farmer was also shown a summary of how their farm would be affected by the scenarios (for example, see Table 5.8). We then explored their reactions to the prescriptions and their willingness to co-operate in landscape based planning and management through a discursive, open-ended interview. Each interview took one to two hours.

Of the 17 farmers interviewed, none completely rejected the proposals for any of the possible landscapes and none were strongly opposed to redirecting their farm management to a comprehensive whole landscape. For example, three farmers faced a 75 per cent reduction in arable in potentially flooded riverine areas, yet were prepared to contemplate the prospect in a spirit of goodwill, subject to an adequate compensation package. Only two farmers had any deeply held reservations, and these were primarily resistant to the 'predetermined' nature of prescriptions.

All of the 17 interviewed had lost income in the previous 18 months, and three were in serious trouble, facing the unenviable prospect of laying off labour. None saw any foreseeable income security, and three had no intention of passing the farm on to the family. None was too enthusiastic about reliance on new agridiversity schemes. They simply did not trust either the government or the European Commission to deliver. The uncertainty of MAFF funding for nominated transitional schemes of economic support was an additional factor in limiting choices amongst the farming community.

One farmer summed up the feelings of almost all of the others with regard to taking on more agri-environmental schemes:

- the finance must be guaranteed
- the commitment from the deliverers must be long term, in that there must be the political will and financial support to see it through
- farms in general have less money to spend on schemes such as this, with less freed labour for the necessary maintenance. Cash is not always a sufficient incentive
- there must be serious momentum behind all this, so there is a need for a fully effective and interventionist project officer with the clout to see things through.

Management incentives and scenario costs

The reaction to buffer strips round streams, and field margin prescriptions were universally favourable. All farmers would be willing to enter into such arrangements given the right level of incentive, though a majority would wish to see only selected hedges and field margins treated. Given appropriate reform of agricultural support payments, this element of the prescriptions could be attained by blanket cross-compliance (for example through restructured arable area payments) without incurring substantial negotiation and project officer costs.

In contrast, the proposal to restore wetlands, extensive grassland and seasonal flooding to formerly dry arable land within the floodplain presented formidable difficulty. The outcome would mean a loss of arable area subsidies, little in the case of new livestock income, reduced opportunity for dry grass production, and a massive restructuring of capital assets. Livestock would have to be catered for in new buildings, and existing grain stores converted into local business enterprises. This scale of change would require long-term financing and close co-operation between the planners and the enterprise agencies, so that new and refurbished buildings could be suitably located and designed.

One farmer responded to the prospect of floodplain restoration with the following question; what size of combine should I now buy? What cow numbers should I plan for? What size of milking parlour should I design? How many people will I now employ? These are typical of the kinds of highly uncertain, yet critical financial and management issues that any whole landscape management plan has to address. Interestingly, at the end of the interview, this farmer, facing a prospect of transferring over half of his land to wet meadow, was not funda-mentally opposed. 'The important thing is to make a living, not necessarily to produce food', he mused. Another commented, 'I've practised proper rotations. I've put muck back on the land. If I can afford it, I'd like to start on something like this. All farming is going to be difficult for the next few years. There is bound to be enormous pressure for diverse sources of income.'

Box 5.4 summarises the consequences for this farmer of converting management into each of the three scenarios. For the character landscape scenario, income loss due to arable conversion would amount to £5,000 per year. There would only be a gain if woodland planting on the released arable land was provided at a grant level to recognise this loss. For the biodiversity conservation scenario, arable losses would amount to £19,500 annually, dairy losses £90,000 annually and beef losses £7,500 annually, making an annual total of £117,000. For the supplemented biodiversity conservation scenario the annual losses would be £135,000. The farmer estimated at least £50,000 capital costs would be involved in the subsequent restructuring. The full compensation package for each of the 31 participating farms could not be calculated, as each farmer had no clear idea of the complete mix of losses to both revenue and to capital assets as a result of the scenario-induced restructuring.

All farmers recognised that, in order to implement such scenarios, there would have to be a change of philosophy. At the time of the interviews, farmers were not keen on agri-environment schemes, regarding them as unreliable. Yet all farmers believed that if there was real dialogue, then it becomes possible to work together for a common aim. 'I think farmers would act on their own interests,' said one, 'but if they spent time enough to discuss the issues, there would be more co-operation and less individualistic action.' In general, farmers favoured a menu of compulsory and voluntary elements to any package of implementation.

The issue that divided the respondents more than any other was the possibility that the new landscapes would only be socially justified if made accessible to the public. This is always a tricky matter, and has not been compulsory previously, although with the implementation of an extended rights to roam may yet change this situation.

Discussion

Linking landscape ecology to scenario development

In the Oxfordshire study, the conservation stakeholders consulted during scenario development sought generalised prescriptions to increase the amount and quality of available wildlife habitat within the landscape. By drawing on analyses of the ecological survey data and published studies, we were able to demonstrate substantial ecological benefits that would result from implementing these scenarios.

Box 5.4 Farm 162: possible annual compensation requirements for the three landscape scenarios

Losses of productive income in each scenario (figures in £ p.a.)

	2: Landscape character	3a: Biodiversity conservation	3b: Biodiversity conservation – supplemented
Arable loss	1,500	19,500	22,500
Dairy loss	2,400	90,000	103,500
Beef loss	–	7,350	8,750
TOTAL	3,900	116,850	134,750

The land 'lost' to production in scenarios 3a and 3b would go into field margins (47 and 43 acres respectively), buffer strips (23 and 22 acres) and wet marsh on the flood plain (218 acres in both cases). The difficult calculation to make is how these changes will impact on the farm overall. Some 20 per cent of the farm will revert to floodplain marsh. This will offer opportunity for very extensive grazing, not dairying or profitable beef production. The farmer is converting the farm in stages to organic production, with the livestock enterprises (dairy and beef) being fundamental parts of the whole farm approach. Therefore, the compensation would need to assess any changes in capital requirements. Operation on the farm would be permanently altered capital invested in dairy buildings and machinery and beef buildings will no longer be earning income. In theory compensation of the gross margin level will allow the rest of the farming operations to cover the increased production costs necessary, but a radical change in farm operation will necessitate further compensation to accommodate the change in farm lifestyle, if the public benefits assumed to flow from the changes are to be realised.

Some 40 per cent of all intensive grass would be lost. The dairy herd would drop by a comparable proportion. In practical terms the farmer would be looking for compensation for previous investments in dairy buildings, silage machinery and storage facilities, and slurry/wastes storage facilities.

Individual family farm management and compensation agreements would be necessary (with consequent increases in administration costs) to cater for the operation of the scheme. This example shows some of the key questions that would need to be asked.

For example, in biodiversity conservation scenarios (3a and 3b), hedges would be cut on a rotation of 2–3 years to give a variety of structures in the landscape at any one time, and would not be cut smaller than a minimum of two metres in height and two metres width. In fieldwork, significantly more bank voles and common shrews were found in wider hedges, and bird species composition was primarily related to hedge height and width (although shrub composition did have some secondary effects). A study by Green *et al.* (1994) also concluded that taller hedges support a higher density of most bird species, though some species such as linnet and yellowhammer show a preference for shorter hedges. Rotational cutting of hedges provides a variety of structures within the landscape at any one time, and will therefore increase overall faunal diversity. Similarly, previous ecological studies show that the unsprayed field margins sought for these scenarios would support substantially higher densities of flowering plant species, invertebrates and birds (Sotherton, 1991; Wilson, 1994; Feber *et al.*, 1996; Kleijn and Verbeek, 2000), including figurehead species familiar to farmers such as the common partridge – now scarce in most arable landscapes (Potts and Aebischer, 1993). Although the prospect of biodiversity increases in these scenarios is clear and unequivocal, predictions are largely qualitative. For example, it is not be possible to quantify the number of species that might be gained, particularly where the future composition, nutrient dynamics and successional trajectory of newly created habitats is uncertain as in the valley floodplain.

Alternatively, scenarios can be designed to give quantifiable single species outcomes for emblematic or Biodiversity Action Plan species. In one example, GIS-based models of species occurrence have been linked to spatial data on known landscapes to predict altered patterns of treecreeper distribution for differing scenarios of woodland extent and buffer area creation in the fragmented woodland landscape of East Anglia (Swetnam *et al.*, 1998). In other recent work, multiple regression models have linked survey data for two farmland bird species, skylark and yellowhammer, to aspects of agricultural management, such as the extent of spring cereals, organic fields and field boundary characteristics. These were then used to predict altered abundance of the target bird species in differing scenarios of farm management, both in the original Oxfordshire study area and also in an English Nature habitat restoration trial project area (Bradbury *et al.*, 2000; Wilson, *et al.*, 2000; Whittingham *et al.*, 2000).

Additional benefits from a whole-landscape approach

One principle is clear; as more and more neighbouring farms co-operate in management then not only the scale, but also the type of benefits achieved, can increase in an incremental manner. Theoretical modelling of population viability suggests that some species will only occupy a landscape if habitat patches are present above a threshold frequency – thus step increases in quantity can alter quality (reviewed by Dolman and Fuller 2003; see also Harrison, 1994 and Peterken, 2000). More specifically, in scenarios 3a and 3b of the current study 117 km of field boundaries would be replanted (mean 1.4 km per km²), representing a 28 per cent increase in the hedgerow resource. As well as the direct benefits of additional strips of wildlife habitat, creating this network will enhance connectivity and has the potential to reduce isolation of individual habitat patches, thus increasing the ecological value of existing hedgerows and margins.

Similarly, local implementation of individual buffer strips to ditches and streams may give benefits within isolated tributaries, but has little potential for improvements within main rivers that receive water from many feeder streams. In contrast, integrated implementation throughout the catchment may give additional benefits, such as decreased sediment loading, improved water quality and amelioration of spate flows, with consequences for biodiversity, utility and recreation (Muscutt *et al.*, 1993; Edwards and Dennis, 2000). Thus the benefits accruing from one farmer's management may be enhanced, or alternatively eroded, by their neighbours' activity, so that the value of an individual buffer strip can increase with cross-boundary compliance.

Building consensus landscapes

Despite a concern that the objectives of management for amenity and for bio-diversity conservation may potentially conflict, participants in the stakeholder validation workshop noted substantial convergence of the 'character landscape' towards elements of the 'biodiversity conservation' landscapes. Furthermore, amenity practitioners responded positively to the additional benefits offered by the more rigorous ecological prescriptions of the biodiversity landscapes, once these had been interpreted and presented with the aid of visual images. There appears to be great potential for scenario visualisation as a tool for building consensus between these differing stakeholders.

Another theme to emerge during stakeholder validation, was the ecological trade-off between generalised prescriptions applied across the entire landscape, versus localised targeting of resources. For example, hedgerow restoration and unsprayed arable field margins would provide widespread wildlife habitat and increased connectivity. However, despite much theoretical analysis the supposed benefits of corridor networks have rarely been studied in the field (Harrison and Bruna, 1999), while their function will differ greatly between species. Targeting new habitat into a network of thin strips can dilute the quality of the created habitats, through sub-optimal location and linear configuration giving increased exposure to damaging edge effects. In contrast, greater benefits may result from locating the same resources in contiguous blocks adjacent to existing sites of conservation interest. The restored habitat may be of better quality due to both a reduction in edge effects and an increase in colonisation opportunities, while the existing valuable habitat may be buffered against further degradation. For further discussion of the trade-off between corridor networks versus habitat blocks, see Kirby (1995) and Dolman and Fuller (2003).

Such divergence highlights the value of explicitly formulating and visualising scenarios of possible future landscapes. Presenting scenarios in roundtable workshops serves to stimulate debate and discussion amongst stakeholders, identify areas of agreement and points of departure, and provides a basis for negotiating towards a consensus scenario.

Visualisation of scenarios to farmers

At the outset of the study, fewer than half of the farmers in this west Oxfordshire landscape would have co-operated for an integrated ecological and scenic landscape. These data applied to the interviews that took place before the GIS maps and VRML displays were shown. In contrast, during the final round of interviews and scenario presentation, none of the farmers rejected even the most extreme of the proposed whole landscapes. Of the seven farmers (24 per cent) who in the initial interviews were most opposed to conforming and co-operating within a whole landscape, only one remained lukewarm towards whole landscape management when presented the scenarios at the end of the study. This farm manager operated a profitable and intensive large-scale operation. The other six recognised the value of the concept on seeing the visualisations and interpretation, though all required reassurance that the incentive package had to be right. The conclusion here is that an assiduous project officer targeting management to highest payoff should be in a strong position to negotiate a 'whole landscape' deal.

Their responses will have been significantly influenced by the deterioration in farm incomes, but the outcome also suggests that when high quality visualisations were presented, farmers could see that their responsibility to the landscape as a whole was critical (O'Riordan *et al.*, 2000).

Conclusion: prospects for designing whole landscapes

It is also important to recognise that the tools for 3D landscape visualisation from GIS databases have improved rapidly and now allow much greater realism and interactivity than at the time of the Oxfordshire study (see Sheppard, 2000; Woolley, 2000; Dockerty *et al.*, 2001 for examples). Other significant developments concern the necessary data for such applications, examples being the enhanced availability of high-resolution colour aerial photography for most of the UK (Jones, 2000) and the planned release of new map products by the

Ordnance Survey in autumn 2001. The later will include Digital National Framework™ data with polygon boundaries and enhanced feature coding that should simplify many aspects of GIS database construction.

Should the Rural Development Programmes couple to modulation aimed at landscapes and not just farms, then there is genuine scope for a more interactive and communal approach to landscape design. There is little doubt that the tools are coming into place. There is also more encouragement over bringing all relevant interests together for constructive dialogue. Furthermore, the mood of the times favours participatory approaches to planning and landscape design. This study shows that it is indeed possible to stir the imagination and generate a collective sense of landscape stewardship. The task now is to engage in a wider debate as to the efficiency and feasibility of whole landscape design and to encourage the local authorities and principal agencies to co-ordinate their policies and management prescriptions to promote such a viable concept. Given these favourable circumstances then surely the time is right to take one or two land management initiatives and convert them to excitingly managed whole landscapes, based on principles of sustainability and biodiversity enhancement.

Acknowledgements

This research was supported by an ESRC grant (award No. L 320 25 32 43) within the Global Environmental Change programme. Additional support has been provided by the Arkleton Trust, the Ernest Cook Trust and the Esmee Fairbairn Charitable Trust. The Ordnance Survey (http://www.ordsvy.gov.uk) generously supplied Land-Line® vector mapping and Land-Form Panorama® elevation free of charge for the purposes of the project. Sophie Lake carried out the ecological field survey.

References

Andrews, J. (1994) *A New Force in Nature Conservation: The Habitats and Species Directive 92/43/EEC. A Report to The Wildlife Trusts* (Lincoln, RSNC).

Bradbury, R.B., Kyrkos, A., Morris, A.J., Clark, S.C., Perkins, A.J. and Wilson, J.D. (2000) 'Habitat associations and breeding success of yellowhammers on lowland farming', *Journal of Applied Ecology*, 37: 789–805.

Buckingham, H., Chapman, J. and Newman, R. (1999) 'The future for hay meadows in the Peak District National Park', *British Wildlife*, 10: 311–18.

CC (1987) *Landscape Assessment, a Countryside Commission Approach.* CCP 423 (Cheltenham, Countryside Commission).

CC (1996) *The Countryside Character Programme* (Cheltenham, Countryside Commission).

CEC (1979) *Council Directive 79/409/EEC on the Conservation of Wild Birds* (Brussels, Commission of the European Communities).

CEC (1992) *Directive 92/43 on the Conservation of Natural Habitats and Wild Fauna and Flora* (Brussels, Commission of the European Communities).

CEC (1997) *Council Regulation 1757/1999 on the Support of Rural Development* (Brussels, Commission of the European Communities).

CNP (1997) *Wild by Design: An Exploration of the Potential for the Creation of Wilder Areas in the National Parks of England and Wales* (London, Council for National Parks).

Cobb, D., Dolman, P.M. and O'Riordan, T. (1999) 'Interpretations of sustainable agriculture in the UK', *Progress in Human Geography*, 23: 209–35.

Cosgrove, D. (1984) *Social Formation and Symbolic Landscape* (London, Croom Helm).

Dockerty, T.D., Lovett, A.A., Appleton, K.J. and Sünnenberg, G. (2001) *Climate Change Impacts on Landscape: New Approaches to Visualising Rural Landscape Change*. JEI Working Paper, Jackson Environment Institute (Norwich, University of East Anglia).

DoE (1994) *Biodiversity: The UK Action Plan* (London, HMSO).

DoE (1995) *Biodiversity: The UK Steering Group Report. Volume 2: Action Plans* (London, HMSO).

Dolman, P.M. and Fuller, R.J. (2003) 'The processes of species colonisation in wooded landscapes: a review of principles', in J.K. Humphrey, A. Newton, J. Latham, H. Gray, K. Kirby, E. Poulsom and C. Quince (eds) *The Restoration of Wooded Landscapes: Forestry* (Edinburgh, Forestry Commission).

Dower, J. (1944) 'The landscape and planning', *Journal of the Town Planning Institute*, 30: 92–102.

Doyle, S., Dodge, M. and Smith, A. (1998) 'The potential of web-based mapping and virtual reality technologies for modelling urban environments', *Computers Environment and Urban Systems*, 22: 137–55.

Dunning, J.B., Danielson, B.J. and Pulliam, H.R. (1992) 'Ecological processes that affect populations in complex landscapes', *Oikos*, 65: 169–75.

Edwards, A.C. and Dennis, P. (2000) 'The landscape ecology of water catchments: integrated approaches to planning and management', *Landscape Research*, 25: 305–20.

ENDS (2001) *ENDS Report 316; May 2001* (London, Environmental Data Services Ltd.).

ESRI (1997) *Understanding GIS: The Arc/Info Method Version 7.1* (Cambridge, Pearson Professional).

Everett, S. (2001) 'Conservation news: land and agriculture', *British Wildlife*, 12: 369–71.

Feber, R.E., Smith, H. and MacDonald, D.W. (1996) 'The effects on butterfly abundance of the management of uncropped edges of arable fields', *Journal of Applied Ecology*, 33: 1191–205.

Forman, R.T.T. (1995) *Land Mosaics: The Ecology of Landscapes and Regions* (Cambridge, Cambridge University Press).

Fry, G.L.A. and Sarlov-Herlin, I. (1995) 'Landscape design; how do we incorporate ecological, cultural, and aesthetic values in design principles?', in G.H. Griffiths (ed.) *Landscape Ecology: Theory and Application* (Aberdeen, IALE-UK).

Green, R.E., Osbourne, P.E. and Sears, E.J. (1994) 'The distribution of passerine birds in hedgerow during the breeding season in relation to characteristics of the hedgerow and adjacent farmland', *Journal of Applied Ecology*, 31: 677–92.

Harms, W.B. (1995) S'cenarios for nature development', in J.F.T. Schoute, P.A. Finke, F.R. Veeneklaas and H.P. Wolfert (eds) *Scenario Studies for the Rural Environment* (Dordrecht, Kluwer Academic Publications).

Harrison, S. (1994) 'Metapopulations and conservation', in P.J. Edwards, R.M. May and N.R. Webb (eds) *Large-Scale Ecology and Conservation Biology* (Oxford, Blackwell Scientific Publications).

Harrison, S. and Bruna, E. (1999) 'Habitat fragmentation and large-scale conservation: what do we know for sure?', *Ecography*, 22: 225–32.

Hartman, J. and Wernecke, J. (1996) *The VRML 2.0 Handbook: Building Moving Worlds on the Web* (New York, Addison-Wesley)

Jones, A. (2000) 'UK imaging – putting you in the picture', *GI News*, 1: 43–5.

Kirby, K.J. (1995) *Rebuilding the English Countryside: Habitat Fragmentation and Wildlife Corridors as Issues in Practical Conservation*. English Nature Science, Report No. 10. (Peterborough, English Nature).

Kleijn, D. and Verbeek, M. (2000) 'Factors affecting the species composition of arable field boundary vegetation', *Journal of Applied Ecology*, 37: 256–66.

Lovett, A.A., Kennaway, J.R., Sünnenberg, G., Cobb, D., Dolman, P.M., O'Riordan, T. and Arnold, D. (2002) 'Visualising sustainable agricultural landscapes', in P. Fisher and D. Unwin (eds) *Virtual Reality in Geography* (London, Taylor & Francis).

MacFarlane, R. (2000a) 'Achieving whole-landscape management across multiple land management units: a case study from the Lake District Environmentally Sensitive Area', *Landscape Research*, 25: 229–54.

MacFarlane, R. (2000b) 'Building blocks or stumbling blocks? Landscape ecology and farm-level participation in agri-environmental policy', *Landscape Research*, 25: 321–31.

MAFF (2000) *England Rural Development Plan, 2000–2006* (London, Ministry of Agriculture, Fisheries and Food).

Matlass, B. (1997) 'Moral geographies of the English Landscape', *Landscape Research*, 22: 141–56.

Meinig, D.W. (ed.) (1979) *The Interpretation of the Ordinary Landscape* (New York, Oxford University Press).

Muscutt, A.D., Harris, G.L., Bailey, S.W. and Davies, D.B. (1993) 'Buffer zones to improve water quality: a review of their potential use in UK agriculture', *Agriculture, Ecosystems and Environment*, 45: 59–77.

Opie, J. (ed.) (1971) *Americans and Environment* (New York, Harper and Row).

Ordnance Survey (1997) *Land-Line User Guide: Reference Section* (Southampton, Ordnance Survey).

O'Riordan, T. and Sayer, M. (1999) *Climate Change, Water Management and Agriculture*. PA99–05, CSERGE (Norwich, University of East Anglia).

O'Riordan, T., Lovett, A., Dolman, P.M., Cobb, R. and Sünnenberg, G. (2000) 'Designing and implementing whole landscapes', *Ecos*, 21: 57–68.

Peterken, G.F. (2000) 'Rebuilding networks of forest habitats in lowland England', *Landscape Research*, 25: 291–303.

Pollard, E. (1977) 'A method for assessing changes in the abundance of butterflies', *Biological Conservation*, 12: 1115–134.

Potts, G.R. and Aebischer, N.J. (1993) 'Population dynamics of the grey partridge *Perdix perdix* 1793–1993. Monitoring, modelling and habitat management', *Ibis*, 137 Suppl. 1: 29–37.

RSPB (2001) *Wading Upstream: The Success of Agri-Environment Schemes for Breeding Waders* (Sandy, Royal Society for the Protection of Birds).

Rutherford, A. and Hart, K. (2000) 'The new Rural Development Regulation: fresh hope for farming and England's countryside', *Ecos*, 21: 69–75.

Sheppard, S.R.J. (2000) 'Visualisation software: bring GIS applications to life', *GeoEurope*, 9: 28–31.

Siriwardena, G.M., Baillie, S.R., Crick, H.Q.P. and Wilson, J.D. (2001) 'Changes in agricultural land-use and breeding performance of some granivorous farmland passerines in Britain', *Agriculture Ecosystems and Environment*, 84: 191–206.

Smith, S. (1997) 'A dimension of sight and sound', *Mapping Awareness*, October: 18–21.

Sotherton, N.W. (1991) 'Conservation headlands: a practical combination of intensive cereal farming and conservation', in L.G. Firbank, N. Carter, J.F. Darbyshire and G.R. Potts (eds) *The Ecology of Temperate Cereal Fields*, 32nd Symposium of the British Ecological Society with the Association of Applied Biologists (Oxford, Blackwell Scientific Publications).

Swetnam, R.D., Ragou, P., Firbank, L.G., Hinsley, S.A. and Bellamy, P.E. (1998) 'Applying ecological models to altered landscapes. Scenario testing with GIS'. *Landscape and Urban Planning*, 41: 3–18.

Whittingham, M.J., Swetnam, R.D., Wilson, J.D. and Perkins, A.J. (2000) *Ecological Modelling to Predict the Response of Farmland Bird Species to Habitat Restoration:*

A Case Study. A Report to English Nature (Sandy, RSPB, University of Oxford and CEH).

Wilson, P. (1994) 'Managing field margins for the conservation of the arable flora', in N. Boatman (ed.) *Field Margins: Integrating Agriculture and Conservation.* BCPC Monograph No. 58: 253–8 (Farnham, BCPC Publications).

Wilson, J.D., Swetnam, R.D., Whittingham, M.J. and Bradbury, R.B. (2000) *Designing Lowland Landscapes for Farmland Birds. A Report to English Nature.* (Sandy, RSPB, University of Oxford and CEH).

Woolley, K. (2000) 'Photorealistic imaging of GIS data', *Geoinformatics*, 3: 12–15.

Chapter 6
Management of urban regeneration and conservation in China
A case of Shanghai

Jiantao Zhang

This paper aims first, to develop a methodological framework for the study of the management of urban regeneration and conservation in China; and second, to evaluate current management practice. Shanghai has been chosen as a case study, as it has experienced large-scale urban regeneration and its urban conservation system is relatively advanced. China has experienced rapid socio-economic development during the last two decades. Similar to the situation in many other Asian countries, large-scale urban regeneration has been undertaken in most Chinese cities and this has seriously threatened the traditional and vernacular built environment of those cities. To protect its built heritage and environment, China established an urban conservation system in the late 1980s. However, the national policy framework of the system is largely incomplete and the urban conservation practice varies between different local authorities. The balance between urban regeneration and conservation has become a hard task for China's local planning authorities. Furthermore, the study of China's urban regeneration and conservation is only at a beginning and lacks a theoretical foundation.

Some studies (Ruan 1995: 37–42; 1996: 208; 2000: 214–21; Wang 1996) have suggested various general problems relating to the management of China's urban regeneration and conservation. Local planning authorities lack national and local legislation and policies for control over changes in China's urban areas. They also lack necessary planning tools and sufficient financial support to ensure the implementation of local conservation area plans (Dong 1999: 24–5; Wang 1996: 15–16; Wang *et al.* 1999: 70–81; Yuan 1999). The protection of conservation area character has to give in to local priorities of economic development and urban regeneration. Similar to urban areas in other developing countries, China's urban areas also face great pressure from rapid socio-economic development. In most cities conservation submits to the considerations of economic development or urban renewal which are regarded as the major commitments of local

Selected as the best paper at the 2003 Congress of the Asian Planning Schools Association; submitted by the Asian Planning Schools Association. © Jiantao Zhang.

government (Geng 1996; Ruan 1995, 1996). The public lacks sufficient under-standing and knowledge of conservation and they are more concerned with practical issues relating to their immediate interests, especially with regeneration (Ruan 2000: 26–42).

No national policy has been developed in China to instruct local government on the management of urban regeneration and conservation. Local planning authorities decide and adopt policies and measures by themselves and their urban areas are managed through the local development control system. According to the Urban Plan Making Regulations (Ministry of Construction 1991), local planning authorities should make Local Controlling Detailed Plans, which are the basis for the zoning system to manage urban areas. In the practice of urban area management, some cities, such as Beijing, Shanghai and Suzhou, have adopted a zoning system based on Local Controlling Detailed Plans, whereas some other cities, such as Nanjing, Wuhan and Luoyang, have adopted a discretionary system based on Local Comprehensive Plans (Wang *et al.* 1999: 112–75). Urban regeneration and conservation in China are thus basically local planning issues and their practice varies between different local authorities. In general, local planning authorities in China have tried to exercise control over changes in urban areas so as to protect area character. However, limited by practical conditions, the authorities' management of urban regeneration and conservation has been largely insufficient and ineffective.

Shanghai is the economic centre and the largest port of China. It contributes one eighth of the national financial revenue and one fourth of the country's total exports. Besides its economic contribution, it is also an important cultural centre in China. Shanghai is the most important city in China's modern and contemporary history (Wang *et al.* 1999: 155). It has the largest amount of, and most valuable, built heritage from China's modern history and is one of the 99 National Historic Cultural Cities in China. Since the mid-1980s, Shanghai, like other Chinese cities, has experienced rapid social-economic development and consequential large-scale urban redevelopment. Therefore the city is chosen as the case study city for this research.

This article has two objectives. The first is to develop a methodological framework for the study of the management of urban regeneration and conservation in China. The second is to apply the framework to management practice and to evaluate this practice.

Theoretical framework

Conzen's ideas of townscape management have been developed by some researchers of the Urban Morphology Research Group into two lines of research. One line examines the agents responsible for urban landscape changes and the other explores the role of public planning in the management of those changes. The two lines are closely interrelated and may be regarded as having substantiated Conzen's concept of townscape management, which has become a major concern in geographical urban morphology (Whitehand 1992: 3). They are consistent with the Conzenian tenet that townscape represents the accumulated experiences of successive generations. In these studies, townscapes are viewed much more as the transmitters of signals about the societies which created them as they are of particular physical artifacts and patterns. The townscape and the societies creating it are synthesized and it thus becomes a part of social geography (Whitehand 1992: 2).

The foci in studies of townscape management are on urban landscape changes, the agents responsible for changes and processes of change. Consequently, several aspects are studied: changes; agents; interrelationships and interactions between agents; the planning of change and the implementation of planning policies; and processes of change. The elaborate processes of change and the intricate interactions between agents are identified, and agents' influences on changes are investigated and evaluated. Decision-making processes are reconstructed and management policies, procedures and implementation are scrutinized. This type of study thus provides a fundamental understanding of the evolution of urban landscape changes and the society and activities which created those changes. Moreover, local planning authorities' management of change is also examined, and this provides a basis from which to offer guidance on the future development of decision-making and management of urban landscapes.

The main method used in this type of study is that of the detailed case study and the unit of analysis is individual change. Local planning authority data sources, including planning applications and building applications, are the major sources complemented with correspondence and interviews with different agents. This approach and the adoption of local authority data sources are largely the contribution of Whitehand, whose work is regarded (Denecke and Shaw 1988b: 6) as a substantial and innovative extension of Conzen's morphogenetic studies. Larkham has utilized Whitehand's methods and sources in the scrutiny of urban landscape change and the management of change in urban areas. The work of these researchers has provided a considerable development of Conzen's initial concept of townscape management.

Townscape management studies have been successfully carried out in either commercial cores or residential areas, or in both types of areas, with a particular emphasis on conservation considerations (for instance, Barrett 1993; Jones and Larkham 1993; Larkham 1986, 1990, 1996; Larkham *et al.* 1988; Larkham and Lodge 1997; Vilagrasa 1992; Vilagrasa and Larkham 1995; Whitehand 1984, 1989, 1990, 1992; Whitehand and Carr 1999; Whitehand *et al.* 1992; Whitehand *et al.* 1999). These studies provide not only an understanding of urban landscape change in the areas, but also a scrutiny of the different agents responsible for change, the effectiveness of planning authorities' control over change and the management of the areas. Thus they constitute an essentially methodological basis from which to formulate theories about and policy recommendations for the practice of management of urban regeneration and conservation.

Informed by the townscape management concept, the study of urban regeneration and conservation management can be focused on changes in urban areas, on the agents responsible for changes and on the processes of change (Figure 6.1).

Changes are examined in terms of their numbers, types and external characteristics. Similarly, agents, mainly initiators and architects of changes, are examined in terms of their numbers, types, characteristics and their inter-relationships. These examinations identify what has happened in the urban area and who was responsible. Archival analysis is the main method for these examinations with local planning authority data sources, consisting of files relating to planning and building applications, as the major sources, complemented by field surveys and interviews with key actors.

The investigation of the processes of change emphasizes the interactions between different agents and their implications as well as the public policies of the management of change. These are the key issues in the study of the management of urban regeneration and conservation. Management policies, procedures and their implementation are examined. Decision-making processes and processes of changes are re-constructed. Thus this process of study identifies how changes happened in urban areas, how agents have affected changes and

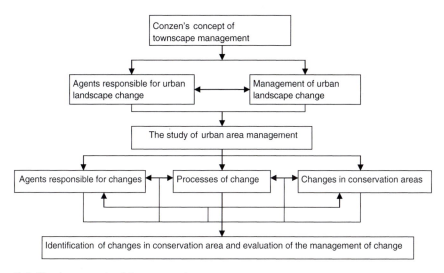

6.1 The framework of the research

how changes were managed, thereby assessing the effectiveness of management. Due to the need to examine quite large spatial instances over an extended time period, detailed case studies, which adopt individual changes as the unit of analysis, are the most suitable method for this investigation. Local authority data sources and interviews with agents (when considering contemporary or recent historical changes) are the major sources for this investigation.

Research methodology

Yin (1994: 1) has suggested that there are five kinds of research strategies (Table 6.1), with the choice of a particular strategy depending on three conditions: (i) the type of research question; (ii) the control an investigator has over actual behavioural events; and, (iii) whether the focus is on contemporary or historic phenomena.

The major research question of this research project is concerned with explaining how the proposed framework can be applied to the study of the definition and management of China's urban regeneration and conservation, which are essentially explanatory research issues. The research focuses on contemporary urban planning practice which is composed of complicated operations and processes and is beyond the researcher's control. The application and testing of the proposed framework need to be traced over time and need in-depth investigation into real-life contexts rather than deliberately controlled circumstances. Therefore, the case study is advanced as the appropriate strategy for the research.

Generally, case study research can be classified into two types, a single-case study and multiple-case studies (also termed as comparative case studies) (Yin

Table 6.1 Relevant situations for different research strategies

Strategy	Form of research question	Requires control over behavioural events?	Focuses on contemporary events?
Experiment	How, why	Yes	Yes
Survey	Who, what, where, how many, how much	No	Yes
Archival analysis	Who, what, where, how many, how much	No	Yes/no
History	How, why	No	No
Case study	How, why	No	Yes

Source: Yin 1994: Figure 1.1

1994: 14). The use of the single case study should meet three major conditions (Yin 1994: 38–41): (i) the case has a set of critical conditions which can meet the requirement to test a well-formulated theory; (ii) the case is an extreme or unique case and the study of it can provide specific findings which cannot be derived from other cases; and, (iii) the case provides the researcher with an opportunity to observe and analyze a phenomenon, event or incidence previously inaccessible to other studies. The key for a multiple-case study is that each individual case study consists of a 'whole' study and can produce separate and complete conclusions (Yin, 1994: 49). The evidence from multiple cases is often considered more compelling and the overall study is therefore regarded as being more robust (Herriott and Firestone 1983, cited in Yin 1994: 45). Shanghai has 11 conservation areas. The areas have different types of urban form and character and have experienced different types and degrees of development pressure. Their urban fabric change has been managed in view of their specific situation (SMUPB 2000: 8–12; SUPDI 1999: 4–10; Wang 1998: 5–17). The research adopted here was that of a Conzenian approach to the study of urban landscape change and the management of urban landscape. Such studies have been carried out in both commercial centres and residential areas. In view of the different types of cases studied in previous research, multiple-case studies are the preferred choice for this research. Therefore two of Shanghai's conservation areas, representing different types of urban areas in Shanghai, have been chosen as case study areas for the research.

Detailed case studies (Larkham 1996: 166–7; Whitehand 1981: 146) of individual development projects within the selected conservation areas formed the basis for the research, which examined the entire process of particular development projects: 'why' and 'how' changes happened in the areas, how these changes affected the character of the areas, and, how the local planning authorities managed changes and protected the character of the areas. The selection of case study development projects was therefore primarily based on the different scale and types of projects and different types of developers found in the case study conservation areas. The major methods used in this part of research were interviews with the case officers and developers and the analysis of approved planning application documents. For each case study development project, the researcher intended to interview the responsible case officer and the developer.

Case studies

The Si Nan Conservation Area (SNCA)

Three development projects in the SNCA have been selected for study: one was a single new commercial building initiated by private developer; one was a replacement of rows of modern Li-Long houses initiated by a quasi-governmental developer; and, the third was a large-scale replacement of old Li-Long houses over 23 blocks by a private developer.

The Central Plaza Project: The first case is the Central Plaza Project (Figure 6.2), involving a new high-rise office building and partial demolition and alteration of a historic building. Details of the project were acquired by interview with Fan Zhang (2000), a case officer of the SMUPB responsible for the project. In company with Shanghai's other commercial centre conservation areas, the SNCA experienced the impact of high-rise building developments during the 1990s, when a group of high-rise office buildings was built along the east end of Mid Huaihai Road. The Central Plaza development was the first building among this group of high-rise office buildings and was initiated in 1994 by a Hong Kong speculative real estate agency on a site containing a historic building which had originally been the Conseil Municipal office of the French Settlement, which had become a high school after 1949 and had already been relocated to new premises. The building was constructed in 1909 in the neo-classical style and was designated as a Shanghai Municipal Excellent Modern Building (SMEMB) in 1993.

6.2 The Central Plaza

Source: Researcher's photograph, 2000

Before formally making the proposal, the developer had long negotiations with the SMUPB case officers on the details of the scheme. Due to the limited size of the site, the proposed new building would have to be erected within the protection area of the historic building, but the Excellent Modern Historic Building Preservation Regulations (SMPC 1991) had stated that no new building, alteration or addition can be approved in such an area. However, as the first large-scale overseas urban investment project in Luwan District, the Luwan District Government expected it would be successful and asked the SMUPB to approve this proposal with favourable conditions. Thus, this development proposal was approved by the SMUPB in early 1997 as an exceptional case and it was required to comply with specific conditions set by case officers.

Among the conditions attached to the approval of the proposed new building, the SMUPB required that the new development did not touch the historic building, whose façade was required to be preserved intact. The SMUPB permitted the demolition or alteration of the internal structure of the historic building according to the function and nature of the proposed office project, but it set out conditions on the new internal structure and decoration of the historic building. The authorized new building could be high-rise in form and should be designed as a background foil to the historic building.

However, after considering the detailed site survey and initial architectural drawings, the developer was still concerned that the limited size of the site and the specified floor-area ratio (FAR) would not provide an adequate profit. Further negotiations with the SMUPB followed and the Bureau modified its original conditions to permit the demolition of the rear part of the historic building and the conjunction of the new building with the historic building. The façade and roof of the undemolished part were to be strictly preserved and posters and signs on it were to be cleared so as to recover its original appearance.

The final detailed application for this project was approved by case officers of the SMUPB in 1997. Complying with the modified planning conditions, the developer spent RMB[1] 30 million on the alteration of the historic building to integrate it as a podium to the new high-rise office building (if had it been demolished and a totally new podium built, the expense would only have been RMB 4 million). To meet the SMUPB's conditions on alterations, the developer invited a US architectural consultant, who was assisted by Shanghai local architectural consultants, to design the project. He searched for, and used, materials from many places outside Shanghai which were the same as, or consistent with, those of the original building.

The case officer (Zhang, F. 2000) felt that, in order to make an advertise-ment of this partial retention of a SMEMB as part of a new building, the developer and his consultants tried their best to preserve original characteristics of the historic building and to integrate it with the new building as its podium. The development met the SMUPB's requirements to preserve the appearance of the retained part of the historic building and to make the style and appearance of the new building harmonious with that of the historic building. This case was valuable as experience of the practice of control over developments involving the coexistence of historic buildings and new buildings in Shanghai's conservation areas. However, after the alterations had been completed, the interior decoration of the historic building too was modernized and thus did not conform to the style of its external appearance. So, after this case, the SMUPB began to control not only the external appearance but also the internal character of historic buildings in such alteration or even rebuilding projects.

In this case the developer played the major role in deciding the characteristics of the new high-rise building and the partial demolition of the historic building. Economic profit was the developer's major concern of the project. The Luwan District Government was also involved in the case because of its concern with the economic development of the area. The case officers of the SMUPB were rather reactive to the developer's and consultants' proposals. Under pressure from the developer and the Luwan District Government, the case officers made concessions to the developer's proposals and could only ensure the preservation of the front façade of the historic building. Indeed, whatever efforts the SMUPB had made, the original character and historic value of the historic building would have been lost after its partial demolition and alteration and the change of land use. Moreover, the erection of a new high-rise building has changed original internal arrangement of the plot, and the imposing volume and glazing glass façade of the new building form a sharp contrast to the low-rise brick buildings on its neighbouring areas and have thus changed the townscape and character of the SNCA dramatically.

The Tai Ping Qiao Area Regeneration Project: The second case is the Tai Ping Qiao Area Regeneration Project, an example of a large-scale development on 23 blocks and involving a group of historic buildings. Details of the project were basically acquired by interviews with Wenhai Zhang (2000), a case officer of the SMUPB responsible for the project, and with Qing Guo (2000), a senior staff member of the Shui On Company responsible for the planning of the project. The Tai Ping Qiao Area mainly consisted of seriously deteriorated old Li-Long houses which by the 1990s required immediate replacement. However, the First Congress site, which had been designated as a SMEMB in 1989, was within the project area. According to the strict preservation requirement for SMEMBs, old buildings within the development control area of the site had to be preserved with only internal alterations being permitted. In 1996 the Luwan District Government suggested to the Shui On Company (from Hong Kong) that it carry out a regeneration project of the Tai Ping Qiao Area, which included the First Congress site. After an initial analysis the Shui On Company accepted the suggestion. Due to the effect of the Asian Economic Crisis, however, the initiation of the project was delayed until 1998. In that year the Shui On Company invited the US design consultant SOM to be their planning consultant for the project. The Shui On Company proposed that the old residential buildings be converted to commercial uses, and that all their façades and roofs as well as their original materials be preserved, while part of their internal structure and decoration be altered.

In addition to the group of protected traditional buildings, the company also proposed the creation of a large, man-made lake in the centre of project area to provide a pleasant landscape improvement for the area. The developer felt that to balance the money which would be spent on preservation and the lake, they needed to build speculative residential and office high-rise buildings on the remaining part of the project area to make a profit. Despite the less intensive development of the small preserved site and the lake, most of the project area would thus be occupied by highly intensive development. The FAR for different individual buildings within the project ranged from 4.0 to 6.0 and building density ranged from 30 per cent to 70 per cent. This provided an average FAR of 4.18 and an average building density of 43 per cent for the project area. Although the proposed average building density was lower than the building density before regeneration, the proposed average FAR was 2.5–3 times of that before regeneration. According to SOM's first proposal, the townscape of the project area would change dramatically after regeneration, from a traditional 2–3 floor, high-density Li-Long housing area to an intensive high-rise city centre like those of Hong Kong and other international metropolises (Figure 63).

Considering the need for regeneration and the efforts to conserve the buildings on the First Congress site, the SMUPB approved this proposal with conditions later in 1998. During negotiations, the case officers had asked the Shui On Company to reduce the building density in its proposal (Zhang, W.H. 2000). After minor modifications, the Shui On Company in fact succeeded in persuading planning officers to approve their proposed density through taking account of the open space reward condition in Shanghai local zoning regulations[2] which was applicable to the proposed lake. Another reason for planning officers to accept this proposal (Zhang, W.H. 2000) was that they did not think the prospects for implementation were good. Due to its intensity and the large area covered, the time to complete the project would be quite long, and the case officers doubted whether there would be sufficient finance and enough demand in real estate market to support the project. So it was possible that the Shui On Company would come back to the SMUPB to modify its proposal during that extended period.

The company's proposals to regenerate the traditional residential buildings on the controlled site were designed by the US design consultant Wood/Zapata

6.3 Envisaged townscape of the proposed development of the Tai Ping Qiao Regeneration Project. The preserved old Li-Long houses are on the near end of the man-made lake, low-height and high-density.

Source: The SMUPB planning application

and had started in 1999. The proposals divided this part of the project area into two groups of buildings, the preserved traditional old Li-Long housing including the First Congress site, and, the new modern-style buildings. Changes of use were involved in both groups: the former, mainly to comply with the SMUPB's preservation requirement, were proposed for use as restaurants, pubs and other small-scale commercial buildings while the latter were to be larger commercial buildings. The Shui On Company emphasized that the contrast between the small-scale traditional Li-Long houses and the large-scale modern commercial building was deliberate, i.e. to act as a foil to the historic townscape. Although planning officers had reservations on that point, and were concerned about the impact of proposed commercial activities on the solemn milieu of the First Congress site (Zhang, W.H. 2000), the argument on architectural style was deemed to be subjective. Local planning authorities usually held a noncommittal attitude on such matters, unless there were approved plans providing detailed requirement on style. According to the Conservation Plan for the First Congress site,[3] the company's proposed nine-storey modern buildings were required to be reduced to six floors to control their height as the background for the site. Seeing the generally positive response to the altered traditional Li-Long houses, the Shui On Company has subsequently wanted to change those modern style buildings into traditional vernacular style and has been negotiating with planning officers on this issue.

In this case, regeneration pressure was the major reason for the Luwan District Government to initiate the Tai Ping Qiao Area Regeneration Project. However, the developer, the Shui On Company, was the decisive actor in the project and economic profit was its major concern. Facing the need for regeneration, the SMUPB could only approve the Company's proposals involving groups of speculative high-rise buildings, although the Bureau succeeded in preserving facades of the old Li-Long houses on the First Congress site according to the Conservation Plan for the site. According to the approved planning application for the project, the Tai Ping Qiao Area, currently a traditional residential area with old Li-Long houses, will experience dramatic morphological changes of building fabric, land-use and town plan patterns after the regeneration, and will become a modernized commercial centre occupied by high-rise buildings.

The Huihai Fang Project: The third case is the Huihai Fang Project designed to replace four rows of ordinary, modern Li-Long houses by six-storey, modern-style public housing flats. Details of the project were basically obtained by interviews with Zhihao Ren (2000), a case officer of the SMUPB responsible for the project, Xianhong Li (2000), a planning officer of the Luwan District Urban Planning Bureau familiar with the project, and Xingjian Fan (2000), the Deputy General Manager of the Yong Ye Company responsible for the project. The project was carried out by the Yong Ye Company, a quasi-governmental company belonging to the Luwan District Housing and Real Estate Bureau, a department of the Luwan District Government. The project was initiated in 1997 as an experiment for the regeneration of traditional Li-Long housing in the Luwan District. Because of the large investment involved and the lack of profit, the private sector was not usually interested in such projects. Shanghai's District Governments, however, facing regeneration pressure from local residents, were used to assigning this type of job to quasi-governmental companies. Similarly, this project was assigned to the Yong Ye Company by the Luwan District Government.

The original buildings in the project area were three-storey, modern Li-Long houses built in 1932. There were altogether 220 households living in the buildings. The Yong Ye Company's own architects, without making a planning application, prepared a demolition and re-building scheme, began the project in June 1998 and completed it in March 1999. The first household moved back into the new buildings in June 1999 with 217 of the total 220 households eventually moving back.

The aim of the Huaihai Fang Project was to rebuild the original flats, each of which was shared by several households, into larger flats, each of which was for a single household. Due to this requirement for increased building space, the new buildings were six-storeys high and their depth was greater than the original. The FAR of the project area increased from 1.1 originally to 2.1 after rebuilding, while the sunlight distance ratio[4] between each building after rebuilding was 0.86 and does not meet the minimum requirement of 0.90[5] in Shanghai local zoning regulations. Not only the density, but also the architectural style changed after the rebuilding – the traditional vernacular Li-Long houses were replaced by modern style flats. Similar building replacements happened to other regeneration projects of the same kind, such as the Shenping Street Project, and the Yueyang Road Project. An application was submitted for retrospective approval of the project after its completion and was approved by the SMUPB in December 1999.

Planning officers (Ren 2000; Li 2000) thought the Huaihai Fang Project had largely changed the original building fabric and damaged the character of the area. The Yong Ye Company expressed different views (Fan 2000). The primary objective of such projects was to ameliorate residents' living condition. Limited by insufficient finance and confined by plot size, it was impossible to double the living space for every household while preserving the original area character of the area. The company preserved the original plot pattern of the project area and tried its best to preserve original building character as much as possible, by imitating the architectural style and façade design of the original buildings in designing the new buildings. The project cost the company RMB 45 million and up to the present (2000) there was still a RMB 17 million deficit. The company thought overseas architectural consultants who were not familiar with local architecture would not be appropriate in designing such a project concerned with traditional vernacular buildings, because their design might deviate from vernacular style. Planning officers were thought to be too idealistic in pursuing conservation goals, while actually overlooking difficulties in conservation work which would prevent others engaging in such work. Compared to the different views of the planning officers and the Yong Ye Company, the residents' opinions acquired by the researcher from informal interviews were quite simple. Almost all the residents were satisfied with the project and some even thought the project was better than their expectations. Most thought the new buildings were good in style and design, although the townscape and area character aspects were neglected by the residents.

The Huaihai Fang Project is a specific case. The project was initiated because of the need for regeneration. The Yong Ye Company carried out the project without employing an architectural consultant or submitting planning and building applications to the SMUPB. The company thus was the only agent deciding the characteristics of the four public housing flats of the project, and the SMUPB failed to exercise development control over the project. Although the original plot pattern was preserved in the project, the original vernacular style three-storey modern Li-Long houses was replaced by totally different, modern-style six-storey flats and the existing townscape of the area was also changed. Therefore the project was a new building project and its sunlight distance ratio failed to meet the technical requirements in the Shanghai local zoning regulations. However, considering the project was a non-profit regeneration project initiated by the Luwan District Government to benefit local residents (Ren 2000), the SMUPB approved the application of the project despite it being submitted after the completion of the project.

The Heng Shan Conservation Area (HSCA)

The HSCA is larger than the SNCA and has many more developments initiated by government and institutions, than the latter area. As a traditional upper-class residential area, development there had some different characteristics from those in other areas, especially commercial centres. Governmental developments were different to others, in that the local planning authority's control over it appeared more complicated than control over other types of development. There were several cases, as follows.

A New Government Development Project: The high-rise development in the Xingguo Hotel, the guesthouse of SMG, located on the west side of Xingguo Road, was a case of government development.

Responsible for most of the municipal government's entertainment work, the hotel had had a large deficit for a long time. To balance the deficit the hotel needed more business income besides government work and thus new guest buildings were needed. Therefore the hotel proposed to build a new high-rise guest building. However, the hotel contained three villas, which were SMEMBs and whose preservation requirement could conflict with the high-rise building proposal. Regarding that, the municipal government negotiated with the SMUPB for favourable conditions for the high-rise building proposal. The SMUPB agreed that the high-rise guest building proposal could be approved but its height was required not to exceed the limit set out in the preservation requirement for the three SMEMBs.

In 1998 the Xingguo Hotel began to discuss detailed proposals for the new high-rise guest building with planning officers. To meet preservation requirements for the three preserved villas, planning officers required the new building to be outside the garden containing those villas. Therefore the only site available for the new building in the hotel was the rear-service base which was north of the garden. According to the preservation requirements for the three villas, new building was required to keep a minimum distance of 150 metres from them. Confined by the strict requirements, the new building could only be slab-shaped. Hence planning officers set no further requirement on building shape but made detailed provisions for the building façade. The architects, Hawk Architectural Consulting from the US, and the local Huadong Architectural Design Institute, complied with the planning officers' conditions in the design and the building satisfied the planning officers in its simple and elegant style, material and colour as well as its harmony with the preserved villas (Figure 6.4).

A new development project of the Nanjing Area Command of the Chinese Air Force: Besides these local government developments, there were other non-local government developments, amongst which army developments made up a large part. A development by the Nanjing Area Command of the Chinese Air Force was such an instance.

The origin of the developments could be traced back to 1986 when SMG reached an agreement with the Nanjing Area Command of the Chinese Air Force to permit the Area Command to choose three sites in Shanghai for its development. One site in Mid Huihai Road, one in Julu Road and the other in Yuqing Road, all within the HSCA, were chosen. Due to the nature of the

6.4 High-rise guest building of Xingguo Hotel

Source: Researcher's photograph, 2000

ownership of the estate, development in Yuqing Road was denied while developments on the other two sites were approved.

The development in Mid Huihai Road, a private guesthouse of the Area Command, began in 1989 and was earlier than the other one in Julu Road. Considering the existing character of low-density, low-rise buildings and plenty of green space, the SMUPB was very cautious in dealing with that proposal and reported it to the Deputy Mayor responsible for urban development for a decision. After the Deputy Mayor approved it, the SMUPB set conditions for the proposal. The new building's height was required to be no more than 24 metres, the upper limit for mid-rise buildings. Conditions for the building façade and style, as well as for the plot layout and traffic, were set in detail to control the development's impact on its surroundings, notwithstanding the fact that there was no conservation area or conservation plan at that time. Despite the building's strict compliance with planning conditions, many residents around expressed negative comments on it to the SMUPB, thinking it was clumsy and degraded the townscape there.

In 1995 the Area Command began to propose a new hotel building on that site for external commercial services. Knowing that residents were afraid that the hotel would debase the townscape and character of the area and cause environmental problems of noise, traffic, crowd, light, and signage. Hence they appealed to the Xuhui District Government and the SMUPB to strongly oppose the proposal. To ease the approval of the proposal, and at the request of the Area Command, planning officers of the SMUPB explained their requirements for the proposal to residents and promised meticulous control over the proposal in an effort to persuade them to accept it. Meanwhile, planning officers set critical conditions on the proposal and its details to keep their promise. After long negotiations and modifications, the proposal was approved at the end of 1997. But in 1998 the Central Government issued an order to prohibit the military force from conducting commercial business. Thus the development had to be terminated and the approved application was aborted. Seeing that, the Area Command proposed to erect several temporary buildings on the site first and to lease them to others, and then to build private flats when funding was available. In view of the residents' deep concern with the development on that site, planning officers set detailed conditions on the proposed temporary buildings and required them be built as permanent buildings and not be leased to small retailers, which might impair the character of that area. The application was approved in April 1998 after all conditions were accepted. While under construction, one building breached the planning condition which required a minimum safe distance to protect an old tree on the site and this was publicized by the local media. The Local Park and Green Space Authority investigated the issue and fined the Area Command.

The Rebuilding of a detached house in Julu Road: Just opposite to that development, on the other side of Julu Road, there was a development of a private detached house. It serves as a comparison to the army development.

The building was originally shared by several households. In 1999 a Taiwan businessman brought the house to live in and proposed to restore it. Because of its severe deterioration, it could not be renovated by refurbishment or minor alteration. Therefore the owner applied to the SMUPB for the total rebuilding of the houses. Considering that the area was characterized by a group of similar house, case officers required the house to be rebuilt the same as the original in every detail and its structure to be fortified more strongly and sustainably than the original. Complying with these conditions, the owner invited architects to formulate a meticulous design of the house and the satisfactory application was approved in December 1999.

The Dingxiang Flats Project: Different from preceding cases of owner-occupier residential development, speculative residential development was another major group of residential developments. The Dingxiang Flats were an instance.

The development was located on the west boundary of the HSCA and was within an upper-class residential area of modern high-rise buildings. The 31-floor high-rise building proposal for Dingxiang Flats, received by the SMUPB in May 1997, was congruous with other high-rise buildings in that area in style, height and appearance. Case officers agreed to that proposal in general but required the developer to solve the problem that the proposed building would shade the rear buildings and thus could not fulfill relevant items in the local zoning regulations. After modification of the layout of proposed building, the problem was solved and the application was approved in 1997.

The Shenda Shopping Building Project: Besides types of development mentioned above, commercial developments and institutional developments were also important types in the HSCA. The Shenda Shopping Building was an instance of a commercial development.

That development was to the north of a distinctive SMEMB, a historic Scandinavian-style villa full of imaginative characteristics (Wu 1997: 119), and therefore the SMUPB set strict conditions on the development's height and appearance. After receiving the proposal in April 1996, case officers held many negotiation meetings with the developer, architects responsible for the development and specialists of planning and architecture, to discuss the proposal as well as the planning conditions on it. Knowing the special situation of the development, the developer and the architects co-operated with case officers well. The building height of the initial proposal slightly exceeded the limit in the planning conditions and case officers thus carried out on-site sight analysis using surveying instruments to examine whether that height was permissible. After site examination, a new height limit was set and it was required to be complied with. Under that condition, the shape of the proposed building was designed to increase gradually from south to north and reach the height limit exactly. Building in that shape was to reach the highest FAR under the height limit, while its FAR was still under the limit in the planning conditions. Besides height, architectural style was another focus of the proposal. Usually there were two ways to make new buildings in harmony with old buildings: imitation or contrast. A previous development to the south of the preserved historic Scandinavian villa adopted pinnacles to be in concert with it, and this was widely criticized as an absurd mimic of the villa, spoiling the villa's architectural interest as well as the townscape of that area (Ma 1999). Planning officers held a similar idea on the design of that development. Considering difficulties in imitating the distinctive style of that villa, agreement was reached that the proposed building could be a modern style with the background slightly contrasting to that historic villa. The style and appearance of the proposed building should be simple and reserved. Those conditions were fulfilled in the proposal.

Generally case officers were satisfied with this development in that they had good communication with the developer and the architects, and the proposal conformed to all planning conditions. They also thought that the effect of planning conditions on architectural style was not obvious, since the proposal already met the condition of a height limit which would hide the proposed building entirely behind the historic villa and therefore whatever style the proposed building was, it would not affect the historic villa's image if people viewed the historic villa in front of it. That consideration was problematic, because most people saw the historic villa from the road, where they could see it and the proposed building simultaneously and the latter's style would obviously affect the former.

The application was approved in 1996, but due to a lack of funds, the development was suspended for about four years and the uncompleted building damaged the townscape severely (Figure 6.5).

The development projects of Huashan Hospital: The development projects of Huashan Hospital were an instance of institutional development in the HSCA.

Due to a lack of space, Huashan Hospital was split into an outpatient department and an inpatient department, which were located in two separate sites close to each other. The outpatient department was located in front of Shanghai Hotel in the same block, which caused inconvenience to both. In the late 1980s, the Huashan Hospital and the Shanghai Hotel reached an agreement that the hotel would pay the hospital the money to relocate residents in the same block of the inpatient department, so that the outpatient department could join the inpatient department in the same block and the hotel would obtain the original

6.5 The unfinished development of Shenda Shopping Building (seen from the east)

Source: Researcher's photograph, 2000

land of the outpatient department. Based on that agreement, the Huashan Hospital invited the Shanghai Architectural Design Institute to prepare a master plan for its united site. The plan was approved by the SMUPB in the early 1990s and it divided the hospital into three parts: inpatients, outpatients and technical support. Accordingly, an 18-floor, high-rise patient building was built in 1993 on the place where those relocated residents lived previously. Due to the increasing number of inpatients, another 21-floor patient building was built to the southwest of the old one in 2000. Because of the special functions and requirements of those patient buildings, planning officers set no specific conditions on their proposals and just required them to meet the general zoning. Although they kept enough distance within the red line of Changle road, which was south to them, because of the narrow width of that road compared to the imposing height of the buildings, people on that road still felt the buildings were depressing (Figure 6.6).

According to the master plan, besides those patient buildings composing an inpatient department to the south of the hospital, the current technical support department would remain in the middle and the outpatient department would be arranged in the north where there were small retailers and residential houses at the time. There was a detached residential house designated as one of the third 162

6.6 The depressing view of the high-rise patient buildings of Huashan Hospital from Changle Road

Source: Researcher's photograph, 2000

SMEMBs in 2000 in the place for the outpatient department. Architects designing buildings for the new outpatient department had recognized that house's character and preserved it in the master plan, although at that time that building had not yet been designated. Since the master plan of the hospital was a controlling detailed plan made in the early 1990s, a building detailed plan has been made recently for the incoming development of an outpatient department. According to the 1991 Excellent Modern Historic Building Preservation Regulations, there was no development allowed in the protection area of that SMEMB. Considering the specific function and requirement of hospital buildings, case officers agreed that new buildings could touch that SMEMB under the prerequisite that they could not damage that building and their style, shape, colour, material and appearance should fulfill planning conditions. Following planning officers' instructions, the building detailed plan was still under deliberation.

The development of Huashan Hospital extended over a relatively long period of one decade and was still in progress. The case officer (Wang 2000) said to the author that because of its special functional requirements, the SMUPB could only require buildings of the hospital to meet some basic planning conditions, although the high-rise patient buildings had already ruined the townscape of that area (Figure 6.7). That was the general situation with the institutional development of special functions.

Conclusions

Based on the above detailed investigation into processes of urban landscape changes in the two case study conservation areas, a number of issues deserve further discussion.

6.7 Inside Huashan Hospital: high-rise patient buildings in sharp contrast to the SMEMB

Source: Researcher's photograph, 2000

The first group of issues is concerned with the direct agents of urban landscape change in the study areas, particularly those who were the initiators. Their different motives resulted in changes of different kinds in the townscape and area character: private-use development appeared more sensitive to the character of the existing landscape than did commercial and speculative development. This situation was obvious in the comparison of development in commercial centres with those in residential areas. Amongst private use developments, some initiated by government and special institutions, like the cases in HSCA, were more incongruous with existing landscapes than other private use developments, especially residential developments. Domestic (mainly local) initiators showed more understanding of, and respect for, existing landscapes than southeast Asian initiators (most of whom were speculative developers and whose major concern was profit). The latter influenced the townscape and character of Shanghai's conservation areas (particularly those commercial centres) largely by introducing foreign elements, the modern high-rise buildings and large-scale developments, which were completely different from the existing local urban landscape. That situation was particularly apparent in commercial centres. Architects played a less influential role in the landscape changes and their major influences were on the visual aspects of those changes. There was no clear difference between domestic (mainly local) architects and foreign architects in their consideration of, and regard for, existing landscapes, which manifested in their design.

The second group of issues is concerned with the local planning authorities' management of, and control over, urban landscape changes in the conservation areas. There were subtle traces of urban landscape management in conservation areas. Planning officers hoped to, and did, exercise control over those changes, although in many cases the outcomes were not as ideal as they had expected. There were several factors contributing to this situation.

First, local planning authorities lacked a coherent strategy for management. There appeared to be no long-term objective for conservation areas and in many cases planning officers made their decisions based on individual buildings rather than on a wider area. That was especially so in commercial centres, which may be partly due to the diverse character of those areas. The diversity of new developments even aggravated the incoherence of management in those areas. In residential areas, whose townscapes were relatively more consistent, area character was considered to a greater degree. Also those distinctive, historic and protected buildings, some of which had specific preservation plans and local legislative protection, received much more attention than did ordinary buildings.

Second, planning tools for management were insufficient. Shanghai's local legislation did not provide detailed and practicable regulations for conservation area control. Except for the SMEMBs, ordinary buildings in conservation areas could only be protected by common zoning regulations. Local planning authorities' incapacity to control signs in conservation areas was a result of the deficient local legislation. Also there were few detailed policies and conservation plans to support management. Planning officers could only treat many cases with discretion while the effects were limited due to the lack of legislative and policy support.

Third, current measures are insufficient to allow monitoring and to ensure the implementation of planning conditions, which made development control in conservation areas less restrictive and effective.

Fourth, external pressures and non-administrative factors interfered in local planning authorities' management and control. Economic and redevelopment pressures, as well as interference from other parts of local government and some initiators, significantly affected planning officers' decisions in some cases, such as the Central Plaza development in SNCA and several governmental developments in HSCA.

Finally, there were differences between local planning authorities' stated policies and priorities for landscape management and those shown in practice. Those differences were caused by several factors: the policies and priorities were too general to implement; effective and sufficient legislative and planning support for those policies and priorities was lacking; external pressures and interference intervened in development control; and other agents' influences affect development control. Therefore, in many cases urban landscapes appeared as by-products of development resulting from co-ordination, rather than from coherent planning objectives. However, despite all those reasons, local planning authorities exercised influences, though not coherent and effective management, on changes in conservation areas.

The third group of issues is concerned with the perceptions, interrelationships and interactions of different agents, particularly of initiators and planning officers. Different agents had different perceptions of landscape changes and areas, which were bearing upon their different standpoints and concerns. Initiators' perceptions came largely from their motives of development and their knowledge of the area, which closely related to their provenance. That was reflected in their development proposals. Planning officers' perceptions were mainly based on the existing landscape and were more conservative than initiators. Similarly, residents' perceptions, which appeared mainly in residential areas, were also largely restricting on the existing landscape, and were based on their self-interest and self-sense of the place. Two instances which revealed residents' perceptions were the case of the development of Nanjing Area Command of Chinese Air Force in Mid Huihai Road, where residents showed strong opposition to new developments; and the case of Huihai Fang, where residents were satisfied with the redevelopment. Clearly, there were differences between residents' perceptions.

The perceptions of each agent guided their attitudes and actions in the development of change. The actual urban landscape changes were the results of interactions between different agents and in most cases they were different from each party's initial perception. Local planning authorities encouraged initiators' first contact before submitting formal applications. More communication was also encouraged and in most cases planning officers communicated sufficiently with initiators and architects as well as with other involved parties, despite the fact that those communications were sometimes not accepted. Initiators and architects played active roles in the interaction with other parties while planning officers and residents were reactive and sometimes passive. In the majority of cases, the final change largely accorded with the proposal of the initiator and architect, while the planning officers' conditions comprised a minor part of the change. In a few cases, planning officers' conditions were crucial to the change and sometimes even more important than the proposal of the initiator and architect. Whatever case it was, residents' opinions influenced the change indirectly and had no concrete effect on the change. They influenced changes through the local planning authorities' development control system. All changes were outcomes of complicated interactions between multiple parties and in many cases they were more likely the results of reconciliation between parties rather than just the objectives of planning or management.

Several factors brought particular difficulties to the local planning authorities' execution of development control. Government and army initiators used to exercise great pressure on local planning authorities and in some cases planning officers had to make concessions to them on planning conditions. In a few specific cases, planning officers acted as a mediator between initiators and residents, rather than their legitimate role of executing planning control. Some speculative developers also exercised pressure on local planning authorities, directly by themselves or indirectly through local government. That economically-driven pressure was closely related to the general local priorities of economics and redevelopment, which deeply affected local planning authorities' policies and actions. Besides initiators, sometimes residents also exercised pressure on local planning authorities to affect changes closer to their expectations. As learned from planning officers, that situation has happened more and more, recently and has become a trend.

Whatever motives behind their action, there was a general tendency of increasing attention to conservation and preservation from each party involved in urban landscape changes. Initiators began to realize the importance of respecting the surroundings of their developments, and some of them hoped to make preservation and conservation an advertisement for them. Residents recognized the significance of the townscape in their living environments, as well as its quality. Local planning authorities were moving towards an effective planning of urban regeneration and conservation. Above all, conservation and preservation have become part of a local consensus. As a news reporter (Ma 1999) has written:

> After large-scale redevelopment of Shanghai's central city, the focus of planning has shifted to the conservation and restoration of Shanghai's historic buildings and areas ... as a city towards the 21st century, Shanghai needs not only high-rises to reflect its modernity, but also distinctive old buildings and areas to demonstrate its long-standing history and culture ...

Previous studies (Dong 1999: 24–5; Geng 1996; Ruan 1995, 1996; Wang 1996: 15–16; Wang *et al.* 1999: 70–81; Yuan 1999) have argued that despite the difficulties involved, conservation area policies can survive the pressure of economic development, urban regeneration and renewal in other cities of China. Here it is argued that the local case studies, e.g. the Xin Tian Di Project, support the view that Shanghai's conservation area policies can survive the pressure of economic development, urban regeneration and renewal, although this is not an unqualified survival. The survival of conservation area policies in China, as found in earlier studies and in the present local case studies in Shanghai, has a close relationship with several factors.

The first factor is the locally variable pressure of economic development and urban regeneration on urban conservation, which has been found in many cities of China and in different parts of these cities. As might be expected, where development pressure is great and is not fully resisted, conservation policies may give way to forms of cosmetic protection at best. Where development pressures are less, the presence of a clear and well-acknowledged conservation policy and instruments make policy survival much stronger (although the deteriorated physical condition of many buildings and lack of funds may make restoration and positive action quite difficult). The second factor is the often different attitudes of local governments towards conservation areas, and urban regeneration and conservation. The local case studies have shown that local planning authorities endeavoured to control developments in conservation areas and to protect the character of the areas, whereas other departments of local governments usually tended to pursue economic and urban development at the cost of urban conservation. This factor has also been found in other studies (Geng 1996; Ruan 1995, 1996). The third factor to be considered is the lack of a consensus over the protection of conservation areas between local governments, local planning professionals, the general public, developers and other involved parties. For instance, in the Huaihai Fang Project, although local planning officers thought the original historic buildings deserved conservation, local residents, the local district government and the developer held the opposite view and pressed for the demolition of original buildings. The final factor is the feasibility of conserving the built fabric of the areas. For instance, in the Tai Ping Qiao Regeneration Project, most of the original old Li-Long houses were seriously deteriorated and their conservation was found to be impracticable (Zhang, W.H. 2000). Therefore, with these factors, the survival of conservation area policies under the pressure of economic development and urban regeneration and renewal, is a qualified one only and continues to be a hard job for local planning authorities and local governments in China.

China has experienced rapid social-economic development during the last two decades. Similar to the situation in many other Asian countries, large-scale urban regeneration has been undertaken in most Chinese cities due to rapid development and this has seriously threatened the traditional and vernacular built environment of those cities. To protect its built heritage and environment, China established an urban conservation system in the late 1980s. However, the national policy framework of the system is largely incomplete and urban conservation practice varies between different local authorities. The balance between urban regeneration and conservation has become a hard task for China's local planning authorities. Furthermore, the study of China's urban regeneration and conservation is only at a beginning and lacks a theoretical foundation.

Notes

1   RMB is the currency used in People's Republic of China. One RMB equals approximately to US$0.122.
2   Item 20, Section 3, and Appendix 2 of the *Technical Directions of City Planning and Administration (Land-use and Building Administration)* (SMG 1994).
3   *The Preservation and Restoration Plan for the site of the First Chinese Communist Party Congress* (SUPDI 1996).
4   The sunlight distance ratio is a technical requirement to keep the minimum north–south distance between two neighbouring buildings so as to ensure necessary sunlight on the north building. The ratio equals the north–south distance between the two buildings divided by the height of the north building. Details are in Section 4, the *Technical Directions of City Planning and Administration (Land-use and Building Administration)* (SMG 1994).
5   Item 28, Section 4 of the 1994 *Directions*.

References

Barrett, H. (1993) 'Investigating townscape change and management in Urban Conservation Areas: the importance of detailed monitoring of planned alterations', *Town Planning Review*, 64(4): 435–56.

Denecke, D. and Shaw, G. (eds) (1988a) *Urban Historical Geography: Recent Progress in Britain and Germany*, Cambridge: Cambridge University Press.

Denecke, D. and Shaw, G. (1988b) 'Introduction', in D. Denecke and G. Shaw (eds) *Urban Historical Geography: Recent Progress in Britain and Germany*, Cambridge: Cambridge University Press.

Dong, L. (1999) 'Bei Jing Jiu Cheng Bao Hu Mao Dun Fen Xi Ji Dui Ce Jian Yi (The analysis and suggestion to solve problems in the conservation of Beijing's Old City)', *Cheng Shi Gui Hua (City Planning Review)*, 23(2): 23–8.

Fan, X.J. (2000) The researcher's interview with Xingjian Fan, the Deputy General Manager of the Yong Ye Company, on 10/11/2000, about the Huaihai Fang Project.

Geng, H.B. (1996) 'Jiu Cheng Geng Xing Xue Shu Yan Tao Hui Zong Shu (Summary of the Urban Renewal Conference)', *Cheng Shi Gui Hua (City Planning Review)*, 20(1): 10–11.

Guo, Q. (2000) The researcher's interview with Qing Guo, a senior staff member of the Shui On Company responsible for the planning of Tai Ping Qiao Regeneration Project, on 05/12/2000, about the Tai Ping Qiao Regeneration Project and the Xin Tian Di Project.

Jones, A.N. and Larkham, P.J. (1993) *The Character of Conservation Areas*, Report commissioned from 'Plan Local' for the Conservation and Built Environment Panel, London: Royal Town Planning Institute.

Larkham, P.J. (1986) 'Conservation, planning and morphology in West Midlands Conservation Areas, 1968–84', unpublished PhD thesis, Birmingham: University of Birmingham.

Larkham, P.J. (1990) 'Conservation and the management of historical townscapes', in T.R. Slater (ed.) *The Built Form of Western Cities*, Leicester: Leicester University Press.

Larkham, P.J. (1996) *Conservation and the City*, London: Routledge.

Larkham, P.J. and Lodge, J. (1997) 'Testing UK conservation in practice: the case of Chartist villages in Gloucestershire', *Built Environment*, 23(2): 121–36.

Larkham, P.J., Booth, P.N., Jones, A.N., Pompa, N.D. and Whitehand, J.W.R. (1988) *The Management of Change in Historical Townscapes: A Discussion of Current Research*, School of Geography, University of Birmingham Working Paper Series No.42, Birmingham: University of Birmingham.

Li, X.H. (2000) The researcher's interview with Xianhong Li, a planning officer of the Luwan District Urban Planning Bureau, on 08/11/2000, about the Tai Ping Qiao Regeneration Project and the Huaihai Fang Project.

Ma, M.L. (1999) 'Liu Xia Wen Hua, Liu Xia Li Shi, Liu Xia Yin Fu ... Ju Jiao Shang Hai Feng Mao Jian Zhu Bao Hu Gong Cheng (Save the culture, save the history, save the melody ... focus on townscape and building conservation projects in Shanghai)', *Wen Hui Daily (Wen Hui Bao)*, 24 April: 6.

Ministry of Construction of China (1991) *Urban Plan Making Regulations*, Beijing: Ministry of Construction of China.

Ren, Z.H. (2000) The researcher's interview with Zhihao Ren, a planning officer of the SMUPB responsible for the Huaihai Fang Project, on 23/10/2000, about the project.

Ruan, Y.S. (1995) 'Dang Jin Jiu Cheng Gai Zao Zhong De Yi Xie Wen Ti (Some problems in present old city regeneration)', *Cheng Shi Gui Hua Hui Kan* (*Urban Planning Forum*), 101: 57–8.

Ruan, Y.S. (1996) 'Jiu Cheng Gai Zao He Li Shi Ming Cheng Bao Hu (Urban renewal and historic city conservation)', *Cheng Shi Gui Hua* (*City Planning Review*), 20 (1): 8–9.

Ruan, Y.S. (2000) *Li Shi Huan Jing Bao Hu De Li Lun Yu Shi Jian* (*The theory and practice of the conservation of historic environment*), Shanghai: Shanghai Scientific and Technological Press.

SMG (Shanghai Municipal Government) (1994) *Technical Directions of City Planning and Administration* (*Land-use and Building Administration*), Shanghai: SMG

SMPC (Shanghai Municipal People's Congress, the local legislation authority of Shanghai) (1991) *Excellent Modern Historic Building Preservation Regulations*, Shanghai: SMPC

SMUPB (2000) *Shang Hai Shi Li Shi Jian Zhu He Feng Mao Di Qu Bao Hu Yu Li Yong Ji Zhi Yan Jiu* (*The Study of the Mechanism of the Preservation and Utilization of Shanghai's Historic Buildings and Townscape Areas*), Shanghai: SMUPB.

SUPDI (1996) *Yi Da Hui Zhi' Di Qu Jian She Feng Mao Bao Hu Yu Gai Zhao Gui Hua* (*The Preservation and Restoration Plan for the Site of the First Chinese Communist Party Congress*), Shanghai: SUPDI.

SUPDI (1999) *Shang Hai Shi Li Shi Wen Hua Ming Cheng Bao Hu Gai Jian Yu Fa Zhan Guan Xi Ji Chu Yan Jiu* (*The Study of Relationships between the Conservation, Regeneration and Development of the Historic Cultural City Shanghai*), Shanghai: SUPDI.

Vilagrasa, J. (1992) 'Recent change in two historical city centres: an Anglo-Spanish comparison', in J.W.R. Whitehand and P.J. Larkham (eds) *Urban Landscapes: International Perspectives*, London: Routledge.

Vilagrasa, J. and Larkham, P.J. (1995) 'Post-war redevelopment and conservation in Britain: ideal and reality in the historic core of Worcester', *Planning Perspectives*, 10(2): 149–72.

Wang, B. (2000) The researcher's interview with Bing Wang, a planning officer of the SMUPB responsible for the development projects of Huashan Hospital, on 20/12/2000, about the project.

Wang, J.H. (1996) 'Li Shi Wen Hua Ming Cheng Bao Hu Nei Rong Ji Fang Fa (The content and methodology of historic cultural city conservation)', *Cheng Shi Gui Hua (City Planning Review)*, 20 (1): 15–17.

Wang, J.H., Ruan, Y.S. and Wang, L. (1999) *Li Shi Wen Hua Ming Cheng Bao Hu Li Lun Yu Gui Hua (The Theory and Planning of the Conservation of Historic Cultural Cities)*, Shanghai: Tongji University Press.

Wang, Y.H. (1998) 'Shang Hai Li Shi Feng Mao Di Duan Bao Hu Ce Lue Yan Jiu (The study of tactics in the conservation of historic districts in Shanghai)', unpublished Master's thesis, Shanghai: Department of Urban Planning, Tongji University.

Whitehand, J.W.R. (ed.) (1981) *The Urban Landscape: Historical Development and Management: Papers by M. R. G. Conzen*, London: Academic Press.

Whitehand, J.W.R. (1984) *Rebuilding Town Centres: Developers, Architects and Styles*, University of Birmingham Department of Geography Occasional Publication, No. 19, Birmingham: University of Birmingham.

Whitehand, J.W.R. (1989) 'Development pressure, development control and suburban townscape change: case studies in south-east England', *Town Planning Review*, 60(4): 403–20.

Whitehand, J.W.R. (1990) 'Townscape management: ideal and reality', in T.R. Slater (ed.) *The Built Form of Western Cities*, Leicester: Leicester University Press.

Whitehand, J.W.R. (1992) *The Making of the Urban Landscape*, Oxford: Blackwell.

Whitehand, J.W.R. and Carr, C.M.H. (1999) 'The changing fabrics of ordinary residential areas', *Urban Studies*, 36(10): 1661–77.

Whitehand, J.W.R. and Larkham, P.J. (eds) (1992) *Urban Landscapes: International Perspectives*, London: Routledge.

Whitehand, J.W.R., Larkham, P.J. and Jones, A.N. (1992) 'The changing suburban landscape in Post-war England', in J.W.R. Whitehand and P.J. Larkham (eds) (1992) *Urban Landscapes: International Perspectives*, London: Routledge.

Whitehand, J.W.R., Morton, N.J. and Carr, C.M.H. (1999) 'Urban morphogenesis at the microscale: how houses change', *Environment and Planning B: Planning and Design*, 26(4): 503–16.

Wu, J. (1997) *Shang Hai Bai Nian Jian Zhu Shi: 1840–1949 (The History of Shanghai's Architecture: 1840–1949)*, Shanghai: Tongji University Press.

Yin, R.K. (1994) *Case Study Research: Design and Methods* (2nd edn), Thousand Oaks, CA: Sage.

Yuan, X. (1999) 'Qian Yi Wo Guo Li Shi Jie Qu Bao Hu De She Hui Jing Ji Ji Chu He Cao Zuo Guo Cheng (The socio-economic basis and operation of China's historic district conservation)', *Cheng Shi Gui Hua (City Planning Review)*, 23(2): 41.

Zhang, F. (2000) The researcher's interview with Fan Zhang, a planning officer of the SMUPB responsible for the Central Plaza Project, on 14/11/2000, about the project.

Zhang, W.H. (2000) The researcher's interview with Wenhai Zhang, a planning officer of the SMUPB responsible for the Tai Ping Qiao Regeneration Project and the Xin Tian Di Project, on 27/11/2000, about the two projects.

Chapter 7

Ecological-economic zoning in the Brazilian Amazon region

The imperfect panoptism

Henri Acselrad

When faced with the complexities of concrete social and territorial dynamics, technical discussions on ecological and economic zoning (EEZ) applied to Brazil's Amazon region display the anti-Cartesian anguish of purportedly holistic planning. Allegations of methodological difficulties and of gaps in the "political sustainability" of EEZ display what de Certeau has called "an enormous remainder made up of multiple and fluid cultural systems, located between the ways space is used and planning is done." Such methodological difficulties express the tension between the geometrized, static and relatively homogenous space of zoning-driven idealizations, and the territory as it is actually used as form-content in a process of change. Contradictions arising from experiences with EEZ in the Amazon region show us that if we take the three moments of its application – pre-understanding the field of action, configuration of the proposed order and social mediation – the domain of political action is not restricted to the moment of final decisions, but rather runs through the entire process. Zoning provokes a reinterpretation of resource rights that runs up against the notion of a consensus supposedly grounded in the "ecological truth of the territory," as unveiled by the force of practice and by classificatory imagery.

From the second half of the 1980s onward, the debate on territorial planning in the Amazon began to include elements of environmental discourse so that an appeal to an ecological rationale, presented as a requirement for territorial organization in the region, gained ground. Ecological-economic zoning (EEZ) is the instrument that has since then been closely associated with the territorial materialization of this rationale. The idea that the projects of authoritarian developmentalism, funded by multilateral organizations, had resulted in "ecological and social disorder" became so established that the World Bank itself endeavoured to

Submitted by the National Association of Urban and Regional Postgraduate and Research Programmes (Brazil).

Originally published as 'O zoneamento ecologico-econômico da Amazônia e o panoptismo imperfeito', in *Planejamento e Territorio*, 15–16 (2001/2): 53–75. By kind permission of the Federal University of Rio de Janeiro. © Henri Acselrad 2004.

include environmental concerns in order to correct the emblematically disastrous impacts of recent projects, such as the Northeastern Brazil Integration Development Project, or POLONOROESTE. After 1986, a new kind of project, the Rondonia Agrocattle and Forestal plan, or PLANAFLORO, was thought up as a way of making economic development and environmental preservation compatible in the forested zones of the state of Rondonia. EEZ was seen there as a key factor through which the project would provide knowledge of the land, identify the territory's potential, and classify areas according to various desirable patterns of use. The federal government's Ecological-Economic Zoning Program was set up in 1990 initially only to cover the Legal Amazon, but it was formally extended in 1992 to the whole country.

The prestige of zoning as a promising instrument for ecologically-based territorial planning has since then been taken into account whenever successive governments have proposed programs, legal instruments, hierarchies, financial packages and institutional restructuring for planning in the Amazon region. The Our Nature Program in 1989, the Steering Committee for Amazonian EEZ set up in 1990, and the Pilot Program for the Protection of Tropical Rainforests financed by the G7, starting in 1991, are some of the landmarks in this process. In these various situations, EEZ has taken on different contents, more or less restricted to the internal domain of public bureaucracies, development agencies, and technical consultancies and with a more or less effective concrete existence – albeit limited, except in the state of Rondonia – in the sociopolitical reality of the Amazon. In these situations, in which international financing conditions, regional and national political agreements, as well as pressures from international and local NGOs and social movements, varied in their configuration and relative weight, the idea of EEZ was being outlined with different emphases, motivations and argumentative strategies.

It has been described in a wide variety of ways, ranging from "strategically important knowledge for defending the Amazon without guns," as Brigadier Marcos Antonio Oliveira (Oliveira 1995: 34), coordinator of the SIVAM (Amazon Surveillance System) project, pointed out, to an ecologically and socially counterproductive instrument, sustained by "an eco-technocratic alliance combining the old authoritarianism and the new green movement," in the words of economist Manfred Nitsch (1994: 508), international consultant to the Pilot Program for the Protection of Brazilian Tropical Rainforests, funded by the G7. Legal-political controversies arose over the lack of transparency in the way in which EEZ was carried out and financed, culminating in the series of public hearings on the Inspection and Control Motion in the National Congress in 1995. Its political relevance was then upheld on the argument that EEZ was needed to provide a scientific basis for the granting of tax incentives in the Amazon, pursuant to Decree Law no. 153/1991. Enforcement of this law was hindered, however, as its technical coordinator (Schubart 1995: 41) admitted, by "the problem that zoning has not been concluded."

The diversity of standpoints and controversies surrounding EEZ evokes what De Certeau (1995: 234) called "an enormous remainder," consisting of multiple and fluid cultural systems, situated between the ways of using space and the planning process. What will be shown here is that the steps leading to the "ecological planning" of the Amazon territory – within the context of the inherent fragility of the regional public sphere – suggest that this "remainder" is present within the planning action itself. In other words, the ecological rationale applied to territorial planning has been the subject of different discursive constructions, which become analytically relevant as expressions of social dynamics which can themselves be seen, as De Certeau (1995: 234) puts it, as the "ebb and flow of murmurs in the advanced regions of planning."

Conjunctures and discourses

In October 1988 the Sarney government set up the Program in Defense of the Ecosystem Complex of the Legal Amazon, currently called the Our Nature Program.[1] Drafted in response to national and international pressures on the government to reduce the rate of deforestation of the Amazon rainforest, the program was intended to "control the rational occupation and exploitation of the Legal Amazon on the basis of territorial organization" (Cruz 1993). An inter-ministerial working group was then set up to study and create measures concerning the protection of the environment, indigenous communities and populations involved in the extractivist process, taking its inspiration from the methodology of PMACI – Program for the Protection of the Environment and Indigenous Communities, launched in 1985 with the basic concern of controlling settlement and mitigating impacts arising from paving the BR-364 highway in the state of Acre.

In the run-up to the UN Conference on the Environment and Development (UNCED 1992), a new inter-ministerial working group was set up[2] to analyze the ecological-economic zoning work in progress and propose measures that would expedite its execution in the Legal Amazon, considered then a priority by the central government (SAE/PR 1990: 9). With Decree no. 99,540 of 21 September 1990, it was superseded by the Ecological-Economic Zoning Program and its Steering Committee chaired by the Secretariat for Strategic Affairs. EEZ therefore began as an alternative form of territorial planning in the Amazon by the federal government, replacing the earlier action by the development agency SUDAM. The results of SUDAM's technically and politically defunct loan and tax incentive policy had been considered undesirable, leaving it too weak to discuss options for regional development or strategic scenarios and with no financial or technical resources to coordinate public policies in the region. EEZ was considered the right solution for presenting political answers to the constant pressure for the return of incentives, which would thus be bound to the standards legitimized by EEZ (Amigos de Terra 1994).[3] Zoning then became a territorial dimension of what has been called "ecological modernization" – a set of policies to minimize environmental risk by identifying "vulnerabilities" and creating institutional arrangements and regulatory practices to imprint an appropriate level of temporality – the much desired "sustainability" – on the forms of territorialized appropriation of resources.[4]

The contradictions of such an enterprise, however, did not take long to be felt. In June 1994, the Environmental Diagnosis of the Legal Amazon was already in its final stage and the IBGE (the federal Brazilian Geographical and Statistical Institute) had submitted to the Secretariat of Strategic Affairs (SAE) the second phase of its program, on creating alternatives to government actions, when a public hearing was held in the Commission for the Protection of the Consumer, the Environment and Minorities, to discuss the proposed ecological-economic zoning of the Legal Amazon. The purpose of the meeting was to publicize the information on the environmental diagnosis of the Amazon that the IBGE had passed on to the SAE and to identify intra-government disputes in relation to EEZ. At the meeting, representatives of civil society demanded greater participation in the Ecological-Economic Zoning Commission and criticized the lack of inter-government cooperation, questioning "the lack of effective coordination between the state EEZs, lack of government cooperation to carry out the EEZ measures and the lack of transparency in relation to information gathered by SAE" (Vianna 1994: 63).

The Environmental Diagnosis, which was the responsibility of the IBGE, was itself dogged by administrative problems[5] and by conceptual differences with the SAE. With the intention of overcoming these problems and completing this environmental diagnosis, the SAE signed an agreement with the Brazilian Foundation for Sustainable Development (FBDS) and the Foundation for Science, Applications and Space Technologies (FUNCATE) with no prior tendering process and without establishing the amounts to be transferred from public coffers to these two private organizations. Bearing in mind the non-transparency and ambiguities of the SAE/FBDS/FUNCATE agreement, the Commission for the Protection of the Consumer, the Environment and Minorities called for an inspection and control motion in the House of Representatives to explain the SAE's administrative procedures regarding the Legal Amazon Ecological-Economic Zoning Program.

Members of the House were concerned about the suspected irregularity in the way the aforementioned agreement had been signed; the exclusion of organized civil society from access to information and from the zoning preparation process; the presumed damage to public interests, since there would be a transfer of state functions to private companies; the risk that the lure of tax and loan incentives would lead to a number of hasty studies, concerned only with approving resources; and, lastly, the lack of clarity in the method by which the "environmental vocations" of the land would be established by those conducting the zoning.

Such contradictions and uncertainties, which culminated in the 1995 Inspection and Control Motion in Congress, pointed to the prevalence of a number of different views which, during the fifteen years since the first attempts at EEZ in the Amazon, had merged and varied in strength as the circumstances imposed different directions on the zoning. The first view saw EEZ as a practice of know-how, area classification and standards production. Another emphasizes EEZ as a project involving development, financing, execution of works and procurement of equipment. A third attitude highlights the role of the zoning function in the organization, incentive and surveillance of economic activities; and a fourth emphasizes those aspects of this territorial policy instrument relating to participation, social control and negotiation of development projects.

The first view focused on EEZ as an instrument of knowledge, paying more attention to data production activities, ways of classifying space and drawing up rules. It involved planning professionals, and technical and legal advisors discussing land observation scales, mapping techniques, database entries and digitalization. The classifications adopted depended on basic concepts such as "environmental systems," "environmental vulnerability," "sustainability," and methodological precepts such as "holism," "systematism" and "dynamic analysis." Research institutions were involved in setting up laboratories and geo-processing centers. Occasionally, difficulties of a cognitive nature arose, such as resorting to out-of-date data as a basis for specific policies, as well as the incompatibility between the scale of economic data and the breakdown required to cope with the ecological processes (Amigos de Terra 1994: 21).

The second attitude sees in EEZ the possibility of satisfying self-interest, and is held either by companies and institutions in the business of design work, execution of works and equipment procurement, or by authorities wanting to benefit from the results of zoning. Some authors point out, for example, the "absolute cynicism" with which the governor of Rondonia, who won the 1994 elections after attacking EEZ during the election campaign, began the second round of zoning of the state only to fulfill the contract with the World Bank (Carvalho 1996: 49; Millikan 1997: 28). On the other hand, in 1996, the central government audit court ordered the summons of a former governor and two of his secretaries for not having passed on to the executive federal agencies of PLANAFLORO resources from the World Bank for this purpose (Millikan 1996: 44). "One of the possible factors 'convincing' the members of Congress, who by a large majority approved zoning as state law, was the state government's argument that without zoning there would be no

PLANAFLORO or its resources for development," according to the Interim Assessment of PLANAFLORO undertaken by UNDP (1996: 25) consultants. Also in the fundraising sphere, the Director-Superintendent of the private FBDS, although acknowledging that "IBGE and FUNCATE did the work," justified the Foundation's retention for itself of 30 percent of the funds transferred by CISCEA – Commission for Implementation of the Aerospace Control System – to carry out the EEZ by declaring: "our performance was marvelous, fantastic, because we are the best in the country."[6] Priority areas for zoning may in fact be selected in the light of pre-established interests. As congressman Salomão Cruz said at a public hearing in the House of Representatives, the Roraima government, for example, chose the Raposa/ Serra do Sol area because of its interest in building a local hydroelectricity plant.[7]

The third attitude toward zoning sees it as an instrument of power over the organization, incentive and surveillance of activities. Different government agencies overlap in their activities relating to green territorial organization – the Ministry of the Environment in coastal management, EMBRAPA in agro-ecological zoning and the SAE itself in EEZ. But disputes have also arisen between federal and state agencies, as in the clash between federal land policies and state territorial organization by EEZ in Rondonia. EEZ has also become an instrument restricting the indiscriminate dissemination of incentive-based projects which, pursuant to the Decree no. 153/1991, have been assessed according to their compatibility with zoning by federal agencies such as SAE, MME, INCRA and FUNAI. The loss of decision-making power on incentives immediately led SUDAM – the Amazonian development agency – to draft a document in 1994 that held eco-development focusing on bio-industries, ecotourism and genetic engineering as a goal, and EEZ as a strategic axis. In view of the strong presence of federal agencies such as INCRA and IBAMA in certain states in the Amazon, internal bargaining tended to include the appointment of local directors to federal agencies, complicating the political scene that conditions the execution of land use policies.

The last view mentioned above highlights the need for EEZ to acknowledge alterity, attributing to this land-use policy instrument a participatory role in the bargaining over development alternatives. Representatives of NGOs, social movements and Congress demand the involvement of society in the EEZ debate, the democratization of access to its information and respect for socio-cultural diversity at the different stages in its preparation. The creation of collegiate institutions has, on the other hand, reflected the concerns of governments to respond to outside pressures and to maintain their political legitimacy. Civil society representatives in such institutions have generally acknowledged that they do not have sufficient power to be heard and decisively influence government policies. NGOs record that the collegiate agencies meet rarely, are reluctant to discuss strategic questions in depth and often have their meetings disrupted by inflamed speeches of politicians involved in local oligarchies. Also visible is the growing reluctance of agencies to make accusations of irregularities in the performance of government bodies, out of fear of reprisals, such as funding cuts and the refusal to grant other requests (Millikan 1997: 30; 1996: 40).

Different conjunctures will account for the prevalence of any one of these views at different times. The run-up to the UN Conference on the Environment and Development (UNCED), for instance, was marked by the view of self-interest in expecting to obtain outside resources. In the post-UNCED period the rationale of power prevailed, in an attempt to occupy the space opened up by the ecological theme, to recycle the national security discourse in ecological terms, and to put the strategies of segments of the business sector in their place. The apparent trend in the second half of the 1990s pointed to an accommodation between the different lines in the sense of forming what some called the "political sustainability of ecological programs." The World Bank seems, in this sense, to be becoming less preservationist: the Moist Areas Agenda that succeeds PLANAFLORO in Rondonia, for example, is considered to be more developmentalist than the preceding project. NGO participation in environmental projects, on the other hand, is gradually focusing more on their technical expertise and the cooperative nature of the services they provide.

The changing circumstances surrounding the discourse on EEZ – a land classification practice that is based on appealing to scientific authority to legitimize the relatively arbitrary nature of the division – only reinforce the perception that this planning instrument may involve a number of different views of the land, building up knowledge of different subjects, outlooks and orders, on the basis of which it may seek to know and represent them.

EEZ and the end of the frontier (or how to learn about things for the market)

Strategic and methodological texts about EEZ associate the economic-ecological rationale with the intent to "completely appropriate the land," "fully use the area" and "fully integrate the region into Brazil," as well as with achieving "total quality in the use of space," the use of an "holistic approach that permits consideration of all opportunities for using the area and natural resources, portraying the real situation with everything in it"[8] and establishing "total surveillance" over it.[9] The aim is to set up a single holistic and all-embracing whole to which the territorialized social diversity would be subordinate. In the EEZ methodology adopted by the Secretariat for Strategic Affairs since 1997, there is a noticeable analogy between the space to be planned and the business idea: the goal is to attain the full productive capacity of the territory, "optimizing the use of space" and attributing to it "technical efficiency compatible with international competition."[10]

This view of the Amazon space as a single technical-material or mercantile whole is not, however, without consequences for the specifically diversified social fabric of the region, characterized by the presence of the extended market and the capitalist frontier. This frontier is the setting for both alterity and the simultaneous expression of multiple historical times that shapes the unity of diversity (Martins 1996). Trying to deal with the Amazon as a technical-material whole would therefore be to deny the frontier, to reduce its social diversity to mere "geographic difference," and to subjugate alterity to the temporal unity of the market/world. This non-dialectic totality leads to denial of conflict and to symbolic non-consideration of diversity. This denial may occur as a result of reducing the other to the condition of pure Nature – as when EEZ classes certain communities as being in a natural state – and through the promotion of certain areas and social players to the status of bearers of "competitive potential." This discursive totality consequently merges both the demographic frontier of "civilization" and that of the market still based on relations of personal domination, as well as the economic frontier that converts land into capital. Eventually, therefore, it symbolically destroys the diversity of situations and historical times that capital itself normally brings together without destroying them.

The symbolic strength of this totalization is mitigated, however, by the intention to show that EEZ can be both a technical and a political instrument (Schubart 1994). The different discourses on EEZ methodologies can be seen to be permeated with substantial internal ambiguities arising from the proposed two-edged nature of this territorial planning instrument. EEZ can be seen as a means of technically identifying environmental facts, regarded separately from what are called the anthropic characteristics of occupation, and also as a way of diagnosing eco-social situations in transformation. It may be understood either as an instrument for identifying the natural vocations of spatial cells by their competitive edges in the world market or as a means of characterizing equi-problematic zones for bargaining processes and legal-political regulation.

The methodological principles used in the various technical documents on the Amazon EEZ thus display internal ambiguities relating, on the one hand, to the intention to produce objective knowledge of the physical and social realities of the territory, where potentials and vulnerabilities are determined without any reference to the subjects of assessment, and, on the other, to the acknowledgment of the fact that EEZ consists of a diagnosis of territorialized historical processes, expressed through the characterization of "equiproblematic zones," based on points of view whose legitimacy should, therefore, be constructed.

It is difficult, however, not to perceive that the so-called technical component of EEZ clearly contains the elements of a political project: that of the technical encounter of the country with itself, the achievement of the land's potential, and a project of territorial occupation that imagines it has technical efficiency compatible with international competition. With the disputes "technically" settled, the land is seen as a purely material substrate for international competitive integration. And the "regional players" of development – now "sustainable" – are merely the developers of the "vocations" dictated by the world market and interpreted by the planners. An explicit political component of EEZ would, in turn, include the mechanisms that could lead to the desired patterns of land occupation and use of natural resources via investments, taxes, public charges, environmental policies, the planning of public works and infrastructure, etc. (Schubart 1994). This political component would contain the means for implementing the technical component, an expression of an agenda of competitive integration regarded as the inevitable outcome of identifying the vocational potential of a territory, which is assumed to be an objective fact, waiting to be learned. For EEZ, learning about the territory is thus learning about "things for the market." Its vocations will be those highlighted by the supposed demands of the world market, to the exclusion of all other demands and agendas, which often conflict and tend to be ignored. Whereas in other situations in the Amazon, as Alfredo Wagner de Almeida recalls, "the ignorance of social processes acted implicitly as a form of social control" (Almeida 1993b: 23), it is now expected with EEZ that learning about the technical potential of things will explicitly legitimize the absorption of conflicts among different territorial projects, or rather express, yet again, the way in which planning methodology ignores them.

Geopolitical control of the territory and "environmental order" (or how to learn about things for control)

Ecologically based territorial policies such as EEZ establish an ecological division of labor, furthering a spatial framework of uncertainties and possible models for the organization of economic activities in the area. Social practices are, in turn, reduced to their technical-productive dimensions in it. In proposing the technical standardization of the territory, EEZ sets up a discourse on the government of things as a way of justifying the government of people and social practices in the area. In the case of the Amazon, particularly, the search for power over things has in recent years replaced the discourse of sovereignty over the territory as the driving force behind policies to control the social occupation of the area. The government of people and things on the land has thus come to overlie the traditional geopolitical concern for the preservation of sovereignty.

The plan to build the Transfrontier Highway, discussed in Congress in 1991, proposed to build farming villages as "pioneer settlements," justified by a military concept of surveillance, inspection and defense of strategic natural resources as well as the need to "repress clandestine activities" (Almeida 1993a: 70). In the terms of the report by congressman Vicente Fialho, settlements would act as a support for police action and military maneuvers to "eliminate and repress drug trafficking, fires, smuggling, illegal mining and logging, invasion of indigenous lands and possible guerrilla movements" (Almeida 1993a: 70). Also in 1991, those in charge of the Calha Norte project called for the installation of "civil housing nuclei," considered fundamental to the success of military operations in the framework of what they called the "vitalization of the border." Furthermore, the idea was to extend the Calha Norte throughout the Amazon, creating conditions "that would facilitate the ordered occupation of such an extensive area, with the correct use of its arable land, the preservation of areas where extractivism was most appropriate, and the organized exploitation of its vast mineral wealth and water resources for the benefit of the whole of society."[11] The proposal of "consolidating national power along the border and its access roads would imply identifying fertile soils and mineral wealth and the predatory use of natural resources" (Brigagão 1996: 21–2). Thus, military thinking moved progressively from the protection of the external borders – the explicit purpose of projects such as the Transfrontier Highway and Calha Norte – to the "ordered occupation of home territory," arguing that in sparsely inhabited areas the involvement of the military in matters outside their responsibility would be explained "by the fact that they are invariably the only ones there."[12] The subordination in March 1988 of the PMACI – Program for Protection of the Environment and Indigenous Communities – to SADEN – the Advisory Secretariat on National Defense to the President of the Republic (a body that was then taking over from the Secretariat-General of the National Security Council) – confirmed the trend towards a militarization of environmental and indigenous questions in the Amazon. It was also SADEN that was at the forefront of the Interministerial Explanation of Motives for the Our Nature Program in October 1988. The consolidation of borders thus justified the proposal for territorial planning measures with regard to both the regulation and correction of the exploitation of natural resources, and the legality of the activities undertaken in the Amazon.

With the Amazon Declaration in 1989, in the context of the Amazon Cooperation Treaty, the technological and ecosystem aspects that are the basis of ecological security began to take center stage. In 1993, the National Defense Council approved the Amazon Protection System (SIPAM), as an expression of "a new strategic idea" that "redefines the conventional, limited concepts of security. Through broader security mechanisms, this strategic apparatus," stated the SAE (Strategic Affairs Secretariat) documents, "must take care of the repression of and preventive measures against projects that may cause distortions and devastation to ecosystems" (Brigagāo 1996: 42). The Amazon Surveillance System (SIVAM), a project worth 1.4 billion dollars, almost half of which was allocated to data collection, eventually subsidized SIPAM with environmental monitoring using sensors, radar, satellite images, an integrated telecommunication system, artificial intelligence tools and the pinpointing of irregular activities. The military involvement in projects of this nature occurred in the context of what a former Secretary for Strategic Affairs called the "existential anguish" of the Armed Forces, in the perception that the military had "ceased to be important players in the country's modernization, and were consequently looking for more room at the core of the State power" (Flores 1995: 7). Their involvement in projects to bring the national security doctrine applying to the Amazon up to date in technico-ecological terms was not, however, untrammeled. Military sectors argued that the difficulties faced by government agencies to operate effectively in the area meant that the vast amount of sophisticated information provided by the remote detection technologies would be worthless.[13] Agents with financial interests, in turn, used the imbroglio over tenders for equipment supplies to SIVAM to call on the government to heavily subsidize banks in difficulties. Faced with the reluctance of his allies in the government to release the funds requested by the banks in distress, Senator Antonio Carlos Magalhāes shrewdly declared in 1995 that "SIVAM is dead." It was alleged that not enough was known by the remote surveillance system managers about the events that SIVAM was meant to monitor – some engineers, for example, had made the laughable suggestion during a scientific meeting that the intention was "to identify clandestine drug laboratories from mercury pollution indicators."[14]

Despite all these setbacks, the justifications for SIVAM result deep down from an appropriation of the emerging idea of "ecological security" adapted to legitimize the military presence in the Amazon. On the international scene, the notion of ecological security has been evoked to justify population control projects in less industrialized countries on the neo-Malthusian premise that population pressure on scarce resources is the main cause of conflicts (Homer-Dixon 1994).

A "militarization of sustainability" has been occurring alongside the appearance of what may be called an "environmental-military" complex, bringing the environment into the information era and legitimizing vast investments in land control technologies and systems. In the Brazilian case, SIPAM is presented as a basis for the sustainable development of the vast Amazon ecosystem, while SIVAM is shown to have two facets, as a military project to defend the airspace, and as a system for monitoring information on mineral, forest and water resources, and human movements and settlements.

This model for interpreting internal conflicts as being started by environmental issues, as tending to fragment nation states or make them more authoritarian, and as being apt to cause splits in international security, was developed by Thomas Homer-Dixon in 1994. It soon became popular in the field of international policy, and in the US Department of State especially, as being applicable to the cases of Haiti, Rwanda and Chiapas in Mexico. The spread of such a model can certainly be explained by the desire to legitimize high military spending, while large corporations in the aerospace and telecommunication sectors are striving to cope with the loss of the generous contracts of Cold War times. These two forces compete fiercely as a basis for the effective discursive meeting between the environment and national security.

The crisis in African countries has allowed certain voices to account for internal political conflicts as the result of too large a population struggling for scarce resources: "There is a whole new set of what may be called biological national security issues," according to the spokespersons of this environmental neo-Hobbesian view: "environmental destruction, explosive population growth, the rapid spread of disease and the emergence of entirely new diseases. It is widely understood that these things hurt Africa. What is not understood is that they can also hurt America. Chaos is the best incubator of disease and disease is an incubator of chaos" (Goldberg 1997: 35) they conclude. Argumentative strategies of this kind have formed the back cloth for changes in North American defense policies. In the light of representations that "competition for scarce resources is an ancient factor in human conflict, causing destructive violence and tension between countries," the US Secretary of State, in her speech on Earth Day in 1997, established "ecological security" as a rhetorical device for presenting social and political problems in an environmental wrapping (Conca 1998: 42).

After 1991, the annual document on the US National Security Strategy started to include environmental issues among its topics, while the use of military satellites for environmental surveillance became the most important embodiment of the new environmental outlook of national security. Based on georeferenced data, quantitative analyses of the population/resources/conflicts ratio began to guide some steps in the new defense policies. One example is the US Defense Intelligence Agency's diagnoses identifying ecological degradation in Lake Victoria as a "cause of potential instability in East Africa,"[15] as was the presence of US military personnel promoting sustainable development in Africa assisting fisheries and water resources management.[16]

In the case of Brazil, the advent of remote sensing and remote event detection technologies renewed the strategic debate on the organization of land occupation in border regions, despite the political setbacks that had marked the history of SIVAM. They also sparked off proposals for environmental protection and to combat illicit actions. On one hand, the production of environmental information was now considered an instrument for the defense of territorial sovereignty and resistance against supposed threats of international intervention in the Amazon.[17] On the other hand, projects such as EEZ and SIVAM can be seen together as methods for the simultaneous remote detection of ecological processes and illicit practices. Geo-referenced environmental information is thereby considered an integral part of the database used for specifying illicit practices. The SIVAM environmental surveillance unit is consequently expected to provide information for the crime surveillance unit. Remote surveillance therefore requires a double reference order – environmental and legal. For the purposes of remote detection, this order will correspond to a predetermined arrangement of people and things in the area, as established in the geo-reference database:

> The geo-reference database is fundamental. If we do not know the location of the mineral provinces, the main indigenous villages, areas of conflict, the main areas of human intervention with regard to the removal of hardwoods, SIVAM cannot start working at all on its surveillance units
>
> (Brigadier M.A. de Oliveira)[18]

Legality will then be seen as men and things being in their proper places. Illegality and environmental disorder will, in turn, be reflected in humans and things not being "in their proper places."[19]

> If we have a certain aircraft flying in a certain direction to a certain point, it may be just a chance event the first time, a normal flight; the second time, we should pay a little more attention; the third time, this air traffic is suspicious. But for this, it is important to have the information for each unit.
>
> (Brigadier M.A. de Oliveira)[18]

The more the surveillance system by itself is credited with the ability to identify illicit actions, the more this assumed order will be supposed as legitimate:

> If it is suspect, it is not the controller who will say it is or classify it as suspect or otherwise; the merging of the data we have available is what will tell us if there is prospecting or some other kind of illegal work going on. The system itself will make the first logical deductions.
>
> (Brigadier M.A. de Oliveira)[18]

The information itself would therefore – on a quasi-natural basis – hold the conditions of the legal and environmental territorial order in objective form in the digital system. This view of the socio-territorial order as quasi-natural does, however, have serious consequences once we realize that the hybrid "living map" handling technologies are making the difference between surveillance and simulation increasingly tenuous. Surveillance by remote detection is, in fact, characterized by the use of technologies that virtually reduce data transmission time to zero. The electronic signals/images of objects and events may thus be taken for their real counterparts, and the imaginary and the real can be considered coincident, so that the distance between virtual and real control tends to disappear.

This rationalizing view that orders the world of things reminds us of Bentham's utilitarianism which, in the eighteenth century, aimed to produce a hydraulic system of pleasures, damming and channeling human psychology towards the productivity of the body (Foucault 1977). In the "greening" of the territory-based economy, in turn, an ecological viewpoint will aim to dam, channel and produce a systemic adjustment of the economic flows in the territory, and provide for a productive channeling of the economic flows of Nature. Added to the former concern about wasting psychic energies in early modern times is now the concern about wasting the elements of the material world. While in Bentham's panoptic view, a biopower would strive not to waste its subjective productive assets, the ecological view of an ecopower will seek not to waste its territorial productive assets. While the former wondered about what to do on the land, disciplining people, their bodies, surfaces and gazes on the basis of a political anatomy focusing on subjugation, the latter wonders what to do with the land, defining legal and illegal practices, and rationally distributing technical and economic processes. Whereas the panoptic gaze sought never to be seen by those watched, but only to be imagined, the ecological gaze is always placed high above the players being watched, looking down from a planetary, global competitive or intergenerational viewpoint.

The "greening" of remote detection practices will thus represent a moment in the appropriation of the land by power strategies, state projects of symbolic investment that promote both a "sociodicy" – the annihilation of the social content of space by establishing a "natural Nature" – as well as an economic meaning of space in areas of "ordinary Nature." It will, therefore, be necessary to discover in practice the weight of the specific aspects, contingencies and subtleties of the concrete social terrain in order to see socioterritorial telematic control as the cause of uncertain orders, "open cosmologies of an imperfect panoptism" (Graham 1998: 486). Furthermore, in the sociopolitical conditions of the Amazon, a project that seeks to add an architecture of positions, applied to individuals and locations, to an engineering of arrangements applied to flows and processes, would quite likely be among the ambitions of what could be called a "more than imperfect panoptism."[20]

Other orders

EEZ is part of the geopolitical imaginary contained in the discourse of development. Just as explorers' maps represented the space of colonialism and administrative maps represent that of the nation-state, resource zoning maps represent the space of development. Zoning based on agricultural science was disseminated in this way by the FAO and UNESCO in the 1960s and 1970s, when they produced soil maps of vast regions of the world, in the idea that the charting of soil aptitudes would help identify those economic uses that were considered appropriate, increasing the food supply without degrading the soils (Deutsch Lynch 1996: 8). In the 1980s and 1990s, the World Bank, UNDP and FAO turned their attention to what was becoming a "tropical rainforest crisis," and focused their programs on rationalizing the use of resources via forest projects such as TFAP – the Tropical Forest Action Plan, begun in 1985. A globalizing view of natural resources materialized after the 1987 Brundtland Report, linking forest protection, climate balance and the question of biodiversity. Globalization of the view of natural resources was then associated with the discursive production of development areas to be protected – as a rule, places were considered "without culture or time," such as parks, biosphere reserves and ecological corridors (Zenner in Deutsch Lynch 1996: 9). Conservation ecology was the basis for deciding upon legitimate uses, so that local populations and their traditional cultures were often considered alien to the scientifically determined vocation of the territory. This happened partly because land tends to be more ambiguous and varied than the abstract categories formulated by land use planners or the proponents of environmental preservation (Vandergeest and Du Puis 1996). On the other hand, rationalization of the gaze by means of EEZ is the vector of a sort of geometrization of the environment, instiling in it a visual order, which configures a space organized by the gaze. EEZ thus evokes a type of sociopolitical geometry, expressed in the spatial distribution of social forms and founded on solidarity between a scientific discourse – that of ecology – and the utopian and harmonious representation of a social geometry. The desired ecological order would result from this structural consolidation between the material and the ideal, the outcome of an assimilation between social degradation and disorder in nature. This has been an ongoing procedure since the eighteenth century, when it was thought that those spaces of nature regarded as unhealthy and repulsive would be those occupied by a disorganized and marginalized society. Assimilation of the natural in the social and political was consolidated in the revolutionary ideas of that time, by the emblematic expression of Bernard de Saint Pierre: "the tree is a republic" (Luginbuhl 1992: 22). Rousseau and Montesquieu also formulated the problem of social order in the terms of a sociopolitical geometry: society would be the space structured by the relations between extent and volume, expansion and contraction, presuming an isomorphism between the geometries of material space and sociopolitical order (Fernandes 1993: 112).

Nevertheless, the construction of such a visual order in border regions should necessarily imply the contradictory handling of the relation between identity and alterity, between a national center and peripheral social forms. The non-substantialist relational border is defined as a game between structured and unstructured zones, between order and disorder, the old and the new, where the occupation of new territories becomes confused with the building of the nation. On the border, space is considered an unknown zone, empty, without history, a non-place, the subject of general initiatives to create environmental reserves or to promote national defense. There, EEZ will perform a volunteer geography, which manufactures regions while reducing history to indicators of the intensity of human pressure, calculated in homogenous interchangeable areas, and described by the quality of the soil and resources sustained by it (Schavoni 1997: 269).

Through EEZ, the "acceptable presences" and "unacceptable practices" are defined in terms of borders, when in fact the presences and practices are interconnected by complex interactive processes. Procedures of inclusion and exclusion may thereby arise from undue extracts and separations between the different portions of the territory, appropriate for procedures that tend to characterize groups and their activities in dual categories, such as indigenous and non-indigenous, park or farming areas, public or private property. This small group of meanings may, consequently, result in the marginalizing of populations that do not adapt to those categories, and who are considered inefficient in their use of resources or destroyers of nature (Vandergeest and Du Puis 1996: 4). The EEZ maps tend to freeze the system of rights of access and use of resources, which is often flexible and mutable. Long-term land rotation agroforestry strategies, for instance, are not easily accommodated in the cartography of resources. The spatial distribution of rights is not compatible with the cartographic language of the national planners of natural resource use. The analytical problem of the border areas is not solved, then, by referring to landmarks or architectural forms, but to mobile spatial fields of social agents. On the other hand, as time passes, the more we must deal with a complex geographic reality that is increasingly hard to pin down in terms of surfaces, zones and, therefore, borderlines and frontiers (Cambrézy 1995: 132). World Bank specialists, for example, say that the Amazon zoning must be associated with "efforts to reduce migration rates by disseminating information elsewhere in Brazil, particularly in the states from which most migrants come" (Banco Mundial 1992: 29). In other words, it is found that compliance with the objectives demarcated in the zones cannot be achieved by actions located in these same zones: the socio-technical pattern of occupation of each zone depends on a set of interconnected processes widely distant in space.

This set of contradictions, expressed in the rationalizing illusions of EEZ, could not but leave its mark in the actual results expected from use of this instrument. According to INPE data, despite SEEZ (socio-economic-ecological zoning) surveillance of PLANAFLORO, from 1991 onwards, Rondonia state had one of the highest rises in deforestation rates, the average annual rate having tripled between 1989–91 and 1992–5, a time when heavy investments had been made in zoning, implementing conservation units, environmental inspection, and so on (Millikan 1998a: 9). A noteworthy feature of the spatial distribution of deforestation was the advance of land clearance and burnings in a number of areas placed under restrictive use in the first round of SEEZ as well as within the various state conservation units (Millikan 1998b: 15).

The advancing deforestation reflected the occurrence of what some call a "de facto zoning." The absence of political agreements that could sustain the EEZ project may explain the rise of this kind of "market counter-zoning," seen in the rush for land that damaged the integrity of the zones established in the first round of SEEZ in Rondonia and which created the expectation that the second round, which started in 1996, would result in a reduction in the area of environmental preservation zones (Pedlowski 1998a). The decrees signed by the state government in 1990 and 1994 had already bowed to pressure from cattle farmers and lumbermen by relaxing restrictions on deforestation, and an unofficial agenda was followed on the official pretext that there was a need to assuage the anxieties of small farmers mistakenly included in the protected zones (Millikan 1996: 48). UNDP consultants were led to acknowledge that, should it fail to resist the pressures to alter the zoning, "there would be the permanent risk that the second costly round of SEEZ would be modified haphazardly, because of various demands and interests through the local Assembly" (UNDP 1996: 25).

A particularly crucial question in the implementation of the socioeconomic-ecological zoning of Rondonia, was the precarious nature of what might be called its political sustainability by the various groups of the local population. The intention that SEEZ should administrate the social use of space, according to Millikan, came up against the paucity of democratic and transparent spaces for dialogue between the public authorities and civil society in order to prevent the privatization of public policies by the political and economic elites of the Amazon and a repetition of the failure of the authoritarian planning of space that had already been tried in the Amazon (Millikan 1996: 44–5). "The first round of Zoning between 1986 and 1988," says Millikan, "was addressed by the Rondonia government and World Bank as an essentially technical exercise, and not as a participatory process involving negotiations between several spheres of the public authorities and the various segments of civil society" (Millikan 1996: 45–6). It was quite common to have local politicians speak out against the zoning, describing it as a straitjacket imposed by the World Bank and non-government organizations to prevent the economic development of the State (Millikan 1998b).

The contradictions demonstrated by the EEZ experiment in the Amazon show, therefore, that if the three stages in its development are considered – the initial understanding of the sphere of action, the design of the proposed arrangement, and social mediation – the field of political intervention is not limited to the moment of the final decision but pervades the whole process (Lussault 1995: 172). Once mapping has begun, a new *locus* of negotiation and potential conflict over access to resources takes center stage. The zoning process thus ushers in a reinterpretation of rights to resources (Peluso 1995: 388) that ends up clashing with the so-called consensus supposedly based on the "ecological truth of the territory," as revealed by the power of the classificatory images.[21]

Discourses on living systems and political order have been in close communication since ancient times, providing the language with numerous biological metaphors for politics. In ecology, the "natural" ecosystem – undisturbed by catastrophes or human exploitation – represents order in nature, stable and permanent, conservable as something similar to itself for long periods. This kind of semantic load would be sufficient to neutralize any potential divergences between different types of intelligibility. Today, however, as Stengers and Bailly (1987) recall, the notion of order, around which these different interpretations revolve, is increasingly seen to be partial, as a translation of a presupposed ideal, which neither the potential of nature nor that of selective evolution, could guarantee. The idea of interdependence of populations within the same system and the idea of stability were no longer directly related (Stengers and Bailly 1987: 228–9). When human relations are recognized as based around the word and symbolic exchange, they are distinguished by the fact of being outside any natural order. This order cannot then be explained as a reduction in the arbitrary – typical of the description of natural phenomena against a background of neutrality – but rather as the suspension of an indetermination of relations that explicitly or implicitly imply a classification and thus an ethic. There would, therefore, be a multitude of ways for the ecological stabilization of practices (Stengers and Bailly 1987: 229).

The difficulties in building the political covenants to sustain EEZ thus reflect the peculiarity of environmental management as a locus of a diffuse interest. What these drawbacks suggest is that, contrary to what is often claimed, the purpose of "green" territorial planning is not the construction of a consensus around superior guidelines that transcend the diversity of practices, but rather a symbiotic agreement in which each player would seem to be interested in a certain type of success of the other, but for their own reasons (Stengers 1996). Such an agreement would not result, then, from a merging of particular interests in submission to a higher good, but from an intrinsic process that Stengers calls "mutual-capture," where players that "co-invent" each other are part of the other's reference, though each to their own account. Each co-invented player in this relationship would, therefore, be interested in the other also remaining in existence, given the inevitability of the interaction of their practices. In order that this kind of relationship can include some form of stability, it should, consequently, be recognized that it does not refer to a single interest higher than itself, but to multiple projects of conflicting co-invention of the territory and of the players in its construction.

Acknowledgement

Cecilia Mello and Maria Nilda Bizzo helped with the survey of the literature used as a basis for this paper

Notes

1 Decree no. 96,944 dated 12/10/88.
2 Decree no. 99,193 dated 27/03/90, amended by Decree no. 99,246, dated 10/05/90.
3 Decree no. 153 dated 25/06/91 prohibited the granting of tax incentives to projects that implied deforestation of primary forest areas and destruction of ecosystems. The projects to be given incentives have since then been instructed pursuant to EEZ, having consulted SAE, IBAMA, INCRA and FUNAI. The loss of decision-making powers on incentives led SUDAM to draft a document in 1994 "Ação Governamental na Amazônia" referring to an eco-development directed at the "bio-industry, eco-tourism and genetic engineering" as a goal and to EEZ as a strategic axis.
4 The idea of ecological modernization describes the process by which political institutions internalize ecological concerns about the proposal to reconcile economic growth with solving environmental problems, giving emphasis to technological adaptation, promotion of the market economy, belief in cooperation and consensus (Blowers 1997).
5 According to the then president of IBGE, the diagnosis was jeopardized by the cut in the IBGE budget to a third of its normal budget, accompanied by a wage reduction, strikes, scarce technological and human resources, bureaucratic impasses for the release of funds and equipment procurement at the required rate, loss of autonomy for financial and personnel management, all within the context of galloping inflation (free translation). Cf. S. Schwartzman, Public Hearing 26/10/95: 36.
6 cf. E. Salati and W. Schindler, Public hearing, 25/10/1995: 49, 52.
7 cf. Public hearing, 7/11/1995: 40.

8   cf. Secretaria de Assuntos Estratégicos, Detalhamento da Metodologia do ZEE, Brasilia, 1997.

9   "With SIVAM, each kilometre of the Amazon will be controlled, according to information from Brigadier Marco Antonio de Oliveira, president of the Steering Committee of SIVAM" (Brigagão 1996: 48).

10 cf. Secretaria de Assuntos Estratégicos, Detalhamento da Metodologia do ZEE, Brasilia, 1997: 12.

11 cf. C.Tinoco, Exposição do Ministro de Estado do Exército, in Diário do Congresso Nacional, 5/4/1991, (Almeida 1993a: 70).

12 cf. C.Tinoco, op. cit. (Almeida 1993a: 70).

13 "On what roads is SIVAM going to use its mobile radars?," asked the former head of the General Staff of the Military Command of the Amazon, Gen. T. Sotero Vaz, cf. *Folha de S. Paulo* newspaper, 5/5/1995: 12.

14 cf. R. Bonalume Neto, "The country is not able to operate SIVAM data," in Folha de S. Paulo, 27/11/1995: 1–6.

15 cf. J. Brian Atwood, "Towards the Definition of National Security," Remarks to the Conference on New Directions in U.S. Foreign Policy, University of Maryland, College Park, November 2. Excerpted in Wilson Center, Environmental Change and Security Project Report, Spring 1996: 85–8, in Hartmann 1997: 15.

16 cf. K. Butts, "National Security, the Environment and DOD," in Wilson Center, Environmental Change and Security Project Report, Spring 1996, in Hartmann 1997: 15.

17 cf. Brigadier M. A. de Oliveira, Depoimento à Comissão de Defesa do Consumidor, Meio Ambiente e Minorias. Câmara dos Deputados. Proposta de fiscalização e controle no 11, Notas Taquigráficas – Audiência Pública, Brasilia, 14 December 1995: 42.

18 Ibid.

19 "All those reports may be associated with the reports on illicit actions that will be used for another unit. If there is anything wrong happening in this region, we will identify what there is in this region. It is much easier to know what the region has so that we can associate some illicit practice," cf. Brigadier M. A. de Oliveira, Comissão de Defesa do Consumidor, Meio Ambiente e Minorias. Câmara de Deputados (House of Representatives) (Oliveira 1995).

20 "The image standard," according to the SAE technical documents, "is the result of combinations of spectrum responses of the physical and biotic variables and of the actions resulting from economic activities." The "graphic homogeneity of the image standard," it goes on, "defines spatialization and permits the preliminary identification of the environmental unit" (SAE/PR 1995: 8). Guillot (in Cambrézy 1995: 50), in turn, warns about the approximate nature of the results of remote sensing of the environment and meteorology, its degrees

of accuracy being heavily dependent on the uncertain ability to recover physical parameters from the rays reflected by objects.

21 "Is practice (planning) based on imagery, not becoming involved in a sophistry where the content of the proposal might be less important than the perfection of its record – a phenomenon that fast diffusion of new technologies, in a community seduced by technical instruments, only makes more accentuated?" (Lussault 1995: 192).

References

Almeida, A.W.B. (1993a) "Continentalização dos conflitos e transformações na geopolítica das fronteiras," *Reforma Agrária*, 23(3): 69–106.

Almeida, A.W.B. (1993b) *Carajás – A Guerra dos Mapas*, Belém: Falangola.

Amigos da Terra (1994) "A harmonização das políticas públicas com os objetivos do programa piloto para as florestas tropicais Brasileiras," São Paulo: Friends of the Earth International/Grupo de Trabalho Amazônico.

Banco Mundial (1992) "Relatório da equipe de avaliação do Projeto de Manejo dos Recursos Naturais de Rondônia," Washington.

Blowers, A. (1997) "Environmental policy: ecological modernization or the risk society," *Urban Studies*, 34(5–6): 845–71.

Bonalume Neto, R. (1995) "País não teria como operar dados do Sivam," *Folha de S. Paulo*, 27 November: 1–6.

Brigagão, C. (1996) *SIVAM, Inteligência e Marketing*, Rio de Janeiro: Record.

Câmara Dos Deputados. Proposta de fiscalização e controle no. 11, de 1995 (Deputies Ivan Valente e Gilney Viana); Comissão de Defesa do Consumidor, Meio Ambiente e Minorias. *Notas Taquigráficas – Audiências Públicas* (Tema: esclarecimento sobre o Programa de Zoneamento Ecológico-Econômico). Brasília, 10/10/1995; 18/10/1995; 19/10/1995; 25/10/1995; 26/10/1995; 7/11/1995; 21/11/1995; 14/12/1995.

Cambrézy, L. (1995) "L'Information géographique à la représentation carto-graphique," in L. Cambrézy and R. De Maximy (eds) *La Cartographie en Débat*, Paris: Karthala-Orstom.

Carvalho, H.M. (1996) "Resgate histórico e analítico do forum de ONGs e movimentos sociais que atuam em rondônia," mimeo, OXFAM: Porto Velho.

Certeau, M. (1995) *A Cultura no Plural*, Campinas: Papirus.

Conca, K. (1998) "The environment-security trap," *Dissent*, summer: 40–5.

Cruz, A.L. (1993) "O zoneamento ecológico-econômico da Amazônia legal," *Projeto de Políticas Públicas*, Brasilia: IEA (Institute of Environmental and Amazon Studies).

Deutsch Lynch, B. (1996) "Marking territory and mapping development, protected area designation in the Dominican Republic," Comunicação apresentada em Latin American Studies Association. Mimeo.

Fernandes, T.S. (1993) "Modernidade e geometrias – a representação da ordem na obra de Emile Durkheim," *Cadernos de Ciências Sociais*, Lisbon, 12/13: 107–48.

Flores, M.C. (1995) "Rumos para defesa," *Jornal do Brasil*, newspaper, 1 April.

Foucault, M. (1977) *Vigiar e Punir*, Petrópolis: Vozes.

Goldberg, J. (1997) "Our Africa problem," *New York Times Magazine*, 2 March: 34–81.

Graham, S. (1998) "Spaces of surveillant simulation: new technologies, digital representation and material geographies," *Environment and Planning D, Society and Space*, 16(4): 483–504.

Guillot, B. (1995) "Imagerie satellitaire et estimation des précipitations," in L. Cambrézy and R. De Maximy (eds) *La Cartographie en Débat*, Paris: Karthala-Orstom.

Hartmann, B. (1997) "Population, environment and security – a new trinity," *Political Environments*, Special Security Issue, 5: 8–17.

Homer-Dixon, T. (1994) "Environmental scarcities and violent conflict," *International Security*, 19(1): 5–40.

Luginbuhl, Y. (1992) "Nature, paysage, environnement, obscurs objets du désir de totalité," in M.C. Robic (ed.) *Du Milieu à l'Environnement, Pratiques et Représentations du Rapport Homme Nature depuis la Renaissance*, Paris: Economica.

Lussault, M. (1995) "La ville clarifiée. Essai d'analyse de quelques usages carto- et iconographiques en oeuvre dans le projet urbain," in L. Cambrézy and R. De Maximy (eds) *La Cartographie en Débat*, Paris: Karthala-Orstom.

Martins J.S. (1996) "O tempo de fronteira – retorno à controvérsia sobre o tempo histórico da frente de expansão e da frente pioneira," *Tempo Social*, 8(1): 25–70.

Millikan, B. (1996) "Participação popular em projetos financiados pelo Banco Mundial: o caso do plano agropecuário e florestal de Rondônia (PLANAFLORO)," Porto Velho: Oxfam.

—— (1997) "Políticas públicas e desenvolvimento sustentável em Rondônia: situação atual e abordagem para um planejamento participativo de estratégias para o Estado," Rondônia: PNUD/Seplan-RO.

—— (1998a) "Comentários preliminares sobre a 'Agenda Úmidas: Diretrizes Estratégicas para o Desenvolvimento Sustentável de Rondônia'," set. Mimeo.

—— (1998b) "Zoneamento sócio-econômico-ecológico no estado de Rondônia – análise de um instrumento de ordenamento territorial na fronteira Amazônica," Brasília: PNUD/PLANAFLORO.

Munn, N.D. (1996) "Excluded spaces: the figure in the Australian Aboriginal landscape," *Critical Inquiry*, Spring, 22: 446–65.

Nitsch, M. (1994) "Riscos do planejamento regional na Amazônia brasileira: observações relativas à lógica complexa do zoneamento," in M.A. D'incao and I.M. Silveira (eds) *Amazônia e a crise da modernização*, Belém: Museu Paraense Emilio Goeldi.

Oliveira, M.A. (1995) "Depoimento na audiência pública da proposta de fiscalização e controle," no. 11/95 sobre ZEE da Amazônia Legal, Brasília.

Pedlowski, M.A. (1998) "O papel do Banco Mundial na formulação de políticas Territoriais na Amazônia – o caso de Rondônia," *Cadernos IPPUR*, 12(2): 157–80.

Peluso, N.L. (1995) "Whose woods are these? Counter-mapping forest territories in Kalimantan, Indonesia," *Antipode*, 27(4): 388–402.

SAE/PR (Secretaria de Assuntos Estratégicos) (1997) "Detalhamento da metodologia do ZEE," Brasília.

SAE/PR (1990) "Programa de zoneamento ecológico-econômico con prioridade para a Amazônia Legal," Report GT/90: Brasilia.

—— (1995) "As fases e as etapas do zoneamento ecológico-econômico do território Nacional," Brasília.

Schavoni, G. (1997) "Las regiones sin historia: apuntes para una sociologia de la frontera," *Revista Paraguaya de Sociologia*, 34(100): 261–80.

Schubart, H.O.R. (1994) "O zoneamento ecológico-econômico e o ordenamento territorial: aspectos jurídicos, administrativos e institucional, presented at a workshop: *Zoneamento Ecológico-Econômico: Instrumento para o Desenvolvimento Sustentável dos Recursos da Amazônia*, Manaus: INPA.

—— (1995) Testifying to the Commission for the Protection of the Consumer, the Environment and Minorities. House of Representatives. Inspection and Control Motion no. 11, shorthand notes – Public Hearing, Brasilia, 14 December 1995

Stengers I. (1996) *La Guerre des Sciences*, Tome 1, Paris: La Découverte; Les Empecheurs de Penser en Rond.

Stengers, I. and Bailly, F. (1987) "Ordre," in I. Stengers (ed.) *D'une Science à l'Autre – des concepts nomades*, Paris: Seuil.

UNDP (1996) *Avaliação de Meio Termo*, Brasília: Mimeo.

Vandergeest P. and Du Puis, M. (eds) (1996) *Creating the Countryside – the Politics of Rural and Environmental Discourse*, Philadelphia: Temple University Press.

Viana M.A. (1994) "O zoneamento ecológico-econômico e a sociedade civil," in *Seminário Diversidade Eco-social e Estratégias de Cooperação Entre Ongs da Amazônia*, Belém: FAOR – FASE.

Acronyms

CISCEA	Commission for Implementation of the Aerospace Control System
EMBRAPA	Brazilian Agricultural Research Corporation
FAOR	East Amazonian NGO Forum
FBDS	Brazilian Foundation for Sustainable Development
FUNAI	National Foundation for Indigenous People
FUNCATE	Foundation for the Space Science, Applied Research and Technology
IBAMA	Brazilian Institute for the Environment and Natural Resources
IBGE	Brazilian Institute of Geography and Statistics
INCRA	Agrarian Reform National Institute
MME	Environment Minister
PLANAFLORO	Rondonia Agrocattle and Forestal Plan
PMACI	Program for the Protection of the Environment and Indigenous Communities
POLONOROESTE	Northeastern Brazil Integration Development Program
SADEN	Advisory Secretariat on National Defense to the President of the Republic
SAE	Strategic Affairs Secretariat
SEPLAN-RO	Rondônia State Planning Secretariat
SIPAM	Amazon Protection System
SIVAM	Amazon Surveillance System
SUDAM	Superintendency for Amazonian Development
SEEZ	Rondonia socio-economic-ecological zoning
TFAP	Tropical Forest Action Plan
UNCED	United Nations Conference on the Environment and Development

Chapter 8
Walking in another's shoes
Epistemological challenges in participatory planning

Karen Umemoto

Growing cultural diversity brings new challenges to the practice of planning. In participatory planning, this diversity poses challenges related to communicating across culture-based epistemologies and soliciting the voices of multiple publics. This article explores five challenges that planners face when working in communities where the cultural background of residents is different from one's own. These challenges are: (1) traversing interpretive frames embedded in culture, history, and collective memory; (2) confronting otherness in the articulation of cultural values and social identities; (3) understanding the multiple meanings of language; (4) respecting and navigating cultural protocols and social relationships; and (5) understanding the role of power in cultural translation.

Cultural diversity in metropolitan cities has changed the world of planning. Planners are confronting an increasing array of issues with explicit cultural dimensions such as public provision of multilingual services, permitting of non-English storefront signage, siting of religious temples, and the preservation of sacred sites, to name just a few (Edelstein and Kleese 1995; Jennings 1994; Saito 1998). Cultural diversity is also evident in planning processes, as people of diverse cultural backgrounds are a growing presence in institutions of planning. Planners hear from an increasing number of cultural groups who speak in more than one hundred languages in world cities such as Los Angeles and New York City. And planning staffs of municipal governments and policy-making agencies are becoming more diverse, especially racially and ethnically. This diversity presents many challenges to planners. One of the most difficult is to design and facilitate planning processes that can accommodate cultural differences, for this requires planners to extend their thinking into other epistemological worlds – like walking

Selected as the Chester Rapkin award winning paper (the best paper in the Journal of Planning Education and Research, volume 21), and submitted by the Association of Collegiate Schools of Planning (USA).

in another's shoes. Not only is this difficult (and some would say impossible), it is a skill seldom emphasized in professional training.

In this article, I outline some of the epistemological challenges involved in facilitating participatory planning processes in multicultural settings. Epistemological challenges are those arising from the existence of multiple worldviews rooted in history and culture. We generally understand that there are culturally specific norms, values, and ways of interpreting the world that, if not understood, can hinder the participation of historically marginalized groups, even in the most well-intentioned planning efforts. This article explores specific challenges involved in soliciting "voices from the borderlands"[1] so that we might better capture the richness that our diversity offers. The challenges outlined below are those that have to do with the accommodation of multiple epistemologies in planning processes and do not speak to the equally important issue of reconciling controversies arising from differences in epistemologies.[2] The task of mediating between divergent cultural paradigms represents an even greater set of challenges that planning scholars have begun to explore (Forester 1999; Healey 1999). For now, I present those epistemological challenges that planners face in working with communities with distinct and non-Western cultural identities, drawing many of the examples from a neighborhood visioning project in the Hawaiian Homestead community of Papakolea. I begin with a brief discussion of the concept of culture, the academic turn toward issues of epistemology, and the relevance of epistemic issues to planning in a multicultural society.

Culture and epistemology

There is a growing sensitivity toward culture and cultural difference in the study and practice of planning. Recent literature addressing diversity in planning can be organized into several main areas: theories of difference in planning, diversity in planning processes, models for planning in multicultural society, and the impact of planning and identity politics in communities of color. Debates surrounding the first category, theories of difference in planning, were rejuvenated amidst postmodern critiques of liberalism and modernism (Harvey 1989; Parpart 1993; Soja 1989; Watson and Gibson 1995; Nicholson 1990). Planning scholars explored specific ways in which different experiences and cultural worldviews shape the meaning and design of place (Beall 1997; Fincher and Jacobs 1998; Hayden 1995; Marchmand and Parpart 1995; Pratt 1998; Rakodi 1991; Sandercock 1998a, 1998b). A number of planning theorists have come to argue that race, ethnicity, gender, sexual orientation, and disability are among salient identity boundaries that demarcate differently situated knowledge, arguing that planners should simultaneously facilitate the articulation of difference and the search for common ground within planning processes.

A second and related set of discussions has focused on the conceptual and practical problems of designing planning processes that can facilitate deliberative democratic discourse in multicultural or diverse settings (Baum 1994; Beall 1996, 1997; Forester 1998; Healey 1997; Innes and Booher 1999; Qadeer 1997). Collectively, they have explored issues of power and communication, institutional structures, identity politics, and social conflict as they shape participation and outcomes in the planning process. Others have developed more practical guides or models for planning in diverse communities, including indigenous communities (Guyette 1996; Hamdi and Goethert 1997; Jojola 1998; Minerbi 1999). These works underscore the importance of cultural values as a foundation for the development of plans. They also suggest ways to develop culturally appropriate methods for involving groups and individuals in the planning process. These guides complement the many empirical works (including case studies) that highlight useful lessons from planning practice, especially in historically oppressed or marginalized communities (Beall 1997; Catlin 1993; Anderson 1996).

There is also a rich body of empirical research that chronicles the misdeeds of planning and related problems facing women and communities of color (Boger and Wegner 1996; Bullard *et al.* 1996; Gillette 1995; Goldsmith and Blakely 1992; Greed 1994; Little 1994; Massey 1994; Massey and Denton 1993; Oliver and Shapiro 1995; Ong 1981; Sandercock 1998a; Yiftachel 1994). Case studies have examined development projects that have threatened ethnic communities (Heskin 1991; Silver 1984; Thomas 1997; Woods 1998), environmental justice movements in communities of color (Bullard 2000; Faber 1998), and the application of Western development theories in the non-Western world (Hettne 1990; Mehmet 1995; Peattie 1987). Tales of social movements, unjust treatment of indigenous peoples, or paternalistic good intentions gone awry have provided rich fodder in theoretical critiques of modernist paradigms. There are also recent works on the contemporary politics of planning involving racial and other intergroup controversies (Chang and Leong 1994; Dear, Shockman, and Hise 1996; Forsyth 1998; Goode and Schneider 1994; Keith and Pile 1993; Saito 1998). These controversies have helped to reframe discussions of planning and civil society in multicultural cities (Douglass and Friedmann 1998; Okin 1994; Young 1995).

Within planning literature dealing with issues of diversity, there is increasing attention to questions of epistemology (Healey and Hillier 1996; Hillier 1998; Sandercock 1998b; Sandercock and Forsyth 1992). Epistemology is the theory of the nature and grounds of knowledge. It has been described as a way of knowing and a way of understanding the world.[3] It can be explained as an interpretive lens through which one makes meaning of events, actions, words, and symbols. Epistemological differences are more than mere differences in experience, but are the differences in how individuals and groups make sense of those experiences.

Epistemologies designate what can be known, who could know, and what constitutes evidence. An epistemological framework is a product of a social process and, as such, is constantly changing and transforming like the history and culture within which it is embedded. Sandercock (1998b) suggests six ways of knowing that constitute an epistemology of multiplicity for planning practice: through dialogue; from experience; through gaining local knowledge of the specific and concrete; through learning to read symbolic, nonverbal evidence; through contemplation; and through action planning. She and others who advocate "planning for multiple publics" (Sandercock and Forsyth 1992) argue for a celebration of difference while addressing the problems of inequality and exploitation.

It is important to clarify the relationship between culture and epistemology by taking note of the evolution of the fundamental concept of culture. Anthropologists can trace usage of the concept of culture as moving from "culture as everything learned and produced" to "systems, codes and programs of meaning" (Friedman 1994: 69). The notion of culture in early anthropology was associated with a people's defining characteristics, that is, those attributes that made a people distinctive from others, whether it was language, religion, technology, or kinship systems. In other words, culture was studied as a collection of attributes attached to particular groups of people. But a shift in the early 1900s abstracted the concept of culture from those who possess it. Social scientists began to focus on signs, symbols, tools, and beliefs. Culture became seen as a system of relations by which people adapted to their environment rather than a collection of attributes.

Today, and especially in the United States, culture is largely understood as a symbolic or cognitive construct by which meaning is made of the world. It is widely acknowledged that culture, along with identity, is socially constructed and contested and is dynamic rather than static. Culture can be described as "a relatively unstable product of the practice of meaning, of multiple and socially situated acts of attribution of meaning to the world, of multiple interpretations both within society and ... between societies" (Friedman 1994: 74). Culture is generally acknowledged as a product of societal contests over meaning, albeit distributed in society based on social position (Barth 1989). As our concept of culture has taken a turn toward epistemology, it is appropriate that explorations into planning theory also pay closer attention to these issues. While not to conflate culture and epistemology, I find it useful for heuristic purposes to discuss cultural differences in terms of differences in epistemologies.

I refer to a type of planning that is attentive to differences in epistemology among culturally defined groups as culture-based planning. Culture-based planning legitimizes multiple epistemologies and, theoretically at least, gives them equal standing in the spirit of pluralism. The inclusivity of this approach gives culturally defined groups discursive forums to express their preferences and visions in planning processes. It also creates space to question the culturally based normative assumptions underlying existing structures and institutions (Healey 1999). The exercise of this discursive power can lead to institutional and social transformation. Social movements can grow in these spaces of discourse and, in their development, put forth political claims based on declarations of culture-based rights.

Culturally distinct groups have traditionally been identified as ethnic or religious. This article, however, is written to apply to any number of social boundaries that delineate a distinct epistemic standpoint, such as race. Race as a social category has historically (at least in the United States) been one of the most salient social identity boundaries in society. The lasting legacies of colonialism, immigration, slavery, political domination, and socioeconomic stratification survive either in the realm of lived experience or collective memory. Race, along with ethnicity, class, gender, sexual orientation, and other social identity markers, represents group boundaries that can be described as sharing distinct epistemic lenses based on a shared history and vantage point. This is not to homogenize any such group, as crosscutting identities further distinguish subgroups within any of these categories. Nor is this to say that a given identity boundary connotes the same meaning to all groups or individuals categorized within them. The cultural group I focus on in this article is technically regarded as ethnically Hawaiian and racially Polynesian or Pacific Islander in federal census books. While there is a great amount of diversity within this Hawaiian community, I focus here on the epistemic lens based largely on a shared Hawaiian identity.[4]

Five challenges for culture-based planning

If we are to recognize multiple epistemologies and acknowledge that inter-pretations of experience are contested and constructed, there are two major types of challenges that planners face. One has to do with the reconciliation of epistemological differences between cultural groups. A second has to do with the ability to accommodate diverse epistemologies in planning processes. In this article, I focus mainly on the latter, discussing five challenges that planners face when working in a community in which the cultural background of its residents is different from one's own. They are (1) traversing interpretive frames embedded in culture, history, and collective memory; (2) confronting otherness in the articulation of cultural values and social identities; (3) understanding the multiple meanings of language; (4) respecting and navigating cultural protocols and social relationships; and (5) understanding the role of power in cultural translation.

I draw examples from a community planning project in the Hawaiian Home-stead community of Papakōlea in central Honolulu, Hawai'i. Papakōlea is a community of 270 families with a total resident population of 1,500. Papakōlea was established as a homestead community for Native Hawaiians in 1934, with an amendment to the 1921 Hawaiian Homes Commission Act (42 Stat. 108). The Hawaiian Homes Commission Act was designed "to enable native Hawaiians to return to their lands in order to fully support self-sufficiency for native Hawaiians and the self-determination of native Hawaiians in the administration of this Act, and the preservation of the values, traditions, and culture of native Hawaiians."[5] By law, homestead land is reserved for those who are of no less than 50 percent Native Hawaiian ancestry. In Papakōlea, the vast majority of residents are of Native Hawaiian or part Hawaiian ancestry, with the exception of several families and the spouses of legal homesteaders.

As a community with a strong Native Hawaiian identity, Papakōlea and planning activities there hold valuable lessons for planners concerned about participatory planning in multicultural societies, especially where ethnic, racial, and cultural identities are distinct and salient. Ethnicity (or nativity for those who consider the category of Hawaiian to designate national origin) is the most salient identity boundary in this community for historical reasons. As a brief background, the indigenous monarchical government of the Hawaiian Islands was overthrown in 1893 with the cooperation of the US armed naval forces. In 1898, the United States annexed Hawai'i despite its own acknowledgement of the illegality of the initial overthrow. In 1959, Hawai'i became the fiftieth state of the United States. Throughout the span of colonization, Native Hawaiians suffered land dispossession, disease, displacement, and disempowerment. Public law 103–150, passed by the US Congress in 1993, acknowledged these wrongs and apologized "on behalf of the people of the United States for the overthrow of the Kingdom of Hawai'i."[6] This history is relatively fresh in the collective memory of Native Hawaiians and is retold through "talk story,"[7] rituals, educational curricula, music, performing arts, and literature.

A visioning process was facilitated by a steering committee led by officers of the Papakōlea Community Association (the homestead association of residents), officers of Kula No Na Po'e Hawai'i (a nonprofit educational and cultural organization serving the homestead), and several social workers with the Queen Lili'uokalani Children's Center.[8] Graduate students in the Department of Urban and Regional Planning and the School of Social Work at the University of Hawai'i at Manoa and several faculty, including myself, were also invited as members of the steering committee. Students in a service learning practicum designed a series of planning exercises in cooperation with the steering committee to solicit ideas from residents as to their visions for the future. More than 300 individuals participated in a five-month process starting in fall 1997. The visioning process in Papakōlea addressed a number of areas including health, education, culture, economics, and family life (see the Vision Statement in Table 8.1). Collectively, these vision statements can be said to reflect the aspirations of the community from a culturally defined worldview.

Table 8.1 Vision statement for Papakōlea

Papakōlea: A Vision for the Future

Our home is Papakōlea,
a community where the spirit of *lōkahi* and *aloha*
inspires self-reliance and participation
to share knowledge of our culture
and respect of *'ohana*.

Residents assume a responsibility
to create a community with strong identity,
spirit and pride. Our participation nurtures our growth
in education, economic well-being and improved health
conditions
for generations to come.

Our vision for:

Economic Development
To enhance self-reliance, we bring together the resources and talents of our community to create jobs and economic opportunities.

Culture
Our culture is based on living the values of *'ohana, aloha, laulima, lōkahi* and *mālama*. We are bound by our pride and respect for the cultural legacy of our kuāpuna.

Education
The wisdom and guidance of our *kūpuna* serve as the pathway toward academic and social achievement.

'Ohana
Our families thrive as members share the values of *aloha, kōkua* and *kuleana*. Our *'ohana* will preserve and nurture the spirituality of this community.

Environment
Our wise use of the 'aina will strengthen our community. Pride of home and respect for our people are nurtured by those who pass on the history of this land.

None of the six students or two faculty members from the university was of Native Hawaiian ancestry. About half the group was born in Hawai'i or lived there for ten years or longer and had become involved in Native Hawaiian culture, politics, or family life. I was among those with the least background in Hawaiian history, culture, and contemporary issues as a relative newcomer to the state. My own epistemic lens was shaped growing up in Los Angeles as a third-generation Japanese American woman. My limited familiarity with Hawai'i was through friends whose families were from there and from the short two years during which I had lived there prior to this planning project.

It would be naive to think that one could know the world from someone else's shoes. Nor is it realistic to think that one could become conversant in an unlimited number of cultural paradigms. It is not unrealistic, however, to create the foundation for social learning that emphasizes multiple epistemologies within planning processes. We can facilitate explicit discourse in a way that Iris Young (1995: 142) argues can lead to enriched democratic discussion "if we regard differences of social position and identity perspective as a resource for public reason, rather than as divisions that public reason transcends." She suggests three ways that planning can bolster communicative democracy: (1) by making participants understand their experiences as perspectival and partial, (2) by moving discourse from claims of self-interest to appeals to justice, and (3) by enhancing the social knowledge of participants in the course of expressing, questioning, and challenging differently situated knowledge. The following discussion is aimed at deepening our understanding of how planners can understand and facilitate discourse among differently positioned lenses.

Traversing interpretive frames embedded in culture, history, and collective memory

Planners tread delicately on the social and cultural maps of the community that residents construct individually and collectively in their minds. When a planner enters a community, he or she enters into a cultural setting at a particular historic moment. Culture, history, and collective memory shape the interpretive frames through which meaning is made. Cultural norms, values, and ways of knowing form the basis of judgment and shape the quality of interaction along with history as lived or remembered. One's mental map and historical lens are shaped by unique personal experiences as well as factors associated with group membership such as age, ethnicity, race, gender, religion, participation in social networks, and roles played in a society (Geertz 1973; Mach 1993). Communities may vary in the extent to which all its members share a particular reading of history, since different versions of a community's history often coexist. In any case, planners are confronted with the challenge of interacting and facilitating interaction among individuals who may see the world from distinct interpretive lenses – worldviews embedded in the culture, history, and memories of a community.

Interpretive frames become apparent during the course of interaction between a planner and members of a community, but often first arise as problematic in the early stages when a planner enters a community. In multicultural cities, planners often work in communities in which the ethnic or racial background of residents is different from their own. The stronger the racial or ethnic identification within a geographic community, the more likely residents share a collective memory that is marked by the relevance of race or ethnicity and the more likely that the racial or ethnic background of a planner may be a factor in initial inter-actions. This may influence how a planner is viewed and the attributions made as to a planner's motives or intentions. Actions and gestures are interpreted from a lens colored by history. For communities that have faced oppressive or discrimina-tory treatment and feel they have done so due to their racial or ethnic identi-fication, the memory of past experiences with outside institutions is often saddled with ambivalence toward those whom they identify with the dominating group. In the United States, this tension is most often found, at least initially, when white planners enter nonwhite communities. With the multicultural face of contemporary urban conflicts, these tensions often also exist between nonwhite groups as well.

As a Hawaiian homestead community, the people of Papakōlea feel a strong pride in Hawaiian identity and view themselves as a distinctively Native Hawaiian community. This identity in being Native Hawaiian is defined in the backdrop of a cultural renaissance and the maturation of the movement for Hawaiian sovereignty. Many important figures, including musicians and cultural artists, have emerged from Papakōlea. As the only homestead in an urban area, Papakōlea is somewhat distinct from other homesteads in the occupational and economic background of its residents. Similar to other Hawaiian communities, Papakōlea faces a high rate of unemployment, health problems, overcrowding, and other socioeconomic problems relative to other ethnic groups. At the same time, those who live there are very aware of the fact that its location in urban Honolulu also offers greater access to social services, jobs, transportation, educational institutions, and other amenities that enhance their well-being.

Despite differences with other Hawaiian communities and among Papakōlea residents themselves, there is a strong and pervasive feeling that the mere fact of being Hawaiian bears a great influence on their lives. As a Hawaiian homestead community, there is a blood quantum requirement to gain rights to the land.[9] But even more significant is the knowledge of the history of colonialism and the residual patterns of social prejudice, inequality, and economic and political marginalization. On one hand, there is awareness that their Hawaiian homestead status may distinguish them in the eyes of outsiders in a problematic way, yet they understand the cultural wealth of the community from which they have drawn strength and support.

This history and collective memory of the past frames how actions and events in the present are viewed. Part of the living history in Papakōlea is the memory of university staff examining Native Hawaiians as objects of research, which was never seen by residents to produce anything of benefit to those under study. The feeling that "we've been studied to death" is partly a result of the proximity of the homestead to the primary research university in the state and the fact that it is the only homestead located in urban Honolulu where the vast majority of state and local agencies are headquartered. Collaborations were often weighted in favor of outside partners. Social researchers often focused on the problems in the community, with little attention to its beauty and richness. Many residents felt labeled by university experts as a problem population, leading to further disenfranchisement. When we from the university entered the community, we entered the memory of this past and the feelings of resentment toward those affiliated with the institution. The racial and ethnic composition of our team (a mixed group but none of Native Hawaiian ancestry) also colored initial interactions due to reasons both historical and cultural.

While it may not be possible to overcome historical barriers, there are steps that planners can take to better prepare themselves to work in and with communities with strong cultural identities. Study of the history of a community from the viewpoint of those who live there as well as from other sources is an important step in culture-based planning. Planners can gain a better understanding of how present activities may be interpreted and given meaning based on past practices. It was important for us, especially before diving into the project, to learn about the history of Papakōlea and its living memories. This learning took place through reading, videotapes, and "talking story" with residents, community leaders, and others knowledgeable about the community. It helped us identify issues that needed to be clarified, like the purpose and process of visioning and the nature of the partnership between the university and community. It was important to assure residents that the planning process was community-led and ownership of the project rested in the community association. And it was important for residents to receive the product of the visioning project that took the form of a booklet containing a summary of the process and results of the visioning activities. Not only was it important to understand the past as conveyed from the standpoint of residents, but it was important that those with whom we worked understood that the university team valued that history and their worldview.

Confronting otherness and the articulation of cultural values and social identities

Planning can be an intimidating process, bound up with an institutional history that has not always welcomed community participation in a serious way. For many segregated communities of color, racial prejudice and marginalization from these processes have given planning a bad name (Sandercock 1998a; Woods 1998). For proprietors and residents whose communities were bulldozed by midcentury urban redevelopment programs, planning was often viewed as a tool of the rich and powerful. For these and other reasons, planners may confront unwilling communities more often than expected when soliciting participation (Forester 1999; Kaufman and Alfonso 1997). On top of this more basic challenge, culture-based planning, at least in theory, invites individuals to express culturally distinct viewpoints, values, and visions.

Given a checkered history with planning and subsequent perceptions of planning as a mainstream activity, planners may find residents less than forthcoming about their views and opinions, especially those that residents see as specific to their cultural group. But if the expression of cultural values and social identities are to be an accepted practice in planning, planners face the task of facilitating planning processes that allow for that expression. This challenge is twofold, involving (1) trust between the planner and a constituent public that enables value articulation within planning processes, and (2) the design and utilization of culturally appropriate planning methods and techniques.

Revealing one's values, including those that are culturally specific, can be a socially sensitive process for any participant. Not every cultural group, personality type, or state of mind finds it easy to articulate its values. Nor is everyone willing to reveal them publicly. Trust that what one may share will not be ridiculed or used against them at some future time is a necessary condition for the articulation of cultural values in planning. Many immigrant and colonized groups in the United States have experienced the denigration or exploitation of their language and cultural practices, either in the form of social marginalization or policy mandate. Examples can be found in cases in which native language use or religious practices were forbidden or discouraged as well as in cases in which cultural knowledge was exploited for others' profit. Collective memories of these experiences can temper a community's willingness to engage in meaningful and intimate dialogue. Building trust between a planner and a constituent along with trust between participants is oftentimes not a well-defined step in the planning process. However, the establishment of trust and a safe environment can make or break a culture-based planning process.

Trust is a critical component of the creation of a safe environment for the articulation of cultural values. Also critical is the invitation to express those values and beliefs that may be considered culturally unique or specific to a group.

Especially if the facilitating planner is not fluent in the language, belief systems, or norms of a group, participants may not refer to words or symbols that are culturally specific. The same is often the case in the presence of other cultural groups, whether out of politeness to others or protection of information. The more that residents may feel alienated from institutions of governance, the greater that planners associated with those institutions can be viewed as disempowering and potentially insensitive, regardless of the intentions of that particular planner. This otherness is reinforced if there is a lack of other common associations or identity boundaries that the planner may share with those in a given community. Through verbal and nonverbal gestures, planners can set a tone or atmosphere that can encourage or discourage such sharing. When planners appropriately make culturally explicit references as part of facilitative dialogue, for example, planners can convey a sense that cultural expression is welcomed and valued.

Culturally appropriate planning processes and techniques can also facilitate the expression of identity and cultural values. This includes participatory formats that are compatible with methods of expression from concerned epistemological positions. For example, there are many cultures within which storytelling is a commonly used method of passing on knowledge or sharing an understanding of self or a place and time. This is particularly true for those who share a strong oral tradition. Official hearings that give residents five minutes at the microphone to share their input are the least effective for these purposes for obvious reasons. Instead, as is said in Hawai'i, "talk story" (sharing stories in the oral tradition) may be a more natural or comfortable mode of expression. In the Hawaiian language, there is the word *mana'o*, which can be explained as an inner thought given to others as a powerful gift of how one understands the truth. To ask someone to "give us your *mana'o*" can be a sign of respect that also curries the attention of all those present. In addition to oral forms of expression, opinions or thoughts may also be conveyed through *hula* or other forms of art (Blaich 1999). Woods (1998) eloquently described the important role of music and poetry in conveying blues epistemology and cultural identity in his chronicle of arrested development in the Mississippi Delta. What planners can often find in artistic traditions and rituals is a social critique of current conditions along with the values, dreams, and hopes of a people or community.

In the Papakōlea project, the steering committee selected visioning as a first step in its community planning process. The technique of visioning is highly amenable to the identification of values, norms, and cultural practices within a community. Rather than beginning a planning process with the identification of particular problems, assets, project ideas, or physical design concepts, visioning began by allowing a community members to step back and dream about their desired future in broad and sweeping terms. Talk story, drawing, letter writing, imaging games, and other interactive techniques were employed.

One of the products of these processes was a vision statement, an articulation of the values and identity of a community. From the visioning process, one general statement and five area-specific statements emerged along with many ideas for concrete projects and programs. The first part of the general vision statement read as follows (see Table 8.1 for the full text):

> Our home is Papakōlea,
> a community where the spirit of *lōkahi* and *aloha*
> inspires self-reliance and participation
> to share knowledge of our culture
> and respect for *'ohana*.

As a process codesigned by steering committee members who were residents themselves, visioning exercises allowed participants to express their values and sense of self-identity in explicit terms. The language of the vision statement reveals a set of values that places importance on working together, love for one another, Hawaiian culture, and the family. The use of such commonly used Hawaiian words captures a sensibility that cannot be precisely translated into English terms, but their meaning is widely understood among young and old.[10]

While Papakōlea is somewhat unique as a homestead community legislated specifically for Native Hawaiians, it is possible to design culturally appropriate methods in other types of communities (many communities may identify them-selves as being a multicultural community while recognizing the unique identities of each ethnic or racial group within it). Certainly, there are additional challenges in culture-based planning in heterogenous communities. Baum (1994), for example, warned of cases where minority groups may acquiesce to a more dominant group through the course of deliberations. This underscores the role that planners can play in tailoring processes according to culturally appropriate means of expression and creating a respectful and equitable forum for deliberations (Sandercock 1998b; Forester 1999). Instead of trying to develop universal, value-free methods and practices, designing processes for many modes of expression may allow us to capture a wider diversity of voices.

Understanding the multiple meanings of language

Language carries with it the power to discourage or encourage, repress or release, legitimize or degrade. How planners phrase what they say, how they choose their words, and how they convey their message can affect the extent to which a constituency of people participate in or withdraw from a planning process. Epistemology, as a lens for interpretation, mediates how messages are relayed and how they are received. Simple language may travel through complex interpretive frames through which meaning is given as well as read (Hall 1980). Not only do problems of interpretation arise in translating between different languages, but meaning can also be distorted or misread among speakers of the same language. Here, for heuristic purposes, I will address the less obvious problem of interpretation and social meaning among common language speakers.

Words acquire meaning through lived experience as well as in the passing on of cultural practices from one generation to the next. Words in the English language can acquire meaning unique to a particular group. The use of words in the planning process can occasionally trigger an unintended reaction based on differences in the meaning that select words evoke. In the case of ethnic communities where history and culture may lend unique meaning to words, planners are confronted with the task of clarifying the meaning of words or symbols to ensure that participants and potential participants in the planning process share the same understanding.

This was one of the first challenges we encountered in the visioning process in Papakōlea. Among many of the elders, the term visioning had an almost sacred meaning. We learned after some confusion that visioning is a term that many of the *kūpuna* or elder generation use to refer to a highly personal and private practice. It usually takes place while in a dream state and is also a form of communication with deified ancestors or *'aumakua*. The term *hihi'o* refers to a dream or vision and *hō'ike* refers to seeing, knowing, and understanding (Pukui *et al.* 1979). It is sometimes practiced in search of an answer to some question or dilemma. It is done under special circumstances and for situations of sufficient import as to warrant such sacred practices. When it was announced that university students would facilitate a visioning project in Papakōlea, a number of the *kūpuna* called the president of the Papakōlea Community Association to voice their objection. What business would university students have conducting visioning in Papakōlea? It was only after the different meanings of visioning were clarified that the *kūpuna* gave their consent and university partners were educated about this use of the term.

What was not but what should have been done in this case was to change the name of the project to something other than visioning so as to avoid the possible altering of the traditional meaning of the word, especially one with reference to sacred cultural practices. Hindsight tends to be clearer than the view at that moment. Rather than looking at the problem as a misunderstanding that simply needed clarification, we should have caught the fact that the problem was a manifestation of cultural difference in the use of language. Problematized in this way, the choice to change the name of the planning process would have been much more obvious. To keep the term visioning (as we did), we privileged the mainland use of the word over the Hawaiian usage. While this is a clear call, there are other cases where there may be reason to continue use of a word to clarify its meaning. For example, collaboration may be one such word. Collaboration can be interpreted in several ways, one with very positive connotation in reference to working together in mutual support on equal terms toward common goals. But it can also connote working in partnership with an enemy force to sabotage another. Given the pervasive use of collaboration in the world of community building and nonprofit organizations, it may make more sense to use the word and clarify its meaning as is situationally appropriate so that a shared understanding is developed over time.

Heskin (1991) also noted a similar problem in his case study of a multiracial tenant organizing drive in Los Angeles that began in the 1970s. Misunderstandings between Latino-speaking and English-speaking residents grew out of the poor quality of language translation at meetings. The less-than-professional skills of selected translators (among other problems) led to distrust and suspicion along racial cleavages. Heskin refers to Molina (1978) in noting the absence of "natural cross-links" among the residential population. Natural cross-links, or what I discuss later as cultural translators, play an important role not only in translating from one language to another but also in reaching mutual understanding in interpretation across cultural paradigms.

While it is impossible to know where language discrepancies may lie, it is important to know that they exist. Being watchful of possible discrepancies helps us in navigating the minefields of discourse. It is certainly an important aspect of a developing sensibility about epistemological multiplicity. A sensibility alerts us to potential language or interpretive dissonance. It helps us know what to listen for. It helps us pay attention to innuendo and connotation that can be found in narrative, tone, or silence. And it helps us to understand the potential sources and the nature of conflicts that result from these differences.

Respecting and navigating cultural protocols and social relationships

Cultural protocols are also embedded in epistemology. Protocols are situationally defined codes of etiquette that can take on greater relevance in more formal meetings or gatherings. Broadly speaking, they cover a range of behaviors, such as the way one addresses another, deference to an understood social hierarchy, symbolic offerings, attendance or nonattendance at sacred or social events, norms of exchange and reciprocity, and even the manner in which discussions are facilitated. Protocols reflect how a group understands what can be known and by whom, who has the right to legitimize knowledge, and who has voice or standing to make knowledge claims. Planners representing formal institutions are trained in the science of modernity. Truth and knowledge are scientific discoveries with legally defined proprietary rights. Political contests have determined the processes by which knowledge claims are suppressed or voiced. Officially practiced procedures for planning may not be compatible with those protocols followed within a culturally defined community. Planners who enter a community without knowledge of practiced protocols can do or say things (intentionally or not) to silence or alienate participation among affected groups of people. Conversely, the demonstration of appropriate protocols can greatly enhance participation.

One of the dilemmas for planners in confronting cultural protocols is an ethical and moral one. One can make the case that protocols confer power and often reinforce age-old social hierarchies. Historically practiced protocols may go against contemporary understandings of equality and freedom of speech. Frequently, there are divisions within communities based on political differences, personal histories, or conflicts of interest. Recognized protocols can reinforce divisions or uphold the status quo. There can even be disagreements between factions as to the proper protocol at any given point in time. And it is not uncommon for women to have less standing according to traditional practices (Rahder 1999; Slocum *et al.* 1995). For planners working in the advocacy or empowerment traditions, following existing protocol may seem counterproductive to the promotion of a communicative democracy.

In Papakōlea, there were no major factions to speak of and, in fact, most of the board members of the two community organizations were women. The social hierarchy that did exist did not have negative bearing on attempts to organize resident participation in the planning process. The organizational leaders had a great deal of respect among the residents there. It was clear, in this case, that to follow protocol would only enhance participation. At the same time, protocols were not always clear, nor were there set expectations that we from the university should follow them, given the fact that we were not of Native Hawaiian ancestry. Notwithstanding, there were basic protocols that the steering committee did adhere to.

The clearest example of the importance of protocol was the need to get the blessing from the *kūpuna*, or the elders in the community. Gaining the permission of the *kūpuna*, especially those who had played leadership roles in the community's past, was essential to launching the planning process. Cultural protocols (e.g. paying homage to a generational hierarchy) exist in many communities, though they may differ in specific norms and practices. In Hawaiian communities and in many communities today – such as Papakōlea, where traditional values are very much alive – there remains a great deal of respect for the elders and respect for a certain amount of hierarchical structure based on age, generation, and experience. Hawaiian words are commonly used to refer to various age groups, from the *kūpuna* down to the *'ōpio* (teens) and *keiki* (younger children). The steering committee led by residents was careful to make sure that the visioning process gained participation from all age groups, starting with the *kūpuna*.

A planning process to chart the road ahead necessarily sought the wisdom of the *kūpuna* about the past and the dreams and desires of the youth who will live the distant future. While there was deference to the elders, the input of each age group was accorded equal respect, as value placed on generational groups was based on a consciousness about the continuity between the past and the future. Visioning exercises were consequently tailored to each age group. For example, among the exercises conducted, the *kūpuna* were asked to compile a timeline of significant events in the history of Papakōlea and map the sites of historic events, landmarks, significant places, and sacred sites. Exercises designed for teens, in contrast, focused on what they envisioned for their future and what they would like to change within their surroundings. After all the groups had documented their input, a *pā'ina* or meal gathering to share ideas among participants was held. Other protocols were abided, including the offering of pule (blessing or prayer) at the start and finish of meetings and events.

But planners often find themselves in fragmented communities where cultural protocols can represent barriers to mass participation. In some of these instances, leaders or gatekeepers might see benefits in more democratic participation and support an inclusive process. When interests or ideology stand against broad participation, however, planners face a difficult ethical dilemma. Depending on the role the planner sees himself or herself playing in view of the various traditions of planning (Friedmann 1987; Forester 1989), one may choose to respect cultural protocols or, in other instances, challenge them. In either case, a reflective planner can make thoughtful decisions, but only by understanding the social structures and cultural norms within a community. This understanding enables planners to proceed with fuller knowledge of the implications of their actions. Would, for example, a particular approach to a planning process destabilize traditional hierarchical relationships? Moreover, planning efforts that do not acknowledge existing protocols can undermine them inadvertently, resulting in unintended consequences. One of the most difficult but important challenges that face advocacy planners is to determine whether challenging cultural protocols would result in an increase in quality of life from the eyes of those directly concerned. The discussion on ethics goes beyond the scope of this article, but is critical to any deliberation and underscores the need to traverse cultural paradigms to make grounded ethical decisions.

Understanding the role of power in cultural translation

In communities with strong cultural identities and distinct cultural protocols and practices, planners often seek the aid of cultural interpreters (if they do not serve this role themselves). They are people who are culturally rooted in a traditional community and who are equally versed in the language of modernity.

They often serve as bridges and help to identify differences in interpretation and facilitate cross-cultural communication. Oftentimes, cultural translators represent the sector of a community who are well-educated in mainstream professional institutions, yet who maintain connections to community organizations, social networks, and cultural practices (Heskin 1991).

In translating across epistemological frames, opportunities to exercise power are expanded within culture-based planning processes. This may take place in two major ways: (1) by elevating the influence or standing of cultural translators, and (2) by legitimizing multiple epistemologies and acknowledging cultural claims. Moral and ethical issues arise in each of these cases. Who should be given standing? Whose cultural interpretation is legitimate? Whose epistemological frame should we make judgment by? What aspects of culture are compromised in translation? How does the necessity for translation affect the construction of culture itself? Reflective practitioners involved in culture-based planning face these questions and more.

The influence of cultural translators relative to other participants in a planning process is elevated in the act of selecting an individual or group of individuals to play such a role. Especially in state-initiated planning processes, cultural translators can insert their biases in various ways. As intermediaries, they gain greater standing by being given recognition and official roles by planners or government agencies. This can amplify their voice in discussion throughout the planning process and potentially contribute to the types of distortions in discourse that Forester (1989) and others have warned us of. They can help to frame issues in the selection of analogies and references used to explain problems or ideas. Depending on who might serve as the cultural interpreter, their service may privilege those factions within a community with whom they have better relations. This can skew participation in favor of some social networks over others. The introduction of cultural translators also comes with the risk of formalizing cultural beliefs that may, in fact, be contested within that cultural community. Cultural translators may explain cultural practices based on their own beliefs without reference to other alternative interpretations that may coexist. They may also have their own class or other interests at stake and can abuse their standing to support cultural claims in protection of those interests.

On the other hand, cultural translators can play a key role in facilitating discourse across worldviews. In the case of immigrant communities, bilingual or multilingual translators can provide language translation. Aside from this, they can identify historical episodes that planners should be familiar with, given the nature of a specific planning project. They can provide a map of the social networks in a community and the historic and current relationship between those networks and organizations. They can advise planners as to cultural protocols, communication styles, and cultural symbols so that planners can effectively approach a community and design appropriate participatory processes. Cultural translators can also open doors that may otherwise be difficult to gain entry to. Often, translators can vouch for the integrity of a planner to a larger group, if they are so inclined, smoothing the way for discussion and relationship building. They can also alert planners when questions about the planner or the process may arise within a community but may not be directly communicated to the planners by participants themselves. Rumor and misunderstanding can often be avoided or minimized when there are cultural translators committed to the planning process and to open communication between planners and participants.

The challenge is to realize the benefits that cultural translators can bring while minimizing the potential pitfalls that may accompany them. In the most ideal scenario, democratically elected representatives committed to inclusiveness from those communities can play this role so that there is no need for planners to make a selection from the outside (Medoff and Sklar 1994). Community leadership that is inclusive and committed to the overall well-being of a neighborhood or jurisdiction is vital to culture-based planning processes (or any planning process, for that matter). When these individuals can translate across cultural and epistemic divides while avoiding additional distortions they can effect on the process, the benefits of culture-based planning can be maximized. Planners normally work under less ideal circumstances, however. While there is no blueprint for identifying or working with cultural translators, it is helpful to be aware of the potential problems that may be involved.

In the case of Papakōlea, community leaders and organizers played a central role in all aspects of the project and worked very closely with students and faculty throughout the visioning process. This ensured that the process and the end product (including the specific wording of the vision statements) were overall reflective of the cultural norms, beliefs, and practices of their community. The active role of residents, however, did not make translation an easy task. There were difficulties despite these favorable conditions. One the major difficulties the steering committee experienced was explaining the purpose of the visioning project to the community. The fact that planning in Hawaiian Homelands was historically conducted by the jurisdictional agency, the Department of Hawaiian Homelands (DHHL), and planning in more traditional Hawaiian communities was conducted on a more incremental basis meant that the visioning project was not easily understood. References to Papakōlea's history and stories about previous community-initiated projects were most effective in explaining the purpose and process; cultural translators (in this case, residents) had this knowledge and were able to find reference points and analogies that the community as a whole could more readily understand. A second difficulty was the understanding of time. This had more to do with the culture of the university as an academic institution than to Papakolea. Many communities do not share the same understanding of time as those in the university who are ruled by the deadlines of semester and quarter systems. While I am employing a broadened use of the term culture here, it is nonetheless important to point out that there are different measures and meanings of time and that these differences often warrant a more detailed clarification of expectations, commitments, and timelines. Especially when there are unequal resources (whether real or perceived) among participants, the timeline of the more dominant institution can easily prevail and impose unnecessary hardship on communities, as was initially the case in this ongoing university-grassroots partnership.[11]

Code-switching and community-led planning

How can we begin to tackle these challenges? The epistemological challenge of planning in culturally diverse cities involves designing methods and developing sensibilities to identify multiple epistemologies and facilitate the articulation of dreams and desires from diverse worldviews. There are at least two approaches we can consider. One option is to find planners who can code-switch. Code-switching in language studies refers to the process that multiple language speakers undergo when moving from one language to another. Code-switching indicates a change in a set of codes and symbols that are themselves part of a cultural paradigm (Auer 1998). When one code-switches, one alters one's interpretive as well as vernacular framework in communication with others who share the same language and cultural sensibilities. There are an increasing number of people who have grown up in two or more cultural environments, such as children of immigrants who experience one cultural environment at home and another at school or those who have lived in different countries. This ability to code-switch, however, is difficult to teach in planning schools.

Certainly, the adoption of certain policies sensitive to issues of multiculturalism calls for this ability of planners to code-switch. In Hawai'i, for example, the Environmental Council of the State of Hawai'i adopted guidelines in 1997 for assessing cultural impacts as part of environmental assessment processes. Cultural impact assessments include information relating to the practices and beliefs of a particular cultural or ethnic group that may be affected by a proposed project. Guidelines encourage assessors to include "traditional cultural properties or other types of historic sites, both man made and natural, including submerged cultural resources, which support such cultural practices and beliefs" (Environmental Council 1997: 2). This necessitates the solicitation of cultural knowledge by planners who can translate across epistemic frameworks, drawing from a wide range of sources – from court records to Hawaiian genealogical chants and legends. Planners engaging in this type of work constantly translate from one cultural paradigm to another in making their assessments. They often find themselves immersed in non-Western epistemology to gain an adequate understanding of cultural impacts and are then asked to communicate these understandings in a Western language and format. This ability to code-switch is a specialized skill and is difficult to teach in planning schools.

Another alternative to code-switching in community planning may be the practice of community-led planning (Hamdi and Goethert 1997; Slocum *et al.* 1995). Planners actively engage in community-based planning, that is, facilitating participatory planning at the community or neighborhood level. But too seldom do we consider community-led planning as a practice in multiculturalism. Community-led planning involves community members in the design and facilitation of community-based planning processes in the tradition of empowerment planning (see Friedmann 1992; Hamdi and Goethert 1997; Krumholz and Forester 1990; Rocha 1997). While this may not be possible or ideal in all situations, I argue that planners would do well to consider this approach when working in culturally defined or multicultural communities. It is rare for a planning agency to have a staff that is culturally representative of the population it serves. More often than not, community planners are working with communities in which there are cultural groups with whom they are not intimately familiar. One alternative to planners facilitating planning processes (with or without the help of cultural translators) is to seek out willing residents who can work with the different constituencies within a community. Together, planners and residents can co-design processes that are culturally appropriate and value cultural differences. This furthers the goal of social learning and capacity building in the spirit of deliberative practice (Forester 1999; Young 1990). Designing and facilitating a planning process can also help develop skills and abilities that may carry into subsequent implementation stages of planning and development.

Community-led planning processes make it easier to overcome otherness by shifting the locus of power (at least at that micro-level) to members of those communities. Community-led planning has a capability of mobilizing members by tapping the power of the "we" voice that does not resonate in the otherness of the "you" voice. This power can elicit meaningful thoughts and feelings from groups who are sensitive to the language of marginalization and can be transformative in a way that an imposed process can never be. In addition, there is arguably one less type of distortion in communication since much more of the discourse takes place among those who share the same epistemology. And in community-led planning, as in the case of Papakōlea, there is no need to select cultural interpreters on the part of planning institutions. Interpreters can arise from within a community-led process. Shifts in power relations that result are less a result of outside intervention and more the result of an internal process, thus limiting the power of distortion that planners might exert.

There are countless examples of community-led planning projects nationally. Perhaps one of the best known of the many projects in the United States is the Dudley Street Neighborhood Initiative (DSNI). DSNI has been studied as a model of "multiracial, mutual progress and holistic community development" involving a diverse community of Latino, African-American, and European-American residents (Medoff and Sklar 1994). This is one example in a long legacy of campaigns and movements for community empowerment. While many of the current efforts can trace their roots to the social movements of the 1960s, this tradition predates the founding of the United States as a nation-state. Jojola (1998) reminds us that Native Americans have maintained a tradition of self-governance and tribal planning as demonstrated by the founding of the All-Indian Pueblo Council, an alliance of tribal groups in the American Southwest that continues to the present.

Many of these examples of community-led planning are historically tied with empowerment planning and insurgent planning, usually in opposition to prevailing planning practices. However, the growing acceptance of community planning and multiculturalism in professional practice and public policy opens new opportunities for community-led approaches that facilitate dialogue across divergent epistemologies. In Canada, Qadeer (1997) notes that the diverse cultures of ethnic communities are beginning to be acknowledged and aired as part of the planning process. Opportunities for culture-based, community-led planning are also present throughout the United States. For instance, numerous local government agencies have initiated visioning, benchmarking, and local planning projects, often handing the initiative over to citizens groups within diverse ethnic communities. Also, many ethnic enclaves are initiating their own planning processes while distinguishing their distinct cultural heritage. In 1999 in Los Angeles, for example, the Thai Community Development Corporation, along with other residents, community organizations, and businesses, secured the designation of Thai Town for a six-block section of the city following a community-led planning process.

There are also specific pieces of legislation that require the participation of cultural experts or those who are literate in a specific cultural paradigm. In Hawai'i, for example, a 1990 set of revisions (Act 306) to the Hawai'i Revised Statutes (chap. 6E) provided increased protection for Native Hawaiian burial and reburial sites in the state of Hawai'i. It also established island burial councils under the administration of the Department of Land and Natural Resources, State Historic Preservation Department. These burial councils are composed of mainly Native Hawaiians, along with representatives of landowners and developers who make decisions regarding the preservation or relocation of Native Hawaiian burial sites. Historically, many of these decisions were reliant on the sole expertise of Western-trained anthropologists. Through the work of various Native Hawaiian organizations, there is a growing recognition of the legitimacy of "native ways of knowing" in documenting the history, significance, and meaning of various wahi pana or legendary sites (Freitas 1999).

Training planners to code-switch and engaging in community-led planning process are two strategies for accommodating multiple epistemologies in planning processes. However, these two strategies do not guarantee that the challenges discussed will not arise at a later point of interface between other cultural groups or between historically marginalized groups and established agencies. The recognition of Los Angeles's Thai Town, for instance, created unintended but unresolved tensions with non-Thai residents and business owners within the designated area. Healey (1999) articulates the challenges of multiple and contested claims as they shape and are shaped by changing institutional relations. Within the context of this larger problem, however, code-switching capabilities and community-led processes allow for the temporal, physical, and discursive space to articulate oneself on one's own terms. Hopefully, this provides an opportunity for the type and depth of participation that may not be possible under existing institutional practice. How to transform institutions so that they better accommodate discourse among multiple epistemologies is yet to be fully explored. For now, it is my hope that the discussion of these challenges in participatory planning can lead to more thoughtful planning practice on these day-to-day matters of culture.

Acknowledgements

I would like to thank the steering committee of the Papakōlea visioning project and reviewers for their support and helpful comments.

Notes

1 This phrase is drawn from Leonie Sandercock's (1998b) book chapter of the same title.

2 If we accept that culture is a constructed and dynamic concept, the declaration of claims is at once political and transformative. It is political in the sense that the definition of cultural claims results in tangible wins and losses within the existing polity. And it is transformative in that embedded in the laws and rules that govern institutions are incentives and disincentives that often shape the definition of culture. Depending on how cultural concepts are defined, some may be made better off and others worse off from their respective standpoints. Disagreements about these definitions can arise, often creating much division within cultural groups who may have different viewpoints or who may be affected differently based on how cultural concepts are defined. The formulation

of culture-based rights creates a new set of alliances and divisions that transform power relations within and between culturally defined groups.

3   Feminist and ethnic studies scholars have contributed greatly to our theoretical understanding of the epistemological chasms in our society. Feminists have used the phrase "women's ways of knowing" (Belenky *et al.* 1986) to distinguish women's epistemologies from those of men. Multiple identity boundaries – race, ethnicity, gender, religion, nativity, language, sexual preference, occupation, or other identity markers – are embraced as well as ascribed, and vary in salience across situations and circumstances (Pratt 1998). The convergence of these and other boundaries designate possible subject positions from which groups view reality. Race, ethnicity, gender, and class remain among the most salient boundaries of identity as well as designators of difference in US society.

4   Though Native Hawaiians can trace their migration to other islands in Polynesia (mainly Tahiti), ethnic identity as Hawaiians was the more salient identity in the contemporary period during which the visioning project took place. Hawai'i was an independent monarchy before the conquest by Europeans in the late 1800s and was under US territorial rule until 1950, when it became the fiftieth state admitted to the United States.

5   As stated in Article 1A., Purpose.

6   US Public Law 103–150 was passed on 23 November 1993 by the 103rd Congress Joint Resolution 19 "to acknowledge the 100th anniversary of the January 17, 1893 overthrow of the Kingdom of Hawai'i, and to offer an apology to Native Hawaiians on behalf of the United States for the overthrow of the Kingdom of Hawai'i."

7   "Talk story" in this context refers to informal as well as formal discussions or conversations by which stories are shared in the oral tradition to pass on knowledge and history.

8   Visioning is a process utilized by community planners and corporate strategists alike and is often the first step in a fuller strategic planning process. It is a process whereby participants are encouraged to freely dream about the future without regard to any practical constraints. Facilitators construct exercises that allow one to envision what the future can be – both desirable and undesirable. Participants identify shared values and articulate them in the form of vision statements.

9   According to the original Hawaiian Homes Commission Act (Act of 9 July 1921, c. 42, 42 Stat. 108), Native Hawaiian means "any descendant of not less than one-half part of the blood of the races inhabiting the Hawaiian Islands previous to 1778."

10 According to the Hawaiian-English dictionary (Pukui and Elbert 1986), *lōkahi* is defined as unity, to make peace and unity, or to be in agreement. *Aloha* has many meanings, including love, affection, compassion, mercy, pity, kindness,

and charity. There are also many kinds of *aloha*, such as *aloha'aina*, or love of the land or one's country. *'Ohana* refers to the family, relative, or kin group.

11 Fitting the visioning project into a semester timeline to accommodate faculty and students proved to be a curse and a blessing. The time schedule resulted in a fairly quick product that the community was able to use to pursue funding for identified projects, but the intensity of the work put a heavy strain on community leaders who had many other responsibilities at that time. In evaluating the visioning project, all partners agreed that conforming to the university semester schedule was a mistake and that the project would have been more successful if conducted during a two-semester period.

References

Anderson, M.B. (1996) *Development and Social Diversity: A Development in Practice Reader*, Oxford: Oxfam.

Auer, Peter (ed.) (1998) *Code-switching in Conversation: Language, Interaction and Identity*, New York: Routledge.

Barth, F. (1989) "The analysis of culture in complex societies," *Ethnos*, 54: 120–42.

Baum, H. (1994) "Community and consensus – Reality and fantasy in planning," *Journal of Planning Education and Research*, 13(4): 251–62.

Beall, J. (1996) "Urban governance: why gender matters," United Nations Development Programme (UNDP) Gender in Development Monograph Series No. 1.

—— (ed.) (1997) *A City for All: Valuing Difference and Working with Diversity*, London: Zed Books.

Belenky, M.F., Clinchy, B., Goldberger, N. and Tarule, J. (1986) *Women's Ways of Knowing: The Development of Self, Voice, and Mind*, New York: Basic Books.

Blaich, B. (1999) "Towards collective creativity: enfolding artsmaking into participatory planning practice." Area of concentration paper, Department of Urban and Regional Planning, University of Hawai'i at Manoa.

Boger, J.C. and Wegner, J. (eds) (1996) *Race, Poverty and American Cities*, Chapel Hill, NC: University of North Carolina Press.

Bullard, R.D. (2000) *Dumping in Dixie: Race, Class, and Environmental Quality*, 3rd edn, Boulder, CO: Westview.

Bullard, R., Eugene Grigsby III, J. and Lee, C. (1996) *Residential Apartheid: The American Legacy*, Los Angeles, CA: CAAS.

Catlin, R. (1993) *Racial Politics and Urban Planning: Gary, Indiana 1980–1989*, Lexington, KY: University Press of Kentucky.

Chang, E.T. and Leong, R.C. (eds) (1994) *Los Angeles – Struggles Toward Multiethnic Community: Asian American, African American and Latino Perspectives*, Seattle, WA: University of Washington Press.

Dear, M.J., Shockman, H.E. and Hise, G. (eds) (1996) *Rethinking Los Angeles*, Thousand Oaks, CA: Sage.

Douglass, C.M. and Friedmann, J. (1998) *Cities for Citizens: Planning and the Rise of Civil Society in a Global Age*, Chichester: John Wiley.

Edelstein, M.R., and Kleese, D.A. (1995) "Cultural relativity of impact assessment: Native Hawaiian opposition to geothermal energy development," *Society and Natural Resources*, 8: 19–31.

Environmental Council (1997) *Guidelines for Assessing Cultural Impacts*. Guidelines adopted by the Environmental Council, state of Hawai'i, 19 November.

Faber, D. (ed.) (1998) *The Struggle for Ecological Democracy: Environmental Justice Movements in the United States*, New York: Guilford.

Fincher, R. and Jacobs, J.M. (eds) (1998) *Cities of Difference*, New York: Guilford.

Forester, J. (1989) *Planning in the Face of Power*, Berkeley, CA: University of California Press.

—— (1998) "Rationality, dialogue and learning: what community and environmental mediators can teach us about the practice of civil society," in C.M. Douglass and J. Friedmann (eds) *Cities for Citizens: Planning and the Rise of Civil Society in a Global Age*, Chichester: John Wiley.

—— (1999) *The Deliberative Practitioner: Encouraging Participatory Planning Processes*, Boston, MA: MIT Press.

Forsyth, A. (1998) *Constructing Suburbs: Competing Voices in a Debate over Urban Growth*, London: Gordon & Breach.

Freitas, K. (1999) "Na wai e mālama i nāiwi: Who will care for the bones?" Student paper, Department of Urban and Regional Planning, University of Hawai'i at Manoa.

Friedman, J. (1994) *Cultural Identity and Global Process*, London: Sage.

Friedmann, J. (1987) *Planning in the Public Domain: From Knowledge to Action*, Princeton, NJ: Princeton University Press.

—— (1992) *Empowerment: The Politics of Alternative Development*, Cambridge, MA: Blackwell.

Geertz, C. (1973) *The Interpretative of Cultures: Selected Essays*, New York: Basic Books.

Gillette, H. Jr. (1995) *Between Justice and Beauty: Race, Planning, and the Failure of Urban Policy in Washington, DC*, Baltimore, MD: Johns Hopkins University Press.

Goldsmith, W.W. and Blakely, E.J. (1992) *Separate Societies: Poverty and Inequality in US Cities*, Philadelphia, PA: Temple University Press.

Goode, J. and Schneider, J. (1994) *Reshaping Ethnic and Racial Relations in Philadelphia: Immigrants in a Divided City*, Philadelphia, PA: Temple University Press.

Greed, C. (1994) *Women and Planning: Creating Gendered Realities*, London: Routledge.

Guyette, S. (1996) *Planning for Balanced Development*, Santa Fe, NM: Clear Light.

Hall, S. (1980) "Encoding/ecoding," in Centre for Contemporary Cultural Studies (ed.) *Culture, Media, Language: Working Papers in Cultural Studies, 1972–79*, London: Hutchinson.

Hamdi, N. and Goethert, R. (1997) *Action Planning for Cities: A Guide to Community Practice*, Chichester: John Wiley.

Harvey, D. (1989) *The Condition of Postmodernity*, Oxford: Blackwell.

Hayden, D. (1995) *The Power of Place: Urban Landscapes as Public History*, Cambridge, MA: MIT Press.

Healey, P. (1997) *Collaborative Planning*, London: Macmillan.

—— (1999) "Institutionalist analysis, communicative planning and shaping places," *Journal of Planning Education and Research*, 19: 111–21.

Healey, P. and Hillier, J. (1996) "Communicative micropolitics: a story of claims and discourses," *International Planning Studies*, 1(2): 165–84.

Heskin, A.D. (1991) *The Struggle for Community*, Boulder, CO: Westview.

Hettne, B. (1990) *Development Theory and the Three Worlds*, New York: John Wiley.

Hillier, J. (1998) "Beyond confused noise: ideas toward communicative procedural justice," *Journal of Planning Education and Research*, 18(1): 14–24.

Innes, J.E. and Booher, D.E. (1999) "Consensus building as role playing and bricolage – toward a theory of collaborative planning," *Journal of the American Planning Association*, 65(1): 9–26.

Jennings, J. (ed.) (1994) *Blacks, Latinos, and Asians in Urban America: Status and Prospects for Politics and Activism*, Westport, CT: Praeger.

Jojola, T.S. (1998) "Indigenous planning: clans, intertribal confederations, and the history of the All Indian Pueblo Council," in L. Sandercock (ed.) *Making the Invisible Visible: A Multicultural Planning History*, Berkeley, CA: University of California Press.

Kaufman, M. and Alfonso, H.D. (eds) (1997) *Community Power and Grassroots Democracy: The Transformation of Social Life*, London: Zed Books.

Keith, M. and Pile, S. (eds) (1993) *Place and the Politics of Identity*, London: Routledge.

Krumholz, N. and Forester, J. (1990) *Making Equity Planning Work*, Cambridge, MA: Blackwell.

Little, J. (1994) *Gender, Planning and the Policy Process*, Oxford: Pergamon.

Mach, Z. (1993) *Symbols, Conflict, and Identity*, Albany, NY: State University of New York Press.

Marchmand, M. and Parpart, J. (1995) *Feminism, Postmodernism, Development*, London: Routledge.

Massey, D. (1994) *Space, Place and Gender*, Cambridge: Polity.

Massey, D. and Denton, N. (1993) *American Apartheid: Segregation and the Making of the Underclass*, Cambridge, MA: Harvard University Press.

Medoff, P. and Sklar, H. (1994) *Streets of Hope: The Fall and Rise of an Urban Neighborhood*, Boston, MA: South End Press.

Mehmet, O. (1995) *Westernizing the Third World: The Eurocentricity of Economic Development Theories*, London: Routledge.

Minerbi, L. (1999) "Indigenous management models and protection of the Ahupuaa," *Social Processes in Hawai'i*, 39: 208–25.

Molina, J.M. (1978) "Cultural barriers and interethnic communications in a multi-ethnic neighborhood," in E. Lamar Rodd (ed.) *Interethnic Communication*, Athens, GA: University of Georgia Press.

Nicholson, L.J. (ed.) (1990) *Feminism/Postmodernism*, New York: Routledge.

Okin, S. (1994) "Gender inequality and cultural differences," *Political Theory*, 22 (February): 5–24.

Oliver, M.L. and Shapiro, T.M. (1995) *Black Wealth/White Wealth: A New Perspective on Racial Inequality*, New York: Routledge.

Ong, P. (1981) "An ethnic trade: the Chinese laundries in early California," *Journal of Ethnic Studies*, 8(4): 95–112.

Parpart, J. (1993) "Who is the 'other': a postmodern feminist critique of women and development theory and practice," *Development and Change*, 24: 439–64.

Peattie, L.R. (1987) *Planning, Rethinking Ciudad Guyana*, Ann Arbor, MI: University of Michigan Press.

Pratt, G. (1998) "Grids of difference: place and identity formation," in R. Fincher and J.M. Jacobs (eds) *Cities of Difference*, New York: Guilford.

Pukui, M.K., and Elbert, S.H. (1986) *Hawaiian Dictionary: Hawaiian–English, English–Hawaiian*, Honolulu, HI: University of Hawaii Press.

Pukui, M.K., Haertig, W.E. and Lee, C.A. (1979) *Nānā i ke kumu* [Look to the source], Vol. 2. Honolulu, HI: Hui Hanai.

Qadeer, M.A. (1997) "Pluralistic planning for multicultural cities – the Canadian practice," *Journal of the American Planning Association*, 63(4): 481–94.

Rahder, B.L. (1999) "Victims no longer: participatory planning with a diversity of women at risk of abuse," *Journal of Planning Education and Research*, 18(3): 221–32.

Rakodi, C. (1991) "Cities and people: towards a gender-aware urban planning process?" *Public Administration and Development*, 11: 541–59.

Rocha, E. (1997) "A ladder of empowerment," *Journal of Planning Education and Research*, 17: 31–44.

Saito, L. (1998) *Race and Politics: Asian Americans, Latinos and Whites in a Los Angeles Suburb*, Champaign, IL: University of Illinois Press.

Sandercock, L. (1998a) *Making the Invisible Visible: A Multicultural Planning History*, Berkeley, CA: University of California Press.

—— (1998b) *Towards Cosmopolis: Planning for Multicultural Cities*, Chichester: John Wiley.

Sandercock, L. and Forsyth, A. (1992) "Feminist theory and planning theory: the epistemological linkages," *Planning Theory*, 7/8: 45–49.

Silver, C. (1984) *Twentieth-century Richmond: Planning, Politics and Race*, Knoxville, TN: University of Tennessee Press.

Soja, E. (1989) *Postmodern Geographies*, London: Verso.

Slocum, R., Wichhart, L., Rocheleau, D. and Thomas-Slayter, B. (eds) (1995) *Power, Process and Participation: Tools for Change*, London: Intermediate Technology.

Thomas, J.M. (1997) *Redevelopment and Race: Planning a Finer City in Postwar Detroit*, Baltimore, MD: Johns Hopkins University Press.

Watson, S. and Gibson, K. (eds) (1995) *Postmodern Cities and Spaces*, Oxford: Blackwell.

Woods, C. (1998) *Development Arrested: The Blues and Plantation Power in the Mississippi Delta*, London: Verso.

Yiftachel, O. (1994) "The dark side of modernism: planning as control of an ethnic minority," in S. Watson and K. Gibson (eds) *Postmodern Cities and Spaces*, Oxford: Blackwell.

Young, I. (1990) "The ideal of community and the politics of difference," in L.J. Nicholson (ed.) *Feminism/Postmodernism*, New York: Routledge.

Young, I. (1995) "Communication and the other: beyond deliberative democracy," in M. Wilson and A. Yeatman (eds) *Justice and Identity*, Wellington: Allen & Unwin.

Chapter 9
Urban planning and intergroup conflict
Confronting a fractured public interest

Scott A. Bollens

Cities across the world are confronted by a growing ethnic and racial diversity
that challenges the traditional model of urban planning intervention focused
on individual, not group, differences. This article examines urban planning
in three ethnically polarized settings – Belfast, Jerusalem, and Johannesburg
– to ascertain how planners treat complex and emotional issues of ethnic
identity and group-based claims. Four models of planning intervention –
neutral, partisan, equity, and resolver – are examined through interviews
with over 100 planners and policy officials. The article outlines the significant
implications of these cases in terms of the limitations and potential contributions of American urban planning to effectively accommodate ethnic and
cultural differences.

> But you cannot show me – even supposing democracy is possible between
> victors and the people they have captured – what a democratic space looks
> like.
>   What effect can the mere shape of a wall, the curve of a street, lights
> and plants, have in weakening the grip of power or shaping the desire for
> justice?
>
>   Anwar Nusseibeh, quoted in Sennett (1999: 274)

This article examines planners' roles and responsibilities in addressing issues of
race and ethnicity and explores how planners think and act when working in
ethnically or racially polarized societies. It is based on interviews with over 100
urban planners and policy officials in the politically contested cities of Belfast,
Jerusalem, and Johannesburg.

Selected as the Best Paper of the *Journal of the American Planning Association*, Volume 68;
submitted by the Association of Collegiate Schools of Planning.

In one sense, these cities are extreme in the magnitude and durability of their conflicts. A deep, intractable type of urban conflict – urban "polarization" – occurs in these cases where ethnic and nationalist claims overshadow distributional questions at the municipal level (Benvenisti 1986; Boal and Douglas 1982). In US cities, there is a belief maintained by all groups that the existing system of governance is capable of producing fair outcomes, assuming political representation of minority interests. Coalition building that can defuse and moderate intergroup conflict remains possible across ethnic groups (Nordlinger 1972). In contrast, governance in polarized cities is perceived by at least one ethnic community as either illegitimate or structurally incapable of producing fair societal outcomes to subordinated ethnic groups (Douglas and Boal 1982; Romann and Weingrod 1991). Compared to cities in liberal democracies where the socio-economic dimension of conflict is primary, in polarized cities ethnocultural and territorial dimensions dominate (Yiftachel 1998). In polarized cities, urban planners must contend with both broader ideological conflict and the specific planning issues of daily urban life.

Despite these differences in the nature of urban conflict, the assertion in this article is that North American planners can learn from overseas examples of deep ethnic conflict about how planners treat complex and emotional issues of ethnic and racial identity and group-based claims. The ethnic fracturing of many cities in North America and western Europe creates a public interest that bears signs of fragility and cleavage similar to the infamous polarized cities studied here. With American cities frequently divided geographically by ethnicity, race, and income, patterns of domination are expressed through physical and symbolic division and spatial fragmentation (Goldsmith and Blakely 1992; Marcuse 1995; Massey and Denton 1993). Fear of "the other" is not only felt at the level of individual behavior but becomes intertwined in urban planning decisions (Sandercock 1998). The terrorism of September 11, 2001, has brought violently into the foreground questions concerning the appropriate balance of urban security, individual freedom, and cultural diversity.

A commonality between most American and western European cities, on the one hand, and ethnically polarized cities, on the other, is that planners in both are responsible for coping with the manifestations of supra-urban forces. In the case of polarized cities, these forces are historically based on conflicting political claims involving ideology, ethnicity, and nationalism. In other cities, these forces are unprecedented migration, globalization of economic production, and the rise of minorities and civil society (Sandercock 1998). That many influences impacting cities are external – whether ideological in the case of polarized cities, or due to globalization or foreign immigration – can lead to the conclusion that local planning is impotent and derivative. Thus, urban planners were found to be silent on the urban impacts of foreign immigration, and the urban perspective was regarded as distinctly a secondary matter (Friedmann and Lehrer 1997). The "low politics" of cities become dismissed as unimportant compared to the "high politics" of states and their promotion and protection of national interests (Rothman 1992).

This article first reviews how American planning has approached issues of race and cultural difference. It then investigates how urban planners have addressed ethnic challenges in the cities of Belfast, Jerusalem, and Johannesburg. In the conclusion, I outline implications of these overseas case studies for American planners who want to deal with cultural difference more effectively.

Planning, race, and ethnicity

The record of urban planning and policy in the United States is stained by the fact that housing, zoning, and development policies have frequently excluded and distanced Blacks and other minorities from opportunity and wealth (Judd and Swanstrom 2002; Massey and Denton 1993; Thomas 1994). Recent urban treatises point out lessons concerning race heard before. They describe policymakers' "ambivalent message on matters of race" (Sugrue 1996: 18), the failure to "manage the process of racial succession in an effective and humane manner" (Cummings 1998: 3), how racial prejudice and conflict stunted efforts to stop city decline (Thomas 1997), and how the "specter of race" has fundamentally shaped urban policy (Gillette 1995). Documentation of differential impacts of public actions across racial and ethnic subgroups has challenged conventional planning on the basis of environmental justice (United Church of Christ Commission for Racial Justice 1987).

The planner's role in addressing racial and ethnic division has not been clearly articulated. Sennett (1999: 274) observes that "the politics of conflict is hard to relate to urban design." The planning profession has at times sought to address the problems of racial division in America, in particular through efforts at advocacy planning beginning in the 1960s and equity planning more recently (Krumholz and Clavel 1994). Yet, the racial issues that planners wrestled with in the 1960s haunt us still (Thomas 1994). Hartman (1994: 158) asserts that planning has had "little to do with the realities of current struggles around racism and poverty." Mier (1994: 239) states that planners are "facilitators of social exclusion and economic isolation" unless they consider race and diversity as the first way to frame planning problems. Even the recent communication-based, critical pragmatic view of planning, states Beauregard (1999: 53), is "silent about important tensions that emanate from multiculturalism" and group-based claims.

Professional organizational introspection about planners' roles amidst racial and ethnic difference is not lacking. A forum after the 1992 Los Angeles riot evaluated the roles of planners in addressing and shaping core social equity issues

(APA 1992). The American Planning Association's Agenda for America's Communities steering committee then produced a book that argued for a "new comprehensiveness" that explicitly includes the concept of community equity (APA 1994). However, this notion of equity tended to be deprived of its color and cultural components.[1] Planners' professional stances regarding race and ethnicity have often been found to be detached, uncertain, and ambivalent. Hoch (1993: 459) observes that the "professional protocol of the expert advice giver and dutiful public servant does not acknowledge the complexity of racial justice issues, and, in fact, seems to simplify the problem." The limitations of liberal reform seem unable to address the cultural differences that divide racial groups. Krumholz and Clavel (1994) observed the difficulties faced by politically left-of-center White professionals when they plan for communities of color. In the United Kingdom, planning has been criticized for being "insensitive to the systematically different needs and requirements of the population and, in particular ... some black and ethnic communities" (Thomas and Krishnarayan 1994: 1899).

Often, planners confronting an ethnically or racially fractured public interest use professional coping skills that distance them from the core issues. Baum (1999) finds that planners commonly view themselves as disinterested, objective, scientific observers who are outside culture, who bear no biases, and who use universal norms when making evaluations. When dealing with issues having strong value conflicts, Morley and Shachar (1986) assert that planners commonly adopt nonideological postures and seek to legitimize an objective methodology of planning. Krumholz and Clavell (1994) found that liberal planners had an inadequate language of race interaction and fell back on labels emphasizing class and neighborhood themes more than explicitly racial ones. In the face of ethnic change in neighborhoods or commercial areas, planners relied on urban design, traffic/parking, and occupancy standards to slow the pace and impacts of change and often assumed a neutral stance toward users' ethnicity (Qadeer 1997). Discussions about racial difference can also produce an anxiety that stifles talk about other types of differences within the community (Baum 1998).

Multiculturalism is challenging planning today even more fundamentally than did criticism in the 1960s and 1970s. It takes issue with the scientific approach of modernist planning and policymaking that uses a universal value system (Baum 1999). While the need for advocacy and equity planning assuredly still exists, planning now is called upon to recognize different cultures and worldviews as authentic, enduring, and worthy of efforts to sustain them (Burayidi 1999; Thomas 1996). Such differing value systems are a defining characteristic of ethnically polarized cities and also appear to be an increasing attribute of planning and resource allocation debates in North American and western European cities.

In terms of planning and city building, multiculturalism poses significant challenges related to such issues as the ethnic character of urban design amidst neighborhood change, regulation of ethnic business and commercial enclaves, housing occupancy standards and cultural differences, and multilingual signage (Qadeer 1997). Multicultural planning also implies an increased sensitivity toward the use and perception of urban space, including issues of residential self-segregation and public park use (Loukaitou-Sideris 1995; Sen 1999). It connotes the need to assess impacts of proposed plans across identifiable subgroups of the population (Pinel 1994). Planning educators and researchers are also grappling with the issues of cultural diversity. The Planning Accreditation Board (2001) requires that the "multicultural and gender dimensions" (p.23) of the city be taught, and that "respect for diversity of views and ideologies" (p.25) be inculcated during planning study. And a survey of planning academics found the ability to plan in a multicultural environment to be a critical skill for planners (Friedmann and Kuester 1994). Yet, planning educators face criticism for emphasizing quantitative methodologies that send the signal to students to keep their distance from communities and for neglecting courses that could help students learn about culture and individual, group, and community psychology (Baum 1999). Cultural differentiation and change "remains a relatively understudied process in urban planning" (Friedmann 1996: 97).

Studying urban planning amidst a fractured public interest

The cities of Belfast, Jerusalem, and Johannesburg encapsulate deep-rooted cleavages based on competing nationalisms and arguments over political control and group rights. Each provides multi-decade accounts of urban planning and management in contested bi-communal environments.[2] Field research consisted of three months of interview-based research in each city.[3] Interviews focused on the influence of ethnic polarization on the city's institutional context, formulation of development goals, public agenda setting, decision making, and policy implementation, and on how urban policymaking in turn constrains or opens opportunities for conflict alleviation. The primary policies studied were land use planning, economic development, housing construction, capital facility planning, social service delivery, community participation, and municipal government organization. These policies can maintain or disrupt territorial claims, they can distribute economic benefits fairly or unfairly, they can provide or discourage access to policymaking and political power, and they can protect or erode collective ethnic and cultural rights.

The research dealt with the subjective as well as objective characteristics of planning amidst intense conflict. I was interested in how interviewees made sense of their everyday activities and professional roles. In particular, I observed closely the interplay between the professional norms and values of planning and the more emotion-filled ideological imperatives that impinge daily upon the professional's life. The distortions, the omissions, the emphases on some issues and not others, and the definition of urban issues and constituents were all part of the story I wish to tell of urban policymaking amidst contested ethnicity.

I examine four planning strategies that urban regimes might adopt under conditions of political and ethnic polarization.

1   A neutral urban strategy distances itself from issues of ethnic identity, power inequalities, and political exclusion. In this strategy, planning acts as an ethnically neutral or "color-blind" mode of state intervention responsive to individual-level needs and differences. This approach is rooted in the Anglo-Saxon tradition and is commonly applied in liberal democratic settings (Yiftachel, 1995). Planners channel disagreements between ethnic groups away from sovereignty- and identity-related issues toward day-to-day service delivery issues solvable through planning procedures and professional norms (Forester 1989; Rothman 1992).
2   A partisan urban strategy, in contrast, furthers an empowered ethnic group's values and authority and rejects claims of the disenfranchised group (Yiftachel 1995). Planners seek to entrench and expand territorial claims or enforce exclusionary control of access (Lustick 1979; Sack 1981).
3   An equity strategy gives primacy to ethnic affiliation in order to decrease intergroup inequalities. Criteria such as an ethnic group's relative size or need are used to allocate urban services and spending. Equity-based criteria will often be significantly different from the functional and technical criteria used by the ethnically neutral professional planner (Krumholz and Forester 1990.) An equity planner is much more aware than a neutral planner of group-based inequalities and political imbalances in the city and recognizes the need for remediation and affirmative action policies based on group identity.
4   The final model – a resolver strategy – seeks to connect urban issues to root causes of urban polarization: power imbalances, competitive ethnic group identities, and disempowerment. Planners challenge the impacts, and even authority, of government policy and attempt to link scientific and technical knowledge to processes of system transformation (Benvenisti 1986; Friedmann 1987).

Belfast: neutral planning and ethnic stability

Sectarian issues don't intrude into our considerations. We do land use planning, that's it. What difference would it make in land use planning terms in any event. Catholics need all the housing, schools, churches, shops, and facilities, just like Protestants do.

George Worthington, Head, Belfast Planning Service (interview)

Belfast is a city pervaded by an overlapping nationalist (Irish/British) and religious (Catholic/Protestant) conflict. Since 1969 it has been a violent city of sectarian (ethnic) warfare. The urban arena is hypersegregated and of strict sectarian territoriality, with antagonistic groups separate but proximate (see Figure 9.1). In 35 of the city's 51 electoral wards, 90 percent or more of the population share a single religion (Northern Ireland Registrar General 1992). Intercommunity hostilities have required the building of 15 "peaceline" partitions – ranging from corrugated iron fences and steel palisade structures, to permanent brick or steel walls, to environmental barriers or buffers (see Figure 9.2). The city of

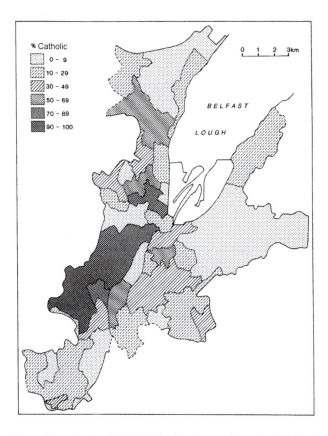

9.1 Percentage of population that is Catholic, electoral wards of Belfast urban area, 1991

Source: Boal (1994). Reprinted by permission.

9.2 Cupar Way peaceline wall separating Catholic Falls and Protestant Shankill neighborhoods, 1995 (Photo by Scott A. Bollens)

Belfast, similar to Northern Ireland as a whole, has a majority Protestant population. The 1991 city population of 279,000 was about 57 percent Protestant and 43 percent Catholic (J. McPeake, interview). The Catholic percentage has been increasing over the last few decades due to higher birth rates and Protestant out-migration to adjoining towns.

Religious identities coincide strongly with political and national loyalties. The allegiances of Protestant "unionists" and "loyalists" are with Britain, which since 1972 has exercised direct rule over Northern Ireland. Catholic "nationalists" and "republicans", in contrast, consider themselves Irish and commit their personal and political loyalties to the country of Ireland. In addition to differences owing to political allegiance, Catholics criticize discrimination by Northern Ireland governments in terms of access to jobs, housing, and social services. Since the imposition of British "direct rule" in the midst of sectarian conflict in 1972, legislative power for the province had been held by the British House of Commons, resulting in "an almost complete absence of representative participation and accountability" (Hadfield 1992: 6). A significant alteration of Northern Ireland governing institutions and constitutional status was specified in a 1998 political agreement. Some legislative and administrative authority in the province has been transferred from Britain to a directly-elected Northern Ireland Assembly, in which Protestants and Catholics share power, but continuation of this devolution is dependent upon further progress on disarmament and police reform issues.

The primary urban policymaker in Belfast, under the Northern Ireland Act of 1974, has been the Department of the Environment for Northern Ireland (DOENI). Within or connected to the DOENI are three major entities. The Town and Country Planning Service is responsible for creating the policy framework within which growth takes place and for regulating development. Belfast Urban Area (BUA) plans have the force of law and establish a broad policy framework within which more detailed development proposals can be determined. Almost all planning and project applications are reviewed by the Planning Service for consistency with the area plan. The Belfast Development Office (BDO) promotes physical regeneration and implements revitalization grant programs. And the Northern Ireland Housing Executive (NIHE) is responsible for construction of public housing, the rehabilitation and maintenance of existing units, and the allocation of public housing units to needy households and individuals.

Belfast Urban Policy Since 1972[4]

The operative principles for Belfast urban policymakers and administrators have been (1) to manage ethnic space in a way that reflects residents' wishes and does not exacerbate sectarian tensions; and (2) to maintain the neutrality of the government's role and image in Belfast, not biased toward either "orange" (Protestant) or "green" (Catholic). Since 1972, strong efforts have been made to base policy decisions on rational, objective, and dispassionate measures. However, the imperatives of containing urban violence dictate that policymakers condone the strict territoriality of the city, one which imposes tight constraints on the growing Catholic population while protecting under-utilized land of the declining Protestant majority. Although objective need dictates it, housing planners "simply cannot say there is to be a Catholic housing estate in an area that is traditionally Protestant" (J. Hendry, interview).

Planning efforts since the 1960s for the Belfast urban area have emphasized physical and spatial concerns, separating them from issues of localized ethnic conflict (Boal 1990). The *Belfast Regional Survey and Plan of 1962* (Matthew 1964) made no mention of the ethnically divided nature of Belfast. A subsequent detailed plan for the area did take note of ethnic divisions, but stated: "It would be presumptuous, however, to imagine that the Urban Area Plan could be expected to influence religious as well as economic, social and physical factors" (Building Design Partnership 1969: 5).

The 1977 plan, *Northern Ireland: Regional Physical Development Strategy 1975–1995*, supported a government role accommodating of ethnic demarcations. It stated that:

A situation now exists where generally people are prepared to be housed only in what they regard as "their own areas." Whilst every effort will be made to break down these barriers, it will inevitably take many years to remove them completely. In the meantime the position as it now exists must be recognized and taken into account in the development of new housing areas.

(DOENI 1977: 41–2)

The *Belfast Urban Area Plan 2001* (DOENI 1990) neglects issues of sectarianism by defining them outside the scope of planning. DOENI (1989: 2) states that "it is not the purpose of a strategic land use plan to deal with the social, economic, and other aspects involved." The department stated that the contentious "non-planning" issues of housing and social service delivery are outside the agency's specific domain (DOENI 1988). Not one of the strategic objectives of the 2001 plan involves explicitly an ethnic or sectarian issue. Even the bread-and-butter of land-use planning work – the forecasting of total and subgroup populations – is excluded from the plan, due likely to its ethnic and political sensitivity.

In contrast to town planning policy, development-oriented agencies by necessity address sectarian realities more directly. The NIHE acknowledges interfaces and peacelines as "locations where conflict can quite frequently occur and where the Housing Executive is seeking to manage and maintain homes on an impartial basis" (NIHE 1988: 2). In building housing near these areas, the NIHE utilizes pragmatic tactics on a case-by-case basis within the limits set by sectarian geographies. At times, the NIHE has built walls or other physical barriers as part of a housing development if they are deemed necessary by national security agencies for stabilizing inter-communal conflict (NIHE 1988). The BDO also, by necessity, confronts sectarian issues more directly than the planning service. Two main physical tactics have been used: creation of neutral land uses between antagonistic sides and the justification of physical alterations in interface areas based on the forecasted economic benefits of BDO-sponsored projects. Whereas the first method seeks to distance opposing sides through neutral infrastructure, the second method seeks economic gains for both sides and could facilitate nontrivial alterations to sectarian territoriality (Murtagh 1994).

Planners' neutral, hands-off approach to ethnicity has sacrificed the development of a strategic plan that could guide housing and development decisions. Accordingly, public actions by government units like NIHE and BDO have primarily been ad-hoc tactics rather than strategic acts, project-based rather than area-based, and reactive instead of proactive. Planning in the strategic and comprehensive sense has been marginalized; there has been "no coherent and strategic planning response to the [ethnic] Troubles" (K. Sterrett, interview).

Instead of providing a guide for managing sectarian space, Belfast town planning "has entrenched itself behind the wall of the physical planning, where social, economic and sectarian issues are pushed outside the wall" (J. Hendry, interview).

Planners' perceptions

The Belfast urban policy approach of color blindness has served organizational goals well in overcoming the discriminatory legacy of the pre-1972 Unionist-controlled Northern Ireland government. Operating within the most contentious policy arena of housing, the NIHE has maintained much integrity as a fair allocator of public housing units through difficult times. W. McGivern (interview), former Belfast regional director of NIHE, states that "the main reason we exist is because we have credibility.' Amidst intense conflict, the DOENI "is practicing the art of the possible, in a circumstance where they are in a sectarian trap and they know it" (J. Hendry, interview). G. Mulligan (interview) acknowledges the inefficiencies of ethnic segmentation, but states that "planning does not want to say how the society or economy should change." Rather, government's proper role is to passively reflect in its policies the needs and demands of residents and neighborhoods. The principle underlying government involvement has been to "follow the wishes of the people" (D. McCoy, B. Neill, P. Sweeney, interviews). Divisions in society are viewed as based on deep-rooted feelings and reinforced through terror. As such, "changes have to come from within people; government cannot change people's minds" (R. Spence, interview).

Government officials operating amidst ethnic polarization do not want to be seen as "social engineers." Benign efforts by government to "artificially" bring people together are viewed as stimulative of intercommunity tensions. D. McCoy (interview) states that in Belfast's sectarian complexity "government should not impose a top-down macro view of how the city should work; rather, it should be responsive and sensitive to the needs and abilities of local communities." G. Worthington (interview) claims that "We must recognize the realities of the situation. If we shifted color, the end result would clearly not work. We're not about making social engineering decisions, or ones that would be perceived as such." Government sticks as close as possible to objective standards and must watch the meanings behind their language in public documents because "words can cause a lot of trouble here" (W. McGivern, interview). D. McCoy (interview) describes the pressured bureaucratic environment of urban policymaking: "There are too many opportunities for mistakes. We are under the microscope all the time." The author found that internal discussions within government agencies show a greater sensitivity to ethnic realities than government's public stance would indicate. One planner (B. Morrison, interview) describes this internal recognition: "It was as if we were carrying out a plan for two cities that happened to overlap each other." Nevertheless, planners remain steadfast in not speaking explicitly in public forums about ethnicity and urban policy.[5]

Planners in Belfast defend their neutral posture of technical land use competence. Town planner B. Morrison (interview) views the stance as beneficial. "Planning works quite well behind the scenes," he states; more deterministic actions by government are best left to others. In contested public discussions, "it can be useful for planners to adopt the technical and professional role because it allows them the ability to avoid confrontation" (K. Sterrett, interview). In the sectarian battleground of Belfast, "there is a sense of almost persecution where planners retreat into narrow technical roles" (B. Neill, interview). The town planning process becomes one viewed by planners as properly regulatory, not proactive and intervening. The comments of B. Morrison (interview) are illuminating:

> Our regulatory role is our reason for being. To do this cleanly and properly, you would have nothing to do whatsoever with anything proactive. This posture as regulator influences us in terms of what we can outwardly do, or be perceived as doing.
>
> (B. Morrison, interview)

In the end, government's approach to urban policy in Belfast is characterized by a set of self-limiting features. There is separation of the town planning function from ethnic issues and the fragmentation of policy along division and department lines. Combined, these factors decrease government's ability to mount an ethnically sensitive strategy that would be multidimensional (physical, social-psychological, economic, and human development) and integrative of planning, housing, and development agencies. Thus, interventions by units such as BDO or NIHE are left adrift on the strong sectarian seas of Belfast, neither anchored nor navigated by an integrated set of city-building principles. P. Sweeney (interview), DOENI advisor, asks a disturbing question: "In a deeply fractured society, was there not a need for government to be more proactive, to be more progressive? Planners stand accused and guilty. They needed to manage the environment rather than simply reacting."

Jerusalem: partisan planning and contested space

> From the very first, all major development represented politically and strategically motivated planning.
>
> Israel Kimhi, City Planner, Jerusalem (1963–86) (interview)

Conflicting Israeli and Palestinian claims on territory intersect with Jewish and Muslim religious heritages in this city that defies exclusivity (Elon 1989; I. Matar, interview). A politically undivided Jerusalem under Israeli sovereignty is a fundamental Israeli position, while Palestinians speak of Jerusalem as the capital of a state of Palestine, staking claim to the city's eastern sector. These conflicting aspirations create a city of "intimate enemies" – a life of encounters, proximity, and interaction, yet remote, extraneous, and alienated (Benvenisti 1995). Having a 1996 population of 603,000 within its disputed borders, the city is a site of demographic and physical competition between two populations. The social and political geography of Jerusalem has included a multicultural mosaic under the 1920–48 British Mandate and two-sided physical partitioning of Jerusalem into Israeli- and Jordanian-controlled components during the 1948–67 period, the division demarcated by a 1949 armistice agreement. Since 1967, it has been a contested Israeli-controlled municipality three times the area of the pre-1967 city (due to unilateral annexation) and encompassing formerly Arab East Jerusalem. The international status of East Jerusalem today remains as occupied territory. Jewish demographic advantage (approximately 70 percent Jewish, 30 percent Arab) within the Israeli-defined borders of Jerusalem translates into Jewish control of the city council and mayor's office (Municipality of Jerusalem 1997). This control is solidified by Arab resistance to participating in municipal elections they deem illegitimate. The West Bank, populated by approximately 1.7 million Palestinians and about 150,000 Jews, surrounds Jerusalem on three sides (Palestinian Central Bureau of Statistics 1998; Peace Now 1997).

Israeli Urban Policy Since 1967[6]

Since 1967, the Israeli central government has shaped or preempted the goals and strategies of local planning as sovereignty goals shape the built landscape. The primary goals have been to extend the Jewish city geographically, strengthen it demographically, and build Jewish neighborhoods so that political division of the city would never again be possible (B. Hyman, interview). Israeli urban policies based on issues of national security, the unification of the city, and immigrant absorption have overridden or contradicted municipal planning policies. The central government sets down the basic parameters of urban and metropolitan growth, and the local government is left with the application and translation of these national goals onto the municipal scale.

Such central government guidance of Jerusalem growth is facilitated by an Israeli regulatory planning system that is highly centralized (Alexander *et al.* 1983; Hill 1980). Of particular significance, regional district commissions dominated by central government representatives have strong oversight power over local "outline" (statutory) plans prepared by municipalities, approval power over most local building permits, and hear appeals on local rejection. In contrast, local planning commissions have limited independent powers of area-wide plan making and project review. National interests have frequently been implemented by active, development-oriented institutions and organizations and the granting of powerful developmental budgets to development ministries. This aggressive developmental planning system involves a maze of agencies and organizations. The most important governmental body from the viewpoint of urban growth and development in the Jerusalem region is the Ministry of Housing and Construction, involved with the development of housing, infrastructure, and roads. Prominent among semigovernmental entities is the Israeli Lands Authority, which controls extensive public land holdings (93 percent of Israel proper is owned publicly) and influences development through land release.

Figure 9.3 displays the post-1967 growth and development patterns that follow from national political objectives. Large Jewish communities – Ramot Allon,

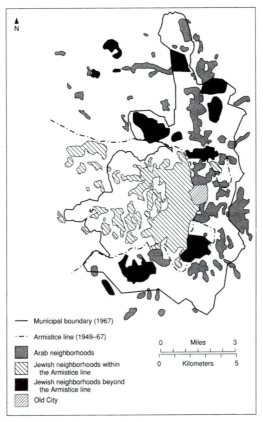

9.3 Jewish and Arab neighborhoods within Israeli-defined borders of Jerusalem, 1991

Source: Benvenisti (1996). Reprinted by permission.

Pisgat Zeev, Neve Yaakov (see Figure 9.4), East Talpiot, and Gilo – have been built in strategic locations throughout the annexed and disputed municipal area. Because Jewish security was an overriding concern, the establishment of a "critical mass" of Jewish residents after 1967 was viewed as essential to Jewish safety and self-confidence (Y. Golani, B. Hyman, interviews). Of the approximately 27 square miles annexed after the 1967 War, the Israeli government has expropriated about 33 percent and has used this land to build Jewish neighborhoods. Since 1967, 88 percent of all housing units built in contested East Jerusalem have been for the Jewish population (B'Tselem 1995). Neighborhoods built in East Jerusalem are home today for over 160,000 Jewish residents.

Disproportionately low municipal spending in Arab neighborhoods cements Jewish advantage. Interviewees (both Israeli and Palestinian) cited consistently at least an 8-to-1 spending ratio in Jewish versus Arab neighborhoods. Amirav (1992) documents that no more than four percent of the infrastructure development budget ever flowed to Arab areas. These estimates are well below the expected share of spending based on the Arab population of the city (30 percent). A city report (Municipality of Jerusalem 1994) acknowledges these huge gaps, documenting more than one half of Arab areas having inadequate water provision and no sewage system.

In addition to facilitating Jewish development in disputed areas, Israel has restricted the growth of the city's Palestinian communities to weaken their claims to Jerusalem. This has been achieved through land expropriation, zoning regulations that constrain Palestinian rights to development, use of road building

9.4 Jewish neighborhood of Neve Yaakov in annexed part of Jerusalem, 1994 (Photo by Scott A. Bollens)

to restrict and fragment Palestinian communities, restrictions on building volume in Palestinian areas, and an intentional absence of plans for Arab areas. The lack of outline plans, a "politically conscious" decision in part (I. Kimhi, interview), made it extremely difficult for Palestinians to gain building permits, because these plans are a necessary condition for permit approval. As a result of these restrictions, only 11 percent of annexed East Jerusalem, at most, is vacant land where the Israeli government allows Palestinian development (S. Kaminker 1995; K. Tufakji, interview). In the last five years, the Municipality of Jerusalem began to prepare outline plans for Arab sectors of the city. However, they often have incorporated "hidden guidelines" that restrict Arab growth (S. Kaminker, interview). Examples of these include intentionally wide road standards that close off development opportunities for rows of building lots consumed by the road, low floor area ratio requirements (0.15–0.25 is common in Arab areas, compared to up to 3.0 in Jewish communities), and strict height standards.

There also exists an ill fit between the Western standards incorporated into Israeli plans and the realities of Arab development processes and ownership patterns. Or, as former city engineer E. Barzacchi (interview) proclaims, "The answers we town planners give to the Arab population are technically 'right' and interesting, but are absolutely irrelevant." For example, development in the Israeli planning system is premised on there being clearly defined private ownership boundaries. However, about one half of the Arab areas in Jerusalem have unregistered land ownership patterns, a legacy of much land being held in community or state ownership under British and then Jordanian control. This allows the Israeli government to boast that, "yes, we have plans" (N. Sidi, interview) for the Arab sector, while knowing that most allowable growth will not come to fruition because implementation tools are lacking. According to J. de Jong (interview), Israel rationalizes, "Look, we gave you the possibilities. If you as a society don't make use of it, we have no responsibility." Former Deputy Mayor M. Benvenisti (interview) states that "Israelis did not plan for the Arab community, but planned just so there would be a plan." Rather than taking proactive responsibility for making their plans and reality meet, Israeli planners use built-in mechanisms that significantly disadvantage the Palestinian community in Jerusalem.

Planners' perceptions

The primary motivation behind my practice of urban planning has been the trauma of the holocaust and the lesson it taught that we cannot count on anybody but ourselves.

Yehonathan Golani, Director Planning Administration,
Israeli Ministry of the Interior (interview)

Israeli planners were aware of the partisan nature of their practice, and there was seldom self-denial about the effects of their planning actions on the city landscape. I. Kimhi (interview) asserts, "We planners have harmed the co-existence of the two nations and peoples. If planned the right way, then both nations can develop here in Jerusalem." Y. Golani (interview) describes himself as an open-minded liberal; yet, "on this issue I cannot be indifferent. I cannot speak objectively. You cannot be objective about this situation." In his discussion of Jerusalem planning, B. Hyman (interview) jumps between functional arguments and political considerations and ultimately states, "It is hard to work out anything that resembles a 'natural solution'." In making professional choices between planning and political criteria, he states, "We are first of all Israelis and officers of the government of Israel. First and foremost." Similarly, E. Barzacchi (interview) reflects upon a 1992–4 Israeli effort, which she co-directed, to plan for metropolitan Jerusalem: "We tried to be scholars, but we were all Israelis. And, I don't think you can be objective. You can try to be scientific; you cannot be objective."

Yet, within this partisan context, Israeli planners give weight to their ability to utilize professional planning expertise in the implementation of these goals. S. Moshkovits (interview), Israeli planning director for the West Bank administration, explains that his goal is to assure "that political expression is done in the most professional way possible." Similarly, B. Hyman (interview) asserts that "we try to make the political decisions sensible from the professional planning point of view." And, U. Ben-Asher (interview), Jerusalem District planner for the Ministry of the Interior, declares that his goal is to "maintain professional principles within this politically determined context." These professional planning techniques are thought to have a moderating effect. I. Kimhi (interview) brings this perception forth: "For the last 27 years, we have made a very clear statement. Everything that was done, though, was done in a humane way. I know how it was done." Similarly, city planner N. Sidi (interview) recounts her distaste of efforts to penetrate Jewish growth into Arab sectors and describes how "sometimes I can find an elegant solution" by proposing alternative sites for proposed Jewish development. Similarly, A. Mazor (interview) recounts how Jerusalem metro-politan planners innovatively utilized the "potential model" to identify areas of greatest urban territorial conflict, describing it as "the use of technical and professional measures to try to resolve conflict."

It was striking that Israeli planners could live comfortably with two worlds – one political, the other stressing objective planning criteria. Planners' personal relationship to political contentiousness seemed an ambiguous one. On the one hand, there was frustration and impotence; on the other hand, attraction and intrigue. Some interviewees were frustrated by the constant politicization of their work and compartmentalized their role by emphasizing professional methodologies and functional arguments. This provided them with a "safe space" within which to address emotion-laden controversial topics. For instance, I. Kimhi asserts the need to "postpone issues of sovereignty; instead, let's talk over the next 5–10 years on a practical level – how we can live together." In contrast, other planners (and frequently the same planners at different times) showed an attraction toward their politically contentious environment. I. Kimhi (interview) recounts planning for a newly unified Jerusalem after 1967:

> It was a most fortunate situation for a planner – that you are needed. We were needed by the politicians – what road to open, what wall to knock down, where is the sewerage, what to do. They simply came to us – we had all the information. We were prepared for this act of reunification. It was a glorious time.

Not all Israeli planners interviewed bought into the partisan style of planning. For example, S. Kaminker, former urban planner with the city, dealt with her frustration by leaving government: "If employed by government, you must be an agent of government. If you can't live within that framework, then you have to leave." She now provides technical planning assistance to Arab communities, but again faces a professional dilemma: "With a heavy heart, I must give away at times the planning principles that I was raised on to meet the political needs [of Palestinians] that are greater today."

Johannesburg: equity planning and urban reconstruction

> Planners have grown up providing services for a well-understood and familiar client – White and affluent.
>
> Tim Hart, SRK Engineers (interview)

Johannesburg anchors a spatially disfigured urban region of enormous economic and social disparities. The region presents dual faces: one healthy, functional and White; the other stressed, dysfunctional, and Black. From 1948 to the early 1990s, the White National Party developed and implemented the policies of apartheid, or separate development. This crushingly exclusionist ideology was forcibly imposed upon the country's 70 percent Black majority seeking basic rights and a proportionate share of power. After the national democratic elections in 1994 brought the Black African National Congress party and Nelson Mandela to power, hope and opportunities for urban change co-existed with awareness by policymakers of the difficulties of bettering the stark conditions of many Black Africans.

The Johannesburg (or central Witwatersrand) metropolitan region contained 2.2 million people in 1991 and by 1997 was home to almost 4 million people (Central Statistical Service 1992; Greater Johannesburg Metropolitan Council 1998). The city's population in the early 1990s was over 60 percent Black (Mabin and Hunter 1993). Racially segregated townships, cities, and informal settlements/shantytowns characterize the urban landscape (see Figure 9.5). Income distribution is grossly skewed in Johannesburg's province of Gauteng. An enormous proportion of basic needs – housing, land tenure, and water and sanitation facilities – is presently unmet. There is an estimated shortfall of 500,000 formal housing units in the province (M. Narsoo, interview.) Black Africans inhabit several different "geographies of poverty" (CWMC, 1993). The two primary locations are Alexandra (see Figure 9.6) and Soweto townships, the latter an amalgamation of 29 townships spatially disconnected from central Johannesburg (South African Township Annual 1993). Formal bricks-and-mortar housing was intentionally underbuilt since urban Blacks were considered temporary and unwanted. Rudimentary hostels were built to shelter workers in

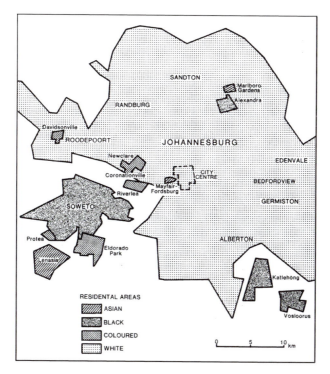

9.5 Racial "group areas" in apartheid Johannesburg, 1991

Source: Parnell and Pirie (1991). Reprinted by permission.

9.6 Squatter shacks in Alexandra Township, Johannesburg, 1995 (Photo by Scott A. Bollens)

industrial and mining activities nearby and have been areas of significant tension politically, ethnically, and physically (Gauteng Provincial Government 1995). In townships, backyard shacks and free-standing shacks on vacant land are character-ized by near-inhuman conditions of living, lack of secure tenure, inadequate standards of shelter and sanitation, and lack of social facilities and services. Outside of townships beyond the urban fringe exist informal shack settlements, which are spatially disconnected from even the primitive services of townships and often erected in areas of geotechnical or political susceptibility (T. Mashinini, interview). Finally, significant "greying" (Black in-migration) has occurred since 1991 in several inner neighborhoods of Johannesburg city, concentrating both poverty and overcrowding.

Urban apartheid policy, anchored by the 1950 Group Areas Act, divided towns and cities into group areas for exclusive occupation by single racial groups. Races were separated by buffer strips of open land, ridges, industrial areas, or railroads in order to minimize intergroup contact (Davies 1981). City centers, environmentally stable and otherwise prestigious areas were zoned White; peripheral areas were zoned non-White and restricted in scope (Christopher 1994). Officially, there existed duality of planning processes – one based on group areas' racial delineations, the other on land use allocation. Yet, in practice, there was harmony between racial zoning and land use planning. Town planning's traditional emphases on efficiency, order, and control were effectively used for ethnic segregation and ordering. As such, the goals and methods of the Group Areas Act "both derived from established planning practices, and enticed town planners into the implementation of racial segregation" (Mabin 1992: 407). In the end, "apartheid proved to be a seductive way of seeing the city for many practitioners and planners who were deeply involved in its implementation" (Parnell and Mabin 1995: 59–60). The town planning profession in Johannesburg went down "the long road of coercion and domination" (J. Muller, interview). "Apartheid planning was terribly effective in achieving its goals," states one interviewee (identity withheld upon request). Yet, the very success of this partisan planning erected functionally and economically unsustainable urban conditions that contributed over time to the downfall of the apartheid system that it worked so hard to support.

Reconstructing urban policy since 1991[7]

From 1991 to 1995, urban leaders and planners engaged as resolvers of core political issues during the transformation of local and metropolitan governance. Officials of the old regime, nongovernmental representatives, and those from the formerly excluded Black communities collaborated in a self-transformative process that changed the basic parameters of local and metropolitan representation, decision making, participation, and organizational structure. City-building issues dealing with day-to-day existence and the Black boycotting of rent and service payments were successfully connected by nongovernmental and opposition groups to root issues of political empowerment and local government reorganization. Discussions transcended sole emphases on the urban symptoms of racial polarization and targeted the need to radically transform apartheid-based urban governance. After complex and difficult negotiations, local and metropolitan government in Johannesburg was restructured to politically combine formerly White local governments with adjacent Black townships. Since November 1995, there have been Black majorities in all four local governments and the Johannesburg Metropolitan Council.

    Concurrent with the political restructuring of local governance was the formulation of alternative urban policies to combat the spatial manifestations of apartheid. The Central Witwatersrand Metropolitan Chamber (CWMC) was established in 1991, in part to develop a vision for future development in the Johannesburg region. This vision – the Interim Strategic Framework (ISF) – indicts the planning profession for its emphasis on regulatory control that seeks order, compartmentalization, and uniformity. Taken to its most extreme form – the Group Areas Act – "mono-zoning creates islands of privilege, vested interest and ownership that residents defend vehemently from perceived 'invasions' from outsiders" (CWMC 1993: 6). As an alternative, the ISF asserts that a spatial form that encourages urban diversity will moderate intergroup tension. The plan states:

> The ISF must thus seek to engender the patterns of urban complexity that undermine the strength of exclusionary areas (and hence conflict) and actively seek the blurring of zone boundaries and the integration of hitherto isolated areas into the mainstream of the urban system.
>
> (CWMC 1993: 11)

Equity-based, postapartheid city-building principles aspire to stitch together apartheid's urban distortions. Key facets of this city building are (1) densification and infill of the existing urban system and (2) upgrading and renewal of those parts of the urban system under stress. The densification approach seeks to encourage growth inward to urbanized areas that have access to employment, services, and facilities, and to fill in apartheid buffer zones. This "compact city" approach would be a primary means to increase opportunities for Blacks to enter the residential and economic fabric of the "White" city (T. Hart, interview). The second policy approach focuses on the upgrading and renewal of those urban fringe areas under stress due to inadequate housing, poor water and sanitation services, and public health hazards. Whereas the first policy approach seeks to transform apartheid space, the upgrading approach aimed at alleviating the many crisis-related needs on the urban remote fringes may over time unintentionally reinforce apartheid racial separation. Another vexing problem in efforts to reconstruct Johannesburg is that although the old centralized apartheid state is gone, land market, economic, and class-based interests now shape urban geography in ways that may produce similar spatial outcomes. In particular, high inner-city land costs, neighborhood opposition, and reliance on private-sector housing provision are obstructing efforts to incorporate the majority into a compact city of urban opportunity.

Urban policy amidst societal transformation has demanded a critical self-evaluation of the basic assumptions of urban planning. A debate among urban policymakers about how best to engage in Johannesburg reconstruction highlights two paradigms having different historic bases and different proponents of dissimilar personal histories and contrasting views of planning goals and skills. The traditional model of town planning in South Africa, derived from British and European foundations, has been focused on regulatory control and spatial allocation and administered in a centralized, hierarchical fashion. Today, not only is this blueprint paradigm discredited due to its alignment with apartheid, but there appears a disconnection between the socioeconomic needs of Black areas and this model of development control. Where Black Africans seek changes in the basic conditions of livelihood, the traditional planning model offers reform-minded, yet ultimately conservative, prescriptions. In response, a new paradigm of "development planning" has emerged that represents a fundamental challenge to traditional town planning.

Development planning seeks to integrate traditional spatial planning with social and economic planning; coordinate development policy objectives across governments, sectors, and departments; and establish participatory processes that empower the poor and marginalized (L. Boya, interview). Development planners have distinctly different personal histories than traditional town planners. Many are Black Africans not trained in the legal and regulatory foundations of physical development control, but rather having experience in nongovernmental organizations and skills related to community development, social mobilization, and negotiation (L. Boya, interview). Development planning in South Africa connotes strongly the empowerment of the deprived majority, according to J. Muller (interview). Traditionally trained town planners fall short here. The lack of community consultation in the town planning model meant that such planners worked in closed rooms in developing spatial frameworks. "You did 'what was best for society' and society had to accept whatever you did," recalls P. Waanders (interview). In contrast, development planners emphasize their role as mediators in the development process between community needs and government resources (T. Maluleke, T. Mashinini, interviews). Development planning, however, remains embryonic in South Africa and its methods appear only broadly articulated. "Nobody has been trained in doing the work that we do," says T. Mashinini (interview).

Planners' perceptions

Town planning and development planning are uneasy bedfellows in their common pursuit of a more humane Johannesburg. Town planning must contend with its image as "old guard," its past links to apartheid implementation, and its lack of connection to community. At the same time, it provides a methodology and technical capacity fundamental to city building. Development planning, meanwhile, is ascendant from community-based struggle and deemed as the way forward for urban South Africa. Yet, it is a young practice whose techniques are not clearly developed, and one that is burdened by demands for it to be all things to all people. When the two faces of postapartheid planning come in contact, one can detect a clash of personalities or comfort zones – town planners rooted to existing systems, rules, and regulations; development planners more proactive and sympathetic to experimentation. L. Boya (interview) wonders "In the future, when we more radically change planning, we will be saying in a sense that 'there is no future in the town planning profession as it is currently structured.' How will they respond?"

Responses from traditional town planners range from defensive rigidity, to counter-attack, to uncertainty, to productive acceptance of the need to change. "Many planners cannot cross the river of change because of this little bible that they have," states P. Waanders, pointing to a thick statute book of planning and zoning regulations. Professional biases are impediments to change: "it is very difficult for many planners to get out of the groove of doing up nice maps and pictures on the wall. It is part of the education system they carry with them" (P. Waanders, interview). Other town planners, however, defend traditional planning's value. J. Eagle (interview) asserts that criticism of traditional planning too simplistically positions planners as technicians worthy of marginalization in the face of emergent community activists. Further, she redirects criticism back at development planning:

> Because development planners know about daily life, they feel they can deal with planning issues and problems. They know about certain aspects of development, and that is important. But we can't just hand all of planning over to them because they don't always have the bigger picture.
>
> (J. Eagle, interview)

Traditional planning's defense of its unique contribution to city building is brought out in other observations. I. Kadungure (interview) states that "community specialists and social workers are needed for communication purposes, but at the end of the day someone else must come in to deal with technical issues such as water provision and engineering capacity." Similarly, J. Muller (interview) states that traditional planning is needed to supply a consciousness of the future to community revitalization efforts, which are commonly reactive and crisis related. A. Kotzee (interview) puts forth a not insignificant contribution of traditional planning – an ability to maintain property values and municipal tax bases, and to assure protection of property rights and investment. While many town planners surveyed expressed professional uncertainty amidst institutional transformation, other traditionally trained planners in government are rising to the challenge. For them, it is an invigorating time to develop new techniques of community consultation or to question assumptions and theories of the past (J. Erasmus, M. Gilbert, interviews.)

Ironically, the new development planning paradigm "is giving a certain credibility to what has been a discredited profession in this country" (J. Muller, interview.) It provides town planning with an opportunity to resurrect itself by employing new techniques that support the ascending paradigm. But town planning must shift away from its control mode into a practice that enables empowerment and capacity building in the interests of social justice (J. Muller, interview). In addition, it must bring into its educational and professional tracks

Black Africans whose local experiences come from community activism and facilitation. Development planning may represent a fundamental shift away from a rigid town planning approach aimed at maintenance and orderly development toward one that is aligned with socioeconomic and reconstruction objectives. It is an historic attempt to create a system of social guidance that utilizes the lessons of social mobilization. If the two faces of postapartheid planning were effectively combined, the result would likely be an altered and Africanized practice of community-based planning encompassing both social mobilization and rational governance.

Conclusions

Belfast, Jerusalem, and Johannesburg shed light on how urban planners and policymakers cope with rival urban communities that interact daily across ethnic divides. Four urban planning strategies are represented in the case study cities. In Belfast, the British government's strategy is to deal pragmatically on a *neutral* basis with the symptoms of political conflict. Protestant/Catholic equity issues are excluded from metropolitan plans, public housing allotment formulae utilize color-blind procedures, and town planning separates its spatial concerns from the broader social issues of housing, social services, and ethnic relations. In Jerusalem, the utilization of land-use planning and regulation as territorial tools constitutes a *partisan* approach to urban planning and administration. Ethnic criteria overshadow functional factors in the distribution of urban benefits such as housing and building approvals, roads, and community facilities. Johannesburg illustrates two roles that postapartheid urban planners have played in reconstructing that city. As *resolvers*, they helped link urban symptoms to root political causes, recognizing that Black political empowerment and restructuring of urban governance were necessary prerequisites to effective urban policymaking. They have also focused on *equity* objectives, addressing the urban symptoms of past racial conflict in their efforts to lessen the gross racial disparities in urban opportunities and outcomes.

The challenges of urban planning in Northern Ireland, the Middle East, and South Africa inform policymakers about the interaction between public policy and group-based claims in the urban setting. Lessons for planning and policymaking appear applicable to the growing number of American multiethnic cities that are not polarized, but come close at times to the ethnic breaking point. The common goal of urban management in both ethnically polarized and nonpolarized urban environments is to accommodate plural needs without sacrificing the soul or functionality of urban life. Policymakers and planners in both types of cities must address the complex spatial, social-psychological, and organizational attributes of potentially antagonistic urban communities. They must be sensitive to the multiethnic environments toward which their skills are applied and to the ways that empowered groups legitimate and extend their power. The problems and principles of city building in polarized cities provide guidance to all those who cope with multiple publics and contrasting ethnic views of city life and function.

Here is what this research implies for American urban planners in terms of how to effectively address group-based claims and multiple cultures in our cities.

Planning is not immune to being used for city-building objectives that are fundamentally at odds with professional ethics

Planning can be effectively used for partisan purposes in such ways that it exacerbates ethnic conflict, creates conditions of urban instability, and paradoxically constructs the perceived need for further partisanship due to its adverse effects on intergroup relations. In Jerusalem and apartheid Johannesburg, public-sector planners have acted as agents of their governments who, even if they have individual qualms, do what is expected of them by their employer. The institutional and organizational context constrains individual planner choice and provides incentives, such as employment security, for continued adherence to politically-based city-building goals.

Neutral, "color-blind" planning, although seen as safe, is both inadequate and difficult to implement in urban circumstances of different group values and trajectories

Neutral planning applied in urban settings of structural inequality does not produce equitable outcomes. The Belfast case illustrates that urban policy that does not take into account the quantitatively and qualitatively different needs of groups will tend to reinforce, not lessen, urban inequalities. Governments must avoid the comfort of acting as benign outsider to racial and ethnic conflict. When urban inequalities of opportunity exist, equity does not imply replication of policy for each identifiable urban group nor numerical balance in government outputs. Rather, it means that policy should be sensitive to the unique needs of each community while keeping in mind the overall good of the city. As illustrated by Israeli planning for Palestinian areas and as brought forth by difficult choices facing postapartheid planning in South Africa, planners should be aware that uniform requirements dealing with land ownership or development may have disparate effects across cultures having different values and customs.

Planners should seek coexistent viability of ethnic and racial groups

In each of the contentious cities studied, proposals to move away from ethnic spatial separation face attack as promoting an unrealistic pro-integration agenda. Yet, a middle approach must exist in such circumstances in order for intergroup tolerance to be nurtured in the urban setting. The goal of policy should not be integration per se, but a "porous" society, where diversity can co-exist and communities are free to interact, if they choose. The goal of urban policy should be accommodation, not necessarily assimilation. Urban policymakers should take stock of color (and ethnicity), not dismiss it, and seek to accommodate the unique needs of each ethnic group. In contrast to the traditional model of ethnic assimilation and its implied residential integration, this approach would seek to expand housing choice and residential differentiation so that diverse individual preferences and needs can be satisfied. In creating these urban environments, planners should take heed from all three cities studied that walls and boundaries (physical or psychological) provide feelings of safety but also tend to reinforce "the other" as threat.

Planning should incorporate social-psychological aspects of community identity into its professional repertoire

For members of an urban ethnic group, psychological needs pertaining to viability, group identity, and cultural symbolism can be as important as objective needs pertaining to land, housing, and economic opportunities. This is illuminated most acutely in the case of Belfast Protestants who feel they are sacrificing too much in current peacemaking efforts. Urban planning should incorporate the nontechnical, subjective aspects of community identity into its toolbox that heretofore has been oriented toward objective and rational methods. Urban planning should, in its methods of analysis and decision making, explicitly account for the importance of ethnic community identity, territoriality, and symbolism embedded in the urban landscape. At the same time, it must be able to address constructively the city's ethnicity when that ethnicity is obstructing the functionality of the urban region in terms of public health, shelter, public services, and economic opportunities. This means that city planners must both respect ethnic territoriality where it constitutes a healthy source of community cohesiveness and break ethnic territorial boundaries where they impose chains that constrain urban functionality and vitality.

Planning education and training should retool and reconceptualize the profession so it can more effectively address ethnic/racial difference

Education of planning students and training of mid-career professional planners should prepare planners to deal with the complex issues of planning amidst ethnic difference. In the case study cities, Israeli planners are restricted by political imperatives in their ability to reconceptualize methods and goals, those in Belfast show a sensitivity to ethnic group differences but are not yet bold enough to display this in public forums, and postapartheid Johannesburg planners are undergoing a critical self-reflection amidst the need to balance community mobilization and government regulation. Planners should be better educated in such topics, as identified by Friedmann (1996) – spatial segmentation, culturally specific forms of urban living, ethnic identity formation, and interethnic and interracial differences. This calls for studio-based workshops in planning schools to involve students in the multidimensional analysis and planning of ethnic neighborhoods. Students and practitioners should be exposed to the rudiments of ethnic impact analysis, qualitative surveying, conflict resolution, and community relations techniques.

Planners should confront the challenges posed by multiculturalism through processes of social learning, not through methodological certainty

In the face of multicultural complexity, the planning profession should not attempt to retreat through professional rigidity but rather engage in processes of social interaction with cultural groups so that their values and visions are incorporated into city planning. Postapartheid Johannesburg planners are highest on the social learning curve, incorporating participatory and human development aspects alongside its traditional spatial and regulatory emphasis. Belfast planners exhibit methodological experimentation but keep it in-house, while Israeli planners' openness to change must unfortunately await a lessening of political tensions.[8] Planning should attempt to understand the unfamiliar terrain of ethnic/racial difference and build new methods appreciative of diversity. Compared to professional detachment, this path poses greater risks to the profession, yet ultimately will provide for its growth, evolution, and enhanced relevance in this century.

Planning – through the spatial, economic, and social-psychological conditions it creates in the built landscape – can play a significant role in addressing the local manifestations of broader societal attitudes concerning ethnicity and race

Planners affect attributes of the urban system – such as viability of ethnic neighborhoods, economic opportunity, socioeconomic integration, and cultural symbolism – in ways that may independently produce or hinder mutually tolerable multiethnic living environments. City policies make a difference. They have intensified urban instability in Jerusalem through their solidifying of relative group deprivation. They have hardened ethnic compartmentalization in Belfast through their emphasis on conflict abeyance and containment. And, after exposing the impractical logic of urban apartheid yesterday, city policies in Johannesburg's future will likely play instrumental roles in the success or failure of reparative social justice. Cities are likely not the primary or direct influence on the level of ethnic or racial tension between competing urban groups, yet they also do not appear to be inert and passive reflectors of larger societal processes and attitudes. Cities matter, and by the nature of the urban assets that they effect, planners have influence.

Planning has the capacity to connect urban issues to root societal problems

The Johannesburg case demonstrates how urban issues can be connected to broader societal ones as day-to-day city problems were connected to root political issues. This potential to connect urban and national issues also exists in Belfast; decision makers there must consider when local policies should be enacted that seek more assertively to build intergroup tolerance and through what means these efforts can be connected to the larger peace process.

This connection between urban and national problems is also evident in the United States. Here, there is mounting awareness that the ways metropolitan areas are structured – including many spatial components amenable to planning policy – are connected to many root problems in our society, including inequality of opportunity, a polarized and anemic democracy, and racial/ethnic anxiety. Urban racial and ethnic segregation, for example, has been indicted for its pervasive societal effects – for creating an inequality of opportunity that has a "long-term debilitating effect on the quality of American democracy" (Altshuler *et al.* 1999: 9), endangering the American dream of getting ahead based on one's own efforts (Hochschild 1995), and constituting "the principal organizational feature of American society responsible for the creation of the urban underclass"

(Massey and Denton 1993: 9). Through progressive planning actions regarding housing, community and economic development, delivery of social services, and management of environmental pollution, metropolitan opportunities can be structured in more equitable ways such that today's separate societies can be connected and a more healthy and genuine democracy can function. Planning and development decisions in today's multicultural cities can establish bridges and links between racial/ethnic neighborhoods or they can build boundaries and figurative walls. The choices we make today will send emotive symbols to future generations about what we either aspire to in hope or accept in resignation.

Acknowledgments

I extend my deep appreciation to the extraordinary individuals who graciously provided me access to the mind and soul of the polarized city – Shalom, Salaam, Peace, Siochain, Vrede, Uxola. I wish to thank specifically Frederick Boal (Queen's University, Belfast), Arie Shachar (Hebrew University, Jerusalem), Chris Rogerson (University of the Witwatersrand, Johannesburg), and peace-builder Meron Benvenisti. The project would not have been possible without the financial support of the United States Institute of Peace, and the Social Science Research Council, Near and Middle East Program.

Notes

1   The broad label of community social and economic disparity is commonly used in the book to subsume ethnic and racial considerations; one indication of this treatment is that *race* and *ethnicity* cannot be found in the book's index. This bears a striking similarity to the lack of explicit reference to *Protestant* or *Catholic* in the Belfast Urban Area Plan *2001*.

2   It is not possible here to address each ethnic or racial conflict in its full richness. To do so would require an account of Jewish/Muslim relations in Palestine over the last 1,300 years, Catholic/Protestant relations since the Protestant plantations in Ulster (Northern Ireland) more than 450 years ago, and Black/White relations in South Africa since the introduction of Europeans over 350 years ago (see Bollens 1999, 2000).

3   The in-person interview was selected over other research techniques because it enables probing to obtain greater data. Thirty-four interviews were conducted in Belfast, 40 in Jerusalem, and 37 in Johannesburg, all between October 1994 and September 1995. Questions were open-ended, which allowed interviewees flexibility and depth in responding and facilitated responses not anticipated by the research design. Strong efforts were made to assure a fair distribution across ethnic groups, and across government and nongovernmental officials. In Belfast,

16 Protestants and 12 Catholics were interviewed (6 not reported); 19 were government officials and 15 were nongovernmental officials or academics. In Jerusalem, 24 Israelis and 15 Palestinians were surveyed; 12 were Israeli government officials, 11 were academics, and 17 were from the Palestinian Authority or nongovernmental organizations. In Johannesburg, 11 non-Whites and 26 Whites were interviewed; 21 were governmental officials and 14 were nongovernmental officials or academics. Interviewees gave written consent to be quoted and individually identified.

4   Assessment of Belfast policy is based on interviews with officials in the DOENI central office, the DOENI Town and Country Planning Service (Belfast Division), the NIHE Belfast Regional Office, the Central Community Relations Unit of the Northern Ireland Office, and with academics who have studied Belfast urban policy.

5   Internal documents that employ a sophisticated analysis of the multiple facets of ethnic geography and how they might impact government action, such as DOENI's 1990 Northgate Enterprise Park report, are commonly not released to the public.

6   Assessment of Israeli policy is based on interviews with current and former government officials in the Municipality of Jerusalem and the Ministry of Interior (Jerusalem District and central government office), Israeli academics who have worked on government projects, and Palestinian officials and researchers in nongovernmental organizations.

7   Assessment of Johannesburg policy is based on interviews with current officials with the City of Johannesburg, the Greater Johannesburg Transitional Metropolitan Council, Gauteng Province, and the South African central government. Many were involved from 1990 to 1995 in the negotiated transformation of Johannesburg local governance.

8   Even during times of great political tension, however, intergroup interaction can continue, at least at the level of professionals. In March 2001, amidst hostilities that began in November 2000, the author participated in a joint workshop of Israeli and Palestinian urban professionals examining the challenges and future options of planning a Jerusalem of mutual acceptance. The March 2001 workshop, held in the Netherlands, was an offshoot of a larger joint effort, begun in 1995, that contributed technical support to the 2000 Camp David peace negotiations. Each group in the Dutch workshop had unofficial connections with their respective governments rather than formal and explicit sponsorship.

Interviews cited

Belfast

John Hendry, Professor of Town and Regional Planning, Department of Environmental Planning, Queen's University of Belfast.

Dennis McCoy, Central Community Relations Unit, Central Secretariat, Northern Ireland Office.

William McGivern, Regional Director – Belfast, Northern Ireland Housing Executive

John McPeake, Assistant Director for Strategy, Planning and Research, Northern Ireland Housing Executive.

Bill Morrison, Superintending Planning Officer, Belfast Divisional Office, Town and Country Planning Service, Department of the Environment for Northern Ireland.

Gerry Mulligan, Central Statistics and Research Branch, Department of the Environment for Northern Ireland.

Bill Neill, Professor of Town Planning, Department of Environmental Planning, Queen's University; Head of Royal Town Planning Institute, Northern Ireland.

Ronnie Spence, Permanent Secretary, Department of the Environment for Northern Ireland.

Ken Sterrett, Town and Country Planning Services, Department of the Environment for Northern Ireland.

Paul Sweeney, Advisor, Department of the Environment for Northern Ireland.

George Worthington, Head, Belfast Divisional Office, Town and Country Planning Service, Department of the Environment for Northern Ireland.

Jerusalem

Elinoar Barzacchi, City Engineer, Municipality of Jerusalem (1989–94); Co-director, Steering Committee, Metropolitan Jerusalem Plan; Professor of Architecture, Tel Aviv University.

Uri Ben-Asher, District Planner, Jerusalem District, Ministry of the Interior.

Meron Benvenisti, author; former City Councilman and Deputy Mayor, Municipality of Jerusalem; Director, West Bank Data Project.

Yehonathan Golani, Director, Planning Administration, Ministry of Interior.

Benjamin Hyman, Director, Department of Local Planning, Ministry of the Interior.

Jan de Jong, Planning consultant, St Yves Legal Resource and Development Center, Jerusalem.

Sarah Kaminker, Chairperson, Jerusalem Information Center; former urban planner, Municipality of Jerusalem.

Israel Kimhi, Jerusalem Institute of Israel Studies; city planner, Municipality of Jerusalem (1963–86).

Ibrahim Matar, Deputy Director, American Near East Refugee Aid, Jerusalem.

Adam Mazor, Co-author, Metropolitan Jerusalem Master and Development Plan; Professor of Urban Planning, Technion Institute; Principal, Urban Institute Ltd. (Tel Aviv).

Shlomo Moshkovits, Director, Central Planning Department, Civil Administration for Judea and Samaria, Beit El, West Bank.

Nira Sidi, Director, Urban Planning Policy, Municipality of Jerusalem.

Khalil Tufakji, Geographer, Arab Studies Society; member, Palestinian-Israeli Security Committee.

Johannesburg

Lawrence Boya, Chief Director, Development Planning, Department of Development Planning, Environment, and Works, Gauteng Provincial Government.

Jane Eagle, Planner, Strategic Issues Division, City Planning Department, Greater Johannesburg Transitional Metropolitan Council.

Jan Erasmus, Acting Deputy Director, Regional Land Use, Johannesburg Administration, Greater Johannesburg Transitional Metropolitan Council.

Morag Gilbert, Deputy Director, Strategic Issues Division, City Planning Department, Johannesburg Administration.

Tim Hart, Urban geographer, SRK Engineers, Johannesburg.

Ivan Kadungure, Reconstruction and Development Programme Support Unit, Office of the Chief Executive; town planner, Soweto Administration, Johannesburg Transitional Metropolitan Council.

Alida Kotzee, Town and Regional Planner, Planning Services Directorate, Department of Development Planning, Environment, and Works, Gauteng Provincial Government.

Themba Maluleke, Project Manager, KATORUS, Department of Local Government and Housing, Gauteng Provincial Government.

Tshipso Mashinini, Deputy Director, Urbanization Department, Johannesburg Administration, Greater Johannesburg Transitional Metropolitan Council.

John Muller, Professor and Head, Department of Town and Regional Planning, University of the Witwatersrand, Johannesburg.

Monty Narsoo, Director of Housing, Department of Local Government and Housing, Gauteng Provincial Government.

Paul Waanders, Chief Director, Planning Services, Department of Development Planning, Environment and Works, Gauteng Provincial Government.

References

Alexander, E., Alterman, R. and Law-Yone, H. (1983) 'Evaluating plan implementation: the national statutory planning system in Israel', *Progress in Planning*, 20(2): 99–172.

Altshuler, A., Morrill, W., Wolman, H. and Mitchell, F. (eds) (1999) *Governance and Opportunity in Metropolitan America*, Washington, DC: National Academy Press.

Amirav, M. (1992) *Israel's Policy in Jerusalem Since 1967*, Working Paper Series No. 102, Center on Conflict and Negotiation, Stanford University.

APA (American Planning Association) (1992) *A Planners' Forum – Social Equity and Economic Development in Planning*, Chicago, IL: APA.

APA (American Planning Association) (1994) *Planning and Community Equity*, Chicago, IL: APA.

Baum, H. (1998) 'Ethical behavior is extraordinary behavior; it's the same as all other behavior – a case study in community planning', *Journal of the American Planning Association*, 64: 411–23.

Baum, H. (1999) 'Culture matters – but it shouldn't matter too much', in M. Burayidi (ed.) *Urban Planning in a Multicultural Society*, Westport, CT: Praeger.

Beauregard, R. (1999) 'Neither embedded or embodied: critical pragmatism and identity politics', in M. Burayidi (ed.) *Urban Planning in a Multicultural Society*, Westport, CT: Praeger.

Benvenisti, M. (1986) *Conflicts and Contradictions*, New York: Villard Books.

Benvenisti, M. (1995) *Intimate Enemies: Jews and Arabs in a Shared Land*, Berkeley, CA: University of California Press.

Benvenisti, M. (1996) *City of Stone: The Hidden History of Jerusalem*, Berkeley, CA: University of California Press.

Boal, F. (1990) 'Belfast: hindsight on foresight – planning in an unstable environment', in P. Doherty (ed.) *Geographical Perspectives on the Belfast Region*, Newtownabbey: Geographical Society of Ireland.

Boal, F. (1994) 'Belfast: a city on edge', in H. Clout (ed.) *Europe's Cities in the Late Twentieth Century*, Amsterdam: Royal Dutch Geographical Society.

Boal, F. and Douglas, J.N. (eds) (1982) *Integration and Division: Geographical Perspectives on the Northern Ireland Problem*, London: Academic Press.

Bollens, S. (1999) *Urban Peace-building in Divided Societies: Belfast and Johannesburg*, Boulder, CO: Westview Press.

Bollens, S. (2000) *On Narrow Ground: Urban Policy and Conflict in Jerusalem and Belfast*, Albany, NY: State University of New York Press.

B'Tselem (1995) *A Policy of Discrimination: Land Expropriation, Planning, and Building in East Jerusalem*, Jerusalem: B'Tselem.

Building Design Partnership (1969) *Belfast Urban Area Plan*, Belfast: Building Design Partnership.

Burayidi, M. (ed.) (1999) *Urban Planning in a Multicultural Society*, Westport, CT: Praeger.

Central Statistical Service (1992) *South African Statistics 1991*, Pretoria: Central Statistical Service.

Christopher, A. (1994) *The Atlas of Apartheid*, London: Routledge.

Cummings, S. (1998) *Left Behind in Rosedale: Race Relations and the Collapse of Community Institutions*, Boulder, CO: Westview Press.

CWMC (Central Witwatersrand Metropolitan Chamber) (1993) *An Interim Strategic Framework for the Central Witwatersrand. Document 2: Policy Approaches*, Johannesburg: CWMC.

Davies, R. (1981) 'The spatial formation of the South African city', *GeoJournal*, Supplementary Issue, 2: 59–72.

DOENI (Department of the Environment for Northern Ireland) (1977) *Northern Ireland: Regional Physical Development Strategy 1975–95*, Belfast: Her Majesty's Stationery Office.

DOENI (Department of the Environment for Northern Ireland) (1988) *Pre-inquiry Response to CTA's Objections to the Draft BUAP*, Belfast: Her Majesty's Stationery Office.

DOENI (Department of the Environment for Northern Ireland) (1989) *Belfast Urban Area Plan 2001: Adoption Statement*, Belfast: Her Majesty's Stationery Office.

DOENI (Department of the Environment for Northern Ireland) (1990) *Belfast Urban Area Plan 2001*, Belfast: Her Majesty's Stationery Office.

Douglas, J.N. and Boal, F. (1982) 'The Northern Ireland problem', in F. Boal and J. N. Douglas (eds) *Integration and Division: Geographical Perspectives on the Northern Ireland Problem*, London: Academic Press.

Elon, A. (1989) *Jerusalem: City of Mirrors*, Boston, MA: Little, Brown and Company.

Forester, J. (1989) *Planning in the Face of Power*, Berkeley, CA: University of California Press.

Friedmann, J. (1987) *Planning in the Public Domain: From Knowledge to Action*, Princeton, NJ: Princeton University Press.

Friedmann, J. (1996) 'The core curriculum in planning revisited', *Journal of Planning Education and Research*, 15(2): 89–104.

Friedmann, J. and Kuester, C. (1994) 'Planning education for the late twentieth century: an initial inquiry', *Journal of Planning Education and Research*, 14(1): 55–64.

Friedmann, J. and Lehrer, U.A. (1997) 'Urban policy responses to foreign in-migration: the case of Frankfurt-am-Main', *Journal of the American Planning Association*, 63: 61–78.

Gauteng Provincial Government (1995, July 27) *Progress Report: Implementation of Housing Investment Plan, Hostels Redevelopment Programme, Flashpoints and RDP*, Pretoria: Gauteng Provincial Government.

Gillette, H. Jr. (1995) *Between Justice and Beauty: Race, Planning, and the Failure of Urban Policy in Washington, D.C.*, Baltimore, MD: Johns Hopkins University Press.

Goldsmith, W. and Blakely, E. (1992) *Separate Societies: Poverty and Inequality in U.S. Cities*, Philadelphia, PA: Temple University Press.

Greater Johannesburg Metropolitan Council (1998) *Greater Johannesburg Metropolitan Council Integrated Metropolitan Development Plan, 1997/98*, Johannesburg: Greater Johannesburg Metropolitan Council.

Hadfield, B. (1992) 'The Northern Ireland Constitution', in B. Hadfield (ed.) *Northern Ireland: Politics and Constitution*, Buckingham: Open University Press.

Hartman, C. (1994) 'On poverty and racism, we have had little to say', *Journal of the American Planning Association*, 60: 158–9.

Hill, M. (1980) 'Urban and regional planning in Israel', in R. Bilski (ed.) *Can Planning Replace Politics? The Israeli Experience*, The Hague: Martinus Nijhoff.

Hoch, C. (1993) 'Racism and planning', *Journal of the American Planning Association*, 59: 451–60.

Hochschild, J. (1995) *Facing Up to the American Dream: Race, Class, and the Soul of the Nation*, Princeton, NJ: Princeton University Press.

Judd, D. and Swanstrom, T. (2002) *City Politics: Private Power and Public Policy*, 3rd edn, New York: Longman.

Kaminker, S. (1995) 'East Jerusalem: a case study in political planning', *Palestine–Israel Journal*, 2(2): 59–66.

Krumholz, N., and Clavel, P. (1994) *Reinventing Cities: Equity Planners Tell their Stories*, Philadelphia, PA: Temple University Press.

Krumholz, N. and Forester, J. (1990) *Making Equity Planning Work: Leadership in the Public Sector*, Philadelphia, PA: Temple University Press.

Loukaitou-Sideris, A. (1995) 'Urban form and social context: cultural differentiation in the uses of urban parks', *Journal of Planning Education and Research*, 14(2): 89–102.

Lustick, I. (1979) 'Stability in deeply divided societies: consociationalisation vs. control', *World Politics*, 31: 325–44.

Mabin, A. (1992) 'Comprehensive segregation: the origins of the Group Areas Act and its planning apparatus', *Journal of Southern African Studies*, 18(2): 405–29.

Mabin, A. and Hunter, R. (1993) 'Report of the review of conditions and trends affecting development in the PWV (Final report),' unpublished manuscript.

Marcuse, P. (1995) 'Not chaos, but walls: postmodernism and the partitioned city', in S. Watson and K. Gibson (eds) *Postmodern Cities and Spaces*, Cambridge, MA: Blackwell.

Massey, D. and Denton, N. (1993) *American Apartheid: Segregation and the Making of the Underclass*, Cambridge, MA: Harvard University Press.

Matthew, Sir R.H. (1964) *Belfast Regional Survey and Plan 1962*, Belfast: Her Majesty's Stationery Office.

Mier, R. (1994) 'Some observations on race in planning', *Journal of the American Planning Association*, 60: 235–40.

Morley, D. and Shachar, A. (1986) 'Epilogue: reflections by planners on planning', in D. Morley and A. Shachar (eds) *Planning in turbulence*, Jerusalem: Magnes Press, Hebrew University.

Municipality of Jerusalem (1994, April) 'East Jerusalem: conflicts and dilemmas – urban coping in the east of the city', unpublished manuscript.

Municipality of Jerusalem (1997) *Statistical Yearbook 1996*, Jerusalem: The Jerusalem Institute for Israel Studies.

Murtagh, B. (1994) *Ethnic Space and the Challenge to Land Use Planning: A Study of Belfast's Peace Lines*, Jordanstown: Centre for Policy Research, University of Ulster.

Nordlinger, E. (1972) *Conflict Regulation in Divided Societies*, Boston, MA: Center for International Affairs, Harvard University.

Northern Ireland Housing Executive (1988) *Coping with Conflict: Violence and Urban Renewal in Belfast*, Belfast: Northern Ireland Housing Executive.

Northern Ireland Registrar General. (1992) *Census of Population 1991: Belfast Urban Area Report*, Belfast: Her Majesty's Stationery Office.

Palestinian Central Bureau of Statistics (1998) *Palestinian Population, Housing and Establishment census – 1997*. Available online http://www.pcbs.org.

Parnell, S. and Mabin, A. (1995) 'Rethinking urban South Africa', *Journal of Southern African Studies*, 21(1): 39–61.

Parnell, S. and Pirie, G. (1991) 'Johannesburg', in A. Lemon (ed.) *Homes Apart: South Africa's Segregated Cities*, Bloomington, IN: University of Indiana Press.

Peace Now (1997) *Settlement Watch – Report no. 9*. Available online http://www.peace_now.org.

Pinel, S. (1994). 'Social impact assessment sensitizes planning', in American Planning Association, *Planning and Community Equity*, Chicago, IL: American Planning Association.

Planning Accreditation Board (2001) *The Accreditation Document: Criteria and Procedures of the Planning Accreditation Board*, Des Moines, IA: Planning Accreditation Board.

Qadeer, M. (1997) 'Pluralistic planning for multicultural cities: the Canadian practice', *Journal of the American Planning Association*, 63: 481–94.

Romann, M. and Weingrod, A. (1991) *Living Together Separately: Arabs and Jews in Contemporary Jerusalem*, Princeton, NJ: Princeton University Press.

Rothman, J. (1992) *From Confrontation to Cooperation: Resolving Ethnic and Regional Conflict*, Newbury Park, CA: Sage.

Sack, R. (1981) 'Territorial bases for power', in A. Burnett and P. Taylor (eds) *Political Studies from Spatial Perspectives*, New York: John Wiley.

Sandercock, L. (1998) *Towards Cosmopolis: Planning for Multicultural Cities*, Chicester: John Wiley and Sons.

Sen, S. (1999) 'Some thoughts on incorporating multiculturalism in urban design education', in M. Burayidi (ed) *Urban Planning in a Multicultural Society*, Westport, CT: Praeger.

Sennett, R. (1999) 'The spaces of democracy', in R. Beauregard and S. Body-Gendrot (eds) *The Urban Moment: Cosmopolitan Essays on the Late 20th-century City*, Thousand Oaks, CA: Sage.

South African Township Annual (1993) 'Johannesburg: IR Information Surveys'.

Sugrue, T. (1996) *The Origins of the Urban Crisis: Race and Inequality in Postwar Detroit*, Princeton, NJ: Princeton University Press.

Thomas, H. and Krishnarayan, V. (1994) ' "Race", disadvantage, and policy processes in British planning', *Environment and Planning A*, 26(12): 1891–910.

Thomas, J. (1994) 'Planning history and the Black urban experience: linkages and contemporary implications', *Journal of Planning Education and Research*, 14(1): 1–11.

Thomas, J. (1996) 'Educating planners: unified diversity for social action', *Journal of Planning Education and Research*, 15(3): 171–82.

Thomas, J. (1997) *Redevelopment and Race: Planning a Finer City in Postwar Detroit*, Baltimore: Johns Hopkins University Press.

United Church of Christ Commission for Racial Justice (1987) *Toxic Wastes and Race in the United States: A National Report on the Racial and Socio-economic Characteristics of Communities with Hazardous Waste Sites*, New York: United Church of Christ.

Yiftachel, O. (1995) 'The dark side of modernism: planning as control of an ethnic minority', in S. Watson and K. Gibson (eds) *Postmodern Cities and Spaces*, Cambridge, MA: Blackwell.

Yiftachel, O. (1998) 'Planning and social control: exploring the dark side', *Journal of Planning Literature*, 12(4): 395–406.

Chapter 10
Beyond labels
Pragmatic planning in multistakeholder tourism–environmental conflicts

Tazim B. Jamal, Stanley M. Stein and Thomas L. Harper

This article advocates a neopragmatic approach to collaborative planning in protected areas characterized by historical conflict among diverse stakeholders. Our example is a multisectoral process initiated to address use and development conflicts in the international tourism destination of Banff National Park, Canada. We show how philosophical presuppositions (essentialism and metaphysical realism) can impede collaboration and exacerbate problems when categories like "environmentalism" and terms like "ecological integrity" are used. Rather than fixing categories and terms up front, a more fluid planning approach is advocated: terms are flexible and meanings emerge through dialogue. Shared descriptions replace contentious categories and terms.

As we embark into the twenty-first century, the World Tourism Organization statistics reveal the robust growth of tourism, with more than 600 million international tourist arrivals in 2000, up from 443 million in 1990. One of the various tourism forms that have attracted the fancy of modern consumers and marketers is nature-based tourism and recreation (e.g. ecotourism), which persistently penetrates remote regions worldwide, while growth continues unabated in iconic landscapes like those represented by Yellowstone National Park (United States) and Banff National Park (Canada). Planners and administrators of such national parks and other protected areas face increasing challenges in managing the popularity of these natural areas as tourism destinations while ensuring their ecological integrity. These are complex domains where planning is often a contested political activity involving multiple, interdependent stakeholders with diverse and possibly divergent interests and values with respect to the natural environment. As the environmental planning and tourism planning literatures demonstrate, issues range from sustainable (tourism) development and public participation in environmental decision making (see Getz and Jamal 1994; Murphy

Submitted by the Association of Canadian University Planning Programs.

© 2002 Association of Collegiate Schools of Planning. Originally appeared in *Journal of Planning Education and Research* 22(2002): 164–77. By kind permission of Sage Publications Inc. www.sagepub.com.

1985; Stabler 1997; Tonn *et al.* 2000) to impact and growth management, planning and risk assessment (e.g. Gill and Williams 1994; O'Brien 2000; Palerm 2000; Weston 2000). But public participation can range from tokenism to genuine resident involvement (Arnstein 1969; Hughes 1995), and developing effective mechanisms for stakeholder involvement continues to preoccupy research and practice. The rise of interest-group pluralism as well as greater recognition of stakeholder interdependence, conflicts, and value differences in the sustainable development of human ecology domains has facilitated this focus on public and private involvement in tourism and environmental decision making. Consequently, multiparty consensus processes are increasingly being employed to deal with natural resource-based conflicts, and researchers, planners, and practitioners have begun to grapple with process issues such as stakeholder representation, negotiation, structuring, and institutional design (cf. Cormick *et al.* 1996; Innes *et al.* 1994; Westley 1995; Healey 1997).

While community-based and stakeholder-centered planning is espoused by many natural resource managers (e.g. the Canadian federal agency, Parks Canada, has public involvement policies in place), the particular processes by which strategic decisions are made and implemented in such collaborations are generally not well understood and neither are the philosophical assumptions that underlie the planning frameworks used. In this chapter, we analyze both philosophical and process-related issues pertaining to stakeholder-based planning and conflict resolution in national park destinations. Our goal is threefold:

1   to advocate a neopragmatic approach to multistakeholder planning processes in domains that are characterized by historical conflict among diverse stakeholders. Our neopragmatic approach (see below) follows contemporary proponents of pragmatism such as Richard Bernstein (1992) and Richard Rorty (cf. Menand 1997) and also draws some key concepts from John Rawls (1985, 1993);
2   to illustrate concretely the theoretical and philosophical argument for this approach using a research study of the Banff–Bow Valley Round Table (BBVRT), a multisectoral process initiated to address ecological, use, and development conflicts involving a diverse group of stakeholders in the international tourism destination and World Heritage Site of Banff National Park, Canada; and
3   to advance practical implications of the neopragmatic approach for addressing tourism development-related conflicts and strategic planning in protected areas.

As discussed by Stein and Harper (1998), neopragmatism is an alternative response to modernism's universalism and postmodernism's relativism. It attempts to retain the Enlightenment virtues of rationality, truth, and objective values, but grounds these within the specific situation and context such that the stories and voices of nondominant groups are able to be heard and involved in open dialogue and decision making. It is nonfoundational, antiessentialist, and nondualistic (in the sense of viewing distinctions as end points on a continuum rather than as absolute dichotomies). Neopragmatism draws on science as a legitimate source of authority but avoids the tendency of Deweyan pragmatists to rely uncritically on science as the primary authority.

This perspective also adopts a much less structured approach to planning and decision making than is advocated by many conventional planning approaches, such as the rational comprehensive planning model, and formal strategic planning approaches (e.g. Ansoff 1988). The approach to planning builds on approaches often referred to as communicative planning – for example, Forester's (1989) progressive planning, Innes *et al.*'s (1994) consensus building, and Healey's (1997) collaborative planning – but seeks to provide a broader theoretical basis. It also suggests certain practical refinements in consensus building or roundtable decision-making processes.

Particularly when it comes to addressing tourism–environmental conflict in domains such as Banff National Park, we argue that seeking agreement on definitions or abstract general principles should not be the starting point for discussion, as this can focus attention on historical differences and further lock people into adversarial stances. It is also counterproductive because it creates a hierarchical planning approach in which action and policy development are limited by the overarching definitions and abstract principles. Joint dialogue and learning among participants might facilitate different, more optimal outcomes if not constrained by such hierarchies. A neopragmatic approach suggests that instead of being fixed at the beginning, definitions of crucial concepts should emerge through dialogue and information sharing during the process, and particular descriptions should replace singular terms that may be contentious or problematic in some other way. Decision making is similarly pragmatic, with discussion focused on searching for, and jointly developing, specific actions and/or policies for particular issues on which there is some agreement. As such, philosophical and metaphysical debates play little or no role in this more fluid, nonhierarchical planning process.

This article offers theoretical and empirical support for this neopragmatic approach to collaborative planning and conflict resolution. In the next section, we provide a brief overview of collaborative tourism planning, followed by a short account of the conflict setting of Banff National Park (Canada) and the Banff–Bow Valley Round Table (BBVRT) case study. A theoretical conceptualization of labeling and category problems is then presented in the subsequent section, illustrated by examples from research conducted on the BBVRT.

Procedural recommendations and implications for multistakeholder planning and collaborative processes are presented in the final section.

Collaborative planning in environmental destinations

In a seminal work, Gray (1989) characterizes collaboration as a flexible and dynamic process involving multiple stakeholders in joint decision making to address issues in the problem domain. A stakeholder is defined here as "any group or individual who can affect or is affected by the achievement of an organization's purpose" (Freeman 1984: 52). Stakeholder-centered collaborative approaches have been employed by (inter-)organizational researchers such as Gray (1989), Roberts and Bradley (1991), Huxham (1996a, 1996b), and Phillips *et al.* (2000). Such processes are commonly based on seeking common ground or consensus on plans, policies, and actions, using techniques such as strategic visioning (Mintzberg 1994; Weisbord *et al.* 1992). Multiparty negotiations and collaborations have been initiated at various levels, including the global and the national, and have been recently enacted in natural resource and public land management (see Pasquero 1991; Susskind 1994; Daniels and Walker 1996; Selin and Beason 1991). Over the past decade in Canada, policies and mechanisms for public involvement in natural resource- and tourism-related conflicts have become increasingly popular, including public hearings and multistakeholder (roundtable) processes (Richardson *et al.* 1993; Cormick *et al.* 1996; Driscoll 1993). This evolution runs parallel with development and visitation pressures on protected areas such as Banff National Park, Canada, which fuel controversy over the use and governance of the national parks.

In the "Canadian Pacific's Rockies," Bella (1987) demonstrated the tension in Canada's national parks, where the railroad interests had first choice of business location in Banff National Park (see Figure 10.1) and in all the other national parks. The conservationist struggles leading to the 1930s National Parks Act enshrined into the act the statement that the parks remain "unimpaired for future generations." However, the conservationists had not argued "purely for the intrinsic value of the scenery" but had "used one economic argument to counter another," insisting on the tourism potential of the beautiful scenery, so the new act "entrenched a system and philosophy of parks for profit" (Bella 1987: 58). This checkered history of Canada's national parks is reflected in the conflict over development and preservation in Banff National Park to this day. In the words of one active environmental group in the park (also present as a participating group in the BBVRT), "the debate is not about keeping people out of the park. It's about the greed that is bent on destroying Canada's most beautiful symbol of its wilderness heritage."[1] Park planners and administrators are particularly vulnerable, caught as they are between the ecological needs of the parks, the political landscape

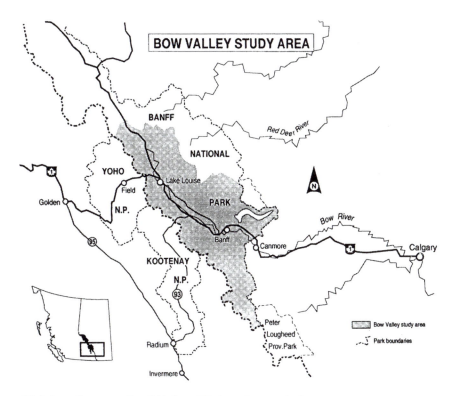

10.1 Location map: Banff National Park and case study area

of tax revenues for government coffers, and the needs of tourists, recreationalists, businesses, and others involved in the "tourism production system" (Britton 1991). The need for new ways to govern the national parks and to manage conflict in such complex destination domains has given rise to stakeholder-centered planning processes such as the Banff–Bow Valley Round Table described below.

Addressing conflict in Banff National Park, Canada

Around 459,000 visitors came to Banff National Park in 1950, with as many as 19 million projected by the year 2020, based on current growth rates (BBVRT 1996). Even with a growth rate of only 3 percent, park visitation could exceed 10 million by the same date, double its current visitation (BBVRT 1996: 53). Within this international tourism destination and World Heritage Site lies the town of Banff (population 7,600), whose continued growth as a service center and destination within the park severely affects the sensitive moraine and natural systems within the narrow Bow River Valley. Visitors spent an estimated $709 million in the park in 1995, and Calgarians account for 60 percent of park visitation. Meanwhile, Parks Canada (the federal agency responsible for the administration of the national parks in the country) has been faced with budget cuts, forcing it to seek revenue-generating alternatives such as increased fees, user-pay policies, and private-sector involvement in running various services. It is not surprising to hear an environmental stakeholder express with some frustration that the park's administrators are "beaten down" by the rationalization of the parks system and the drive to become increasingly efficient and economically sustainable.

Driven by long, sustained conflict over use and development in Banff National Park as well as by distrust over park governance, the Banff–Bow Valley Study (BBVS) was initiated by the (then) Minister of Canadian Heritage, Michel Dupuy, in March 1994. The BBVS Task Force was announced by the minister on 5 July 1994, with the mandate to conduct a comprehensive analysis of the environmental, economic, and social issues in the Bow River watershed within the park. This was to culminate in a set of strategies for the long-term management of the Banff–Bow Valley, "to protect the environmental integrity, as well as the social and economic vitality, of the Banff–Bow Valley for future generations" (*BBVS Newsletter*, 1 May 1995: 2).

A multiparty roundtable was established by the task force as one of the key mechanisms for enabling public input into the task force's report, based on a process of dialogue and consensus decision making. Key stakeholder groups were identified and convened with a sector chair representative for each sectoral interest (see Table 10.1). A mediator was appointed, ground rules were established, and interest statements were developed by each sector. An early task of the roundtable was to assist the task force with constructing a vision for the Banff–Bow Valley. This became a major agenda item between May (when a work plan was compiled) and December 1995. The final products included a core vision, key themes, principles, and values.

Based on discussion in the July, August, and September meetings, the participating groups identified four key negotiation issues, but due to time constraints, they agreed to work primarily on the first two, that is, (1) ecological integrity and (2) appropriate use. Negotiation on these two issues commenced in the September and October meetings and continued to the end of March 1996 (along with other agenda items). The wording of the vision statement continued to take table time up to the end of the December meetings. A report summarizing the roundtable's work was ratified by the sectors and used in the preparation of the task force's report to the minister, which was released to the public by the current minister of Canadian heritage at a media event held in Banff on 7 October 1996. Table 10.1 summarizes the overall study and roundtable process.

The case study and the theoretical position forwarded in the following sections draw on Jamal's (1997) dissertation research, which spanned the duration of the BBVRT process, including the release of the final study report to the public in October 1996 and public meetings in early 1997. Data gathering and analysis were based on (1) in-depth interviews with a dozen participants in the BBVRT (during and postprocess) using purposive sampling to ensure that a broad array of interests and concerns were included in the research, (2) participant observation of the BBVRT meetings (assisted as a volunteer on the Park Users sector), (3) attendance at public meetings related to both processes, and (4) examination of documents related to this initiative.

Interviews were primarily field based and face to face, although a few were conducted over the telephone. An open-ended, semistructured interview format enabled in-depth exploration of (1) the process of convening stakeholder participants; (2) the visioning, negotiation, and consensus decision-making process;

Table 10.1 Overview of the Banff–Bow Valley Study and roundtable process

Process/location	Banff–Bow Valley (in Banff National Park)
Name	Banff–Bow Valley Study Round Table
Representation	Fourteen interest sectors (originally) and provincial Alberta government observer only; sectors included tourism and local businesses, environmental groups (local and national), diverse recreational groups of park users, local municipal government, federal (including national park) representation, local community (Banff) social and cultural interests, and First Nations inhabitants of the area (who dropped out early in the process, reducing the sectors to twelve)
Time frame	Study commenced in June 1994; roundtable meetings were held from February 1994 to March 1994; final report of the task force was submitted in late summer 1996
Structure	Formal – process and procedure agreement (ground rules); external mediator appointed
Initiator	Minister of Canadian heritage
Convenor(s)	Five-member task force (with administrative help from task force secretariat)
Public input	Public forum during roundtable meetings; public meetings; vision statement survey
Product	Vision statement for Banff–Bow Valley, State of the Valley Report, Summary Report of Round Table (March 1996), and so forth; final report of the task force was released to the public in October 1996

and (3) being a participant in this high-profile study and roundtable, that is, the everyday, lived experience of participating in the BBVRT process and the broader community as well as the meanings associated with participation in this context. The major focus of the interpretive approach in this research was this last aspect (3), around which the specific process issues (1) and (2) were explored. A few follow-up interviews were also conducted more than a year after the process ended. Interview quotes are cited anonymously to protect the identity of respondents. Italics, where used in the quotes, are meant to direct the reader to specific concepts or items of interest to the study.

Philosophical problems with labels and abstract concepts

The BBVRT illustrates two general problems that can inhibit effective collaboration in such a domain: the problem of labeling or categorizing (e.g. "environmentalist") and the problem of applying abstract principles, terms, or concepts (e.g. "ecological integrity," "intrinsic value"). We attempt to show below that such general terms, categories, and labels can impede rather than enhance dialogue due to certain philosophical presuppositions that underlie their understanding. We are not suggesting that categories should be avoided entirely but rather that attention should be paid to understanding and dealing with philosophical influences contributing to the development of contentious dichotomies and ambiguities, especially where these enable dominant interests to prevail over effective participation from less powerful stakeholders. A neopragmatic planning approach offers an alternative way to address such issues and influences. We present the two general problems below, using the category "environmentalist" and the term "ecological integrity" to illustrate concretely the philosophical issues (pertaining to essentialism and metaphysical realism). This is followed by the alternative view we advocate, which is also illustrated practically with the help of examples from the BBVRT.

Essentialism and categories: the "environmentalist"

Essentialism is the view that objects have essential properties. An essential property of an object is a property the object could not lack and still be the same object. For example, Bill Clinton could not have lacked the property of being human; he could not have been, say, a mosquito or an automobile. Hence, the property of being human is an essential property of him. By contrast, he could have failed to be a politician – he could have continued to practice law without ever running for public office. Thus, the property of being a politician is not essential to him. Essentialism presupposes that categories or general terms that pick out natural kinds "in the world" have precise definitions that reflect the essence of the category or term. Consequently, those who accept this traditional point of view search for definitions that determine the essence of a category, seeking the essential element common to all uses of the term or category, for example, the category "environmentalist."

While this tradition of essentialism has a long history (e.g. the essentialist tradition stemming from Aristotle), a very simplistic sketch of John Stuart Mill's theory of meaning may help to understand the essentialist problems associated with a label or category such as "environmentalist." Mill states that words have a denotation (roughly, reference) and connotation (roughly, meaning or sense). The denotation of a term is the class of items to which it refers; the connotation is the properties shared by all members of that class. The connotation is roughly associated with the meaning of the term and provides its (essential) characteristics or attributes. These properties or characteristics are rigidly fixed. In an essentialist view, all terms must have these various features (except proper names, which we shall not discuss). The term thus confers "reality" on that to which it refers, in virtue of these certain (essential) properties that determine what it is (its essence). Since the term appears to be consistently definable and "real," it can be used to claim legitimacy (and power).

Consider, for instance, what we mean when we characterize someone an "environmentalist." What do we consider to be the (essential) properties that determine the category "environmentalist" – tree hugger, wilderness lover, volunteer steward and activist for environmental causes, believer in intrinsic value of living things? An environmental participant in the BBVRT commented during an interview that he did not wish to be labeled environmentalist, or preservationist, or conservationist. Why does being an environmentalist constitute a special interest, but being a golfer does not? (remarked another BBVRT environmental respondent with frustration). While it appears to be essentially given, the label "environmentalist" is neither homogeneous nor rigidly fixed, as other studies also note. For example, in a social assessment for a US national forest, two kinds of environmentalists were distinguished by the attributes of preferred outcomes and management preferences (Carroll *et al.* 2000; see also Cronon 1996). Hence, structuring participation in a roundtable-type process into environmental interests versus development/business interests could potentially aggravate differences between the two groups, worsened by essentialist presuppositions associated with the term "environmentalist."

Other challenges to effective participation also ensue from categorizing participants under terms or related categories that could be viewed essentially, such as the "local environment" and "national environment" sectors in the BBVRT. For example, if one lived within the national park but happened to represent a social or cultural sector, did it mean that environmental concerns were the legitimate purview of the environmental sectors only? Another participant than the ones mentioned above expressed such a concern about the structuring of roundtable representation, observing that the labeling of sectoral interests had an artificial and exclusionary aspect:

> Well, I mean, I think the table could be even bigger. I think it could be, we could each partition ourselves down smaller and smaller but to me it doesn't matter what the titles are in the pigeon holes, just get yourself there and get in find a place where you can fit in. It's all artificial, it's *an artificial structure that's imposed on an organic system. So, I mean, anytime you label, you exclude.*
> (Interview, BBVRT participant, November 1995)

As the respondent therefore wondered, was it legitimate to empathize with another sector's view if one is participating in a different sector, categorized by different interests and attributes?

> As you're listening to the dialogue at the table, I'll know exactly what another individual is expressing. I'll be empathizing and then I'll be thinking in my head, is that where I'm supposed to be with my sector's point of view?

This exclusion through labeling noted above is also echoed by a Vermont grassroots activist in Blechman *et al.*'s (1996) study, who says, "We have to break down those barriers of feeling that you're not legitimate unless you really are attached to one organization or one philosophy" (p. 20). She indicates that her views cannot be so easily reduced to being reflected by one philosophy or organization. The difficulty of structuring participation by sectors or interest groups such as environmentalists is that these categories may be viewed as essential. If such terms are polemic or politically charged, an essentialist view may exacerbate conflict or distrust among participants already opposed to each other's positions and/or interests.

To return to the practical issue, when and if a term or its use is contested, this search for its essential meaning or properties can stall a planning process in its early stage. By avoiding labeling a set of beliefs as "environmentalist," for instance, fewer people may reject them outright, and more may be willing to debate them. In domains of historical conflict over use and development, such as Banff National Park, neutral language is more helpful than normative, value-laden categories and concepts such as "environmentalist," "intrinsic value," and "limits" (to growth). Normative language works if we are dealing with a unitary shared culture, but in a domain characterized by conflict among disparate values, it may be exclusionary and detrimental to dialogue and joint decision making to use general terms that come with historical, temporal, and essentialist baggage.

People become committed to the categories they use and often develop a close identification with them, thus making it more difficult to facilitate discussion and dialogue that enable shared understanding of issues and concerns. By just describing their specific beliefs rather than labeling or categorizing themselves as "environmentalist" or "developer," participants may be able to better identify overlapping beliefs that can then provide a basis for dialogue.

Metaphysical realism: ecological integrity

Another way in which terms can take on fixed meaning is by appealing to metaphysical realism. Metaphysical realism is the view that the objects that constitute the world exist independently of the human mind. A strong corollary of metaphysical realism is that language and thought are able to refer to and accurately describe (characterize) the nature of these objects, that is, their properties and the relations they stand in. Thus, our forms of representation (categories, terms, labels) are seen as rigidly fixed and given by the world. So, for example, our analysis indicates that ecological integrity in the parks mandate and policies tended to be viewed through the lens of metaphysical realism in the BBVRT, particularly with respect to its associated corollary that that there is a "fixed relation between terms and their extensions" (Putnam 1990: 27). This leads to the (implied) claim that the term is more legitimate because it refers to a thing that is really in the world, which then becomes a powerful source of normative justification for a particular course of action, as occurred in the roundtable process.

The definition of ecological integrity that was used by the BBVRT and study was fixed early in the process by scientists (primarily) modifying a Parks Canada definition. The interview data and roundtable meetings show the implied metaphysical realism with which this term was associated. For instance, a business stakeholder who was interviewed after the end of the BBVRT meetings described issues that he felt (in hindsight) should have been examined during the BBVRT process, but were not. In the first sentence of the following quote, he refers to the national park's mandate whose meaning was contested by participants – some, such as this business participant, perceived it to be a dual mandate of use and protection, while others, such as the environmental sectors, protested that ensuring ecological integrity was, in fact, the primary mandate of the parks. He then applies his understanding of the mandate, as clarified by the assistant deputy minister, Tom Lee, during a September 1995 roundtable meeting, to explain how the process and he himself had somehow become focused on ecological integrity instead of the broader human use issues related to the park's being a premier international tourism destination. But it was only after the process had ended and he had had some time to reflect that this understanding of a different reality arrived:

As Tom [Lee] says, *it's not a dual mandate, it's one mandate, you know, a multifaceted role for the Park.* The science has got to acknowledge that going in. ... We've got a national transportation corridor. We've got Canada's premier tourism destination, a recreational area that's fundamentally important to western Canadians, we've got to *face reality* here, and it's really only crystallized after the fact [and?] what we should have been saying and perhaps delivering a message, you know, the message there *is that's the reality,* how do you deal with it? And instead the Bow Valley Study addressed it from *ecological integrity [which] means this, this place doesn't have or is unlikely to have ecological integrity and therefore we have to shut the doors.*

(Interview, business participant, January 1997)

The rhetorical manner in which this term became used at the roundtable meetings and in media documents presented a sense of real existence of such a condition, somewhere or sometime. Consider the following concern of one environmental respondent (the full quote appears later in the chapter), which was expressed at the roundtable meetings as well: "We believe clearly that the ecological integrity of the Banff–Bow Valley is really on shaky ground right now." Yet many terms and concepts in the social (including cultural) sciences and in the ecological sciences do not lend themselves to this model of metaphysical realism: they do not refer to an objective thing or property in the world. However, when stakeholders adopt the perspective of metaphysical realism toward a term such as "ecological integrity" or use terms such as "intrinsic value" in an essentialist way or imbue categories such as "environmentalist" with essentialist meanings, it can be detrimental to dialogic processes convened under conditions of conflict between development and preservation interests.

An alternative view

A neopragmatic view of decision making in planning rejects the notion of rigid definition and avoids a reliance on essentialism and metaphysical realism to justify a view. Rather than being fixed, categories are viewed as more flexible and fluid, with properties that are open and changeable. Wittgenstein's idea of family resemblances is, we contend, far more appropriate to interpreting social concepts. Wittgenstein (1969) discussed the example of games, a social concept, to illustrate how there is not one property that can essentially define what a game is. For each denoted class (e.g. game), there is an associated cluster of properties such that some members of the class share some of the properties in the cluster and other members of the class share other properties of the cluster. Together, these properties can be thought of in terms of what Wittgenstein called family resemblances, that is, properties that underlie similarities between different members of the class. The properties with which the terms are identified are open and variable. Hence, the word "game" should not be viewed as having a fixed or essential meaning. Rather, one game is related to another game by the idea of family resemblances. "Instead of producing something common in all that we call language, I am saying that these phenomena have no one thing in common ... but that they are related to one another in many different ways" (Wittgenstein 1969: para. 65).

Similarly, the term "ecological integrity" could be described using the perspective of family resemblances rather than viewing it through an essentialist or realist lens. This philosophical approach is also particularly compatible with neopragmatism for, as Rorty (1979, 1991) suggests, debate about realism is unproductive: the criteria governing discussions should not be which accounts come closer to the truth but rather which accounts are most productive to the human enterprise. In other words, a neopragmatic planning view suggests that the choice of linguistic form should be determined on the basis of the purpose(s) and goals of the planning process and not on the basis of what accords better with reality. Categories such as "environmentalist" and terms such as "ecological integrity" are therefore fluid, that is, they involve characteristics, properties, and descriptions that are open and evolving over time rather than being rigidly definable, fixed, and real. The choice of linguistic forms, categories, names, and labels should be in the service of our goals rather than being their master. Their correctness is determined by how well they serve our purposes rather than how well they conform to reality.

As such, allocating process time to come up with new descriptions, jointly derived definitions, or new terms that replace the use of contentious or ambiguous terms may be more productive than establishing definitions early in the process. This is particularly important when sensitive issues and positions such as limits to growth (see below) are causing serious tensions in negotiations. The following two examples from our analysis of the BBVRT process illustrate how the philosophical concepts in our alternative view may usefully explain certain outcomes and requirements of the collaborative process.

Example: the pragmatic vision statement

Terms such as "limits" or "intrinsic value" were not debated when included in the roundtable's vision for the Banff–Bow Valley, which itself involved a long, drawn-out process of word smithing, as several interview respondents noted. More than one roundtable respondent commented on how the concept of limits to development and visitation in the park was disconcerting to tourism interests in the park:

We believe clearly that the ecological integrity of the Banff–Bow Valley is really on shaky ground right now and there's some serious problems ... six months ago we were hearing that time and time again, "well we just don't believe that," *there was a state of denial* going on. That seemed to have been, they seem to have given up that argument after Tom Lee came out and spoke in September. And Steve Woodley [invited scientist speaker] gave his definition of how they developed [a] definition of ecological integrity. *That seemed to move some of the sectors out of that state of denial.* Now *maybe they just you know, decided not to speak about it* but now I think *we're starting to see it resurface because we're at the point now where we're really talking about putting restrictions and limitations in place*; now *they're starting to fight back.*

(Interview, environmental participant, January 1996)

The concept of limits was hardly discussed at the roundtable or in the workshops, other than in terms of percentages or numbers with respect to growth in the national park. What scenarios shall we project in our futures modeling exercise – one percent, three percent, five percent? Very little discussion at these meetings focused on what limits meant, or the various ways in which impacts might be handled or limits imposed, other than by restricting visitation and population growth. Yet limits made it into the roundtable's vision statement for the Banff–Bow Valley, as did the notion of intrinsically valuing other forms of life, although how the participants interpreted these may have varied considerably:

Just getting stuff like that in the vision I think is a major accomplishment. The word "*limits*" is in there and there may be, around the table there may be *differing interpretations* as to where on the list we place those but at least it's part of the vocabulary now. There may be some things in there that I'm not completely comfortable with but I think *we've moved things along.* ... I mean, we've taken a group of people and *they've agreed* that these are the things that are important to us and we said restraining ourselves for future generations is important to us. We value the intrinsic, *intrinsically value other forms of life.*

(Interview, environmental participant, December 1995)

This vision statement was a pragmatically oriented one that cobbled together a diverse range of beliefs and values into some concrete statements that were not cross-examined early in the process but remained open to interpretation. The visioning process, too, followed a pragmatic approach that avoided philosophical debate about the park, thereby enabling the process to move along. Other than a short debate about the national park mandate (which was settled by inviting the assistant deputy minister to inform the table on the official interpretation of the mandate), the very sensitive issue of the purpose of the national park was not broached. Nevertheless, since the general purpose of a vision statement is to provide an uplifting, forward-looking description of the hopes, values, beliefs, and aspirations of participant(s) in the visioning process, as well as a sense of joint direction, the above discussion does raise the question of how common and consensus based the roundtable's vision statement really was to sector participants and constituents. A business participant and respondent felt the vision statement was a "significant document" in presenting a "negotiated settlement" among the participating groups. This, he said, was a vision statement crafted carefully through a rationally "negotiated agreement" based on "compromise" not consensus because "ideologically," he was "never going to convert" X (an environmental participant). How useful, then, was this exercise if compromise rather than consensus formed the basis of the vision developed?

The applause at the table when the vision statement was finally completed and agreed on by the sector chairs reflected a sense of accomplishment among the participants. References to the vision (and to the jointly developed principles and values that were seen to be an integral part of it) in subsequent roundtable meetings and the positive comments made by respondents during interviews indicate that the participants considered the vision to be helpful in dealing with subsequent process issues. Parks Canada also used the vision statement in the next park management plan (1997). As a participant-respondent noted, conducting this vision exercise early in the overall process allowed observation of other participants" positions, personalities, and interactions, thereby offering an inkling of how process dynamics were shaping up (e.g. relationships among sectors and between sector chairs). The exercise also fulfilled an early process step of enabling participants to develop (an apparent) common ground from which to proceed, without risking being locked into an untenable view or legal position on the desired future of the park. The open-endedness of some meanings in the statement and the nonlegal nature of the visioning exercise thus facilitated the formation of some relationships and understandings among participants, enabling some pragmatic actions and decisions to be made that advanced the process to the issues negotiation phase.

Example: creating new shared descriptions

In the collaborative planning context, a neopragmatic approach suggests that after dialogue and reconfiguration of some beliefs take place, new groupings may be chosen that might encourage consensus between previously conflicting positions, using a new shared description. For participants such as the business one quoted below, who felt that "human experience" was missed out in the debate on ecological integrity, it was a relief to see the task force recommend the development of a heritage tourism strategy for the park (by building on an initiative that had been commenced by another group of stakeholders elsewhere in the park). The new grouping (heritage tourism strategy) and the concept of heritage enabled people to bring in various stories of human presence in the park while acknowledging the ecological importance of this space and place. Since heritage is a concept that enables different appropriations from the past to be brought into the present (Lowenthall 1998), both historical and ongoing human presence can be described in the plan and the park, along with efforts to ensure its ecological integrity.

> *We fundamentally believe in the need to preserve those areas for future genera-*
> *tions.* But I think what we're going to have to do is see if we can't convince
> people that there's a way to embrace the environment and the need to *preserve*
> *the ecological integrity* and at the same time acknowledge the need of the
> human experience.
>
> (Interview, BBVRT business participant, January 1997)

What was important to this business participant was the need to manage the impacts of development rather than focus on the realism of the crisis (of which he said he was not convinced). Rather than debate the crisis or dispute the scientific evidence being presented to prove serious damage to the park's ecological integrity, he adopts a pragmatic view, (re-)interpreting problematic concepts and notions such as the park's dual mandate, crisis, and ecological integrity within a pragmatic framework, seeking specific concrete issues that he could examine in light of his sector's interests and then focusing on solutions that address his stakeholders' needs and goals.

The issues and examples presented above indicate that a neopragmatic approach may be valuable for multistakeholder planning under conditions of historical conflict in protected areas such as national parks. Our analysis of the BBVRT suggests that sensitive terms may not necessarily detract from moving a process along, as long as they are brought in without strict definitions and are not so contentious that they cause conflict to escalate without control. In other words, definitions of such sensitive terms should not be imposed on the participants but rather should be left open and allowed to evolve over time in the process, if they have not been replaced by new shared terms and descriptions by then.

A neopragmatic approach therefore supports an interactive, learning-based approach to planning under conflict that allows new, shared meanings to be formed by participants. However, process managers will need to be able to recognize the philosophical issues that may impede effective participation and negotiation since this has implications for both structure and process. They will need to decide whether to avoid sensitive categories or whether to facilitate dialogue about them, so that participants recognize that terms such as "environmentalist" are not to be used in an essentialist way. They will also require skills and techniques that facilitate joint discussion and learning about (possibly) sensitive, ambiguous, and/or complex categories and terms. While the overall process requires some fluidity in planning so that such dialogic and learning opportunities are enabled to deal with such issues as they emerge along the way, there are a few process areas that are particularly conducive to meaning making in a collaboration, such as the problem-setting phase, the visioning process, and the situation mapping step in collaborative learning (Daniels and Walker 1996). We discuss these and other implications in the final section below.

Implications for multistakeholder planning

As we have attempted to demonstrate above, neopragmatism blurs the line between naming and the object of the naming. Names and their meanings come and go, they evolve over time (hence the varying interpretations of the dual mandate noted later in the BBVRT process, despite attempts to fix one meaning earlier in the process). However, while the neopragmatist's categories and terms can be softer, more flexible, and open, they are not so radically decentered as to make it impossible to fix meaning in any way, nor are they merely conventions dependent on language, as deconstructionist philosophers such as Derrida might have them be (Harper and Stein 1995b). Unlike deconstructionism, neopragmatism attempts to ground meaning, but this meaning is tailored to particular needs in particular contexts, as illustrated in the examples above.

Not surprisingly then, neopragmatism criticizes the search for abstract principles, such as intrinsically valuing other life forms, since it rests on a traditional philosophical position in which there is a hierarchy with abstract principles at the top, from which are deduced more specific principles and then concrete actions. We argue that abstract principles do not have any privileged or absolute position: they are part of an interactive process of holistic mutual adjustment through dialogue and discussion (see Rorty 1991). One is weighed against the other, sometimes modifying principles, other times modifying intuitions (Harper and Stein 1995a). Such an approach is incremental, allowing our beliefs and concepts to evolve and/or emerge over time. This approach is also nonhierarchical, blurring the lines between abstract principles and concrete intuition, between judgment and action, and between theory and practice (Stein and Harper 1998).

A neopragmatic approach to labeling and abstract principles thus offers flexibility for arriving at some form of consensus or agreement since it veers clear of negotiating issues that are fixed by absolutist positions. It is not necessary to define things in sequential or contested categories. Hence, it frees the participants

from seeking hard and fast principles that could do more to damage the negotiations than facilitate movement toward reasonable solutions. Such an approach
does not affect the legitimacy or credibility of particular points of view, but it
does free and open them up to possibilities for new groupings and more fruitful
categories, not because such names are "out there" or have preexisting essences
but because "regrouping things into new kinds ... prove(s) to lend (itself) to
many inductions more relevant than old groupings" (Quine 1969: 128). Such
categorizing or labeling activity is more likely to be helpful during the process
rather than at the very start where entrenched categories, definitions, and positions
may tend to create or exaggerate divisiveness among participants. As beliefs are
reconfigured and shared meanings emerge along the way, a new name, label, or
definition may become a useful shorthand for a new shared (re-)description of a
problematic term.

The fluidity of a neopragmatic planning approach thus enables participants
to address sensitive terms or contentious issues such as limits to growth or
reintroduce them later in the process after some information and activities have
been shared, some concrete agreements have been reached, and joint understandings have emerged along with relationships of respect and/or trust among
(some) players (see Jamal and Getz 1999). This neopragmatic approach offers
several implications for multistakeholder planning and conflict resolution under
conditions of historical and/or escalating conflict.

The concept of person and group in the BBVRT

A neopragmatic approach has particular implications for the concept of interest
groups. In the "Introduction to Briefing Material," Banff–Bow Valley Study,
Round Table, 02/03/95, under the section heading "Structure and Representation," is the following statement: "The Banff–Bow Valley Round Table is
designed to be representative of all genuine concerns associated with the Valley.
The strength of the Table as a planning and decision-making body rests in this
concept of effective representation." Our study suggests, however, that structuring
participants into general interest categories during the early convening stage sets
up barriers to recognizing the interdependence of various constructs (e.g. social-
culture-environmental). As discussed in the previous section, it also facilitates a
social reality of naming with which participants may identify, therefore further
widening the chasm between opposed parties. Hence, both the structuring of
interest groups and the development of interest statements (as was done in the
BBVRT) need to be approached with caution for these reasons. Rather than
recognizing that they are fluid and may change over time in the process, such
interest statements are often interpreted in an essentialist way to be fixed
representations of sectoral and constituent interests and identities.

Much debated and contended in discussions about interest-based stakeholder processes is the concept of a person. Pursuing traditional debates about personal identity, liberals with a Kantian inclination have been criticized by both postmodernists and communitarians for conceptualizing a person as a transcendental, autonomous, and absolutely free agent. Communitarians have a competing concept of the person as a social construction, a product of the environment. Neopragmatists, interpreting Rawls (1993), sidestep this controversy by emphasizing that the concept of a person that is needed for debates about political justice is one appropriate to that purpose; that is, it is "political not metaphysical." In other words, this conception of a person is context bound and not essentialist. Neither is it relativistic, for, as we have argued earlier, a concept (such as "game") is a matter of an overlapping family of resemblances.

So while we reject the attempt to find an essentialist definition, we believe that the concept of the person is still useful and workable from a neopragmatic approach, which does not attempt to rigidly define process rules, participant roles, and contentious categories. Practical decisions about appropriate actions do not require governing principles or debates on metaphysical issues such as the nature of the person, society, the city, or the environment (e.g. whether nature has intrinsic/biocentric or instrumental/anthropocentric value). However, as noted earlier, the process manager has to be aware of the philosophical issues related to this to try and avoid exclusionary effects that may develop due to categorizing participants under labels such as "environmentalist."

Focus on concrete/substantive problems

In issues-oriented negotiation processes such as the BBVRT, where there are such a wide range of interests, values, and goals, as well as deeply entrenched historical conflict, distrust, and volatile tensions, we suggest a neopragmatic approach to decision making that focuses on addressing specific, clearly identified problems and concerns rather than philosophical ones. For instance, a strong concern of several business participants during the issues negotiation phase was to try and understand the impact of proposed strategies/actions on business in the park. Expressing lack of understanding about the science being forwarded to support the ecological concerns of some stakeholders in the process, one business respondent felt it was more important to manage the substantive implications of tangible problems, such as the difficulty of bears and humans vying for the same space in a specific habitat area. To some extent, this supports our claim for a political, not metaphysical, approach to address specific issues, so essentialist debates are avoided. Effort has to be expended, however, to clarify categories and terms that are being viewed in an essential way. If central or contested notions such as intrinsic value or limits are used, it may be best to leave them intentionally vague early in the process, as was done for the BBVRT vision (though, arguably, this was not necessarily by design on the part of the process managers).

If no agreement (consensus) is arrived at on an issue, it may be best to lay aside this issue for a while, perhaps in favor of something smaller, narrower, and more concrete. Our analysis of the BBVRT process suggests that success in solving smaller problems may help move the process along and build confidence for tackling more difficult issues. It follows that environmental conflict resolution processes such as the BBVRT, involving diverse interest groups and community residents in developing a vision and strategies, should be fluid, flexible, and adaptive. Participants and process managers need not commence by seeking underlying principles or fixing each sector's interests into a static, unchangeable interest statement. These concepts need to be explored, discussed, and debated to find out what might be shared beliefs or goals. These can be written up in as neutral terms as possible, so that they are not categorical, normative, or abstract. If used, contested labels can be left vague early in the process. Abstract principles need to be treated as one element in an interactive process of holistic, mutual adjustment rather than as hierarchical, absolute, or universal principles.

More specifically, for environmental planning in a domain of historical conflict, the debate between the environment as an economic resource (having only instrumental value) and the environment as having intrinsic value can be put aside to focus on understanding what should be preserved and how to do this. This helps the process to move forward, aided further by some relationship building, direction setting, and activities such as the visioning exercise. As more than one respondent mentioned, the visioning process in the BBVRT was very helpful in providing them a nonbinding discussion forum that enabled them to ascertain where others stood with respect to their positions and opinions.

Strategic planning and neopragmatic decision making

Our analysis of the BBVRT process indicates the need to pay careful attention to the purpose of the process as well as to the needs and concerns of the participants. While the BBVRT addressed some key substantive issues related to the park's natural environment, a number of cultural, economic, and social concerns and issues were not addressed by several sectors. Planning is not merely an activity conducted in a "black box" or a "garbage can" (Cohen *et al.* 1972). People are involved in anticipatory, relational, and contested narratives (Mumby 1987, 1988) both in strategic planning and in strategic visioning. Their beliefs and values are central to the conflict. So while it is important that participants are able to share and discuss their beliefs and values about the national park and protected area in question, we argued that metaphysical debates (e.g. about intrinsic value of wilderness) should be avoided in favor of a pragmatic approach, particularly under conditions of prolonged conflict and distrust. But this, of course, raises the issue of ensuring that such debates can be engaged in somewhere in the public sphere. Can a multistakeholder collaboration such as the BBVRT provide such a public space for discussion and debate?

The bigger philosophical questions related to the meaning and purpose of a national park experience, and the value of wilderness or wildness, were largely ignored in the BBVRT even if they were raised by a participant. So was the BBVRT a process for setting vision and strategic direction based on understanding the issues, beliefs, and values related to the conflict, or was the process aimed to develop specific strategies and action steps for an already identified and defined problem? The former purpose may require a form of dialogic, interactive, therapeutic mediation or collaborative learning approach (Daniels and Walker 1996; see also Jamal and Getz 1999), while the latter suggests a more instrumental (means-ends), planning-oriented process. Intervention approaches for the former include therapeutic mediation (Barush Bush and Folger 1994) and learning-led planning processes (Westley 1995; Daniels and Walker 1996), which suit the notion of emergent strategy (Mintzberg and Waters 1985; Mintzberg 1994). Westley and Vredenburg's framework (discussed in Westley 1995) characterizes some aspects of a planning-led collaboration, which arguably fits the BBVRT process.

But regardless of whether the process is learning based or planning led, a neopragmatic approach helps participants to move past contentious metaphysical blocks. It falls on the mediator/facilitator and other process managers to recognize and adapt the process to manage the metaphysical challenges in such a way that difference in voice and dialogue, values, and meanings come through in enabling ways, such as through descriptions of beliefs and understandings.

Conclusion

We advanced in this chapter a critical and theoretical explication of a neopragmatic approach to planning and conflict resolution in national park tourism destinations. This approach was then examined further through a research study of multistakeholder conflict resolution in Banff National Park, Canada. The following is a summary of our recommendations.

1   A neopragmatic approach focuses on the political not the metaphysical aspect of issues, purposes, peoples, and planning processes in protected areas; it attempts to overcome the distortions of powerful, traditional philosophical assumptions related to essentialism and metaphysical realism.

2   Principles and definitions need not come first: early agreement is important on those practical concepts needed to address the problem to be addressed

(hence, the importance of dialogue in the early problem-setting phase), but abstract principles do not have any privileged hierarchical position in the process.

3   Flexibility is key: the process should be fluid, flexible, and adaptive. Principles, situational judgments, normative values, and empirical theories are not fixed but explored as required to broaden understanding and agreement, with the help of new shared definitions and/or descriptions. If terms appear contentious or sensitive, they should be left vague until discussion generates new meanings. Alternatively, they may be left out or avoided if the process manager determines this to be the better alternative, keeping in mind the metaphysical traps to be avoided.

4   Trust is crucial: interpretation of what anyone says presupposes a principle of charity (Davidson 1985). The need for trust makes it important to begin decision processes by finding and focusing on areas of agreement, as well as developing shared understandings of issues and concerns. Visioning processes (Weisbord *et al.* 1992), situation mapping (Daniels and Walker 1996), and other meaning-making mechanisms (cf. Jamal and Getz 1999) are conducive forums for enabling relationship and trust building among participants.

5   A neopragmatic approach is therefore helpful for collaborations in which ideological contests and multiple, interdependent stakeholders struggle in a domain of historical conflict over use and development such as national parks and protected areas. Being nonhierarchical, fluid, and iterative, it offers potential for arriving at agreement on contentious issues in the national park domain.

A major contribution of this article is the interweaving of theory and field research, drawing on a diversity of disciplines and study areas such as philosophy, planning, and organizational studies. In complex domains such as national park tourism destinations, an interdisciplinary approach is required if planning research, theory, and practice are to be richly informed. This suggests that researchers will need to pay increasing attention to clearly explicating the philosophical and methodological assumptions that inform their work. It also means that writers and readers of articles such as this one may have to grapple with understanding and disseminating concepts and theories that are not familiar to one's home discipline or field of study. As pressures intensify on the sustainability of local and global ecological and human cultural resources, philosophical clarifications that facilitate innovative, collaborative decision making and conflict resolution become increasingly important. As Goethe says, "He who cannot draw upon three thousand years of history is living from hand to mouth."

Acknowledgment

More immediately than Goethe, Tazim Jamal thanks Dr Chris Menzel (Philosophy, Texas A&M University) for helpful discussion on topics of metaphysics and essentialism, especially the view that traditional metaphysics does not adequately account for complex socially constructed concepts such as ecological integrity. We also thank our anonymous reviewers for their constructive suggestions.

Note

1   W. Francis, Canadian Parks and Wilderness Society (Alberta chapter) representative. Letter to the editor, *Banff Crag and Canyon*, p. 15. Cited in Hanson (1996: 11).

References

Ansoff, A. (1988) *The New Corporate Strategy*, New York: John Wiley.

Arnstein, S.R. (1969) "A ladder of citizen participation," *AIP Journal*, July: 216–24.

Barush Bush, R.A. and Folger, J.P. (1994) *The Promise of Mediation: Responding to Conflict Through Empowerment and Recognition*, San Francisco, CA: Jossey-Bass.

BBVRT (Banff–Bow Valley Round Table) (1996) April, *Summary Report*.

Bella, L. (1987) *Parks for Profit*, Montreal: Harvest House.

Bernstein, R.J. (1992) *The New Constellation: The Ethical-Political Horizons of Modernity/Postmodernity*, Cambridge, MA: MIT Press.

Blechman, F., Crocker, J., Docherty, J. and Garon, S. (1996) "Looking back at the northern forest dialogues: 1988–1995," unpublished manuscript, Institute for Conflict Analysis and Resolution, George Mason University, Fairfax, VA.

Britton, S. (1991) "Tourism, capital and place: towards a critical geography of tourism," *Environment and Planning D: Society and Space*, 9(4): 451–78.

Carroll, M.S., Findley, A.J., Blatner, K.A., Mendez, S.R., Daniels, S.E. and Walker, G.B. (2000) January. *Social Assessment for the Wenatchee National Forest Wildfires of 1994: Targeted Analysis for the Leavenworth, Entiat, and Chelan Ranger Districts* (General Technical Report PNW-GTR-479). USDA Forest Service, Pacific Northwest Research Station.

Cohen, M.D., March, J.G. and Olsen, J.P. (1972) "A garbage can model of organization choice," *Administrative Science Quarterly*, 17(1): 1–25.

Cormick, G., Dale, N., Edmond, P., Glenn Sigurdson, S. and Stuart, B.D. (1996) *Building Consensus for a Sustainable Future: Putting Principles into Practice*. Ottawa: National Round Table on the Environment and the Economy.

Cronon, W. (ed.) (1996) *Uncommon Ground: Rethinking the Human Place in Nature*, New York: W. W. Norton.

Daniels, S.E. and. Walker, G.B (1996) "Collaborative learning: improving public deliberation in ecosystem-based management," *Environmental Impact Assessment Review*, 16: 71–102.

Davidson, D. (1985) "A coherence theory of truth and knowledge," in A. Malachowski and J. Burrows (eds) *Reading Rorty: Critical responses to* Philosophy and the Mirror of Nature *(and beyond)*, Oxford: Basil Blackwell.

Driscoll, K. (1993) "Diversity, dialogue and learning: the case of the forest round table on sustainable development," Ph.D. diss., Queens University, Kinston, Ontario, Canada.

Forester, J. (1989) *Planning in the Face of Power*, Berkeley, CA: University of California Press.

Freeman, R.E. (1984) *Strategic Management: A Stakeholder Approach*, London: Pittman.

Getz, D. and Jamal, T. (1994) "The environment-community symbiosis: a case for collaborative tourism planning," *Journal of Sustainable Tourism*, 2(3): 152–73.

Gill, A. and Williams, P. (1994) "Managing growth in mountain tourism communities," *Tourism Management*, 15(3): 212–20.

Gray, B. (1989) *Collaborating: Finding Common Ground for Multiparty Problems*, San Francisco, CA: Jossey-Bass.

Hanson, L. (1996) "Reconstituting the boundaries of nature: the discursive formation of nature in the debate over the management of Banff National Park," *Avante*, 2(2): 1–16.

Harper, T.L. and Stein, S. (1995a) "Contemporary procedural ethical theory and planning theory," in S. Hendler (ed.) *Planning Ethics: A Reader in Planning Theory, Practice and Education*, New Brunswick, NJ: Center for Urban Policy Research, Rutgers University.

—— (1995b) "Out of the postmodern abyss: preserving the rationale for liberal planning," *Journal of Planning Education and Research*, 14(4): 233–44.

Healey, P. (1997) *Collaborative Planning*, London: Macmillan.

Hughes, G. (1995) "The cultural construction of sustainable tourism," *Tourism Management*, 16(1): 49–59.

Huxham, C. (1996a) "Advantage or inertia? Making collaboration work," in R. Paton, G. Clark, G. Jones, J. Lewis, and P. Quintas (eds) *The New Management Reader*, London: Routledge.

—— (ed.)(1996b) *Creating Collaborative Advantage*, London: Sage.

Innes, J., Gruber, J., Neuman, M. and Thompson, R. (1994) "Coordinating growth and environmental management through consensus building," *CPS Brief*, 6(4): 1–7.

Jamal, T. (1997) "Multi-party consensus processes in environmentally sensitive destinations: paradoxes of ownership and common ground," Ph.D. diss., University of Calgary, Calgary, Alberta, Canada.

Jamal, T. and Getz, D. (1999) "Community roundtables for tourism-related conflicts: the dialectics of consensus and process structures," *Journal of Sustainable Tourism*, 7(3): 356–78.

Lowenthall, D. (1998) *The Heritage Crusade and the Spoils of History*. Cambridge: Cambridge University Press.

Menand, L. (ed.) (1997) *Pragmatism: A Reader*, New York: Vintage.

Mintzberg, H. (1994) *The Rise and Fall of Strategic Planning: Reconceiving Roles for Planning, Plans, Planners*, New York: Free Press.

Mintzberg, H. and Waters, J.A. (1985) "Of strategies, deliberate and emergent," *Strategic Management Journal*, 6(3): 257–72.

Mumby, D.K. (1987) "The political function of narrative in organizations," *Communication Monographs*, 54: 113–27.

—— (1988) *Communication and Power in Organizations: Discourse, Ideology and Domination*, Norwood, NJ: Ablex.

Murphy, P.E. (1985) *Tourism: A Community Approach*, New York: Methuen.

O'Brien, M. (2000) *Making Better Environmental Decisions: An Alternative to Risk Assessment*, Cambridge, MA: MIT Press.

Palerm, J.R. (2000) "An empirical-theoretical analysis framework for public participation in environmental impact assessment," *Journal of Environmental Planning and Management*, 43(5): 581–600.

Pasquero, J. (1991) "Supraorganizational collaboration: the Canadian environmental experiment," *Journal of Applied Behavioral Science*, 27(1): 38–64.

Phillips, N., Lawrence, T.B. and Hardy, C. 2000) "Inter-organizational collaboration and the dynamics of institutional fields," *Journal of Management Studies*, 37(1): 23–43.

Putnam, H. (1990) *Realism with a Human Face*, Cambridge, MA: Harvard University Press.

Quine, W.V.O. (1969) "Natural kinds," in *Ontological Relativity and other Essays*, New York: Columbia University Press.

Rawls, J. (1985) "Justice as fairness: political not metaphysical," *Philosophy and Public Affairs*, 14(3): 223–51.

—— (1993) *Political Liberalism*, New York: Columbia University Press.

Richardson, M., Sherman, J. and Gismondi, M. (1993) *Winning Back the Words: Confronting Experts in an Environmental Public Hearing*. Toronto: Garamond.

Roberts, N.C. and Bradley, R.T. (1991) "Stakeholder collaboration and innovation: A study of public policy initiation at the state level," *Journal of Applied Behavioral Science*, 27(2): 209–27.

Rorty, R. (1979) *Philosophy and the Mirror of Nature*, Princeton, NJ: Princeton University Press.

—— (1991) *Objectivity, Relativism and Truth: Philosophical Papers.* Vol. 1. Cambridge: Cambridge University Press.

Selin, S. and Beason, K. (1991) "Conditions facilitating collaborative tourism planning: A qualitative perspective," paper presented at conference, Tourism: Building Credibility for a Credible Industry. Twenty-first annual conference of the Travel and Tourism Research Association.

Stabler, M.J. (ed.)(1997) *Tourism and Sustainability: Principles to Practice*, Wallingford: CAB International.

Stein, S. and Harper, T. (1998) "Pragmatic incrementalist planning in post-modern society: a normative justification," *Planning Theory*, 18: 3–28.

Susskind, L. (1994) *Environmental diplomacy: Negotiating more effective global agreements.* New York: Oxford University Press.

Tonn, B., English, M. and Travis, C. (2000) "A framework for understanding and improving environmental decision making," *Journal of Environmental Planning and Management*, 43(2): 163–83.

Weisbord, M.R. *et al.* (1992) *Discovering Common Ground: How Future Search Conferences Bring People Together to Achieve Breakthrough Innovation, Empowerment, Shared Vision, and Collaborative Action*, San Francisco, CA: Berrett-Koehler.

Weston, J. (2000) "EIA, decision-making theory and screening and scoping in UK practice," *Journal of Environmental Planning and Management*, 43(2): 185–203.

Westley, F. (1995) "Governing design: the management of social systems and eco-systems design," in L.H. Holling and S.S. Light (eds) *Barriers and Bridges to the Renewal of Ecosystems and Institutions*, New York: Columbia University Press.

Wittgenstein, L. (1969) *On Certainty*, G.E.M. Anscombe and G.H. Wright (eds), D. Paul and G.E.M. Anscombe (trans.) New York: Harper Torchbooks.

Chapter 11

The usefulness of normative planning theories in the context of Sub-Saharan Africa

Vanessa Watson

The article focuses on three contemporary and better-known normative theories of planning: communicative planning theory (Forester, Healey, Innes and others), the Just City approach (Fainstein), and those concerned with the recognition of diversity and cultural difference (Sandercock). Such theories are of great interest to planners who continue to grapple with the problem of overcoming the extreme forms of inequity, division and social breakdown that persist in the cities of Africa. The paper examines some of the central assumptions underlying these theories and considers the extent to which they provide useful direction, or simply attempt to generalize a Western context.

Current normative theories of planning, represented by communicative planning theory (Forester, Healey, Innes and others), the Just City approach (Fainstein) and those concerned with the recognition of diversity and cultural difference (Sandercock), may be of great interest to planners who continue to grapple with the problem of overcoming the extreme forms of inequity, division and social breakdown that persist in the cities of Sub-Saharan Africa.

This chapter takes the position that, as planners, we should only proceed on the basis of a thorough understanding of the socio-spatial and political processes which shape the contexts in which we work (see amongst others Huxley and Yiftachel 2000). It raises the question: given the particular dynamics which currently appear to be shaping many cities in the sub-continent, do these normative theories of planning offer a resource on which planners can draw?

Some justification is required for both the theoretical and contextual focus of this chapter. I recognize that the three normative planning theories considered here do not exhaust the field. Communicative planning theory (which itself has a number of different strands) is frequently held up as a currently dominant theoretical paradigm (Innes 1995), although this is almost as frequently contested

---

Submitted by the Association of African Planning Schools.

(Yiftachel and Huxley 2000). A relatively recent post-modern and cultural-turn scholarship (Storper 2001) has influenced thinking in a number of disciplines, and Leonie Sandercock's work is arguably the best-known example of the application of this perspective in the planning field (Beauregard 1998; Storper 2001). The third example, the Just City approach, represents one position within a much wider normative literature on city form (e.g. Breheny 1992; Lynch 1990), but its strong roots in social theory set it apart from other urban form positions and facilitate the examination of the assumptions which underlie it. These three theories together allow reflection on both planning processes and spatial outcomes in the context of Sub-Saharan African cities. I do not suggest that planning practitioners in such cities generally know about these theories or use them (although some certainly do). Rather, the question of their potential usefulness is posed in a largely hypothetical sense, to explore the issue of theoretical universality.

I use the term 'planning' in this text to refer to those intentional public actions which impact on the built and natural environment, and which are frequently accompanied by political processes of some kind. Planning is also (and not infrequently) initiated by groups other than formal governments, such as non-governmental and community-based organizations, and sometimes business. I therefore use the term planning in the narrower sense, referring to the activity of urban planning or town planning, while recognizing that planning is now used to describe the activities of a wide variety of actors and professionals. I am aware of the fact that the extent to which urban planning actually takes place within the context of Sub-Saharan Africa is highly variable. In some countries law and order has broken down and little intervention is possible; in other contexts planning systems function and planning initiatives are undertaken (see Diaw *et al.* 2001), although forms of planning differ (strongly influenced by particular colonial histories) and their impact may be highly variable across the city.

Two more qualifications are necessary. The focus of this paper is specifically on the *cities* of Sub-Saharan Africa. The intention is not to negate the importance of the rural areas, nor the linkages that these have with the urban areas. However, the three normative theories under consideration have far greater potential applicability in the urban areas: considering their usefulness in the often very different rural areas would unreasonably stretch expectations of their applicability. Finally, I am aware that the Sub-Saharan continent is highly varied, and that reference to it as an entity borders on dangerous over-generalization. However, there are also important social and political commonalities. African scholar Mahmood Mamdani (1996) has argued cogently that these commonalities, rooted in the colonial history of the sub-continent, legitimate the consideration of Africa as a unit of analysis, and in particular, discount the position of South African 'exceptionalism'. While care is taken in this chapter to highlight contextual differences where these have relevance, I proceed on the assumption that some level of generalization is possible.

The chapter is structured as follows. It first examines a number of assumptions on which the three normative theories of planning are based. It then turns to Sub-Saharan Africa, to sketch the context within which planners operate. The chapter concludes with some reflections on the value of the three normative planning theories in resource-poor contexts such as this one.

Three normative theories of planning

With the demise of rational scientific planning as the dominant form of planning theory, the space was opened up for the emergence of a range of new theoretical positions, concerned both to explain planning as a phenomenon and to provide ideas for how planning should be conducted, and to what ends. Some of these theorists, influenced by a growing disillusionment with modernist thinking and technocratic planning, were persuaded that social movements in liberal democracies, and the development of civil society more generally, held the key to social transformation. Their new interest in localized and empirical approaches centres on the empowerment of groups outside (and sometimes against) the state. Of these planning theorists, centre-stage is taken by those associated with communicative planning theory. John Forester (1989) and others after him drew inspiration from Habermas to pose communication as the most important element of planning practice. Interaction (with stakeholders or interest groups), communicating ideas, forming arguments, debating differences in understandings, and finally reaching consensus on a course of action replaces detached, expert-driven plan-making as the primary activity of planners. These ideas are developed in their most sophisticated form by Patsy Healey, who also introduces 'institutionalism' as an explanatory theory of social dynamics to inform the normative position of communicative planning.[1] For the purposes of this chapter, the following aspects of communicative planning theory are important.

Habermas' thinking is central in this work. With a concern to protect and extend democracy, he conceptualizes the 'life-world' (or public sphere) as separate from and outside 'the system' of formal economy and government. Within the life-world it is possible for rational and inherently democratic human beings to reach consensus, and co-ordinate action, through the process of communication (communicative rationality). Here the 'force of the better argument' will determine the final validity of a particular position. Habermas recognizes that communication can be distorted in various ways and puts forward a set of criteria, or discourse ethics, to guide communication processes: if processes are inclusive, empathetic, and open, and if existing power differences between participants can be neutralized, then the outcome of such a process can be considered valid (Habermas 1990a, 1990b). For communicative planning theorists, this has come to mean that the aim of planning is a just process, and that if the process is just, the outcome will be as well (see Fainstein 1995).

Communicative planning theorists echo Habermas' faith in civil society as a source of democracy, and as a vehicle for placing pressure on the state to act more responsively. Healey refers to the 'democratic deficit' (the distance between the state and civil society), and argues that planning '... seeks ways of recovering a new participatory realization of democracy and of reconstituting a vigorous, inclusive public realm that can focus the activity of governance according to the concerns of civil society ...' (Healey 1999: 119).[2] The state, in terms of this position, is therefore downgraded as a role player relative to non-state actors, and civil society is seen as the main standard-bearer of the democratic project.[3]

Habermas' assumption regarding the consensual nature of discourse in the public sphere is also adopted by communicative planning theorists.[4] While writers in this school do not deny the operation of power, the belief still holds that if communication processes are correctly managed (according to Habermas' discourse ethics), then it is possible for voluntary but binding agreements to be reached. Basic to their position is the assumption of universal citizenship, where differences between actors occur only at the level of speech or ideas and can be overcome through argumentation. Thus: '... the power of dominant discourses can be challenged at the level of dialogue; through the power of knowledgeable, reflective discourse; through good arguments; and through the transformations that come as people learn to understand and respect each other across their differences and conflicts' (Healey 1999: 119). Healey refines the idea of universal citizenship further to acknowledge that communicating groups may operate within different 'systems of meaning', which means that 'we see things differently because words, phrases, expressions, objects, are interpreted differently according to our frame of reference' (Healey 1992: 152). The assumption that these differences can be accommodated in a consensus-seeking process remains.

Healey adds two further dimensions to the idea of communicative processes. The first, shared with 'cultural-turn' scholars (for example, Escobar 1994), is the valorisation of 'local knowledge', referring to 'items of information that are mapped and interpreted within the sense-making frameworks and purposes of particular social networks' (Healey 1999: 116). This is different from 'expert' (or sometimes Western) knowledge: it consists of common sense and practical reason, proverbs and metaphors, practical skills and routines, and may be spoken or unspoken. A second dimension, related to the first, is that consensus-seeking processes can have an added benefit in that the shared understanding, mutual trust and 'identity-creation' which are built up, linger on as new 'cultural resources' or 'cultural capital' (Healey 1999: 114), benefiting future planning processes. Also now central in the mainstream development literature, social capital is frequently promoted as a precondition for both economic development and more democratic systems of governance (Mohan and Stokke 2000). It assumes that such relationships of trust and mutual (economic) interdependence can persist over long periods of time, in particular localities, leading to 'bottom-up' processes of development.

The final important aspect of communicative planning theory is its tendency to focus on sub-national levels of government, on individual actors, be they planners or related participants, and on inductive theorizing. To quote Mandelbaum in the introduction to the volume which was a first attempt to define the shape of this new theoretical territory, there is 'a pervasive interest in the behaviour, values, character and experiences of professional planners at work', and in the practices of these planners which encompass 'ways of talking, rituals, implicit protocols, routines, relational strategies, character traits and virtues' (Mandelbaum 1996: xviii). In terms of the long-standing structure–agency debate, the pendulum has clearly swung back to agency, and along with it, an interest in the power of local government and local organizations to take forward the idea of democratic planning. This, again, is not out of line with mainstream development thinking with its focus on local economic and political empowerment (Mohan and Stokke 2000), and with cultural-turn scholarship's interest in how culture and context shapes knowledge and behaviour (Storper 2001). The assumption is that society can be transformed from the 'bottom up', and that just local processes can change the broader distribution of resources and power (Fainstein 1995). Again, Healey is sensitive to this issue, and in her own analytical framework draws on Giddens' theory of structuration to recognize that 'active agency interacts with constraining structuring dynamics …' to influence '… the making and acknowledging of formal rules, … the deployment of material resources … and the frames of reference actors deploy …' (Healey 1999: 113).

Leonie Sandercock's theory of planning in multicultural societies (see Sandercock 1998a, 1998b, 2000) may be regarded as a variant of, or development of, communicative planning theory, although there are some important differences with it. Like the communicative planning theorists Sandercock is strongly influenced by post-modernism[5] and cultural-turn thinking (Storper 2001). She holds with the notion of civil society as an autonomous site of resistance and social movements as primary agents of change. She places her own work within what she terms a 'radical planning model', with roots in advocacy planning, happening most often outside the formal structures of state and economy (Sandercock 1998b). Her work focuses on agency and 'the local',[6] and on the kinds of processes and discourses which shape planning debates. As Beauregard (1998) notes, both communicative planning theorists and multicultural theory shift the emphasis in planning theory from outcomes to process and from consequences to consciousness.

Sandercock's point of departure lies in her idea of what constitutes citizenship and how this is fragmented by identity, and the role of the planner in relation to this question. As opposed to the idea of universal citizenship, her society is structured by relationships between culturally different groups, based on sexuality, ethnicity, gender or race. This diversity requires to be celebrated rather than repressed:[7] that is, the claims of groups need to be recognized and facilitated. It can be argued here that Sandercock is not just interested in recognizing difference in procedural terms (in order to move towards a more homogenous or equal society); she is interested in 'substantive difference', or affirming a society made up of different groups (Storper 2001). This is promoting difference for its own sake.

The role of the planner in such a context is to link knowledge to action to empower oppressed and marginalized groups, to resist exploitation and the denial of their authenticity (Beauregard 1998). How the legitimacy of such claims is to be judged is not clear: Sandercock values the idea of a socially just city, but argues that this *requires* a politics of difference. Identity claims must thus be prior to material claims. This means, it would seem, that notions of what constitutes justice may be culturally specific and need to be uncovered through 'different ways of knowing' (an epistemology of multiplicity) and hence a different relationship between planner and groups. Her faith in 'local knowledge' and the questionable nature of 'expert knowledge' parallels Healey's here. Assumptions regarding the possibility of reaching consensus are present in Sandercock's writing as they are in communicative planning theory. The difference with Sandercock, however, is that she is concerned to build consensus between groups (which affirms and valorizes difference rather than erases it), which could take the form of resistance to the state. There is a difference here from communicative planning theorists who sometimes see the aim of a planning process as being to negotiate emotions and differences and arrive at a collective agenda, accommodated by the state (Beauregard 1998). The issue of power, Foucaultians might argue, thus remains as problematic in multicultural theory as it does in communicative planning theory.

With the demise of rational scientific planning, still other theorists drew on the penetration of Marxist thinking into the planning field. From a normative perspective, interest in a form of planning which achieves redistribution, equity and justice informs the work of Susan Fainstein, and in somewhat different form, that of David Harvey. Fainstein's Just City position is the focus of attention here (see Fainstein 2000).

Fainstein's theoretical base in a 'postmarxist political economy' (which encompasses a more complex view of social structure and social benefits than was envisioned by material analysis) gives rise to a number of commonalities between her position and those discussed above. She, like Sandercock, holds with a society structured primarily by groups rather than classes, but her concerns are less with a planning which aims to valorize and promote the claims (material and non-material) of these groups, and rather with how such groups can benefit from redistributive planning actions.

Fainstein, along with the communicative planning and multicultural theorists, is also concerned with planning processes and participation. But she is closer to Sandercock in seeing her primary audience as the 'leadership of urban social movements', rather than government which may be neither neutral nor benevolent, and she distances herself from communicative planning theorists who 'primarily speak to planners employed by government, calling on them to mediate among diverse interests …' (Fainstein 2000: 468). Her faith in the reformative power of civil society is thus in line with other post-modern normative thinkers, and with neo-liberal development theorists as well. She does, however, concede that certain individuals within the state (progressive officials and 'guerrillas in the bureaucracy') may act in the interests of marginalized groups, leaving the question of whether or not to engage with the state presumably dependent on particular circumstances.

Fainstein is more cautious than Sandercock in terms of accepting the validity of all group claims, and recognizes that some claims can be highly non-democratic. For this reason she is insistent that claims cannot be judged by procedural rules alone. Just processes do not necessarily result in just outcomes, as Habermas would have it. Hence the 'substantive content', or the impacts of decisions, have to be judged as well for their impact on equity and democracy.

The question this raises of course, is how do redistribution and equitable planning occur, and who is to judge claims, if government is not to be trusted and if progressive officials do not exist. Fainstein's vision of the Just City requires a state that is both entrepreneurial and provides welfare (p. 468), and assumes a capitalist world economy and a commitment to economic growth. But as her theory downplays government in the planning process, and as her arguments are addressed primarily to groups outside of the state, it is not clear how this would happen other than through luck or accident. Sandercock is somewhat clearer here: she throws in her lot with marginalized and oppressed groups and relies on their pressure to win gains from the state.

Where the Just City position departs significantly from the other normative planning theories is in terms of its concern with substantive spatial planning outcomes, as well as processes, and the distributive impacts that different spatial forms may imply. Fainstein's inspiration for a spatially Just City is Amsterdam with its physical diversity, high density and socially and economically mixed residential areas. This spatial form is accompanied by, and has benefited from, a welfare state, a strong civil society and public ownership of land. Fainstein makes connections here to the spatial tradition of new urbanism (of which she is also somewhat critical).

There is a growing literature which would support Fainstein's argument that spatial forms have different distributive (and environmental) implications (see for example Jenks and Burgess 2000), and points to the negative social and economic impacts of spatial exclusion in cities (Borja and Castells 1997). While it would seem to be important for a normative planning theory to articulate a position on a central substantive issue such as this, attempts to universalize a particular spatial form worry many other planning theorists. David Harvey (2000: 196) is unhappy about what he calls spatial form utopianism, as it treats space as a container for social action, and usually confines utopianism to the scale of the city.[8] His own normative position, also inspired by goals of justice and equity, is expressed in a set of 'rights', one of which is the 'right to reconstruct spatial relations ... in ways which turn space from an absolute framework of action into a more malleable relative and relational aspect of social life' (Harvey 2000: 251).

The chapter now turns to the context of Africa to sketch the nature of issues confronted by planning.

What is happening to Sub-Saharan Africa?

There is a high degree of consensus in the development literature that the problems faced by Africa (and particularly Sub-Saharan Africa) are more extreme than elsewhere in the Third World or the South. Chabal (1996) identifies four dimensions of this crisis: economic decline, political instability, 're-traditionalisation', and the marginalization of Africa.

The economic crisis in Sub-Saharan Africa is severe: economies today are generally in a worse state than they were at independence. Even World Bank functionaries, usually inclined to 'talk up' development in Africa, now agree that descriptions of its economic performance as 'tragic' and of 'crisis proportions' are 'not exaggerations' (Elbadawi and Mwega 2000: 415). The mean annual growth rate of real GDP per capita has declined steadily since the 1970s (Elbadawi and Mwega 2000) with the result that of the 500 million people in Sub-Saharan Africa, nearly 300 million are living in absolute poverty, and these numbers are growing (World Bank 2001). Moreover, extremely high levels of HIV/AIDS (68 per cent of the world's population living with HIV/AIDS are in Africa, with 3.8 million new infections occurring in 1999 alone (Aids Analysis Africa 2000)) are a major factor undermining possibilities of economic recovery.

Economic decline has been paralleled by political crisis, manifesting itself in warfare, endemic violence and state collapse. Sub-Saharan Africa has a higher incidence of civil war than any other part of the world with 40 per cent of these countries having experienced civil war in the last 40 years (Elbadawi and Sambanis 2000). Writers (see Allen 1999) are now also pointing to new forms of violence on the continent, taking the forms of more frequent and widespread civil wars; dramatic increases in interpersonal violence linked to crime, and the breakdown of civility and respect for law; war-lordism; community-level conflicts often involving the seizure of food or other resources; ethnic conflicts; child slavery;

and violence which targets vulnerable groups such as women, children and refugees.

Chabal (1996) is cautious when referring to what he calls 're-traditionalisation' in Africa, described as a revival of age-old traditions and cultural practices. Seen in its own terms, Chabal argues, it must be understood as tied to questions of identity and adjustment (or resistance) to the particular economic and political circumstances sweeping the continent. Examples of re-traditionalization are to be found in the endurance of sorcery and witchcraft; the revival of African religion and the traditionalization of Christian churches in Africa; the persistence of ethnicity and the increased channelling of violence along ethnic lines; the dominant role played by kinship networks; the persistence of exchange and trade rather than a shift to productive investment, and an overwhelming 'informalization' of urban economies; and the apparent failure of 'modern' (liberal or socialist) politics in Sub-Saharan Africa.

Chabal (1996) points finally to the perception that Sub-Saharan Africa has become irrelevant in world terms, particularly from an economic and political point of view. Hopes that economic problems may be overcome by the opening up of African economies and greater exposure to foreign investment flows have not borne fruit. Africa now accounts for no more than four to six per cent of net global direct investment (Simon 1997) and most of this goes to Nigeria and South Africa. Africa is thus largely being bypassed by foreign private investment, and this is coinciding with dramatic decreases in aid financing as well: official aid flows fell by 48 per cent in the 10 years to 1996 (Bush and Szeftel 1998). Added to this is the 'grotesque charade' of Africa's foreign debt, recently the highest in the world as a proportion of GDP (Leys 1994), with some countries spending over half their foreign earnings on debt servicing.

Attempts to explain the African situation have emerged, over time, from the modernists, from various Marxist and dependency schools, and more recently from those who take a 'cultural turn', privileging explanations rooted in the specificities of political culture. There is also a productive body of policy-related work. While there is a notable lack of consensus between these various explanatory and prescriptive positions, together they do help to throw light on those aspects of economy and society that are relevant for considering the value of the three normative planning theories.

Civil society and the state in Sub-Saharan Africa

A number of authors, from various positions, have questioned conceptions of civil society in Sub-Saharan Africa and have drawn attention to the ways in which it differs from notions of civil society in Western contexts.

How civil society is conceptualized depends to a large extent on the definition of it that is used. Allen (1997) points to the way in which earlier definitions of the concept, which saw it as a *process* by which society seeks to 'breach' and counteract the simultaneous 'totalisation' unleashed by the state (Bayart cited in Allen, 1997), have given way, in the development literature in particular, to a focus on the actors responsible for such a process. Allen terms this the 'associational life' view of civil society, which is based on the assumptions that NGOs (non-governmental organizations) and 'autonomous societal groups' are a significant part of civil society, that they are distinct from the state and often in conflict with it, and that they drive democratization. Civil society is thus viewed as a category, separate from the state, which can be created or improved, rather than something that emerges spontaneously (Allen 1997; McIlwaine 1998). This conception has been operationalized in an analytical sense: writers point to the massive growth of NGOs and social movements in developing countries in recent years as evidence of a growing and flourishing civil society; and in a prescriptive sense: neo-liberal development theory links market liberalization and 'community enablement' with strategies to reduce the role of governments in developing contexts and to channel aid funds to NGOs instead (Burgess *et al.* 1997). The question remains, however, can the growth of NGOs, and grassroots social and political movements, be taken as an indication of the development of civil society and democratization?

Given the relative weakness of indigenous social movements in Sub-Saharan Africa (Crush 1996), NGOs have been viewed by development agencies and donor organizations as central vehicles for development and change. However, in reporting on an extensive evaluation of 'northern' NGOs (those funded and usually staffed by Western donors) in Africa, Marcussen (1996) points to some major weaknesses in NGO performance. Many have taken a 'top-down' approach, and have exhibited a general failure to reach the very poor and foster sustainable economic benefit. NGOs have been described as 'bastions of development' focusing on small enclaves and lacking the ability to up-scale their activities or replicate them. Of particular concern is their tendency to see the state as part of the problem and to try and bypass it, leading to direct competition and conflict with the state, particularly over funding and human resources. This in turn further weakens governments and prevents development ideas from being permanently institutionalized at a broader scale. Marcussen (1996: 420) makes the point that in the Western world the development of civil society occurred organically and in cooperation with government, not in conflict with it. In Africa it has become an artificial and externally driven process orchestrated by organizations whose sphere of influence, relative to the scale of problems, is minor, and whose lifespan (and funding) is unpredictable.

Some writers (particularly those interested in political transition) celebrate a post-1990s 'international momentum of democracy' (Diamond, cited in Bartlett

2000) characterized by the overthrow of authoritarian regimes in Eastern Europe and developing countries and the emergence of a vigorous civil society. In Africa there have been numerous cases in recent years in which one-party governments have been overthrown and replaced by multi-party and 'democratic' political systems. But tracking the results of these political transitions leads a number of researchers to conclude that they should not be simply equated with the establishment of either democracy or civil society. 'Older political logics' do not simply disappear because authoritarian regimes have been challenged (Bartlett 2000). In the case of Zambia (argued by Bartlett to be typical), historically determined social and political conditions permitted the emergence of a dominant group able to exclude major elements of civil society and allow the resurfacing of corruption, nepotism and 'spoils politics'. Or, as expressed by the then Zambian minister of Foreign Affairs: 'If I do not appoint people from my own region, who will?'. Bartlett (2000: 445) concludes that 'the existence of a wide range of civil organizations gives no guarantee that any will articulate norms which further the development of a tolerant or participatory public arena'.

From a wide-ranging review of the literature on social movements in developing countries Walton (1998) finds evidence to support such conclusions. Despite the growth of social movements and moves to democratization, he suggests that participation is still mediated more typically by patron–client relations rather than by popular activism. In the context of Africa, De Boeck (1996: 93) makes the point that understood dichotomies such as state/society or legal/ illegal no longer capture reality. In an 'increasingly "exotic", complex and chaotic world that seems to announce the end of social life and the societal fabric as most of us know it', the state is but one (often weaker) locus of authority along with traditional chiefs, warlords and mafias. Definitions of legal and illegal constantly shift depending on which groups are exerting power at the time. It is a mistake in Africa, Aina (1997: 418) argues, to assume that the relationship of civil society to the democratization process is always progressive, in fact there are often strong conservative trends.

Identity

The issues of group difference and identity are increasingly occupying the attention of writers on Africa. Here the point is repeatedly made that political struggles in Africa are far less like the identity/lifestyle politics which have become so visible in developed contexts and are far more likely to be reactive to material issues and the simple need for survival (Mohan 1997). This has led Mohan to argue that identity is not a useful starting point in understanding political struggles in Africa, or at least it may require a more complete understanding of the relations between materiality and identity.

In the context of the discussion above on the nature of the state and civil society, a number of authors highlight the extremely complex and fluid nature of identity in Africa. Social and economic collapse and turmoil leave many people with little sense of belonging (a process, some argue, which begun with colonial penetration) or little idea of who represents them. One way out of this is to use identity in a highly opportunistic way:

> ... depending on the situation, sometimes religion, sometimes ethnicity may prove to be the determining factor in an individual's identity and behaviour. The organisational versatility of the orders that has made them the primary modes of organisation vis a vis the state lies in their capacity to adapt to this ambiguity, and even capitalise on it ...
>
> (Leonardo Villalon, cited in O'Brien 1996: 63)

Thus identity in Africa is often a product of hybridization, fusion and cultural innovation. It is frequently self-generated and self-constructed, sometimes with a renewed stress on ethnic identity or 'retribalization', sometimes intertwined with global identities (De Boeck 1996). Currently religious commitment offers many young people a way of escaping from social marginalization, and O'Brien (1996: 64) comments that Christian missions are the biggest single industry in Africa today. Students are often in the vanguard of liberation movements, but their role is ambivalent, and may be related more closely to the desire to gain access to government jobs and membership of the ruling elite than to secure democracy. The political impulse of the crowd is above all economically motivated (O'Brien 1996).

The 'dark side' of identity construction in Sub-Saharan Africa perhaps has more in common with other contexts. Identity defines elements of similarity, and simultaneously of difference – of 'the other'. Where the state is weak, social cohesion fragile, and competition for resources desperate, social divisions can, and do, all too easily degenerate into the horrors of ethnic cleansing and genocide.

The economy and informalization

The most striking aspect of Sub-Saharan African economies over the recent past is their growing 'informalization'. As economies have been opened up to global processes of trade (primarily as a result of structural adjustment policies) and domestic manufacture has been decimated, as the world terms of trade have continued to move against primary producers, and as the state, often one of the largest providers of formal employment, has been cut back, people have had to find ways of survival outside of the formal economy. They have moved in large numbers into self-employment (both legal and illegal) or casual wage employment, or have found it necessary to supplement formal wages with informal income generating activities. In 1992 the ILO was estimating that 63 per cent of the total urban labour force of Sub-Saharan Africa was in informal employment, and that this sector would be generating 93 per cent of all additional jobs in urban Africa in the 1990s (Rogerson 1997).

While a heterogeneity of work opportunities is sometimes regarded as inevitable in the new global economy, and while the growing informal sector is sometimes portrayed as a positive sign of entrepreneurialism by neo-liberal policy advocates, the particular nature of informalization in Africa has to be read as predominantly a survival strategy. Most informal activity is in the realm of trade, with little evidence that 'incubating', productive, micro-enterprises are emerging to secure a place in the world (or even regional) economy. Most activities provide few extra jobs and many of these provide low and irregular incomes under very poor working conditions. Most activities themselves are of a 'survivalist' nature, involving little investment, few skills and minimal profit.

These processes have obvious implications in terms of high levels of poverty, inequality and insecurity, but they have implications for other aspects of social and political life as well. In a context of shrinking economies, competition becomes intensified, promoting both the need to draw on a wide range of networks (familial, religious, ethnic etc) and to continually manoeuvre, negotiate and protect the spaces of opportunity that have been created (Simone 2000). Intensified competition, Simone argues, means that economic and political processes of all kinds become open for negotiation and informalization. Networks with the state become particularly valuable, both in negotiating preferential access to resources and in avoiding control and regulation, with the result that, increasingly, '... public institutions are seen not as public but the domain of specific interest groups, and indeed they become sites for private accumulation and advantage' (Simone 2000: 7). The relationship between state and citizens, and between formal and informal actors, thus becomes under-codified and under-regulated, dependent on complex processes of alliance making and deal breaking, and particularly resistant to reconfiguring through policy instruments and external interventions.

Cities in Sub-Saharan Africa

Sub-Saharan Africa, with only 31 per cent of its population in urban areas, is the least urbanized region in the world (Simon 1997), and there are few very large cities. A significant feature is the strong urban–rural ties which still exist, and which keep many people in perpetual motion between urban and rural bases. This strategy of spatially 'stretching the household' (Spiegel *et al.* 1996) functions as an economic and social safety-net, allowing access to constantly shifting economic opportunities as well as maintaining kinship and other networks. As survival in the cities becomes increasingly precarious, rural resources assume greater importance and rural survival strategies begin to penetrate the urban areas – the 'ruralization' of the cities (in terms of productive activities and ways of life) is a term increasingly used to describe changes in cities in Africa (De Boeck 1996). Economic decline has also precipitated more general movement across Africa in search of opportunity. The large-scale (often illegal) movement of people back and forth across the continent, trading drugs and curios, is evidence of this. One implication of this phenomenon is that conceptualizing cities as self-contained entities that can be planned and managed accordingly (as has been the case with past planning efforts in African cities) becomes obviously questionable;[9] another is that the commitment of people to particular urban locales (and what happens in them) becomes more tenuous. As Simone (1999) suggests: connections between social and physical space become progressively disjoined, and frameworks for identity formation and networks are spread across regions and nations, rather than being rooted in specific locations.

Within many cities, highly differentiated patterns of access to resources are reflected in growing spatial divisions between a well-connected elite and the larger mass of the poor. Most African cities developed a formal, well-serviced business and residential 'core' which housed first the colonial masters and subsequently the local political and commercial elite and foreign investors. Many cities also display attempts from the post-colonial period to provide working-class housing in the form of apartments and low-cost site-and-services schemes.[10] In subsequent years, declining state capacity to deliver urban services or regulate the urban environment, together with a rapidly growing urban poor, has resulted in an extensive informalization of the urban fabric and use of urban land. With growing levels of crime, those with wealth barricade themselves into high-security enclaves and carefully choose their movement routes to avoid car hijackings. These parts of the city remain, to varying degrees, well serviced and regulated. Beyond these areas, services are degraded or non-existent, shelters are makeshift, and land occupation and use is unregulated (and frequently highly contested). This does not mean that the organization of these areas is haphazard: Simone (1998) comments that it is difficult to determine where the city begins and ends but also how it is one city, instead of hundreds of quarters and neighbourhoods. In most cities, any new private-sector investment that is occurring avoids such areas, and thus exacerbates the divisions between rich and poor. Even in Cape Town, where the extent of informal and unregulated settlement is far less than in most other cities, the spatial divisions entrenched by apartheid are now being reinforced by the pattern of new investment which confines itself to the wealthier, better serviced and more attractive parts of the city (Turok and Watson 2001). African cities are thus becoming increasingly inequitable in terms of their spatial organization, with the poor excluded spatially and socially from access to the few formal opportunities that cities do have to offer.

In essence, in many cities of the sub-continent, the 'reach' of formal institutions of state authority (and hence of systems of maintaining law and order) is only partial, and there are large parts of many cities which must be considered 'ungoverned'. Here alternative sources of authority (tribal chiefs, warlords and drug lords) hold sway and resist attempts by the state to trespass on their territories. Even in Cape Town, certain of the 'coloured' townships are controlled by gangs (linked to international drug-trade routes) to the extent that they have, at times, taken over from the municipality the allocation of public housing units and the collection of rents. In another example, municipal attempts to initiate an upgrade of an informal settlement in Cape Town were resisted by local warlords with links to sources of tribal authority in the rural areas, as it would have removed their main source of income, which was 'protection' money from shack dwellers (Municipality of Cape Town 1998). Other cities in Sub-Saharan Africa are a long way further down this path of reluctant power sharing.

Using normative planning theories in the cities of Sub-Saharan Africa

Can the three normative planning theories discussed above move forward the debate about planning in Sub-Saharan Africa? Do they offer, at least, a theoretical perspective on the role and positioning of planning in such a context, or do they, as Huxley and Yiftachel (2000: 336) suggest, inappropriately generalize a Western context? I argue below that in some respects they offer important insights that planners in Africa will do well to draw from. In other respects, however, they are based on assumptions regarding the nature of the context in which planning occurs which appear not to hold in this part of the world.

The value of current normative planning theories

Given the nature of much past (and present) planning in Sub-Saharan African cities, which has been either weakly state managed, or donor driven and often sectoral, all three theories usefully draw attention to the importance of civil society-based groups in planning processes, and to the political nature of planning. These theories thus move planning beyond technocratic, corporatist notions, grounded in instrumental rationalism and often insensitive to context. The theories also usefully question the Enlightenment model of the public realm which universalized a white male, European experience, denied others, and imposed the ideal of impartiality on all (Beauregard 1998). The recognition that there are 'different voices' within civil society which represent what may be valid and valuable points of view is vitally important in Africa where societies are anything but homogenous and where some voices are often repressed by violence or tradition. As Storper (2001: 156) has noted, movements to combat racism and other prejudices, and respect for diversity in general, are probably amongst the most important developments of the twentieth century, and in this respect Africa should not be left behind. Sandercock's position that these differences go beyond speech-level 'differences in meaning', and may be rooted in more fundamental cultural differences is also valid: high levels of mobility and turmoil in Africa have resulted in the co-existence of ethnically and culturally diverse groupings with often very different ways of 'seeing and knowing'.

Aspects of Fainstein's Just City approach are also very important for thinking about planning in Africa. In a context in which poverty and survival are the central issues for the vast majority of inhabitants, the question of the distributive effects of planning decisions and of particular planned spatial forms, is crucial. Unless planning in Sub-Saharan African cities can demonstrate that it is about more than the control of land uses, and has a central role to play in addressing development issues, then it is destined to become even more marginalized than it already is. For this reason Fainstein's recognition of the role of the political economy in both determining the nature of urban problems, and in shaping the range of possible planning outcomes, is an important correction to the focus on 'agency' and on 'the local' of the other planning theories. Important, therefore, is her focus on planning at the level of the city as a whole, as opposed to a focus on local group or project initiatives, and how decisions at this wider level set the parameters for more local actions.

Finally all three theories raise useful questions about the project of modernity, evolutionary development theories, and the sense of certainty that pervaded many planning initiatives of the past. In Sub-Saharan Africa, more than in any other part of the 'south', the future appears to be one of steady decline, broken by the occasional enclave of development. If and how this situation will 'bottom out' is not at all predictable, leaving planning (where it can function) with little useful precedent and with few firm foundations on which to chart a way forward.

Where current normative theories are less useful

In other respects these normative theories are based on assumptions regarding civil society, identity, and the possibilities of 'bottom up' development, which are unlikely to hold in the context of large parts of Africa. Just City ideas may also require some modification.

All three normative theories display a faith in the ability of civil society to promote the ideal of democracy, a faith shared by mainstream development theory.

This has translated into the promotion of planning processes carried out by organizations based in civil society either in conjunction with local government or, in the case of Sandercock and sometimes Fainstein, entirely outside of government structures. The assumptions here are that organs of civil society are sufficiently organized to be able to: recognize the need for planned intervention; commit themselves to an organized process of planning which is accepted as well by those who will ultimately be affected by action; engage in a process of consensus-seeking which is democratic and equitable; negotiate any processes or outcomes with formal structures of government; mobilize resources and capacities to carry forward decisions; and maintain involvement with processes of implementation.

The highly dysfunctional nature of civil society in many countries in Sub-Saharan Africa makes it extremely difficult for such processes to occur.[11] Social or grassroots movements are few, fragile and often tied to ethnic interests, and cannot necessarily be relied on to take forward issues of broader public interest. Externally funded NGOs may be better positioned to take such initiatives but the limitations of these organizations have been noted above (also see Mitlin 2001). The point has also been made that the linkages between state officials and politicians, and various groupings outside of the state, are complex and often 'clientelist' in nature: the notion of an independent civil society bringing pressure to bear on government to act more democratically and equitably is seriously at odds with the reality of much of Africa. Moreover, the possibilities of achieving consensus are undoubtedly more difficult in societies fractured so deeply by ethnicity and so motivated, necessarily, by the objective of survival. The exercise of power as a motivating force is present in all such situations, but can manifest itself more overtly and more negatively under conditions of scarcity and instability. Networks of all kinds operate intensively, but are unlikely to be concerned with the place-bound and long-term issues that usually occupy planning. Populations in constant movement, in constant search of ever-shifting opportunities, are not well positioned to commit themselves to lengthy processes of debate and engagement in localized planning initiatives. Unfortunately the hope of building up localized social capital to draw on in future processes also becomes less likely.

The recognition and celebration of identity, as advocated by Sandercock, also needs to be thought about differently, given the continued focus of political struggles in Africa on material rather than lifestyle/identity politics. Fraser (2000) is concerned with identity politics more generally, but her arguments have relevance for operationalizing this approach in Africa. Her concerns are first, that demands for recognition are eclipsing demands for redistribution (in a context of growing economic disparity), and second, that the reification of cultural difference is encouraging separatism and intolerance. The results, she argues, are growing inequalities and a sanctioning of the violation of human rights. Identity politics displace struggles for redistribution in two ways. Some positions cast the roots of injustice at the level of discourse (e.g. demeaning representations), rather than at the level of institutional significations and norms. This strips misrecognition of its social-structural underpinnings. Other positions, associated with cultural theory, assume that maldistribution is a secondary effect of misrecognition and that misrecognition should be considered prior to distributional issues. This appears to be Sandercock's position. Fraser (2000) argues that not only do these positions obscure the real roots of misrecognition, which lie in institutionalized value patterns, but that reification of identity creates a moral pressure for group conformity, obscuring intra-group struggles, such as that around gender.

These ideas suggest that planners, who may be keen to foreground identity issues in the context of Africa, need to proceed with great care. To the extent that they sideline distributional issues, they may exacerbate a central problem in Africa: that of poverty and disparity. There is also the danger of failing to recognize that many expressions of identity in Africa are economically motivated and sometimes opportunistic. Assuming a primacy for identity may have economic consequences that are not entirely predictable or desirable. Perhaps even more important is the tendency in Africa for ethnic identity to form the fault lines for major conflicts, civil wars and genocide. There are indications as well, as Fraser (2000) suggests, that ethnicity covers a multitude of intra-group abuses (female circumcision, child slavery etc.), affecting particularly the more vulnerable in society. At this point in time, reification of identity in simplistic ways may do more harm than good.

A third area of contention has to do with the focus in planning theories on 'the local'. Both communicative planning theory and multicultural theory are concerned with local group processes and the role of agency. Local knowledge is valorized, and the concept of social capital becomes important in stimulating a process of 'bottom-up' development. In the Just City approach, the broader forces of political economy are recognized, but there is nonetheless the assumption that some kind of equity can be achieved at the level of the individual city.

There is no doubt that, in Africa as elsewhere, 'the local' plays an important role in determining processes and outcomes and this recognition is an important corrective to the structural positions of the past. But to marginalize the importance of broader structural forces in Africa's development would also be a major mistake. While global economic forces are playing an increasingly important role in the economies of all countries, Africa has been particularly susceptible to shifts in demand and pricing of primary products, its prime generator of foreign exchange. Most African countries are, moreover, influenced fundamentally by structural adjustment policies and aid programmes imposed on them by the World Bank and IMF. Few aspects of African economy and society are left untouched by these policies and programmes, and it has been near impossible for local initiatives to work outside of them. Growing poverty and political instability are in turn important factors underlying the extremely high levels of population mobility experienced within and between African regions. Local populations are thus neither stable nor cohesive, both preconditions, it would seem, for social capital creation,[12] bottom-up development initiatives, harmonious group processes and a sustained commitment to planning and implementation processes. For the same reasons, inequities at the level of a single city must be traced to dynamics in the rural areas, to other cities and regions, and of course to much wider forces.

The problem with a focus on the local, argue Mohan and Stokke (2000) is that it circumscribes both consciousness and action. If the economic and political base is not rendered problematic, then blame can be simply placed on the inabilities of local groupings or areas to situate themselves correctly in relation to broader forces. This in turn ignores the need for local initiatives to 'scale up' or begin to make global alliances.

A fourth area of contention has to do with the kind of urban form promoted by the Just City approach. There is no doubt that the kinds of spatial principles to be found in a city such as Amsterdam (held up by Fainstein as an example of equitable form) come closer to meeting the needs of a poorer population than do the car-oriented, sprawling and 'monofunctional' environments promoted by much past planning in African cities. They also begin to address the issue of equity at a city-wide level as well as important environmental considerations (Jenks and Burgess 2000). It is for exactly these reasons that these spatial ideas (sometimes called the 'compact city' model) found their way into urban plans in South Africa in the last decade (Dewar 2000; Schoonraad 2000; Todes 2000; Todes *et al.* 2000), allowing some conclusions to be drawn about their viability in resource-poor areas.

The approach assumes relatively high levels of state control over land use in order to define and hold an urban edge and control land invasions. While this may be possible in the context of a city such as Cape Town which has less peripheral informal settlement than other South African cities, and valuable commercialized agricultural land beyond the edge, in other cities the curtailment of informal settlement in this way may be highly detrimental to poorer households which survive through complex urban–rural linkages and marginal local employment (Cross, cited in Todes 2000: 619). The approach also assumes that significant resources are available to develop expensive inner city land and to build housing to high densities, rather than simply provide serviced sites. Few African countries are able to deploy housing funds of the magnitude required. The usual planning response, which is to provide very small serviced sites (to both cut costs and maintain densities) has proved highly unpopular, as larger sites are seen as an economic resource which allows sub-letting and sometimes agriculture. Attempts to achieve compact and more equitable cities also find themselves flying in the face of market forces, which are tending to direct private investment into decentralized and defended enclaves (Turok and Watson 2001), and individual investment into peripheral housing (Bebbington and Bebbington 2001). In South Africa at least, cities have become less equitable in income terms in the years since apartheid, with growing divisions and barriers between the wealthier and poorer parts of cities. Fainstein's Just City idea remains an ideal worth striving for, but also seems to be increasingly unrealizable in a context such as this one.

Conclusion

It is not possible to think about planning in Africa outside of the issue of development more generally, not least because positions on planning are inevitably underpinned by assumptions relating to wider economy and society. In this chapter I indicate a situation in which the development problem is probably more serious than anywhere else. I draw attention particularly to the basic problem of human survival (threatened by AIDS, war and poverty); economic collapse; the inability of governments to represent, regulate or provide; inter-group conflicts of all kinds; cities which are dissolving into desperate factionalism; and the suspension of all moral and legal codes in the struggle to survive. The picture is not homogenous: there are enclaves of economic success and wealth, and there are democratic social movements and NGOs that are doing positive work. But these seem to be the exception rather than the norm.

Modernism, in either its capitalist or socialist forms, has not served Africa well, or at least very unevenly, and neo-liberal development philosophies promoted through structural adjustment policies have been downright destructive. With no new development paradigm on the horizon, post-modernists and cultural-turn scholars retain a faith in civil society and social movements to build democracy and local economic development. Their vision of society is one of a diversity of groups with different values, interacting via porous frontiers and blurred borders (Storper 2001). This is a view not incompatible, Storper argues further, with the friendly, consumerist world of neo-liberalism, and one that is equally depoliticizing. Other positions argue for greater control over global financial flows and a stronger role for the state in order to strengthen its welfare functions, a position now also conceded by emerging 'pragmatic neo-liberalism' (see Sen 1999). But as Storper points out, there is:

> ... a viable intellectual contest right now to determine what degree of regulation capitalism needs in order to attain a reasonable level of stability and social justice. Current efforts to define the nature and degree of political regulation of capitalism have no credible utopian project attached to them.
>
> (Storper 2001: 161)

In the context of Sub-Saharan Africa, policies to reduce the role and power of central governments, to decentralize them and to privatize public services, have been partly responsible for the slide into inter-ethnic conflict, and welfare and service collapse. Many previous governments were inefficient, over-centralized and corrupt, but 'rolling back' the state has been no solution to this. Moreover, in Africa, civil society is generally not cohesive enough or organized enough to carry forward, on its own, either development goals or democratic goals, and a strong civil society is going to require stronger government than now exists. In the same vein, it seems that the globalized economy is not about to bring 'development' to Africa and major structural changes (debt relief, massive assistance for AIDS and anti-poverty programmes, preferential terms of trade, etc.) are an essential precondition for any kind of economic revival.

This lends support to a form of planning in which governments play an important role, but are certainly not the only players. As Yiftachel (1995) suggests, the traditional values of planning which have to do with reform and public interest are as important as ever, as long as reformism does not resort to social control and there is a recognition of a heterogeneous public. It lends support to a form of planning that recognizes that 'the local' both shapes, and is shaped by, broader structural forces, and that local action on its own will be limited and depoliticizing. And it lends support to a form of planning which acknowledges the material basis of identity struggles, in Africa at least, as well as the complex, fluid and crosscutting nature of identity issues. This in turn requires planners to be 'street-wise' when it comes to processes of negotiation: power will prevail over rationality (Flyvbjerg 1998b) and will certainly be more evident than harmonious consensus seeking. Finally it recognizes the social and environmental impact of spatial interventions, and the need for these to respond to the particular demands of context, without resorting to simplified importations from very different parts of the world.

Notes

1 Differences exist between communicative planning theorists (see Tewdwr-Jones and Allmendinger 1998). This paper makes primary use of Healey's work.
2 While this suggests a duality between state and civil society, Healey's institutionalist approach emphasizes social networks which '... weave in and out of the formal institutions of government ...' (Healey 1997: 205).
3 Huxley (2000: 375) points to the potential problem which this raises for planners who are employed by government and are accountable to elected representatives, but who are required to operate in participatory processes and also be directly accountable to 'a public'. Huxley also points to the unquestioned assumption underlying communicative planning theory that planning is the best institutional framework for fostering participatory democracy.

4 This is one aspect of communicative planning theory that has been strongly criticized (see Flyvbjerg 1998a; Huxley 2000; Tewdwr-Jones and Allmendinger 1998).

5 As opposed to Habermas himself who has often been described as a modernist due to his faith in rational processes and the universality of his ideas, and his concept of citizenship.

6 Although she does not disregard the role of political economy, it is downplayed.

7 Beauregard (1998), in comparing the positions of John Forester (a founding communicative planning theorist) and Sandercock, notes that Forester is hesitant about identity politics and wants to de-emphasize difference. Planners are citizens first, and relate to identity second.

8 The problem with this has been well articulated by Graham and Healey (1999).

9 This is not a phenomenon confined to African cities, as Healey (2000) argues.

10 In South African cities these efforts were linked to the apartheid project and the achievement of racially segregated cities. Formal housing and serviced site provision for lower income (black) groups was far more extensive than in other African cities.

11 Critics of communicative planning theory also question the viability of such processes in more stable, economically developed parts of the world (see, for example, Flyvbjerg 1998a; Huxley 2000).

12 The over-riding importance of the local in social capital creation has, anyway, been criticized by those examining the role of broader forces in Putnam's famous case study (Tarrow, cited in Mohan and Stokke 2000).

References

Aids Analysis Africa (2000) 10(5). Available online: http://www.und.ac.za/und/heard/AAA/AAA.htm (accessed June 2000).

Aina, T. (1997) 'The state and civil society: politics, government and social organization in African cities', in C. Rakodi (ed.) *The Urban Challenge in Africa: Growth and Management of its Large Cities*, Nairobi: United Nations University Press.

Allen, C. (1997) 'Who needs civil society?', *Review of African Political Economy*, 73: 329–37.

Allen, C. (1999) 'Warfare, endemic violence and state collapse in Africa', *Review of African Political Economy*, 81: 367–84.

Bartlett, D. (2000) 'Civil society and democracy: a Zambian case study', *Journal of Southern African Studies*, 26(3): 429–46.

Beauregard, R. (1998) 'Writing the planner', *Journal of Planning Education and Development*, 18(2): 93–101.

Bebbington, A. and Bebbington, D. (2001) 'Development alternatives: practice, dilemmas and theory', *Area*, 33(1): 7–17.

Borja, J. and Castells, M. (1997) *Local and Global: Management of Cities in the Information Age*, London: United Nations Centre for Human Settlements (Habitat), Earthscan.

Breheny, M. (ed.) (1992) *Sustainable Development and Urban Form*, London: Pion.

Burgess, R., Carmona, M. and Kolstee, T. (1997) *The Challenge of Sustainable Cities: Neoliberalism and Urban Strategies in Developing Countries*, London: Zed Books.

Bush, R. and Szeftel, M. (1998) 'Commentary: "globalisation" and the regulation of Africa', *Review of African Political Economy*, 76: 173–7.

Chabal, P. (1996) 'The African crisis: context and interpretation', in R. Werbner and T. Ranger (eds) *Postcolonial Identities in Africa*, London: Zed books.

Crush, J. (ed.) (1996) *Power of Development*, London: Routledge.

De Boeck, F. (1996) 'Postcolonialism, power and identity: local and global perspectives from Zaire', in R. Werbner and T. Ranger (eds) *Postcolonial Identities in Africa*, London: Zed Books.

Dewar, D. (2000) 'The relevance of the compact city approach – the management of urban growth in South African cities', in M. Jenks and R. Burgess (eds) *Compact Cities: Sustainable Urban Forms for Developing Countries*, London: Spon Press.

Diaw, K., Nnkya, T. and Watson, V. (2001) 'Planning education in Africa: responding to the demands of a changing context', paper presented at the World Planning Schools Congress, Shanghai, 11–15 July.

Elbadawi, I. and Mwega, F. (2000) 'Can Africa's saving collapse be reversed?', *World Bank Economic Review*, 14(3): 415–43.

Elbadawi, I. and Sambanis, N. (2000) 'Why are there so many civil wars in Africa? Understanding and preventing violent conflict', *Journal of African Economies*, 9(3): 244–69.

Escobar, A. (1994) *Encountering Development*, Princeton: Princeton University Press.

Fainstein, S. (1995) 'Politics, economics, and planning: why urban regimes matter', *Planning Theory*, 14: 34–41.

Fainstein, S. (2000) 'New directions in planning theory', *Urban Affairs Review*, 35(4): 451–78.

Flyvbjerg, B. (1998a) 'Empowering civil society: Habermas, Foucault and the question of conflict', in M. Douglass and J. Friedmann (eds) *Cities for Citizens*, Chichester: John Wiley and Sons.

Flyvbjerg, B. (1998b) *Rationality and Power: Democracy in Practice*, Chicago, IL: University of Chicago Press.

Fraser, N. (2000) 'Rethinking recognition', *New Left Review*, 3: 107–20.

Forester, J. (1989) *Planning in the Face of Power*, Berkeley, CA: University of California Press.

Graham, S. and Healey, P. (1999) 'Relational concepts of space and place: issues for planning theory and practice', *European Planning Studies*, 7(5): 623–46.

Habermas, J. (1990a) *Moral Consciousness and Communicative Action*, Cambridge, MA: MIT Press.

Habermas, J. (1990b) *The Theory of Communicative Action*, Cambridge, MA: MIT Press.

Harvey, D. (2000) *Spaces of Hope*, Edinburgh: Edinburgh University Press.

Healey, P. (1992) 'Planning through debate: the communicative turn in planning theory', *Town Planning Review*, 63(2): 143–62.

Healey, P. (1997) *Collaborative Planning. Shaping Places in Fragmented Societies*, Basingstoke: Macmillan Press.

Healey, P. (1999) 'Institutional analysis, communicative planning, and shaping places', *Journal of Planning Education and Research*, 18(2): 111–21.

Healey, P. (2000) 'Planning in relational space and time: responding to new urban realities', in G. Bridge and S. Watson (eds) *A Companion to the City*, Oxford: Blackwell.

Huxley, M. (2000) 'The limits to communicative planning', *Journal of Planning Education and Research*, 19(4): 369–77.

Huxley, M. and Yiftachel, O. (2000) 'New paradigm or old myopia? Unsettling the communicative turn in planning theory', *Journal of Planning Education and Research*, 19(4): 333–42.

Innes, J. (1995) 'Planning theory's emerging paradigm: communicative action and interactive practice', *Journal of Planning Education and Research*, 14(3): 183–9.

Jenks, M. and Burgess, R. (eds) (2000) *Compact Cities: Sustainable Urban Forms for Developing Countries*, London: Spon Press.

Leys, C. (1994) 'Confronting the African tragedy', *New Left Review*, 204: 33–47.

Lynch, K. (1990) *Good City Form*, Cambridge, MA: MIT Press.

Mamdani, M. (1996) *Citizen and Subject: Contemporary Africa and the Legacy of Late Colonialism*, Cape Town: David Philip.

Mandelbaum, S. (1996) 'Introduction: the talk of the community', in S. Mandelbaum, L. Mazza and R. Burchell (eds) *Explorations in Planning Theory*, Rutgers, NJ: Centre for Urban Policy Research.

Marcussen, H. (1996) 'NGOs, the state and civil society', *Review of African Political Economy*, 69: 405–23.

McIlwaine, C. (1998) 'Contesting civil society: reflections from El Salvador', *Third World Quarterly*, 19(4): 651–72.

Mitlin, D. (2001) 'The formal and informal worlds of state and civil society: what do they offer to the urban poor?' *International Planning Studies*, 6(4): 377–92.

Mohan, G. (1997) 'Developing differences: post-structuralism and political economy in contemporary development studies', *Review of Radical Political Economy*, 73: 311–28.

Mohan, G. and Stokke, K. (2000) 'Participatory development and empowerment: the dangers of localism', *Third World Quarterly*, 21(2): 247–68.

Municipality of Cape Town (1998) *Commission of Enquiry: Crossroads and Philippi Crisis Report*, Cape Town: Cape Town Municipality.

O'Brien, D. (1996) 'A lost generation? Youth identity and state decay in West Africa', in R. Werbner and T. Ranger (eds) *Postcolonial Identities in Africa*, London: Zed Books.

Rogerson, C. (1997) 'Globalization or informalization? African urban economies in the 1990s', in C. Rakodi (ed.) *The Urban Challenge in Africa: Growth and Management of its Large Cities*, Tokyo: United Nations University Press.

Sandercock, L. (1998a) *Towards Cosmopolis. Planning for Multicultural Cities*, Chichester: John Wiley.

Sandercock, L. (1998b) 'The death of modernist planning: radical praxis for a post-modern age', in M. Douglass and J. Friedmann (eds) *Cities for Citizens*, Chichester: Wiley.

Sandercock, L. (2000) 'Negotiating fear and desire, the future of planning in multi-cultural societies', *Urban Forum*, 11(2): 201–10.

Schoonraad, M. (2000) 'Cultural and institutional obstacles to compact cities in South Africa', in M. Jenks and R. Burgess (eds) *Compact Cities: Sustainable Urban Forms for Developing Countries*, London: Spon Press.

Sen, A. (1999) *Development as Freedom*, New York: Alfred Knopf.

Simon, D. (1997) 'Urbanization, globalization, and economic crisis in Africa', in C. Rakodi (ed.) *The Urban Challenge in Africa: Growth and Management of its Large Cities*, Tokyo: United Nations University Press.

Simone, T.A. (1998) *Urban Processes and Change in Africa*, Working Paper 3/97, Dakar: CODESIRIA.

Simone, T.A. (1999) 'Thinking about African urban management in an era of globalisation', *African Sociological Review*, 3(2): 69–98.

Simone, T.A. (2000) *On Informality and Considerations for Policy*, Dark Roast Occasional Paper Series, Cape Town: Isandla Institute.

Spiegel, A., Watson, V. and Wilkinson, P. (1996) 'Domestic diversity and fluidity among some African households in Greater Cape Town', *Social Dynamics*, 21(2): 7–30.

Storper, M. (2001) 'The poverty of radical theory today: from the false promises of marxism to the mirage of the cultural turn', *International Journal of Urban and Regional Research*, 25(1): 155–79.

Tewdwr-Jones, M. and Allmendinger P. (1998) 'Deconstructing communicative rationality: a critique of Habermasian collaborative planning', *Environment and Planning A*, 30(11): 1975–89.

Todes, A. (2000) 'Reintegrating the apartheid city? Urban policy and urban restructuring in Durban', in G. Bridge and S. Watson (eds) *A Companion to the City*, Oxford: Blackwell.

Todes, A., Dominik, T. and Hindson, D. (2000) 'From fragmentation to compaction? The case of Durban, South Africa', in M. Jenks and R. Burgess (eds) *Compact Cities: Sustainable Urban Forms for Developing Countries*, London: Spon Press.

Turok, I. and Watson, V. (2001) 'Divergent development in South African cities: strategic challenges facing Cape Town', *Urban Forum*, 12(2): 119–38.

Walton, J. (1998) 'Urban conflict and social movements in poor countries: theory and evidence of collective action', *International Journal of Urban and Regional Research*, 22(3): 460–81.

World Bank (2000) *World Development Indicators 2000*, Washington, DC: World Bank.

World Bank (2001) *World Development Report 2000/2001*, Oxford: Oxford University Press.

Yiftachel, O. (1995) 'The dark side of modernism: planning as control of an ethnic minority', in S. Watson and K. Gibson (eds) *Postmodern Cities and Spaces*, Oxford: Blackwell.

Yiftachel, O. and Huxley, M. (2000) 'Debating dominance and relevance: notes on the "communicative turn" in planning theory', *International Journal of Urban and Regional Research*, 24(4): 907–13.

Chapter 12
Out of the closet
The importance of stories and storytelling in planning practice

Leonie Sandercock

This article argues that story has a special importance in planning that has neither been fully understood nor sufficiently valued. Planning is performed through story, in a myriad of ways. The aim here is to unpack the many ways we use story: in policy, in process, in pedagogy, in critique, as a foundation, and as a catalyst for change. A better understanding of the work that stories do can make us better planners in at least three ways: by expanding our practical tools, by sharpening our critical judgment and by widening the circle of democratic discourse.

Allow me to introduce you to Martha Quest, the protagonist of Doris Lessing's novel *The Four-Gated City* (1969). Martha is a Marxist intellectual recently arrived in 1950s London from Rhodesia. She sees London as socially deprived and ugly. For Iris, however, a local woman with whom Martha is staying, the neighborhood is a living archive, textured and animated by layers of history and memory (Donald 1999).

> Iris ... knew everything about this area, half a dozen streets for about half a mile or a mile of their length; and she knew it all in such detail that when with her, Martha walked in a double vision, as if she were two people, herself and Iris, one eye stating, denying, warding off the total hideousness of the whole area, the other, with Iris, knowing it in love. With Iris, one moved here in a state of love, if love is the delicate but total acknowledgement of what is ... Iris ... had lived in this street since she was born. Put her brain, together with the other million brains, women's brains, that recorded in such tiny loving anxious detail the histories of windowsills, skins of paint, replaced curtains and salvaged baulks of timber, there would be a recording instrument, a sort of six-dimensional map which included the histories and

Submitted by the Association of Canadian University Planning Programs.

lives and loves of people, London – a section map in depth. This is where London exists.

(Quoted in Donald 1999: 122)

Martha, we might say, 'knows' London through theory. Iris knows it through immersion, through all of her senses, through empathy and love. In the paragraph quoted there is an implicit epistemology of the city, a distinctly feminist epistemology, which is at first sight appealing. It outlines a way of knowing the city through the senses and emotions rather than through (Marxist) theory. In the declaration of the last sentence, 'This is where London exists', there is a truth claim, a claim that to really know the city you need to know the stories in the heads of its entire female population. If we take this literally (which of course we are not meant to) then it is obviously ridiculous, since we could never know the stories of all those 'other million brains'. But even if we did, we would still have to interpret them, make our own sense of them. Is it even true, as a generalization, that inside women's heads there exists a particular kind of knowledge about the city? And why is that knowledge, Iris's perspective in the novel, inherently more valuable than Martha's more analytical perspective? My own answer to this last question is that it is not, that both are valuable and that it is not helpful to think of these different ways of knowing the city as mutually exclusive, or as superior/inferior. But that is the way 'story' is usually thought of, as 'soft', as a woman's way of knowing, as inferior, lacking in rigor.

In response to this kind of marginalizing of story in the social sciences, feminists and others have reasserted its importance, both as epistemology and as methodology. What I want to argue in this chapter is that story has a special importance in planning that has neither been fully understood nor sufficiently valued. In order to imagine the ultimately unrepresentable space, life and languages of the city, to make them legible, we translate them into narratives. The way we narrate the city becomes constitutive of urban reality, affecting the choices we make, the ways we then might act. My argument will be deceptively simple. Stories are central to planning practice: to the knowledge it draws on from the social sciences and humanities; to the knowledge it produces about the city; and to ways of acting in the city. Planning is *performed* through story, in a myriad of ways. I want to unpack the many ways in which we use stories: in process, as a catalyst for change, as a foundation, in policy, in pedagogy, in explanation and critique as well as justification of the status quo, and as moral exemplars.

My approach is not uncritical. Despite increasing attention to and use of story in some of the newer academic fields (feminist and cultural studies, for example), I do not see it as the new religion. We still need to question the truth of our own and others' stories. We need to be attentive to how power shapes which stories get told, get heard, carry weight. We need to understand the work that stories do, or rather that we ask them to do, in deploying them, and to recognize the moral ordering involved in the conscious and unconscious use of certain plots and character types. I believe that a better understanding of the role of stories can make us more effective as planning practitioners, irrespective of the substantive field of planning. Story and storytelling are at work in conflict resolution, in community development, in participatory action research, in resource management, in policy and data analysis, in transportation planning, and so on. A better understanding of the role of stories can also be an aid to critical thinking, to deconstructing the arguments of others. Stories can often provide a far richer understanding of the human condition, and thus of the urban condition, than traditional social science, and for that reason alone, deserve more attention.

In short, I want to make two bold arguments in this chapter. One is about the importance of story in planning practice, research, and teaching. The other is about the crucial importance of story in multicultural planning. Much of what planners do, I will argue, can be understood as performed story. Yet the importance of story has rarely been understood, let alone validated in planning. Story is an all-pervasive, yet largely unrecognized force in planning practice. We do not talk about it, and we do not teach it. Let us get this out of the closet. Let us liberate and celebrate and think about the power of story. Let us appreciate its importance to the twenty-first century multicultural planning project, as a way of bringing people together to learn about each other through the telling of stories.

How stories work

Very few scholars within the planning field have investigated the work of story in planning, and even then, only aspects of it (Forester 1989, 1993, 1999; Mandelbaum 1991; Marris 1997; Throgmorton 1996; Eckstein and Throgmorton 2003). In coming out of the closet about the importance of story, I want to be systematic about the ways, implicit and explicit, in which we use story, and to demonstrate what I mean when I say that planning is performed through story. But first something needs to be said about story itself, because 'story' conveys a range of meanings, from anecdote, to exemplar, to something that is invented rather than 'true', in the sense of strictly adhering to widely agreed-on facts. All three of these meanings are present and demonstrable in the way story is used in planning. In their most developed form, stories have certain key properties, and here I draw on my film school training, and also on Ruth Finnegan (1998), to sketch five of them. First, there is a temporal or sequential framework, which often involves a ticking clock to provide dramatic tension. Second, there is an element of explanation or coherence, rather than a catalogue of one thing after another. Third, there is some potential for generalizability, for seeing the universal in the particular, the world in a grain of sand.[1] Fourth, there is the presence of recognized, generic conventions that relate to an expected framework, a plot structure and protagonists. Aristotle's *Poetics* was our bible on this subject in film school. We learned from him that stories have plot as well as characters, both equally important: and that stories have a beginning, middle and end, a shape or structure. Fifth, moral tension is essential to a good story.

I want to expand on the second and fourth points. A lot has been written about the second point, the element of coherence or explanation. Literary, folklore and myth analysts have argued that there are a number of widely recognized plots: most obviously, the hero's tale, the rags-to-riches tale, the fall from grace, the effects of villainy, the growth to maturity, the Golden Age lost, the pioneer's tale, the stranger comes to town, and, the young man leaves home in order to find himself/make his place in the world/escape from the provincial straitjacket. What do these have to do with stories in and about planning? Let us take a few examples.

1   The conflict between settlers and indigenous peoples in New World countries over land uses and land rights. For indigenous peoples there is a core story that is about paradise lost or an expulsion from paradise. For the settlers, the core story is the pioneer's tale of bravery and persistence in the face of adversity.
2   The story of the young man leaving home to escape the provincial strait-jacket. This may evolve into the urban story of the young gay man who seeks out the big city to find a community of those like him, as well as to feel the freedom of anonymity. Or it may become the story of a squatter settlement in the hills outside town or on the banks of a river, or a homeless encampment in skid row on the edge of downtown. Each of these is a story in which planners get involved at some point.
3   The Golden Age lost. This is a story that recurs in writings about communities and their destruction. Sometimes the villains in this plot are developers. Other times, they are planners.

And so on. Stories in and about planning, even the most seemingly abstract, embody one or more of these recognizable plots.

What about the fourth element of story, generic conventions relating to framework and types of protagonist? Planning or urban stories may seem far more limited in their range of protagonists than fictional stories, because the protagonists often take the form of impersonal forces, (such as capitalism, globalization or the alienation of urban life), but there are also individuals who are seen as embodying these forces (such as wicked developers, alienated gang members, noble community activists) and are portrayed as villains or heroines.

In other words, the moral ordering of the more familiar fictional genres is equally present in stories in and about planning (Finnegan 1998: 9–13).

If we think about the East St. Louis story as told by Ken Reardon (Reardon 1998, 2003), it is possible to see all five story conventions at work. There is a 'temporal sequence' that begins when the University of Illinois is challenged in the State House regarding its community service work, and proceeds through early tentative efforts to do something, followed by setbacks, turning points, crises, obstacles and finally reaches dramatic resolution when we learn that a decade later, $45 million in funds has been committed to the revitalization of the hitherto abandoned neighbourhood. There is certainly an 'element of explanation'. In Reardon's version, this achievement was primarily the product of the faith of certain community leaders, and secondarily the result of hard work on the part of community members. There is 'potential for generalizability' in the way that Reardon draws lessons from this story that may have applicability for other poor communities as well as for university/community partnerships. There is the presence of the 'generic conventions of plot and character'. At one level, the 'plot' is about de-industrialization and globalization, abstract and impersonal forces, but it is also about community resistance and mobilization, coalition building, and the triumph of the human spirit. There are individuals who embody some, but not all, of these abstract forces. The 'noble community activists' have names and brief biographies, as do the 'few good men' who come forward to invest in the community with public or private funds, whereas those who had abandoned the community remain unnamed villains. Finally, the moral ordering of the story is clear. Faith produces a will to act. The capacity to act is enhanced by the university/community partnership. There is also blindness/self-deception in the university's involvement, and that has to be overcome, through the courage and honesty as well as compassion of the community leaders. An ethic of service to others drives the story ...

I want to turn now to the ways in which I see 'planning as performed story': in process, in foundational stories, in stories as catalysts for change, in policy, and finally, in academic stories, as method, as explanation, and as critique.

Planning as performed story

Story and process

For many planning practitioners, the role of story is central, although not always consciously so. Those who do consciously make use of story do so in diverse, and often imaginative and inspiring ways. The best way to demonstrate this is by using some examples, of story as process, and of story being used to facilitate process. But these examples are so varied that I will use sub-headings as guides.

Community participation processes

In community or public participation processes, planners orchestrate an event in such a way as to allow everybody, or as many people as possible, to tell their story about their community, neighborhood, school, or street. We tend to refer to this as drawing on local knowledge, and there are various techniques for eliciting people's stories, such as small group work with a facilitator for each group. What is not always clear is how these collected stories will be used in the subsequent process, but the belief operating here is that it is important for everybody to have a chance to speak, and to have their stories heard. This is linked with an argument about the political and practical benefits of democratizing planning.

If a participatory event is a way of *starting* a planning process, its purpose is most often about getting views and opinions, so the story-gathering is likely to be followed by an attempt to find common threads that will help to draw up priorities. If, on the other hand, the participatory event is a response to a pre-existing conflict that needs to be addressed before planning can move ahead, then the gathering of rival stories takes on more import. In such a situation, practitioners will usually meet separately with each involved person or group and listen to their stories of what the problem is before making a judgment about when and how to bring the conflicting parties together to hear each others stories. In extreme cases, where the conflict is long-standing, relating to generations or even centuries of oppression or marginalization, this is very difficult work, but when done well can be therapeutic, cathartic, even healing.[2]

Mediation, negotiation, and conflict resolution

In one growing branch of planning practice – mediation, negotiation, and conflict resolution – there is a raft of techniques and procedures for facilitating storytelling, and the hearing of stories, in conflict situations.[3] In this kind of work, the ability of a practitioner to make the space for stories to be heard is more important than the ability to tell stories. It is here that the importance of listening to others' stories, and the skills of listening in cross-cultural contexts, is at a premium.

Forester describes a case in Washington State where the mediator, Shirley Solomon, brought together Native Americans and non-Native county officials to settle land disputes. A critical stage in that mediation was the creating of a safe space in which people could come together and 'just talk about things without it being product-driven' (Solomon, quoted in Forester, 2000: 152). Solomon ceremonialized this safe space by creating a talking circle and asking people to talk about what this place meant to them.

Everyone was encouraged to tell their story, of the meaning of the land, the place, to them and their families, past, present and future, the land whose multiple and conflicting uses they were ultimately to resolve. It was this story-ing that got people past 'my needs versus your needs' and on to some 'higher ground', moving toward some common purpose. Solomon describes this stepping aside to discuss personal histories as both simple and powerful, as a way of opening surprising connections between conflicting parties. Or as Forester has it, storytelling is essential in situations where deep histories of identity and domination are the context through which a present dispute is viewed. Stories have to be told for reconciliation to happen (Forester 2000: 157). In terms of process, too, the design of spaces for telling stories makes participants from different cultures and class backgrounds more comfortable about speaking, and more confident about the relevance of the whole procedure. A tribal elder who was present at Solomon's mediation said to her: 'In those meetings where it's Roberts Rules of Order, I know that I either have nothing to say, or what I have to say counts for nothing' (quoted in Forester 2000: 154).

Core story

Another interesting development of the use of story in practice is what Dunstan and Sarkissian (1994) call 'core story'. The idea of core story as methodology draws on work in psychology which suggests that each of us has a core story: that we do not merely tell stories but are active in creating them with our lives. We become our stories. When we tell stories about ourselves we draw on past behaviour and on others' comments about us in characterizing ourselves as, say, adventurous or victims or afraid of change or selfish or courageous. But in telling and re-telling the story, we are also reproducing ourselves and our behaviours. Social psychologists argue that communities, and possibly nations have such core stories that give meaning to collective life (see Houston 1982, 1987). Culture is the creation and expression and sharing of stories that bond us with common language, imagery, metaphors, all of which create shared meaning. Such stories might be victim stories, warrior stories, fatal flaw stories, stories of peace-making, of generosity, of abandonment, of expectations betrayed.

In their work in evaluating the success of community development on a new outer suburban estate developed by a public agency in an Australian city, Dunstan and Sarkissian used an array of research tools: attitude and satisfaction surveys, interviews, focus groups, as well as census and other 'hard' data. When they came to analyze this material, they found contradictions that were not likely to be resolved by collecting more details. In order to go beyond the details and the quantitative scores on 'satisfaction', they explored the notion of core story, drawing on heroic, mythic and meta-poetic language. They scripted such a story of heroic settlers, of expectation and betrayal, of abandonment, and took the story back to the community, saying 'this is what we've heard'. The response was overwhelming, and cathartic. 'Yes, you've understood. That's our story'. The task then, as the social planners defined it, was to help the community to turn this doomed and pessimistic story around. They asked the community how they thought their story might/could/should be changed. Underlying this was a belief that core stories can be guides to how communities will respond to crisis, or to public intervention. As with individuals, some tragic core stories need to be transformed by an explicit healing process or else the core story will be enacted again and again. Renewal and redemption are possible, Dunstan and Sarkissian argue. New chapters can be written if there is the collective will to do so. They suggest four steps towards renewal. The first is a public telling of the story in a way that accepts its truth and acknowledges its power and pain. The second is some kind of atonement, in which there is an exchange that settles the differences. The third is a ceremony or ritual emerging out of local involvement and commitment by government (in this case municipal and provincial) that publicly acknowledges the new beginning. The fourth is an ongoing commitment and trust that a new approach is possible and will be acted on (Dunstan and Sarkissian 1994: 75–91).

This fascinating case study offers some illumination to a more general puzzle in participatory planning: how to turn a raft of community stories into a trustworthy plan, one that is faithful to community desires. To turn the light on inside the black box of that conversion surely requires planners to take their plan back to the community storytellers and say, 'this is how we converted your stories into a plan. Did we understand you correctly?' In a community or constituency where there is only one core story, this is a more straightforward process than in a situation where what the planners have heard is two or more conflicting stories. In the latter situation there is far more working through to do, in order to prioritize and to reach some consensus about priorities.

Non-verbal stories

Depending on the community involved in an issue, video, music or other art forms, may be powerful forms of story telling. In his violence-prevention work with youth in the Rock Solid Foundation in Victoria, British Columbia, Constable Tom Woods initiated a project to create an outdoor youth art gallery and park site along a 500-metre stretch of railway right-of-way between two rows of warehouses. This area, which had a long history as a crime corridor, is now home to the Trackside Art Gallery, where local youths practice their graffiti on the warehouse walls. Woods realized that these teenagers needed a safe site for their graffiti. More profoundly he realized that they needed a space to express themselves through non-violent means, and that graffiti is a communicative art form, a form of story telling (Macnaughton 2001: 5). The potential of planners working with artists in processes like these that encourage story telling has scarcely been tapped.

What emerges then is the use of story in both obvious and imaginative ways in planning processes: an ability to tell, listen to, and invent stories is being nurtured as well as the equally important ability to make the space for stories to be heard.

Story as foundation, origin, identity

I have discussed the notion of core story and how it might be used by planners. There is a related notion of foundational story, a mytho-poetic story of origins, a story that cities and nations tell about themselves. This is particularly relevant to planning in multiethnic, multicultural contexts in which conflicting notions of identity are at play. Look at Australia. The foundational story that Anglo-Australians have been telling for the past 200 and some years concerns the arrival of the brave Captain James Cook, who landed with the First Fleet at Botany Bay in 1788 to establish a colony, and of subsequent heroic pioneers who explored and tamed the land, a familiar story in new world settler societies. On one level this story is mytho-poetic, but on another it is also politico-legal. The founding institutions, and specifically the system of land ownership, were based on the legal concept of *terra nullius*, that is, empty land. This concept rendered invisible the previous 60,000 years of indigenous occupation, as well as their continued presence on the continent.

Towards the end of the twentieth century, growing numbers of non-indigenous as well as indigenous Australians grew increasingly uncomfortable with this founding fiction. Momentum grew for the rewriting of the story of origins. Many of those concerned with celebrating nation-building at the turn of the twenty-first century wanted to tell a more complex origins story, and the foundational myth became contested terrain. Part of the battle was legal and was fought through the High Court. Another part was symbolic and emotional, concerning apology and atonement. That was handled in part by the placing of 'Sorry Books' in all public libraries across Australia. Anyone who wished to could sign one of these books, and thereby publicly apologize to the Aboriginal people for their dispossession. There were also a series of 'Sorry Day' marches throughout 2001, one in each capital city. Half a million people participated in Sydney and 300,000 in Melbourne. The refusal of the Prime Minister (since 1996), John Howard, to make an official apology on behalf of the government continues to anger many Australians, and to be seen as unfinished business in the reconciliation process.

Having participated in the Melbourne march, this was lurking in the back of my mind in the winter of 2002 when I was working in Birmingham, at the invitation of the City Council. Partly in response to race riots in other northern British cities in the preceding summer, Birmingham's politicians were concerned about 'getting it right' in relation to 'managing' ethnic diversity. As I met with various groups in the city, from the city planning staff to workers in a variety of community development programmes, to young black men and Muslim women, I began to hear very different versions of Birmingham's identity. There was a fairly widely accepted founding story on the part of some Anglo residents (who referred to themselves as the 'indigenous' population) that Birmingham was an *English* city (not a multicultural city) and that those who were there first had greater rights to the city than the relative newcomers from the Indian sub-continent, the Caribbean, and so on. This profoundly political question of the city's changing identity clearly needed the widest possible public debate. I suggested that at some point the city was going to have to re-write its foundational story, to make it more inclusive, and open to change. The planning staff were very much implicated in this debate. At the community coalface, and especially in non-Anglo neighbourhoods, these predominantly Anglo-Celtic planners were either reproducing the founding story of 'British Birmingham', or helping to change that story by making their policies and programmes reflect and respect the diversity of the 'new city'.

This is not an isolated example anymore, but a situation increasingly common across Europe in this age of migrations. The need to collectively change (and represent in the built environment itself) these old foundational stories is one of the contemporary challenges facing planners.

Story as catalyst for change

Stories and storytelling can be powerful agents or aids in the service of change, as shapers of a new imagination of alternatives. In my own practice I have used stories in this very obvious way, discovering early on in my planning life (as a research student) that even within one city, it was often the case that one neighborhood had no idea that another neighbourhood was fighting, or had recently fought, the very same battle, and had come up with creative ways of doing this. When people are immersed in local battles, they are often so locally focused that they have no idea what's happening elsewhere. To discover that some other neighbourhood or social movement in your city or country has won some similar battle can be inspiring and galvanizing, and I have found myself in the role of relating such stories and becoming a galvanizing agent. As the world gets smaller, being the teller of stories of how people elsewhere have faced similar or even more dire adversity, and triumphed, is a role I increasingly and sometimes surprisingly find myself playing. When I was invited to Johannesburg in 2000, I was nervous because I felt that I was going into a context in which I had no experience and not much understanding. I could not 'pronounce' on issues there. But I could tell stories about struggles elsewhere and, just as the rest of the world has been inspired by Nelson Mandela, so too were South Africans moved and inspired by the struggles that I described in East St Louis and Sydney. There were processes embedded in those stories that I told, from which people could learn, get ideas, reflect on. The only skill that I bring to this is some sense, some judgment, about which stories are appropriate in what circumstances, and some sense of what constitutes, and how to tell, a good story.

Stories of success, or of exemplary actions, serve as inspirations when they are re-told. I have lost count of the number of times I have told 'the Rosa Parks story',[4] either in class, in a community or activist meeting, when the mood gets pessimistic and people feel that the odds are too great, the structures of power too oppressive and all encompassing. When Ken Reardon tells or writes his East St. Louis story, he is amongst other things conveying a message of hope in the face of incredible odds. This 'organizing of hope' is one of our fundamental tasks as planners, and one of our weapons in that battle is the use of success stories, and the ability to tell those stories well, meaningfully, in a way that does indeed inspire others to act.

In multicultural contexts, there is usually a dominant culture whose version of events, of behaviour, and practices, are the implicit norm. It is also usually the case that those engaged in planning, as a state-directed activity, are members of the dominant culture, and therefore less likely to recognize, let alone question, dominant cultural norms and practices. For a society to be functionally as well as formally multicultural, those norms occasionally have to be held up to the light and examined and challenged. One effective way to do that is through story. Canadian planner Norman Dale has written of the critical importance of hearing the stories of the Haida Gwaii (an indigenous community on the Northwest coast of Canada) in what was meant to be a cross-cultural community economic development project in the Queen Charlotte Islands, sponsored by the provincial government (Dale 1999). After a series of formal meetings with local residents, Dale was struggling to create a space in which the lone Haida representative (whose name was Gitsga) would feel empowered to say anything. Gitsga seemed to have taken a vow of silence, and was on the verge of pulling out of the consultation process when Dale sought him out and encouraged him to return. At the next consultation meeting, there was some informal chat among the white people, before the real meeting began, about the artistic and environmental merits of a sculpture that had been erected on a rock offshore. It had not occurred to anybody to ask the Haida people what they thought. When Gitsga broke his silence to volunteer the information that the rock was sacred to the Haida, there was genuine shock and consternation, leading to an opening up of the whole community economic development planning process to the involvement of the Haida. Planners have a tremendously important role in acknowledging the voices of minority groups, designing meetings in which such groups are comfortable speaking, and encouraging them to speak.

I have one more example of the use of story in planning practices, in the process of policy analysis, formulation, and implementation, before I turn to academic storytelling about planning.

Story and policy

Here I am aided by my colleagues James Throgmorton and Peter Marris, each of whom has done a lot of thinking about the connections between story and policy. In *Witnesses, Engineers and Storytellers: Using Research for Social Policy and Community Action* (1997), Peter Marris argues that the relationship between knowledge and action is not straightforward, and that knowledge itself cannot, has not ever, determined policy. In analyzing various types of and approaches to social policy research, Marris asks why so little of the research produced on poverty, for example, has affected policy. His answers are several. One is that academics are powerful critics but weak storytellers. That is, they fail to communicate their findings in a form that is not only plausible but persuasive. (By contrast, he notes that community actors have great stories to tell, but no means of telling them, except to each other. So the wrong stories win the debates.) Storytelling, he says, is the natural language of persuasion, because any story has to involve both a sequence of events and the interpretation of their meaning. A story integrates knowledge of what happened with an understanding of why it happened and a sense of what it means to us. Stories organize knowledge around our need to act and our moral concerns. The stories do not have to be original, but they must be authoritative (that is, provide reliable evidence marshalled into a convincing argument). The best are both original and authoritative.[5]

To be persuasive, the stories we tell must fit the need as well as the situation. Policy researchers compete with everyone else who has a story to tell, and their special claim on public attention lies in the quality of their observation as well as the sophistication of the accumulated understanding through which they interpret their data. But this truthfulness is not, in itself, necessarily persuasive. Good stories have qualities such as dramatic timing, humour, irony, evocativeness and suspense, in which social researchers are untrained. 'Worse', says Marris, 'they have taught themselves that to be entertaining compromises the integrity of scientific work' (Marris 1997: 58). Writing up policy research is hard work: it is hard to tell a good story while simultaneously displaying conscientiously the evidence on which it is based. However, Marris insists, the more social researchers attend to the storyteller's craft, and honour it in the work of colleagues and students, the more influential they can be. We have to be able to tell our stories skilfully enough to capture the imagination of a broader and more political audience than our colleagues alone.

There are two notions of story at work here. One is functional/instrumental:

bringing the findings of social research to life through weaving them into a good story. The other is more profound: storytelling, in the fullest sense, is not merely recounting events, but endowing them with meaning by commentary, interpretation and dramatic structure.

While Marris seems to confine his advocacy of storytelling to the publishing of research results, James Throgmorton's work addresses the next step, the arts of rhetoric in the public domain of speech and debate. The lesson he wants to impart is that if we want to be effective policy advocates, then we need to become good story-makers and good storytellers, in the more performative sense. In *Planning as Persuasive Storytelling* (1996), Throgmorton suggests that we can think of planning as an enacted and future-oriented narrative in which participants are both characters and joint authors. We can think of storytelling as being an appropriate style for conveying the truth of planning action. However, what should be done, he asks, when planning stories overlap and conflict? How can planners (and other interested parties) decide which planning story is more worthy of the telling?

Throgmorton (1996: 48) draws on Fisher's concept of narrative rationality in claiming that humans are storytellers who have a natural capacity to recognize the fidelity of stories they tell and experience. We test stories in terms of the extent to which they hang together (coherence) and in terms of their truthfulness and reliability (fidelity). But Throgmorton is unhappy with this, reminding us of situations in which two planning stories, both of which are coherent and truthful, compete for attention. What then makes one more worthy than another? Throgmorton suggests that the answer to this question lies in part at least in the persuasiveness with which we tell our stories. Planning is a form of persuasive storytelling, and planners are both authors who write texts (plans, analyses, articles) and also characters whose forecasts, surveys, models, maps, and so on, act as tropes (figures of speech and argument) in their own and others' persuasive stories. A crucial part of Throgmorton's argument is that this future-oriented storytelling is never simply persuasive. It is also constitutive. The ways in which planners write and talk shape community, character and culture. So a critical question for planners is what ethical principles should guide and constrain their efforts to persuade their audiences.

Marris's and Throgmorton's work has very important implications for policy research and recommendations. If planners want to be more effective in translating knowledge to action, they argue, then we had better pay more attention to the craft of story telling in both its written and oral forms. That means literally expanding the language of planning, to become more expressive, evocative, engaging, and to include the language of the emotions. 'Academic story telling', writes Finnegan, 'is ugly in its stark, clichéd monotone manner. We tell the dullest stories in the most dreary ways, and usually deliberately, for this is the mantle of scientific storytelling: it is supposed to be dull (Finnegan 1998: 21). What Finnegan alleges of academic story telling is equally true of bureaucratic story telling. Policy reports produced by government planning agencies, and also by consultants for those agencies, are cut from the same clichéd cloth. They are dry as dust. Life's juices have been squeezed from them. Emotion has been rigorously purged, as if there were no such things as joy, tranquility, anger, resentment, fear, hope, memory and forgetting, at stake in these analyses. What purposes, whose purposes, do these bloodless stories serve? For one thing, they serve to perpetuate a myth of the objectivity and technical expertise of planners. In doing so, these documents are nothing short of misleading at best (dishonest at worst), about the kinds of problems and choices we face in cities.

To influence policy, planners need to learn story, or rather, an array of storytelling modes. But where to learn it? What is the academy teaching?

Story as critique and/or explanation

There is a false binary in our heads that separates planning documents, social scientific research and theorizing, from storytelling, rather than allowing us to appreciate the ways in which each of these employs story. Planning documents, from maps, to models, to GIS, to plans themselves, do in fact all tell a story. Sometimes the story is descriptive, or poses as descriptive, 'this is how things are', 'these are the facts'. But there is no such thing as mere description, or pure facts. There is always an author, the planner as policy analyst, who is choosing which facts are relevant, what to describe, what to count, and in the assembling of these facts a story is shaped, an interpretation, either consciously or unconsciously, emerges. Facts are usually marshalled to explain something and to draw some conclusions for action.

Scholars also use story in their critical writings about cities and planning, sometimes consciously, but usually not. Even unconsciously, however, academic urban stories, even the most seemingly abstract, often exhibit some of the five familiar properties of story that were described in the introduction, drawing on familiar plot lines. There are heroes and anti-heroes, victims and other familiar character types: the witch figure/demon of international capitalism; the two-faced fairy of progress; the insubstantial and ambiguous trickster called post-modernity; and the darling love, long-lost, but in some stories found again, of community (Finnegan 1998: 21). There is a temporal ordering, often on a grand scale, taking us from pre-industrial to industrial to post-industrial cities, or from deindustrialization to the knowledge economy and the space of flows. The most familiar plot is change itself, and the desire to explain it.

Along with the explaining usually comes a valuing. Things were better before, or after, such and such, which then suggests we should go backwards or forwards. Evocative plots, of rural superseded by urban, community by alienation, tradition by modernity, or community triumphing over capital, residents over bureaucracies, squatters over the forces of law and order, are moving stories with which individual readers can identify, positioning themselves in a larger historical narrative. There are stories of times of transition, of new eras, of an old order passing, of lost Golden Ages. There are also some stories, but not many, which foretell a happy ending, if only … If only 'we' would do such and such, then we could live happily ever after.

In other words, academic urban stories and theories evoke basic narrative plots that are familiar to us from other contexts (from fairy tales to movies) and which resonate with us morally as well as intellectually, satisfying or disturbing or challenging us. My point here is not to say that these stories are therefore worthless. On the contrary, they are illuminating and instructive precisely because of these underlying plots, which are all exercises in valuing human activities, in a moral ordering of life and social organization. As with planning documents, the more alert we can be to the underlying story or stories, the better we are able to evaluate them. We need to understand the mechanisms of story, both in order to tell good stories ourselves, and to be more critical of the stories we have to listen to.

As with the myths of other cultures, our planning and academic stories function as sanction and justification for the current order, but also as launching pads for counterversions. Academic stories about planning usually take sides, although not always overtly. Sometimes the side that is being taken is revealed by asking the question, of any narrative, what stories are missing here? In *Making the Invisible Visible* (1998), I critiqued what I call the 'Official Story' of planning's history, by pointing out what that story leaves out. The 'Official Story' portrays planning as a heroic pursuit, often without any fatal flaws, always on the side of the angels, and those who oppose it as irrational, reactionary, or just plain greedy. What this leaves out are the gender, class, race and cultural biases of planning practices; the ways in which planning has served as an agent of social control, regulating (certain marked) bodies in space; and the many stories of oppositional practices, grass roots planning by excluded groups, in opposition to a state-directed mode of planning that has always disadvantaged them.

To imagine the future differently, we need to start with history, with a reconsideration of the stories we tell ourselves about the role of planning in the modern and postmodern city. In telling new stories about our past, our intention is to reshape our future. If we can uncouple planning history from its obsession with the celebratory story of the rise of the planning profession, then we may be able to link it to a new set of public issues, those connected with a dawning appreciation of a multicultural heritage and the challenge of planning for a future of multicultural cities and regions.

The multicultural city cannot be imagined without a belief in inclusive democracy and the diversity of social justice claims of the disempowered communities in existing cities – communities of migrants, indigenous peoples, poor people. If we want to work towards a policy of inclusion, then we need to start from a sound understanding of the exclusionary effects of planning's past practices and ideologies. If we want to plan in the future for and with a heterogeneous public, acknowledging and nurturing the full diversity of all the social groups in the multicultural city, then we need to develop a new kind of multicultural literacy. An essential part of that literacy is familiarity with the multiple histories of urban communities, and the multiple histories of newcomers, especially as those histories intersect with struggles over space and place claiming, with planning policies and resistances to them, with traditions of indigenous planning, and with questions of belonging and identity and difference.

Story and pedagogy

There are a variety of ways of using story in pedagogy: that is, specifically in the training of planners. I will mention a number of them, and then concentrate on the contribution of one outstanding educator. It is not new for planning educators to use story in the form of role play in the classroom (or in problem-solving workshops). The intention is to nudge people beyond their own horizons, into the worlds of others with whom they are in conflict. I have a number of reservations about role play. One is that the effect of asking participants to take on roles with which they are unfamiliar, or opposed to, may simply be to mobilize the worst kind of stereotyping of others' views and positions and behaviours. Another is that some people feel extremely uncomfortable having to be anybody but themselves. This may be more than shyness. For example, the mediator Shirley Solomon, in the case discussed earlier in this article, tells how in one case the attempt at a role play turned into a near-disaster. 'The people couldn't get into it because they just wanted to be themselves ... all these people are very much engaged in these issues, and it's passionate for them. They learned not at all from having to take the other's role ... One of the tribal leaders never got it, couldn't get into it, and just couldn't believe that he wasn't able to represent himself ... The (county) general manager was asked to be a developer. He just didn't want to be a developer. So he tried to do it for a while and then just got aggravated with it' (Solomon, in Forester 2000: 158–9).

I have been inspired by new teaching ideas that emerged from feminist studies in the 1980s. During my decade teaching graduate students in the Urban Planning Program at UCLA I used the device of 'life stories' as a way to explore difficult issues of identity and difference. My students, in their diversity, mirrored the social and cultural diversity of that city, and this occasionally led to tensions in classes. I began each semester asking students to write short stories about the ways that race, gender, ethnicity or disability, had shaped their lives. We then shared those stories in class, and drew on them during the semester, as a way of connecting the personal with the political. I have also used the idea of a 'housing autobiography' when teaching undergraduates about housing issues, asking students to craft a story about the houses they have lived in and how that might have shaped their ideas of the ideal house and neighborhood. When I did this at the University of Melbourne, with students from Hong Kong, Singapore and Malaysia in class as well as Anglo-Australians, it worked very well in bringing out cultural and class stereotypes of the 'normal' house and neighborhood. In general, I have found that the more creative I can be in the classroom (by using music, images, and so on) the more creative is the response of my students in their own papers and in their thinking. They start connecting unusual things, thinking laterally, which is definitely what is needed from planners in the twenty-first century. It was partly feminism, partly my film school experience, and partly the need to find as many ways as possible to connect with my multicultural student group that led me to experiment with story. The results, in terms of wonderful papers and presentations from my classes, have taught me a lot about the creativity that so often lies dormant, undernourished or even discouraged, through our academic straitjackets of 'appropriate', 'objective', 'scientific' papers.

For two decades, the outstanding planning educator John Forester has been a tireless story-gatherer, collecting the details of the working days and lives of a wide range of practitioners in North America and a handful from Israel and Europe, using interviews to get them to describe what it is that they do, always in terms of action rather than theorizing. With minimal editing, these 'work stories' have been published both as transcripts for pedagogical purposes and also, with detailed commentary and interpretation, incorporated into Forester's books as the foundation of his understanding of and theorizing about planning (Forester 1989, 1999).[6]

Over the past decade, Forester has been dogged in his pursuit of under-standing of difference in planning. I see his larger project as an attempt to reshape planning as a practice of deliberative democracy. But as part of that quest, he recognizes 'the challenges of a multicultural planning practice – the ability to anticipate and respond sensitively and creatively to complex differences of standpoint, background, race and gender, cultural and political history' (Forester 2000: 147). His underlying concern, as I interpret his recent work, has been puzzling over what it means to 'respect difference'. He sees the danger of respect conceived as the mere acceptance or appreciation of difference: in that form, respect can stymie dialogue and mutual learning. He is acutely aware that planning conflicts are often about more than resources (such as land, money, facilities). They are also about relationships, and this involves not only personality and politics, but also race, ethnicity, and culture. To learn about how to work success-fully in such cross-cultural or multicultural situations, he has sought out practi-tioners with good stories to tell. One such story, that can do double duty for me in writing here about pedagogy and story in multicultural contexts is the work of Marie Kennedy, who teaches community development planning at the University of Massachusetts in Boston.

Kennedy's undergraduate students are primarily of a working-class back-ground, urban, and older (average age 39). The class works with grass-roots community organizations in the Boston area, around issues defined by those organizations, and in the process, students learn planning skills. The project that Kennedy describes in her interview (Forester *et al.* 1993: 110–22) was in the city of Sommerville, adjacent to Cambridge, near Boston, population around 100,000. Sommerville was in transition from a predominantly white ethnic working-class district to a city with a significant new immigrant population, as well as a new liberal/radical, more educated white group who were moving in from Cambridge. (This latter group had become politically active and pushed the agenda of Sommerville as a Sanctuary City).[7] In the previous ten years the population had changed from 95 per cent white ethnic working class to 25 per cent foreign born (Haitian, Vietnamese, Central American) and this was accompanied by increasing racial tension and incidence of racial violence. Kennedy was approached by the Mystic Welcome Project, an organization of newcomers in the Mystic housing project, the largest public housing project in Sommerville. The question was how to build, or rebuild, a sense of community co-operation and support in this neighbourhood. There was also the challenge of how to bring together several neighbourhood-based organizations in the same area who had nothing to do with each other. For Kennedy the agenda was clear. 'We are explicitly going in with an agenda to build a healthy multi-racial, multi-ethnic community. So the goal is out front. We will have many discussions, and some of them will be heated' (Forester *et al.* 1993: 118).

What I want to draw from this story is how Kennedy prepared her students to work in this situation. The students themselves were diverse in terms of age, gender, race and ethnicity, and mostly working class. For the first month (of a one-year course) she met with the students and concentrated on their own attitudes towards immigrant communities and newcomers, and their own attitudes towards Sommerville as a place.

> We spend the initial time getting their biases and preconceptions on the table … I feel strongly that no matter who we are, we bring our previous experience, our baggage, our preconceptions with us into any planning situation. The first step is to get real clear about what you are bringing … You can either set your baggage aside in order to clearly hear and listen to

other people's experience, or you can check it out against other people's opinions and against facts to see whether your preconception is born out or not.

(Forester *et al.* 1993: 113)

The students all individually took walking tours through the neighborhood and had to figure out how the neighbourhood affected them, whom they saw there, what racial and ethnic and socio-economic groups, what they saw in the physical environment, what their assumptions about it were, whether they thought it would or would not be a 'nice' place to live. Kennedy got all the students to write about Sommerville, and to write about their attitude to newcomer groups and individuals. The writing was done anonymously, and discussed collectively. There was a lot of disagreement among students about their impressions. What came out in the discussions was how different students' backgrounds (growing up, or not, in a public housing project; living, or not, in a neighbourhood of newcomers, and so on) had shaped their reflections on Sommerville. Students were asked to think about the experience of becoming a minority newcomer, maybe the only family that is different from the now-majority community. Some could draw on their backgrounds as minority members to talk about this, and educate their fellow (white) students. Gradually this led into discussions on housing policy, immigration policy, a needs analysis of the area, and so on. But a whole semester was spent in this kind of preparation, before the students started to work with the community group, in the community.

This is a deeply informative account of what it takes to work as an agent of social change in a changing neighborhood, and how important it is to examine one's own preconceptions. It gives us some idea of the detailed personal work that needs to be done in preparation for working in multicultural environments.

In this learning stage, the stories that students tell about themselves, and hear from each other, are crucial in peeling back layers of preconceptions and assumptions about 'others', and about physical, residential environments different from whatever one is accustomed to. In turn, when I read this account of Kennedy's work, I learn new ways of approaching the training of community development planners. Her 'work story' helps my work. Forester's gathering of such stories helps us all. Stories teach. But what do they teach?

Forester's work, in spite of its empirical base, is both ethically and normatively saturated. Despite his disclaimer that 'we sought no particular philosophy or style' when seeking out potential interviewees, he is not merely describing what planners do, in their own words. He wants planners to do good and make a difference, and he searches for stories from practitioners which demonstrate these possibilities (and correspond with his understanding of doing good). His purposes shape his collection of stories. His pedagogical aims in passing these stories on to his students are not simply to convey the skills of these practitioners but also to inspire his students with how those skills are used, that is, for what moral purposes. In Kennedy's case, the purpose is building healthy multiracial, multi-ethnic communities. Herein is perhaps the oldest and most traditional use of stories, as moral exemplars.

Conclusions

There are of course limits to the power and reach of stories and storytelling in planning. Two need to be mentioned in closing. One concerns scale; the other, power itself. I am not claiming that storytelling works in situations of extreme conflict that divide nations, such as contemporary conflicts between Hindus and Muslims in India, or between Zionists and Palestinians in Israel. My examples are drawn from local and regional contexts and from scenarios in which planners have a role and some leverage. Nor am I claiming that storytelling is so powerful that it can or should replace other planning tools. Persuasive storytelling is one form of power at the disposal of planners, but it takes its place in a force field in which there are other powers at work, including the powers of misinformation, deception and lying, which are deployed by fellow planners as well as outside forces opposing planning interventions.[8]

Nevertheless, this article has argued that stories and storytelling are central to planning practice, that in fact we can think about planning as performed story. We have seen stories working as, and in, planning processes, where the ability to tell, to listen to, and to invent stories is being nurtured as well as the equally important ability to create/design the spaces for stories to be heard. When stories work as catalysts for change, it is partly by inspirational example, and partly by shaping a new imagination of alternatives. We have explored the notion of foundational stories that need to be rewritten, whether at the level of the nation, the city, or the neighbourhood. We have heard how story could be critical in policy research and analysis, as well as how the mantle of scientific storytelling may actually handicap our policy causes. We have seen how academics use story, as explanation and as critique of planning practices, and how these stories too can make a difference, can uphold as well as question the status quo. We have explored various ways that stories are used in the training of planners, personal stories, practical stories, moving and inspiring stories. I have also suggested the crucial importance of story in multicultural planning, and demonstrated how particular applications of story contribute to the multicultural planning project.

But there are still too few practitioners or academics who are conscious of or creative about the use of story. My purpose in drawing attention to the centrality of story is, among other things, to suggest that the role of the storytelling imagination could be given far more prominence in the education of planners. A better understanding of the work that story does, or can do, and how it does it, could produce more persuasive plans and policy documents. It could help us to analyze such documents. The creative use of or responsiveness to stories in planning processes can also serve many purposes, including widening the circle of democratic discourse, and shifting participants in such discourses out of their entrenched positions and into more receptive or open frames of mind.

I am advocating both a creative and a critical approach to stories and story-telling. I have talked about the need to deconstruct the 'official story' in relation to planning history. Using stories in planning practice must be open to the same process of critique, including an alertness to the ways in which power shapes which stories get told, get heard and carry weight. Critical judgment will always be necessary in deciding what weight to give to different stories, as well as what stories are appropriate in what circumstances. The telling of stories is nothing less than a profoundly political act.

As cities become more multi-ethnic and multicultural, the need to engage in dialogue with strangers must become an urban art and not just a planner's art, if we are concerned about how we can co-exist with each other, in all our difference. This most ancient of arts begins with the sharing of stories, and moves towards the shaping of new collective stories. 'The storyteller, besides being a great mother, a teacher, a poetess, a warrior, a musician, a historian, a fairy, and a witch, is a healer and a protectress. Her chanting or telling of stories ... has the power of bringing us together' (Minh-ha 1989: 140).

Acknowledgements

My thanks to Bob Beauregard, Jim Throgmorton, John Friedmann and three anonymous reviewers for their careful reading of this article and constructive suggestions. In an expanded form, this article is Chapter 8 of my book *Cosmopolis 2: Mongrel Cities of the 21st Century* (London: Continuum 2003).

Notes

1 This is why I have always been interested in 'gossip' as an everyday way of knowing/interpreting the world, in which people exchange apparently small (but not trivial) stories and search out commonalities and differences, as a way of making sense of their world (see Spacks 1985).

2 Forester (2000), Dale (1999) and Sandercock (2000) all detail such cases.

3 See Fowler and Mumford (1999); LeBaron (2002); Susskind *et al.* (1999(; Thiagarajan and Parker (1999).

4 Rosa Parks was the African American woman who, in Alabama in 1955, refused to move to the back of the bus when white folks boarded. This act of civil

disobedience turned into a year-long boycott of the bus service by Blacks, and gave birth to the Civil Rights Movement.

5   Marris cites Herbert Gans' *The Urban Villagers*, and Michael Young and Peter Willmott's *Family and Kinship in East London* as good examples.

6   The eight volumes of edited transcripts, arranged by substantive content (e.g. 'Mediation in Practice: Profiles of Community and Environmental Mediators') are available from the Department of City and Regional Planning at Cornell University.

7   That is, as a city welcoming of newcomers, with or without the legal papers.

8   For some hair-raising examples of how planners use their data dishonestly and deceptively, see Flyvbjerg *et al.* (2002).

References

Dale, N. (1999) 'Cross-cultural community based planning. Negotiating the future of Haida Gwaii', in L. Susskind, S. McKearnan and J. Thomas-Larmer (eds) *The Consensus Building Handbook,* Thousand Oaks, CA: Sage.

Donald, J. (1999) *Imagining the Modern City*, Minneapolis, MN: University of Minnesota Press.

Dunstan, G. and Sarkissian, W. (1994) 'Goonawarra: core story as methodology in interpreting a community study', in W. Sarkissian and K. Walsh (eds) *Community Participation in Practice. Casebook*, Perth: Institute of Sustainability Policy.

Eckstein, B. and Throgmorton, J. (eds) (2003) *Story and Sustainability: Planning, Practice, and Possibility for American Cities,* Cambridge, MA: MIT Press.

Finnegan, R. (1998) *Tales of the City. A Study of Narrative and Urban Life*, Cambridge: Cambridge University Press.

Flyvbjerg, B., Holm, M.S. and Buhl, S. (2002) 'Underestimating costs in public works projects: error or lie?' *Journal of the American Planning Association*, 68(3): 279–96.

Forester, J. (1989) *Planning in the Face of Power*, Berkeley, CA: University of California Press.

Forester, J. (1993) 'Learning from practice stories: the priority of practical judgment', in F. Fischer and J. Forester (eds) *The Argumentative Turn in Policy Analysis and Planning*, Durham, NC: Duke University Press.

Forester, J. (1999) *The Deliberative Practitioner*, Cambridge, MA: MIT Press.

Forester, J. (2000) 'Multicultural planning in deed: lessons from the mediation practice of Shirley Solomon and Larry Sherman', in M. Burayidi (ed.) *Urban Planning in a Multicultural Society*, London: Praeger.

Forester, J., Pitt, J. and Welsh, J. (eds) (1993) *Profiles of Participatory Action Researchers*, Ithaca: Department of City and Regional Planning, Cornell University.

Fowler, S. and Mumford, M. (eds) (1999) *Intercultural Sourcebook: Cross Cultural Training Methods. Vol. 2*, Yarmouth, ME: Intercultural Press.

Houston, J. (1982) *The Possible Human*, Los Angeles, CA: Tarcher.

Houston, J. (1987) *The Search for the Beloved: Journeys in Sacred Psychology*, Los Angeles, CA: Tarcher.

LeBaron, M. (2002) *Bridging Troubled Waters*, San Francisco, CA: Jossey-Bass.

Macnaughton, A. (2001) 'Constable Tom Woods – the unlikely planner', unpublished term paper for PLAN 502, School of Community and Regional Planning: University of British Columbia.

Mandelbaum, S. (1991) 'Telling stories', *Journal of Planning Education and Research*, 10(2): 209–14.

Marris, P. (1997) *Witnesses, Engineers, and Storytellers: Using Research for Social Policy and Action*, College Park, MD: University of Maryland, Urban Studies and Planning Program.

Minh-ha, T. (1989) *Woman Native Other*, Bloomington, IN: Indiana University Press.

Reardon, K. (1998) 'Enhancing the capacity of community-based organizations in East St Louis', *Journal of Planning Education and Research*, 17(4): 323–33.

Reardon, K. (2003) 'Ceola's vision, our blessing: the story of an evolving community/university partnership in East St Louis, Illinois', in B. Eckstein and J. Throgmorton (eds) *Stories and Sustainability: Planning, Practice and Possibility for American Cities*, Cambridge, MA: MIT Press.

Sandercock, L. (1998) (ed.) *Making the Invisible Visible. A Multicultural History of Planning*, Berkeley, CA: University of California Press.

Sandercock, L. (2000) 'When strangers become neighbors: managing cities of difference', *Planning Theory and Practice*, 1(1): 13–30.

Spacks, P. (1985) *Gossip*, Chicago, IL: University of Chicago Press.

Susskind, L., McKearnan, S. and Thomas-Larmer, J. (eds) (1999) *The Consensus Building Handbook*, Thousand Oaks, CA: Sage.

Thiagarajan, S. and Parker, G. (eds) (1999) *Teamwork and Teamplay*, San Francisco, CA: Jossey-Bass.

Throgmorton, J. (1996) *Planning as Persuasive Storytelling*, Chicago, IL: University of Chicago Press.

Chapter 13
Dilemmas in critical planning theory

Raine Mäntysalo

In this paper, it is argued that Critical Planning Theory is inadequate as a planning theory. It ought to search for means to incorporate the principles of legitimate planning argumentation, derived from Habermas's social theory, to a theory that is able to address planning practices both descriptively and prescriptively – grasping the essence of planning as problem-solving activity that transcends rationality and necessarily manages social relationships. However, Habermas's conceptual separation of communicative and instrumental rationalities, and his total reliance on rationality make such theoretical work inherently problematic. In order to add descriptive and prescriptive capacity, planning theorists have had to look for other theoretical sources, such as pragmatist systems theory and Foucauldian power analytics, which, however, are incompatible with Habermas's theory of communicative action.

The purpose of this chapter is to evaluate Critical Planning Theory (CPT) as a planning theory based on Critical Theory. It addresses the question as to whether CPT can be expected to give rise to a new paradigm of planning theory (Innes 1995) or is it too controversial and inconsistent to claim such a position in the Kuhnian (1970) sense? By Critical Planning Theory is meant the planning theoretical developments since the late 1980s, also placed under the headings of 'communicative' and 'collaborative' planning, where Jürgen Habermas's (1984, 1987) Critical Theory has provided the main theoretical and philosophical foundations.[1] Among the key planning theorists in this 'new planning theory' field are John Forester, Frank Fischer, Patsy Healey, Tore Sager and Judith E. Innes. With the development of their work such normative, interdependent issues as legitimacy, inclusiveness, domination and quality of argumentation in planning have become central in planning theoretical discussion.

Chosen as AESOP Prize Paper for 2003, and submitted by the Association of European Schools of Planning.

Recently the new planning theory has also met some criticism. These critical comments focus on the application of Habermas's concept of 'communicative rationality' in the context of planning. What Habermas means by the concept of communicative rationality is unforced argumentation held in an 'ideal speech situation' between participants where, by making claims and testing their validity in reference to shared 'lifeworldly' criteria, it is possible to achieve consensus on common issues and decisions. The attacks on CPT draw on certain critical observations on the idea of planning as communicatively rational action; it is claimed that critical planning theorists do not explain how communicative rationality in planning can be achieved. CPT is thus claimed to lack prescriptive potential (Tewdwr-Jones and Allmendinger 1998: 1988; McGuirk 2001: 199). Communicative rationality as a concept is said to have a character that is too utopian to function as a model for real life planning practices (Hillier 2000: 50). It does not offer clear advice on how to organize and manage planning processes, and hence it tends to remain as a theoretical ideal not rooted in everyday planning work.

A central aspect of the presumed utopianism of CPT is said to be the conceptual separation of power from communicative rationality. For Habermas, power represents a repressive force that replaces consensus-seeking argumentation with communication based on exchange relationships. In such power-based communication, the coordination of participants' actions can be achieved by appealing to positive and negative sanctions, thereby rendering unnecessary efforts to achieve consensus between the participants (Habermas 1987: 277–81, 310–11). Power 'distorts' communicative rationality (Habermas 1987: 187, 322). Mostly basing their arguments on the Foucauldian approach to power, the critics put the view that in the analysis of actual planning situations the Habermasian understanding of power is unfruitful. By viewing power as a negative 'outer force' that distorts argumentation in planning, one fails to acknowledge the positive, constructive aspect of power – power as necessity in achieving the capability of making and implementing decisions. In communicative planning, too, power is needed in carrying the planning process through, but this aspect of power is fenced out from the idea of communicative rationality.

In their counter-argument, the critical theorists appeal to the distinction Habermas has made between two types of power – power as unnecessary, systematic distortions of communicative action, and power as necessary distortions, publicly acknowledged as legitimate authority. The latter type of power, legitimate authority, would provide 'positive distortions' to communicative action. Notwithstanding the problematic vagueness of this distinction between 'necessary' and 'unnecessary' distortions, the distinction still maintains the general approach to power as an outer distortion. The Foucauldian critics of this approach assert that when power is dissected analytically from action situations this way, the crucial aspect of power as a factor that constitutes the action situations themselves, and subjects involved in them is missed (McGuirk 2001: 213; Hillier 2000: 50; Flyvbjerg 1998: 227).

This dispute over the concept of power between critical planning theorists and their Foucauldian critics is, to a degree, misdirected, since the disputants stand on different philosophical foundations. In planning theory, a common context for a comparative review between the two theoretical traditions can be found by evaluating the explanatory power of each and responsiveness to planning practice. Flyvbjerg's (1998) detailed account of the making and implementation of the traffic plan for Aalborg, Denmark, is a powerful argument in favour of the Foucauldian (combined with Nietzschean and Machiavellian) approach in analyzing and explaining real-life planning processes – whereas attempts to apply CPT in the analyses of actual planning processes are strikingly few. On the other hand, Forester, too, has convincingly developed Habermas's ideas on validity criteria and their manipulation into an analytical framework by which uses of unnecessary power in planning communications can be categorized (Forester 1989: 27–47).

Indeed, Habermas's Critical Theory seems to apply best in the identification of normative principles of legitimate argumentation in planning and this is practically all that critical planning theorists claim they are striving for. This is also their general argument against accusations of utopianism and the lack of prescriptive capacity of CPT. The concept of communicative rationality is not offered as a real possibility, but as a 'yardstick' with which to measure the real planning situations that always lag more or less behind it (Innes and Booher 1999a: 418; Sager 1994: 21, 246). The theory, therefore, is not intended to provide tools for the production of new planning practices but for the critical evaluation of existing planning practices. However, the question of whether the theory can truly serve as a useful empirical tool in the critical evaluation of the factual, normative and expressive validity of real life planning discourses, is still not successfully answered (see Tait and Campbell 2000). Be that as it may, the critical planning theorists' central argument against notions of utopianism and lack of prescriptions is that such criticisms display the critics' misreading of the general purpose of CPT (Healey 1999: 1133).

The crucial questions which remain are whether CPT thus framed can really serve as a planning theory; what should be expected of a planning theory; whether CPT can refrain from an attempt to achieve a methodology of argumentative participatory planning without losing its character as a planning theory; and whether it is a 'theory of valid argumentation in the context of planning' or a theory of planning.

A theory of planning ought to address the basic question – 'what is planning?' (Ramírez 1995: 2). This question raises the issue of the kind of activity being dealt with when studying the activity of planning. Habermas has several categories to different types of human action, but basically his view of human action can be seen as movement between two rationalities – communicative rationality and instrumental rationality. Power-mediated action is oriented towards self-regarded success aiming at instrumentally rational strategies, whereas action oriented towards consensus aims at communicative rationality. A direct application of Habermas's conception of human action leads to a view of planning as activity that alternates between these two rationalities. Does this view truly grasp the essence of planning?

If CPT were satisfied with the task of formulating theoretically the normative criteria of argumentation in participatory planning, it would leave largely unanswered the questions of how participatory planning processes proceed or how they should be developed – how the planning process is organized and planning situations arranged, how planning problems take shape and are solved, how worldviews, attitudes, allegiances and roles evolve in the process and how conflicts are handled. Habermas's Critical Theory poses powerfully for analysts the problems of public accountability and systematic domination in planning, public administration and policy (Forester 1993: 4). It thereby leads us to practical tasks, which take us beyond the goals of Critical Theory. Critical Theory defends practical and political reason, but as a philosophy it cannot solve the problems of society and politics (see Bernstein 1986: 112–14). This cannot be required of any philosophy – not even a philosophy rooted in praxis; but what then about Critical Planning Theory? Should it be considered similarly as a philosophy of participatory planning, rather than a theory – a theory of participatory planning, which would take on the normative-pragmatic challenge of how to achieve legitimate and inclusive planning practices? Although Habermas's theory as a philosophy cannot be required to provide solutions for our societal and political problems, this demand can be made to theorists, who apply Habermas's philosophy to planning theory, especially since planning is a form of human action motivated by the resolution of societal and political problems. It is awkward, to say the least, to retain a philosopher's attitude when applying a philosophy to the field of planning. This is not to argue that critical planning theorists adopt such an attitude, but in this regard they are (conveniently) unclear what their position actually is. Can a planning theory consist of a mere critique of society without addressing society constructively?

In any case, the formulation of a constructive theory of participatory planning is a sensible and justifiable task for a planning theorist, regardless of whether critical planning theorists themselves are willing to take on this task or not. But what could be the use of CPT in this theoretical work? Is it possible to move beyond CPT towards a theory of participatory planning, which attempts to capture participatory planning activity as a whole phenomenon, both descriptively and normatively? Could CPT be integrated into such a normative-pragmatic theory, which utilizes its principles of legitimacy and valid argumentation in planning and its general conception of modern capitalist society?

In the following, these issues will be taken into closer scrutiny. Can CPT be considered as a planning theory, which grasps the phenomenon of participatory planning activity to a sufficient degree, and if not, can it be complemented with other theoretical sources to form one? If the answer is negative to both of these questions, then it is doubtful whether CPT can give rise to a new paradigm of planning theory.

Planning aims to solve problems, not merely to achieve valid argumentation and consensus

As a theory of argumentation in planning, CPT cannot limit itself to identifying the principles of valid planning discourses without losing that which I consider the most essential characteristic of planning discourses. Planning discourses are intended to detect and solve problems we face in our social, political and urban lives. What we need is more than just legitimate and argumentative planning discourses; we need planning discourses that solve our problems and this poses the requirement of integrating the criteria of valid discourses into a methodology of planning as problem-solving activity.

As a planning theory, which acknowledges the character of planning as problem-solving activity, CPT is bound to apply Habermas's theory beyond the limits of its applicability, otherwise analysts would be dealing with a theory of legitimacy in the context of planning instead of a theory of planning. According to critical planning theorists, an ideal planning practice would be based on communicative rationality. The goal of communicatively rational action is consensus based on mutual understanding. What can be done with consensus in planning? Where does it lead us? As I see it, the goal of planning is the ability to cope with complex social problems. Even in an ideal situation, the task of planning would not end with the achievement of consensus. Planning problems are social in the sense that they affect a large number of people from different walks of life, but also in the sense that acting upon them demands social action and commitment. Moreover, they are often complex in the sense that their proper understanding requires cooperative action that transcends sub-cultural contexts of meaning. It follows from the nature of these problems that consensus becomes a necessary factor of successful planning. It is also necessary in order to gain trans-cultural commitment and support behind the making of such binding decisions that are influential enough to make a difference in our social reality. Hence, consensus becomes a constitutive element of our coping with complex social problems. (Mäntysalo 2000: 104).

It would be a misunderstanding of such planning activity to try to determine whether it were communicatively or instrumentally rational. The instrumental search for means is always present in our approach to a problematic situation, but due to the complexity of the situation, the search must often be extended to focus on ends as well. What is needed, then, is an ability to construct the whole framework of ends and means in such planning that reaches the quality of trans-cultural dialogue, but the dialogue is still motivated by the initial search for means, although acknowledging that one needs to find meanings first (or perhaps simultaneously). The basic effort is to mutually orient ourselves to our problematic situation, so that we can formulate plans of coordinated action on it. Rather than consensus *per se*, the issue is how consensus advances our coping with our problematic planning and policy problems. To cope with a planning problem is not the same as to get a planning project done. It means that we get done with the problem, for now – whatever we may decide to do with the project. The instrumentality of consensus is such collective orientation to our world that enables us to make decisions (Mäntysalo 2000; Tewdwr-Jones and Allmendinger 1998: 1983–4; McGuirk 2001: 206–7).

Planning transcends rationality

Planning as world-making

The possibility of communicative rationality is based on the assertion that a shared context of lifeworldly values and understandings is achievable as soon as each participant withdraws from the use of power. There is a good case for a counter-argument that in the present world we lead our lives in a society so differentiated into subcultures that a shared lifeworld is no longer readily (if at all) available (Tewdwr-Jones and Allmendinger 1998: 1979; McGuirk 2001: 213–14; Lapintie 1999: 9–11; Hillier 2000: 50–2). If that were the case, it would not be possible, even in principle, to plan in the fashion of communicative rationality before the participants have mutually created such circumstances, where the differing understandings and goals can be bridged. What kind of activity then is this creation of circumstances for communicatively rational action?

Habermas's theory with its rationality apparatus leads us to observe analytically and critically the created new, not the creation of the new itself. Critical Theory is too 'scientific' to handle the question of creativity[2] – it is a captive of its two rationalities. Can the true essence of planning activity really be found from rationality – communicative or instrumental? Is planning merely a form of rational debate, or a rational means for a given end, or an alternation between the two? Are we here offered an adequate description of what the planner actually does when he plans?

In communicatively rational planning, the participants are expected to make claims about something and to appeal to something that already is there, but where does planning step in? Are we not here reducing planning to a form of reasoned speaking and decision-making and neglecting its potential in world-making? In planning we are not merely debating but also producing the contents (survey results, ideas and suggestions for solutions, contexts for value choices, comparisons to similar cases, and so forth) upon which we debate. Rationality, whether communicative or instrumental, is concerned with the validity or effectiveness of a proposed set of actions in reference to a given criterion or end. It does not address the type of communication that has to do with more fundamental processes of shaping criteria or ends. Habermas's communicative rationality is based on making and testing claims in reference to a given moral-practical horizon of shared understandings, but the key problem in transcultural and pluralistic planning situations is how such a mutual horizon could be found (Rittel and Webber 1973). In its deepest sense, planning is the shaping of shared worlds and, accordingly, the formulation of shared rationalities. Habermas's Critical Theory does not address this crucial aspect of planning, but starts from a situation where we already have a shared world and a shared yardstick of rationality (Mäntysalo 2000: 103). Habermas's communicatively rational dialogue is not genuine dialogue because, as Karatani points out, the participants already have shared rules. For Karatani, shared rules are the outcome of dialogue, not its point of departure (Karatani 1995: 153).

Planning as dialogue

Let us examine the concept of 'dialogue' more closely. Bohm and Peat see dialogue as 'the free flow of meaning between communicating parties' (Bohm and Peat 1992: 245).[3] They emphasize the creative nature of dialogue as a process of revealing and then melting together the rigid constructions of implicit cultural knowledge. Bohm and Peat make a distinction between 'dialogue' and 'discussion' as the two basic forms of discourse (Bohm and Peat 1992: 245). Senge elaborates this distinction by claiming that in discussion different views are presented and defended, whereas in dialogue different views are presented as a means towards discovering a new view (Senge 1990: 247). He argues that discourses in the form of discussion may provide useful analyses of problem situations. In dialogue, complex issues are explored, but in a discussion, decisions are made.

> When a team must reach agreement and decisions must be taken, some discussion is needed. On the basis of a commonly agreed analysis, alternative views need to be weighed and a preferred view selected ... When they are productive, discussions converge on a conclusion or course of action. On the other hand, dialogues are diverging; they do not seek agreement, but a

richer grasp of complex issues. Both dialogue and discussion can lead to new courses of action; but actions are often the focus of discussion, whereas new actions emerge as a by-product of dialogue.

(Senge 1990: 247)

Here Senge associates the distinction between dialogue and discussion with the distinction between *divergent* and *convergent* thinking that Faludi, among others, has used in his *Planning Theory* (Faludi 1973). Faludi suggests that creative planning oscillates between convergent thinking, which corresponds to conscious analyzing and selecting, and divergent thinking, which corresponds to intuitive associating (Faludi 1973: 119). Faludi quotes O. L. Zangwill:

... in convergent thinking, the aim is to discover the one right answer to a problem set. It is highly directed, essentially logical thinking of the kind required in science and mathematics. It is also the kind required for the solution of most intelligence tests. In divergent thinking, on the other hand, the aim is to produce a large number of possible answers, none of which is necessarily more correct than the others though some may be more original. Such thinking is marked by its variety and fertility rather than by its logical precision.

(Faludi 1973: 118)

Faludi concludes that '[w]hen combined, these types of convergent and divergent thinking enable truly creative responses to an ever-changing environment in a way which neither of the two would be capable of providing on its own' (Faludi 1973: 118). When Habermas's concept of communicative rationality is related to these definitions of dialogue and discussion (and divergent and converted thinking) it can be claimed that communicative rationality is more akin to un-dominated discussion than to dialogue. Habermas is more concerned with determining valid methods of evaluating and criticizing arguments than with the actual production of arguments (Mäntysalo 2000: 339).

Habermas's concept of dialogue is too narrow. The central aspect of creativity is missing. In Habermasian dialogue the lifeworld exists as a stable horizon, in reference to which societal ends are rationally derived in an un-dominated argumentation process. The concept does not reach the changing of the lifeworld. Neither communicative rationality, nor instrumental rationality can be used to explain how lifeworld changes and evolves. As Forester comments: Habermas defines explicitly the processes of lifeworld reproduction, but '[h]e does little, though, sociologically, to assess how these processes work, how worldviews, allegiances, identities are elaborated, routinized, established, or altered' (Forester 1993: 126). According to Forester that is the central issue to be addressed in any concrete analysis of political struggle, policy debate, political conflict, or social movement – and this explains part of the difficulty, to this date, of applying Habermas's work directly and concretely to political conflicts.

(Forester 1993: 126)

Forester himself has addressed this issue with his concept 'designing as making sense together'. With the concept he refers to the notion of designing as a shared interpretive sense-making process between participants engaged in practical conversation in their institutional and historical settings (Forester 1989: 119–33).

When form-giving is understood more as an activity of making sense together, it can be situated in a world where social meaning is a perpetual practical accomplishment. Designing takes place in institutional settings where rationality is precarious at best, conflict abounds, and relations of power shape what is feasible, desirable, and at times even imaginable. By recognizing design practices as conversational processes of making sense together, designers can become alert to the social dimensions of design processes, including organizational, institutional, and political-economic influences that they will face – necessarily, if also unhappily at times – in everyday practice.

(Forester 1989: 120–1)

'Designing as making sense together' acknowledges the world-making nature of design, where the participants create new meanings together, regarding ends as well as means (Forester 1989: 126–8). According to Forester, such design work is both instrumentally productive and socially reproductive (Forester 1989: 129–32), but rather than referring to Habermas's theory of communicative action, Forester's description of design activity follows Schön's ideas of designing and planning as 'reflective conversations with the situation' (Schön 1983: 76–104). Schön's theory of reflective action is a powerful influence also on other major critical planning theorists, such as Fischer (1990), Sager (1994) and Innes and Booher (1999a; 1999b). However, the use of Schön's theory in the context of Critical Theory poses philosophical and theoretical problems. The discussion will return to these in the next section.

To Forester's concept 'designing as making sense together', Healey makes an addition – 'while living differently' (Healey 1992: 148). It reveals Healey's attitude of doubt towards hopes of achieving truly shared understanding in trans-cultural communicative planning. Participants may share a concern, but arrive at it through different cultural, societal and personal experiences. They belong to different 'systems' of knowing and valuing that will remain nearer or farther from each other in relation to access to each other's languages. Planning communication should thus focus on reaching an achievable level of mutual understanding for the purposes at hand, while retaining awareness of that which is not understood (Healey 1992: 154).

> Through such processes of argumentation we may come to agree, or accept a process of agreeing, on what should be done, without necessarily arriving at a unified view of our respective lifeworlds. The critical criteria built into such a process of argument encourages openness and 'transparency', but without simplification. If collective concerns are ambivalent and ambiguous, such a communicative process should allow acknowledgement that this is so, perhaps unavoidably so. So the dilemmas and creative potentials of ambiguity enrich the inter-discursive effort, rather than being washed out in the attempt to construct a one-dimensional language.
>
> (Healey 1992: 156)

This approach to planning situations as socially and culturally fragmented contexts where a shared lifeworld is missing, in fact, stresses the view that in planning we need to transcend communicative (and instrumental) rationality. Problems are solved in planning, but beyond that characteristic, and more essentially, planning is about shaping such problem situations, where problems can be identified as rationally solvable. In planning we generate the context for rationality. Cates's comment in her critique of the bounded rationality of incrementalism applies here also – 'What is needed is something other than rationality[1] (Cates 1979: 529).

Participatory planning bureaucratizes itself

Planning as organized participation

Critical planning theorists' theoretical efforts have in large part concentrated on demonstrating and articulating the crisis of former planning theory, which was heavily influenced by systems theory. Simon (1979) introduced the view of systems theory as the theoretical core of planning theory in the 1940s and this theoretical development culminated in the 1960s and the early 1970s. The main counter-argument of CPT against this theoretical tradition is that systems theoretical models of thought turn public planning agencies into technocratic institutions, which aim at efficient control of environmental changes, but which thereby also bypass political conduct. The political treatment of public affairs would hence be superseded by systems rationality, which both defines the problems and offers solutions for them. Instead of being a mere administrative tool, systems rationality would thus become the goal of planning, the supreme value (Fischer 1990: 203–10, 271–4; Forester 1993: 9, 89; Thomas 1982: 15, 21, 25).

Habermas uses systems theory in describing the mechanisms of societal sub-systems that are steered by the media of power and money. The sub-systems are thus presented as control systems, which have the tendency to 'colonize' the lifeworld by their processes of bureaucratization and commodification. However, although Habermas critically approaches the workings of positivist systems thought in this way, he does not seek to restructure the theory. For Habermas systems theory is still an adequate theory to describe the type of rationality that is decisive in the political and economic life of the modern capitalist state. Habermas calls this rationality 'instrumental rationality' – a concept which is a reformulation of Weber's purposive rationality, but also comprises systems rationality. Habermas's communicative action, on the other hand, is based on his concept of communicative rationality – on seeking agreement in social inter-action by making and testing claims of the shared world in reference to three practical criteria – propositional truth, normative rightness, and subjective truth-fulness.[4]

There is a dialectical relationship between the two rationalities, but how does this dialectic actually work? Habermas alternates from one rationality to the other, but does not actually analyse their interplay – that is, how communicative and strategic actions intertwine to produce and reproduce forms of social and societally institutionalized behaviour. We find ourselves at one end of the dialectical relationship between 'system' and 'lifeworld', looking critically at the other end. However, it seems that a proper understanding of planning processes would require a shift in focus to the dialectical relationship itself.

On the basis of Habermas's 'bipolar' theory of society it is difficult to approach constructively the kind of problems that concern public planning and organization dynamics. These issues are placed on the 'system' side. Public planning, signified as 'bureaucratization of the lifeworld', is seen as a potential threat to legitimacy in planning. On the other hand, unconstrained participation aiming at communicative rationality is treated as an ideal form of legitimate conduct. But participation has an inherent tendency to organize, and hence to bureaucratize, itself. What is organized participation, if not a bureaucracy? To address the issue of participation without addressing the organization of participation is half-hearted, if not outright irresponsible, theoretical work (Luhmann 1990: 223). Critical planning theorists speak for participation against bureaucracy without critically recognizing the bureaucratization inherent in participation itself.[5] For example, in a relatively short time, resident associations have developed from *ad hoc* civic movements into well-organized interest groups that have found their institutionalized positions in the local political organizations. The following quotation from Luhmann is illustrative:

Organizations are social systems that produce decisions with the help of decisions. Therefore the strengthening of the possibilities of participation within organizations amounts to an increase of decisions. More decisions are necessary if decisions are shifted to committees where those affected or their representatives have to decide whether they want to agree with a decision or not. Such committees have to be prepared, both regarding the subject matter as well as tactically. The decision process is reflexive. Everyone has to decide how one wants to decide. Most of all, this reflexive decision process has to be discussed in advance. In this way the reflexivity of deciding is shifted to a third level. One has to decide about how a representative ought to decide about decisions.

(Luhmann 1990: 223)

This process has a striking correspondence with normal behaviour in bureaucracies. According to Luhmann, '[t]he normal bureaucratic process constantly makes decisions about decisions. Decisions are made possible or impeded by decisions. Or if one cannot decide about this decision, then it is deferred by decision' (Luhmann 1990: 223). Luhmann argues that this is precisely how one behaves in the participatory procedure (Luhmann 1990: 223–4). 'Like a puppet within a puppet, participation develops into an organization within an organization, into a bureaucracy within a bureaucracy' (Luhmann 1990: 224).

In the light of CPT, the result can be condemned as bureaucracy and praised as participation. As Luhmann remarks, this double evaluation has an immobilizing effect – '[o]ne affirms in principle what one condemns in execution' (Luhmann 1990: 224). Here Luhmann, in fact, describes the double bind[6] of participation that critical planning theorists often produce – because you want to participate, you must reject bureaucratic domination; and because participation itself gets bureaucratized, you have to reject participation.

Critical planning theorists are well aware of the necessity of administrative and managerial work for the success of participatory planning processes:

When participatory research projects fail, the problem most commonly stems from a misbegotten belief – namely, that participation assigns equal weight to all opinions and, worse, that everyone can talk at will (if not all at once). Under these conditions, participatory research opens up a cacophony of miscommunication that easily degenerates into vituperative namecalling. In the absence of a well-structured model of expert-client discourse, including rules of evidence and evaluation criteria, participatory research can be a formula for trouble. To avoid its premature failure, and to avert disillusionment among both experts and clients in the process, it is essential that the ground rules of the alternative model, procedural as well as methodological, be carefully worked out.

(Fischer 1990: 377)

From the conceptual basis of Critical Theory, however, the issue of management in participatory planning is very difficult to attend to. Critical planning theorists often mistake the structural problems of a participatory organization for ideological problems. They offer hopes of democratic liberation in such organizational contexts where these hopes may be structurally impossible to fulfil (Luhmann 1990: 223). When structure is identified with domination, liberation means the same as 'unstructuring'. Our situation becomes unbearable, if our conceptions lead us to condemn as domination the forms of strategic and coordinated action that are unavoidable and ubiquitous in our social relations. These confusions lead to the divorce of ethics and praxis. Social justice is pursued at the price of practical handling of common affairs. We become paralyzed equally.

The distinction between 'socially necessary' and 'socially unnecessary' distortions of communication processes is offered as a defence against this critique. According to Forester, even among critical planning theorists the fundamental difference between the two often goes unrecognized, with the consequence of mistaking the distortions of discourses that are inevitable for domination (Forester 1993: 159; 1989: 33–5, 41–43; Fischler 1995: 17). Habermas himself, according to Forester, 'has no illusions … Rather, he contrasts unnecessary, systematic distortion with what might be called necessary and justifiable, or legitimate, distortion. The former manifests domination; the latter manifests legitimate authority' (Forester 1993: 168).

This distinction between domination and legitimate authority leads to a further problem. How can necessary distortions be legitimated in communicative action that already is distorted by these distortions? How can we justify the terms within which we justify? Moreover, how can we even distinguish between necessary and unnecessary distortions in a distorted speech situation? The distinction can be made only in an 'ideal speech situation', where all use of power, and thus distortion, is absent. As this is an ideal, not a real context of communication, it is likely to render unreal also the distinction between necessary and unnecessary distortions, as a theoretical tool.

The problem with the concept of communicative rationality is that it leads us to attempt to 'rise above' power. We need an alternative theoretical approach, which, instead, would guide us to reflect on our contexts of planning that are not distorted but structured by different forms of contextual power, such as conceptual domination by planning experts, institutionalized economic criteria and the privilege of organized political interests. Such an alternative would acknowledge the unavoidable presence of power in all planning action, even in acts of critique and reflection. Legitimacy in planning would thus be approached with a more humble attitude – as a normative task of improving legitimacy without assuming the possibility, and necessity, of determining universally what constitutes legitimate planning.

Planning as organizational learning

Although CPT speaks for dialogue and social learning, it can address them only passively. By following Habermas, one is able to deduce how planners should act in order to allow social learning to take place – not yet grasping what actually takes place in social learning. In order to add theoretical capability to describe social learning processes in planning, the critical planning theorists have looked for other theoretical sources besides Habermas. In this regard, what has been considered as promising is especially Schön's (1983) theory of reflective professional action.

Schön belongs to the broad scientific tradition of 'Organization Development' (Friedmann 1987: 56–7). Organization Development (OD) is a spin-off of 'Scientific Management', which developed after 1945 mainly to serve large private corporations. Argyris, Schön, Senge and others moved the field gradually away from profit as the sole criterion of management, and brought forth humanistic values and the motive of psychological self-development (Friedmann 1987). OD acted so as to apply systems-theoretical thinking, but approached it from the perspective of American pragmatism (for example James, Peirce, Dewey and Mead).

There are objectives in OD research that are likened to those of Habermas's Critical Theory (Fischer 1990: 365; Huttunen *et al.* 1999: 126). In addition to the shared emphasis on the importance of dialogue, the conception of knowledge as historically and socially situated is a shared characteristic. According to Habermas, a claim is accepted as a true claim if its validity is inter-subjectively agreed upon by the community to which the claim is directed. The OD tradition works with a process concept of knowledge – knowledge is not pre-existing in libraries, in agency documents, in computer files, or in the expert's 'head'; it is rather designed by small task-oriented groups of both experts and clients. Knowledge is the product of a social learning process, which has brought mutual understanding of a problematic situation and simultaneously provided means to alter that situation. Knowledge is tied to specific real-life contexts and to problems and goals that are relevant in those contexts. What is generalizable is not knowledge itself, but the collective learning processes that generate knowledge. Problems are examined from the perspective of actors actually engaged in practice; it is the practice itself that poses the puzzles to be solved. Research attitude and dialogue become aspects of an ongoing practice.

At first glance, OD seems like a welcome complement to Critical Theory. Due to its 'client-orientedness', it harmonizes with the emancipatory principle of Critical Theory. At the same time, it goes further in joining theory and practice and in synthesizing normative and empirical research. It is oriented towards the actual production of practice, not merely aiming to define the normative principles the practice should meet. Whereas Critical Theory offers social learning and dialogue as a well-reasoned and ethical plea, the field of Organization Development goes further and provides a methodology for them.

Still, in general terms the project of OD is rejected by critical planning theorists. And the reason is clear – it is, after all, organizations that are developed. What should be concerned with the maintenance of communicative action has been harnessed in the service of 'system maintenance'. According to Forester, OD theorists formulate our problems of planning and administration as the organization of learning, and thereby bypass important questions of politics and power (Forester 1993: 58).

> The literature of 'learning organizations' teaches us that in a turbulent environment, organizations must be adaptive, flexible, continually testing, 'error-correcting,' and innovating. Still, the 'learning theorists' leave unasked the basic political questions: what ends ought these organizations to serve and who ought to learn what?
>
> (Forester 1993: 53–4)

Forester does not deny that our organizations need to be 'error-correcting' – but then we should remember to ask, '[w]hat sorts of judgments will determine error, undesirable activity, and who will have the power, with what accountability, to make these judgments?' (Forester 1993: 54). Ignoring these questions,

> we are left with the struggle only for organizational survival and self-perpetuation; we are asked to keep the organizations we now have, whether or not 'might makes right,' and only then, if at all, are we to ask what we ought to keep them for.
>
> (Forester 1993: 54)

The critique is continued by Friedmann, who argues that OD is 'primarily a science for boardrooms' (Friedmann 1987: 216). According to Friedmann, its therapeutic programme is mainly addressed to managerial elites, who tend to overlook power in their organizations. The matter is quite different for those who remain outside the executive chambers and council rooms – whether white- and blue-collar workers or the less well-to-do citizens, who frequently experience the depredating effects of power (Friedmann 1987). Fischer, in turn, claims that the theory has become a technique and ideology advanced largely by management consultants who have bypassed the objectives of democratization. Instead they speak of 'participative management' with the aim of making bureaucratic organizations more responsive to change (Fischer 1990: 365).

These criticisms reflect an approach to organizational learning that is framed by the dichotomy between 'system' and 'lifeworld'. What learns in organizational learning is the 'system'. Thus learning takes the meaning of improvement in the 'system's' ability to control its environment, that is 'lifeworld'. This position makes it very problematic to incorporate Schön into CPT, as Forester (1989, 1993), Fischer (1990) and others have done. With Schön's theory, systems theory also creeps in again, only in a revised, pragmatist form.

Indeed, not even Schön will take us very far, in our attempts to approach planning as legitimate organizational learning, since he is primarily concerned with individual reflection, rather than organizational reflection. The very reason why Schön's ideas are so popular among critical planning theorists may be that his main and most cited book *The Reflective Practitioner* (1983) is concerned with how individual professionals learn, not with how organizations learn. Here, in contrast to his former work, Schön does not raise problematic questions concerning the goals and inclusiveness of organizational learning. At the level of organizational learning lurks the 'trap' of putting participation against bureaucracy. Then, organizational learning soon takes the meaning of improvement in the domination of participation.

However, the question of how participatory organizations can and should develop themselves does not fade away by not addressing it. We are already addressing the question, anyway, when we observe individual learning. There is no dividing line between individual and organizational learning (Engeström 1987: 158–61). As Peter Senge argues, learning that changes mental models cannot be done alone: '[i]t can only occur within a community of learners' (Senge 1990: xv). There is an organizational side to every individual learning act. Individuals learn in organizations, and organizational development is triggered by the learning acts of their individual members (Argyris 1992: 123).

Organized activity means cooperation between individuals specialized into performing certain sub-tasks, so that the sub-tasks are coordinated to produce a higher collective task jointly. In an organization, cooperative relations between its members are institutionalized to produce a certain collective outcome recurrently. Through the division of sub-tasks all organizations necessarily involve power relationships and inequalities in members' access to resources and their opportunities to affect decision-making. On the other hand, however, power relationships generated by the coordination of sub-tasks are also necessary for the achievement of collectively beneficial results. This far, CPT has been much more successful in tapping into indications of 'systemic distortion' and 'structural influence' (Sager 1994: 131) in planning as organized activity and organizational learning than in articulating the productive aspects of power in this activity. Even if it were signified as 'necessary distortions' to communicative action, this productive power would still be 'distortions'.

In Habermasian terms, cooperation in a public organization towards a given collective end is describable as a form of activity that approaches 'instrumental rationality'. However, how could this form be combined with 'communicatively rational action', which enables the members to question and evaluate the legitimacy of this collective end and the means used, and, moreover, with the non-rational action of creative planning, where new collective ends and means are shaped? By answering this question we address the methodology of planning as organizational learning. The critical planning theorists may be reluctant to go far in this direction, but even if they wanted to, it would be exceedingly hard with the conceptual tools provided by Habermas. The main stumbling blocks for such work are, first, the conceptual separation of communicative and instrumental rationalities, so that their interplay is basically described as disturbances by one form of rationality on the other; and second, the total reliance on reason, whether communicative or instrumental. Planning work cannot be based on reason alone. Otherwise we would lose the possibility for creativity and development – the fulfillment of the demands posed by the communicatively rational critique of existing ends and means of coordinated action in our public organizations.

Conclusion

In its critical stance towards Critical Planning Theory, this paper joins with a number of other recent reviews of communicative (or collaborative) planning theory (see Flyvbjerg 1998; Hillier, 2000; McGuirk 2001; Tait and Campbell 2000; Tewdwr-Jones and Allmendinger 1998). However, by questioning whether the programme of CPT serves sufficiently as a program for planning theory, my approach is somewhat different. CPT is a theory concerned with planning practices and the normative task of improving their legitimacy and inclusiveness. If CPT, as such a theory, settles in with articulating the principles of legitimate argumentation in planning, then it is bound to be partial as a planning theory. Planning practices aiming at legitimacy and inclusiveness raise many other essential questions to planning theory, besides the question of what are the parameters of legitimate planning argumentation. Other important questions are, for instance, how should the participatory planning process be organized and managed; how do new ideas and capacities for cooperation emerge and how can these be mutually developed and mobilized into coordinated problem-solving activity; how can participatory planning be empowered, and, at the same time, the depredating effects of power in the actual planning work be countered; what are the characteristics of planning and participatory planning as forms of human and social action?

If it is agreed that a theory of participatory planning ought to face the questions of legitimacy, power, openness, quality of argumentation and possibilities for critique, creativity and social learning as challenges to planning methodology, then CPT should be considered as inadequate. Rather than a theory of participatory planning, CPT is a theory of legitimacy in the context of (participatory) planning. To some extent critical planning theorists, such as Forester, Fischer, Sager, Healey and Innes, have attempted to complement CPT with other theoretical sources to constitute such a planning theory. They have combined other theoretical strands with Habermas's Critical Theory to address issues of planning methodology, creativity and social learning. As I have tried to show, there are severe difficulties in incorporating theories of creativity and organizational learning into Habermas's theoretical framework. First, Habermas's concept of dialogue as undominated speech is too narrow in its reliance on communicative rationality and the assumption of a shared lifeworld. It misses the aspect of creativity as non-rational search for meanings and ideas in a possible situation where a shared lifeworld is missing. Second, Habermas's dichotomy between 'system' and 'lifeworld' makes it difficult to make a constructive theoretical contribution to organizational management and learning in planning, without its being signified as an attempt to improve the 'system's' domination over the 'lifeworld'. The theories of public management and organizational learning are largely rooted in systems theory. Efforts to combine theories of this origin with Critical Theory would lead into an epistemological and ideological clash. This clash is already hidden in the critical planning theorists' use of Schön.

Although CPT provides, without a doubt, a crucial contribution to the 'communicative turn' of planning theory, the problem of how it can be related with methodologically and empirically concerned theories of participatory planning is a pressing one. It seems that, in order to be able to address these aspects of planning theory, there has to be a shift from Habermas to other theoretical sources, such as pragmatist systems theory and Foucauldian power analytics, which, however, are incompatible with Habermas's theory of communicative action, including his general conceptions of society and rationality. Therefore, in terms of scientific consistency, the communicative turn of planning theory does not yet deserve to be associated with the term 'paradigm'.

In my own work, I have tried to formulate an alternative theoretical foundation to the theory of participatory planning (Mäntysalo 2000). It stems from a dialectical reorientation of systems theory, utilizing especially the communication-theoretical insights of Bateson (1987) and Wilden (1980). In this line of thought, the 'system' provides the conceptual framework for all aspects of human and social life, including reason, creativity and learning, as well as explicit and implicit forms of power and pathological behaviour. The aim is to view these as inherent aspects and states of a single dialectical planning system, thus enabling one to concentrate on the dialectics of planning activity itself – not dissecting it into two separate strands, each of which is explained by using different theoretical tools, and thus losing the crucial in-between. The aim is also to transcend the dichotomies between the Habermasian and the Foucauldian view, on the one hand, and the Habermasian and the systems view, on the other. With this reorientation of the theoretical foundation, it may be possible to bring together, in a coherent fashion, theoretical contributions to participatory planning that now seem mutually incompatible.

Acknowledgement

I am very grateful to the referees of this chapter, whose insightful remarks helped me to improve my argument considerably.

Notes

1   In place of the concept of 'communicative planning theory' I prefer to use in the context of this article the concept of 'Critical Planning Theory' to indicate its specific reliance on Critical Theory. Communicative planning theory can be understood as a broader concept, which, besides Critical Theory, applies other theoretical sources, too, such as argumentation theory following Perelman and Toulmin, and power analytics following Foucault. With the notion of 'Critical Theory' I refer particularly to the theoretical work of Habermas, as does Forester in his book *Critical Theory, Public Policy, and Planning Practice* (Forester 1993: 163).

2   Undoubtedly there are those who would claim that it is no place for science to study creativity. But if we accepted this, should we not also give up studying planning – or at least admit that science can capture only those aspects of planning that are not connected with creativity? Scientific planning theory is a possibility only if we broaden the limits of science to include research on creativity.

3   The etymological explanation is that '*dia*' means 'to cross', 'through'; and '*logos*' denotes not only 'word' but, more profoundly, 'meaning' (Bohm and Peat 1992: 245). Ramírez, on the other hand, translates 'logos' as 'conversation' (Swedish *samtal*) (Ramírez 1993: 28). In spite of these differing derivations from the etymological origins of 'dialogue' ('crossing meanings', 'crossing conversation'), both sources (Bohm and Peat 1992; Ramírez 1993) conceive of dialogue as 'meaning generating communication'.

4 Habermas 1984: 75. Here Habermas builds on Parsons, who saw culture as consisting of three respective dimensions – factual, moral, and expressive – and who also worked on the theory of validity claims (Heiskala 1994: 94).

5 A notable exception is Healey (1997; 1998) who has elaborated the institutional aspects of collaborative planning.

6 Double binds are activity contexts where there are no alternatives left (Bateson 1987: 335). As one example, Bateson describes a Zen Buddhist lesson between the Zen master and his pupil. The Zen master holds a stick over the pupil's head and says fiercely: 'If you say this stick is real, I will strike you with it; if you say this stick is not real, I will strike you with it; if you don't say anything, I will strike you with it.' The pupil might break out of this immobilizing activity context by reaching up and taking the stick away from the master. (Bateson 1987: 208). According to Wilden, industrial capitalism is in a global double bind: if it stops producing for the sake of producing, it will destroy itself; if it goes on producing it will destroy us all (Wilden 1980: 394).

References

Argyris, C. (1992) *On Organizational Learning*, Cambridge, MA: Blackwell.

Bateson, G. (1987) *Steps to an Ecology of Mind*, 2nd edn, Northvale, NJ: Jason Aronson.

Bernstein, R.J. (1986) *Philosophical Profiles*, Cambridge: Polity Press.

Bohm, D. and Peat, F.D. (1992) *Tiede, järjestys ja luovuus*, trans. T. Seppälä, J. Jääskinen and P. Pylkkänen, *Science, Order, and Creativity*, Helsinki: Gaudeamus.

Cates, C. (1979) 'Beyond muddling: creativity', *Public Administration Review*, 39(6): 527–32.

Engeström, Y. (1987) *Learning by Expanding*, Helsinki: Orienta-konsultit.

Faludi, A. (1973) *Planning Theory*, Oxford: Pergamon Press.

Fischer, F. (1990) *Technocracy and the Politics of Expertise*, Newbury Park, CA: Sage.

Fischler, R. (1995) 'Strategy and history in professional practice: planning as world making', in H. Liggett and D.C. Perry (eds) *Spatial Practices*, London: Sage.

Flyvbjerg, B. (1998) *Rationality and Power: Democracy in Practice*, trans. S. Sampson, Chicago, IL: University of Chicago Press.

Forester, J. (1989) *Planning in the Face of Power*, Berkeley, CA: University of California Press.

Forester, J. (1993) *Critical Theory, Public Policy, and Planning Practice*, Albany, NY: State University of New York Press.

Friedmann, J. (1987) *Planning in the Public Domain: From Knowledge to Action*, Princeton, NJ: Princeton University Press.

Habermas, J. (1984) *The Theory of Communicative Action. Volume 1 – Reason and the Rationalization of Society*, trans. T. McCarthy, Boston, MA: Beacon Press.

Habermas, J. (1987) *The Theory of Communicative Action. Volume 2 – Lifeworld and System*, Cambridge: Polity Press.

Healey, P. (1992) 'Planning through debate: the communicative turn in planning theory', *Town Planning Review*, 63(2): 143–62.

Healey, P. (1997) *Collaborative Planning: Shaping Places in Fragmented Societies*, Planning, Environment and Cities Series, Basingstoke: Macmillan.

Healey, P. (1998) 'Building institutional capacity through collaborative approaches to urban planning', *Environment and Planning A*, 30: 1531–46.

Healey, P. (1999) 'Deconstructing communicative planning theory: a reply to Tewdwr-Jones and Allmendinger', *Environment and Planning A*, 31: 1129–35.

Heiskala, R. (1994) 'Talcott Parsons ja rakennefunktionalismi' ('Talcott Parsons and structural functionalism'), in R. Heiskala (ed) *Sosiologisen teorian nykysuuntauksia* (*Current Tendencies in Sociological Theory*), Helsinki: Gaudeamus.

Hillier, J. (2000) 'Going round the back? Complex networks and informal action in local planning processes', *Environment and Planning A*, 32: 33–54.

Huttunen, R., Kakkori, L. and Heikkinen, H.L.T. (1999) 'Toiminta, tutkimus ja totuus' ('Action, research and truth'), in H.L.T. Heikkinen, R. Huttunen and P. Moilanen (eds) *Siinä tutkija missä tekijä. Toimintatutkimuksen perusteita ja näköaloja* (*Where the Researcher, There the Agent: Principles and Prospects of Action Research*), Juva: Atena kustannus.

Innes, J.E. (1995) 'Planning theory's emerging paradigm: communicative action and interactive practice', *Journal of Planning Education and Research*, 14(3): 183–90.

Innes, J.E. and Booher, D.E. (1999a) 'Consensus building and complex adaptive systems: a framework for evaluating collaborative planning', *Journal of American Planning Association*, 65(4): 412–23.

Innes, J.E. and Booher, D.E. (1999b) 'Consensus building as role playing and bricolage: toward a theory of collaborative planning', *Journal of American Planning Association*, 65(1): 9–26.

Karatani, K. (1995) *Architecture as Metaphor: Language, Number, Money*, trans. S. Kohso, Cambridge, MA: MIT Press.

Kuhn, T.S. (1970) *The Structure of Scientific Revolutions*, 2nd edn, enlarged, Chicago, IL: University of Chicago Press.

Lapintie, K. (1999) 'Ratkaisemattomien kiistojen kaupunki' ('The city of unsettled conflicts') in L. Knuuti (ed) *Kaupunki vuorovaikutuksessa* (*City in Interaction*), Centre for Urban and Regional Studies, C 52, Espoo: Helsinki University of Technology.

Luhmann, N. (1990) *Political Theory in the Welfare State*, trans. J. Bednarz, Jr, Berlin: de Gruyter.

Mäntysalo, R. (2000) *Land-use Planning as Inter-organizational Learning*, Oulu, Acta Universitatis Ouluensis Technica, C 155. Available online http://herkules.oulu.fi/isbn9514258444/.

McGuirk, P.M. (2001) 'Situating communicative planning theory: context, power, and knowledge', *Environment and Planning A*, 33: 195–217.

Ramírez. J.L. (1993) *Strukturer och livsformer*, Report 3, Stockholm: Nordplan.

Ramírez, J.L. (1995) *Designteori och teoridesign*, Report 3, Stockholm: Nordplan.

Rittel, H.W.J. and Webber, M.M. (1973) 'Dilemmas in a general theory of planning', *Policy Sciences*, 4(2): 155–69.

Sager, T. (1994) *Communicative Planning Theory*, Aldershot: Avebury.

Schön, D.A. (1983) *The Reflective Practitioner*, New York: Basic Books.

Senge, P. (1990) *The Fifth Discipline: The Art and Practice of the Learning Organization*, New York: Currency Doubleday.

Simon, H.A. (1979) *Päätöksenteko ja hallinto*, *Administrative Behaviors*, trans. P Rajala, Economy Series 58, Espoo: WeilinandGöös.

Tait, M. and Campbell, H. (2000) 'The politics of communication between planning officers and politicians: the exercise of power through discourse', *Environment and Planning A*, 32: 489–506.

Tewdwr-Jones, M. and Allmendinger, P. (1998) 'Deconstructing communicative rationality: a critique of Habermasian collaborative planning', *Environment and Planning A*, 30: 1975–989.

Thomas, M.J. (1982) 'The procedural planning theory of A. Faludi', in C. Paris (ed.) *Critical Readings in Planning Theory*, Oxford: Pergamon Press.

Wilden, A. (1980) *System and Structure. Essays in Communication and Exchange*, London: Tavistock.

Index

Also available from Routledge

Dialogues in Urban and Regional Planning 2
Bruce Stiftel and Vanessa Watson (Eds)
(Forthcoming 2006)

Healthy Cities in Europe
Alex Tsouros and Jill Farrington (Eds)

Cities without Cities
An interpretation of the Zwischenstadt
Thomas Sieverts

Making European Space
Ole B. Jensen and Tim Richardson

Regional Innovation Systems, 2nd edition
Philip Cooke and Martin Heidenreich (Eds)

Place Identity, Participation and Planning
Cliff Hague and Paul Jenkins

Planning Middle Eastern Cities
Yasser Elsheshtawy (Ed.)

Planning Latin America's Capital Cities
Arturo Almandoz (Ed.)

Planning Europe's Capital Cities
Thomas Hall (Ed.)

AAPS

Association of African Planning Schools
www.gpean.org/jp/0128/2college/aapsschool.htm

Association of Collegiate Schools of Planning
Christopher Silver, President
Patricia Baron Pollak, Secretary
6311 Mallard Trace Drive, Tallahassee, FL 32312, USA
www.acsp.org

ACUPP

Association of Canadian University Planning Programs
David Brown, President
Peter Mulvihill, Secretary
School of Planning, McGill University, 815 Sherbrooke Street West,
Montreal, Quebec H3A 2K6, Canada
www.acupp-apucu.mcgill.ca

Association of European Schools of Planning
Simin Davoudi, President
Gert de Roo, Secretary General
Department of Planning and Environment, University of Groningen, PO Box
800, 9700 AV Groningen, Netherlands
www.aesop-planning.com

ALEUP

Latin-American Association of Schools of Urbanism and Planning
Sergio Flores Peña, President
Universidad Nacional Autonoma de México, Cuidad de México, Mexico
urbanismo@correo.arq.unam.mx

Australia and New Zealand Association of Planning Schools
c/o School of Human and Environmental Studies, University of New England,
Armidale, NSW 2351, Australia
www.une.edu.au/ANZAPS/

**National Association of Urban and Regional Post-graduate and Research
Programmes**
Heloisa Soares de Moura Costa, Presidente
Roberto Luis de Melo Monte-Mór, Executive Secretary
Programa de Pós-Graduação em Geografia – IGC/UFMG, Belo Horizonte,
MG, Brazil
www.anpur.org.br

APERAU

Association for the Development of Planning Education and Research
Michel A. Boisvert, President
Jean-Claude De Brauwer, Secretary
Rue de la Victoire 177, B-1060 Bruxelles, Belgium
www.aperau.org

APSA

Asian Planning Schools Association
Zhiqiang Wu, President
Anthony Yeh, Secretary General
Centre of Urban Planning and Environmental Management, University of
Hong Kong, Pofulam Road, Hong Kong SAR, China
www.apsaweb.org

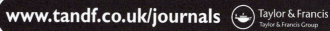